INTRODUCTION TO THE DESIGN AND ANALYSIS OF ALGORITHMS

McGRAW-HILL
COMPUTER SCIENCE SERIES

RICHARD W. HAMMING
Bell Telephone Laboratories

EDWARD A. FEIGENBAUM
Stanford University

BELL and NEWELL   Computer Structures: Readings and Examples
COLE   Introduction to Computing
DONOVAN   Systems Programming
GEAR   Computer Organization and Programming
GIVONE   Introduction to Switching Circuit Theory
GOODMAN and HEDETNIEMI   Introduction to the Design and Analysis of
     Algorithms
HAMMING   Computers and Society
HAMMING   Introduction to Applied Numerical Analysis
HELLERMAN   Digital Computer System Principles
HELLERMAN and CONROY   Computer System Performance
KAIN   Automata Theory: Machines and Languages
KATZAN   Microprogramming Primer
KOHAVI   Switching and Finite Automata Theory
LIU   Elements of Discrete Mathematics
LIU   Introduction to Combinatorial Mathematics
MADNICK and DONOVAN   Operating Systems
MANNA   Mathematical Theory of Computation
NEWMAN and SPROULL   Principles of Interactive Computer Graphics
NILSSON   Artificial Intelligence
RALSTON   Introduction to Programming and Computer Science
ROSEN   Programming Systems and Languages
SALTON   Automatic Information Organization and Retrieval
STONE   Introduction to Computer Organization and Data Structures
STONE and SIEWIOREK   Introduction to Computer Organization and Data
     Structures: PDP-11 Edition
TONGE and FELDMAN   Computing: An Introduction to Procedures and
     Procedure-Followers
TREMBLAY and MANOHAR   Discrete Mathematical Structures with
     Applications to Computer Science
TREMBLAY and SORENSON   An Introduction to Data Structures with
     Applications
TUCKER   Programming Languages
WATSON   Timesharing System Design Concepts
WEGNER   Programming Languages, Information Structures, and Machine
     Organization
WIEDERHOLD   Database Design
WINSTON   The Psychology of Computer Vision

INTRODUCTION TO THE DESIGN AND ANALYSIS OF ALGORITHMS

S. E. Goodman
S. T. Hedetniemi
University of Virginia

McGraw-Hill Book Company
New York   St. Louis   San Francisco   Auckland   Bogotá   Düsseldorf
Johannesburg   London   Madrid   Mexico   Montreal   New Delhi
Panama   Paris   São Paulo   Singapore   Sydney   Tokyo   Toronto

To Dee and Judy

**INTRODUCTION TO THE DESIGN AND
ANALYSIS OF ALGORITHMS**

234567890FGRFGR78321098

This book was set in Helvetica.
The editors were Peter D. Nalle and Laura D. Warner;
the designer was Laura D. Warner;
the production supervisor was Dennis J. Conroy.
The drawings were done by J & R Services, Inc.
Fairfield Graphics was printer and binder.

Library of Congress Cataloging in Publication Data

Goodman, Seymour E
    Introduction to the design and analysis of algorithms.

    (McGraw-Hill computer science series)
    Includes bibliographical references and index.
    1. Electronic digital computers- -Programming.
2. Algorithms. I. Hedetniemi, S. T., joint author. II. Title.
QA76.6.G66   511'.8   76-43363
ISBN 0-07-023753-0

CONTENTS

PREFACE

A representative sampling of undergraduate computer science courses would include the following (with varying titles): (1) introduction to computing, most often via Fortran, Basic, or PL/1; (2) assembly language programming; (3) data structures; (4) discrete structures; (5) machine organization; (6) numerical methods; (7) programming languages survey; (8) business data processing; (9) applications programming; and (10) systems programming. Through this book, we are proposing a course on the *design and analysis of algorithms*.

A first course in computing typically focuses on such topics as the workings of a computer, keypunching and data preparation, the syntax of a programming language, coding, input/output, the elementary aspects and uses of data structures, subroutine and function concepts, the art of debugging, the design of relatively simple programs, some machine-language concepts, and a few applications programs. There are a number of additional topics on programming which are neither covered in a first course in computing nor covered in much detail in any other undergraduate computer science course. These topics include:

1 The complete development, from start to finish, of a reasonably complicated problem for computer solution
2 Algorithm design techniques, such as subgoals, hill climbing, working backward, backtracking, branch and bound, recursion, and heuristics
3 Efficient and correct implementation of stated algorithms
4 Algorithm and program correctness (a matter that all too frequently encourages the question: Does the output look all right?)
5 Measures of algorithm efficiency, complexity, and overall effectiveness
6 Program testing, including tests for correctness, complexity, and general program behavior
7 More sophisticated mathematical thinking (involving probability, for example) required in designing and analyzing programs of reasonable complexity

This text is concerned with all the above-mentioned aspects of computing.

Although a course in the design and analysis of algorithms necessarily involves a significant amount of programming, it is not meant to serve simply as a second (or third) programming course. Consequently, a number of topics which might relate to the design and analysis of algorithms are not discussed in this text; these topics include matters of I/O, debugging techniques, optimizing compilers, and use of library routines. This text is intended to serve as a bridge between the more practical, programming-oriented courses and the more theoretical, mathematically oriented courses in computer science. The algorithms presented have a distinct mathematical flavor because of this orientation and the instructive nature of their design and analysis.

The figure on page ix shows how a course on the design and analysis of algorithms can fit into a typical undergraduate computer science curriculum. To some extent, we see this course as a substitute for the introduction to discrete structures, the course listed in the ACM Curriculum 68 (*Comm. ACM*, Mar. 1968). Although our subject matter has a healthy mathematical content, the level is lower, less theoretical, and less formal than that of an introduction to discrete structures; and the applications to computer science are more apparent.

The mathematical content in the design and analysis of algorithms comprises introductory parts of the subjects of networks, combinatorics, probability, and statistics. These topics are covered not for their own sake but rather for use in algorithmic applications. To establish the correctness or properties of certain algorithms, proofs are presented throughout the book, many of which use mathematical induction. We do not attempt to teach the student how to prove the theorems, but we do expect that he or she will be able to follow their logic.

We also believe that the subject matter in this text plays a central role in computer science. In addition to serving as the first theoretical course in a computer science curriculum, the subject relates well to courses in data structures, programming languages, applications programming, and numerical analysis.

In principle, a student whose background includes one semester of calculus, a first computer programming course, and a high-school-level knowledge of permutations, combinations, and sets should be adequately prepared to read this book. Calculus is used infrequently, but it is regarded as a prerequisite to ensure some mathematical maturity. We have found that the material is slightly difficult for most sophomores and appears to be most appropriate for the junior or senior level.

Since implementation and testing of programs are an important part of the development of algorithms, computer code has to be exhibited. Although some computer scientists may not agree with our choice, we have decided to exhibit all programs in Fortran for the simple reason that it is the only programming language that is close to being universally known. There does not appear to be an alternative that neither forces additional prerequisites nor makes the book so long as to dilute the material of primary interest. For those readers who are familiar with more structured programming languages, we have included an appendix containing Algol or PL/1 equivalents of most of the programs in the text.

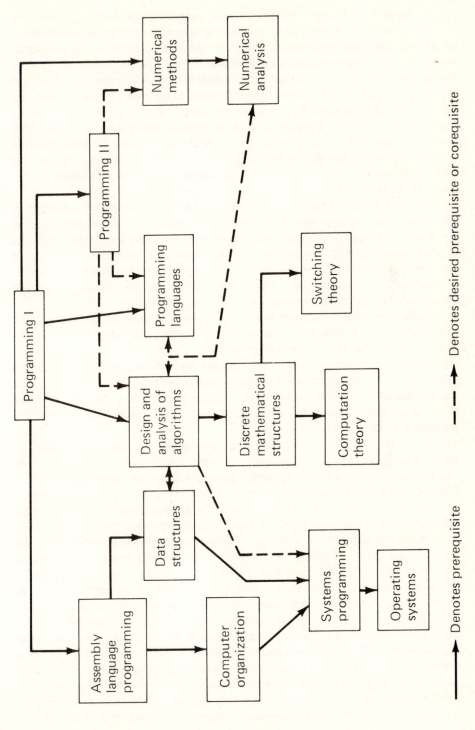

Denotes desired prerequisite or corequisite

Denotes prerequisite

Our format for the presentation of algorithms is a cross between the heavily annotated, step-by-step style popularized by Knuth in the first three volumes of *The Art of Computer Programming* and the Algol-like format that is currently popular in the literature. Constructs such as **do-while** and **if-then-else** are used regularly and implemented in obvious ways. A reasonable effort has been made to adhere to the principles of structured programming. Appendix A summarizes the conventions used to state algorithms in this text.

Chapter 1 is primarily a qualitative introduction to the notions of an algorithm and the basic steps that go into its complete development. Unfortunately, considerations of space do not permit us to develop most of the algorithms in this text in this much detail. In later chapters, some of the development steps have been left as exercises.

Chapter 2 develops several tools that are useful in the design and analysis of algorithms. Elementary concepts of structured programming, networks, data structures, probability, and statistics are considered. For supplementation, an appendix—on sets and elementary proof techniques—is provided at the end of the book. An effort has been made to retain an "algorithmic flavor" throughout this chapter and the appendices and, whenever possible, new algorithms are introduced to illustrate concepts.

A statement should be made about the elementary aspects of probability and statistics covered in Chap. 2. Many interesting and important problems in the design and analysis of algorithms are probabilistic in nature; for example, a strong argument can be made that the most useful measure of the quality of an algorithm is its average or expected performance. On the other hand, we recognize that many students have difficulty with the study of probability and statistics. With this in mind, we have written this text so that an instructor may omit probabilistic material without much trouble.

A number of useful algorithm design techniques are studied in Chap. 3, in which each section includes at least one new problem and/or algorithm. An algorithm for finding a minimum-weight spanning tree is completely developed in Chap. 4, and it is used to illustrate some simple program-testing procedures.

Chapters 5 and 6 contain a variety of examples and applications, most of which reinforce ideas introduced in the first four chapters. Instructors can select topics from these chapters on the basis of class interest, available time, mathematical level, and so forth. Chapter 7 is designed as a reference tool for the reader.

Almost 300 exercises have been included in this text. They vary widely in difficulty; many are open-ended and experimental. The exercises are an important part of the book, and it is hoped that instructors will find time to discuss some of the more interesting and difficult problems in class. Note that the more asterisks (*) preceding an exercise, the greater its difficulty. An exercise with an "L" label will require considerable time. Some of the exercises are "titled" to indicate the coverage of certain subject matter or concepts. Instructors might consider using groups of two or three students for some of the longer and more difficult assignments, particularly those that require extensive program testing.

It is difficult to acknowledge everyone who has contributed time and effort to this book. Many people have read it and offered their comments, constructive criticism, and encouragement; unfortunately, it is not possible to recognize them all individually. Above all, we thank Diane Goodman, our typist and chief debugger. Dana Richards contributed more than half of Sec. 6.1, and Bruce Chartres is responsible for the ecological model in Sec. 3.6. Others who have made major contributions to the manuscript include Linwood Ferguson, Richard Armentrout, and Clay Pendergrast. Thanks are also due to Art Fleck, Harold Stone, Ken Bowman, Wayne Madison, and an anonymous reader for their useful comments. Mouton Publishers kindly gave us permission to use about 12 figures and several pages of text in Sec. 2.2. Diane Spresser, Sandee Mitchell, and Jennifer Ward helped with the exercises and the proofreading of the manuscript. George Eade and Louis Rowley wrote the Algol and PL/1 programs in Appendix C. Last, but not least, we would like to thank the students in our course in the design and analysis of algorithms, who have been such willing guinea pigs for the last three years.

No book of this sort can ever be completely free of "bugs." In spite of the efforts of many people, there undoubtedly remain errors in the text. We would appreciate having these brought to our attention by our readers.

S. E. Goodman
S. T. Hedetniemi

1 THE COMPLETE DEVELOPMENT OF AN ALGORITHM

1.1 INTRODUCTION

It is only fair to start by telling you what we hope to accomplish. Throughout your academic and professional careers people will present you with problems, and you will be expected to use your background in mathematics and computer science to solve them. This will often entail the development of an algorithm. Our purpose in this text is to help you learn how to (1) get started on a problem, (2) design an algorithm that works, (3) implement the algorithm as a computer program, and (4) judge the effectiveness of an algorithm.

This is easier said than done. The world of computing is littered with the remains of computer programs which were once considered to be finished products, but which later were found to be incorrect, inefficient, unintelligible, or worthless for some other reason. Perhaps the simplest explanation for this is that the computer is a relatively new and complex tool and it takes time to learn how to use it well. The skills necessary to use a computer as a powerful instrument for solving problems, particularly mathematical problems, are not easy to acquire.

The objective of this chapter is to make a "first pass" at the concept of the *complete development of an algorithm*, the basic steps of which are:

1 Statement of the problem
2 Development of a model
3 Design of the algorithm
4 Correctness of the algorithm — *Intuitive proofs (informal)*
5 Implementation
6 Analysis and complexity of the algorithm
7 Program testing
8 Documentation

The remainder of the book is devoted to the detailed study and illustration of these fundamental steps. For the time being we shall limit ourselves to brief discussions of algorithms (Sec. 1.2) and the steps leading to their complete development (Sec. 1.3).

1.2 ALGORITHMS

Everyone who has solved problems with the aid of a digital computer has some intuitive idea of the meaning of the word "algorithm." One might even go so far as to argue that it is one of the most central concepts in computer science. The "official" definition from the most recent (1971) edition of the *Oxford English Dictionary* states that the word "algorithm" is an "erroneous refashioning of algorism"; in turn, algorism is considered to be more or less synonymous with algebra and arithmetic, and this definition dates back to the ninth century. Apparently the modern usage of the word is still strictly limited to the computer science community.

Let us first try to verbalize our intuitive ideas. We can loosely define an *algorithm* as an unambiguous procedure for solving a problem. A *procedure* is a finite sequence of well-defined steps or operations, each of which requires only a finite amount of memory or working storage and takes a finite amount of time to complete. We append the requirement that an algorithm must terminate in finite time for any input.

One difficulty with this definition is that the term "unambiguous" is very ambiguous. "Unambiguous" to whom? Or to what? Since nothing is universally clear or vague, the executor of the algorithm must be, at least implicitly, specified. An algorithm for computing the derivative of a cubic polynomial might be perfectly clear to someone who is familiar with calculus, but it may be totally incomprehensible to someone who is not. Thus, the executor's computational capabilities must also be specified.

There are other definitional problems. An algorithm may clearly exist for some task, but it may be difficult or impossible to describe in some given format. The human race has clearly developed efficient algorithms for tying shoelaces. Many children can tie their own shoes by the age of five. But it is very difficult (try it) to give a purely verbal—no pictures or demonstrations allowed—statement of such an algorithm.

This definition obviously has some defects. It is possible to avoid most of these defects by defining "mathematical machines" with very carefully specified capabilities. We then say that an algorithm is any procedure which can be executed by such a machine. Such attempts at defining an algorithm are very deep and difficult mathematically; they are also much too rigid for our purposes.

We would like to retain some of the flexibility and intuitive appeal of the first definition, and yet at least partially remove some of its ambiguities. This is easily done by specifying a "typical" modern digital computer and a language of communication with such a computer, and then licensing a procedure as an algorithm if it can be implemented on this machine using the given language.

This computer will have an unlimited random-access memory in which real numbers, integers, and logical constants can be stored. In one word of this memory we can store a number of arbitrary, but finite, size and can access any word in a fixed, constant amount of time (this may be a bit unrealistic, but it is almost true in practice and is a convenient assumption). This computer is capable of executing a stored program that consists of a reasonable collection of instructions of a basic type, including all standard arithmetic operations, comparisons, branchings, etc. We will usually assign one unit of execution time to each such instruction. Some of our memory can be organized into one-, two-, and three-dimensional arrays (matrices) by simple declarations. When we want to be specific, we will use the Fortran language as a model for the capabilities of our machine.[1]

We have effectively said that we only have an algorithm for solving a problem when we can write a computer program that solves it. This is a debatable issue. Programs on the kind of computer described in the previous paragraph cannot tie shoes. The well-defined steps do not include those necessary to successfully tie shoes. A good argument can be made that we are really dealing with a restricted concept of an algorithm. The human machine is capable of executing a large variety of subtle steps that are beyond the range of our typical computer. However, the restricted definition is just what we want for this book.

The following example of an algorithm illustrates a level of detail that is consistent with our definition. Appendix A contains a detailed discussion of the conventions used to state algorithms in this text.

Consider the simple problem of finding the maximum number in a list of N real numbers R(1), R(2), ..., R(N). The basic idea of the algorithm is to go through the entire list, one number at a time, and remember the largest number that we have seen so far. By the time the entire list is inspected, the largest number will have been retained. You might try to draw a flowchart for this algorithm before reading further.

The notation $A \leftarrow B$ denotes an assignment statement; that is, set variable A equal to the current value of B.

Algorithm MAX Given N real numbers in a one-dimensional array R(1), R(2), ..., R(N), find M and J such that

$$M = R(J) = \max_{1 \leq K \leq N} R(K)$$

In the case where two or more elements of R have the largest value, the value of J retained will be the smallest possible.

Step 0. [Initialize] **Set** $M \leftarrow R(1)$; **and** $J \leftarrow 1$.

Step 1. [N = 1?] **If** N = 1 **then** STOP **fi**.†

Step 2. [Inspect each number] **For** $K \leftarrow 2$ **to** N **do** step 3 **od**; **and** STOP.

   Step 3. [Compare] **If** $M < R(K)$ **then set** $M \leftarrow R(K)$; **and** $J \leftarrow K$ **fi**.† (M is now the largest number we have inspected, and it is in the K*th* position of the array.)

---

[1]Many of the algorithms in this book have also been coded in Algol or PL/1. See Appendix C.

†The **fi** and **od** in this algorithm are used to denote the end of the **if** and **do** constructs, respectively. This will be discussed in more detail in Sec. 2.1.

Algorithm MAX is not in coded form. It is in a form that is generally easier to follow than computer code, but it is expressed in terms of steps which are available in every common computer language. The conversion to coded form is easy. However, this is not always the case. Some algorithms are too complicated for us to make the transition from the preceding verbal form to computer code in one step. At least one intermediate stage of development may have to be introduced.

1.3 THE BASIC STEPS IN THE COMPLETE DEVELOPMENT OF AN ALGORITHM

We will now briefly consider each of the basic steps listed near the end of Sec. 1.1. Our primary interest is to establish the function of each step and to gain some perspective on how these steps combine to form a coherent whole.

Statement of the Problem

Before we can understand a problem, we must be able to give it a precise statement. This condition is not, in itself, sufficient for understanding a problem, but it is absolutely necessary.

Developing a precise problem statement is usually a matter of asking the right questions. Some good questions to ask upon encountering a crudely formulated problem are:

Do I understand the vocabulary used in the raw formulation?

What information has been given?

What do I want to find out?

How would I recognize a solution?

What information is missing, and will any of this information be of use?

Is any of the given information worthless?

What assumptions have been made?

Other questions are possible, depending on the particular problem. Often questions such as these need to be asked again, after some of them have been given answers or partial answers.

Example Jack is a computer marketing representative (salesman) whose territory covers 20 cities scattered throughout Texas. He works for large commissions, but his company will reimburse him for only 50 percent of the actual cost of automobile travel for his business trips. Jack has taken the trouble to figure out how much it would cost him to travel by car between every pair of cities in his territory.   He would clearly like to keep his travel costs down.

What is given?   The primary information is a list of the cities in Jack's territory and the associated cost matrix, that is, a square array with entry c_{ij} equal to the cost of going from city i to city j.   In this case the cost matrix has 20 rows and 20 columns.

What do we want to find out?   We want to help Jack keep his travel costs down.   That is a bit vague.   It really looks inadequate when we ask: How would we recognize a solution?   After giving the matter some thought, we should conclude that we cannot do any better without additional information from Jack.   Does Jack have more customers in some cities than in others?   If he does, or if he has some special customers, Jack might want to visit certain cities more often.   There may be other cities that Jack would not bother to visit unless he happened to find himself in a nearby city.   In other words, we must know more about Jack's priorities and schedule preferences.

Therefore, we go back to Jack and ask him for additional information.   He tells us that he would like an itinerary that would start at his base city, take him to each of the other cities in his territory exactly once, and return him to his base.   Consequently, we would like a list of cities which contains each city exactly once, except for the base city which is listed first and last.   The order of the cities on this list represents the order in which Jack should make the tour of his territory.   The sum of the costs between every consecutive pair of cities on the list is the total cost of the tour represented by the list.   We could solve Jack's problem if we could give him the list with the smallest possible total cost.

This is a good basic statement of the problem.   We know what we have and what we want to find.

Development of a Model

Once a problem has been clearly stated, it is time to formulate it as a mathematical model.   This is a very important step in the overall solution process and it should be given considerable thought.   The choice of a model has substantial influence on the remainder of the solution process.

As you might imagine, it is impossible to provide a set of rules which automates the modeling stage.   Most problems must be given individual attention.   However, there are some useful guidelines.   This topic is more of an art than a science and is likely to remain that way.   The best way to become proficient is by acquiring the experience that comes from the study of successful models.

There are at least two basic questions to be asked in setting up a model:

1 Which mathematical structures seem best-suited for the problem?
2 Are there other problems that have been solved which resemble this one?

The second question is perhaps the most useful one in all mathematics. In the context of modeling it often provides the answer to the first question. In fact, most of the problems that are solved in mathematics tend to be perturbations of previously solved problems. Most of us simply do not have the talent of a Newton, Gauss, or Einstein, and we need a considerable amount of guidance from existing work in order to make progress.

The first question is of more immediate concern. We must choose mathematical objects to represent both what we know and what we want to find. This choice of appropriate structure will be influenced by such factors as (1) the fact that our knowledge is limited to relatively few structures, (2) convenience of representation, (3) computational simplicity, and (4) the usefulness of the various operations associated with the structure or structures under consideration.

Once a tentative choice of mathematical structure has been made, the problem should then be restated in terms of these mathematical objects. This will be a candidate model if we can give affirmative answers to such questions as:

Is all the important information in the problem clearly labeled by mathematical objects?

Is there a mathematical quantity associated with the result sought?

Have we recognized some useful relations between the objects in the model?

Can we work with the model? Is it reasonably manipulable?

Example Reconsider the computer salesman problem presented earlier in this section. Start with the problem statement given at the end of the example.

Have we solved a problem similar to this before? Probably not, in a mathematical sense. But we have all been confronted with routing problems using road maps or mazes. Can we come up with a convenient representation of our problem that is similar to a map?

The obvious thing to do is to sit down with a piece of paper and put down one dot or point for each city. We do not want to get bogged down with drawing the points so that the distance between any pair of points corresponding to cities i and j is proportional to the travel cost c_{ij}. Therefore, put the points down in any convenient way, draw a line between points i and j, and label the line with the "weight" c_{ij}.

This object that we have just created is a special case of what is known mathematically as a *network* or *graph*. More generally, a network is a set of points (in a plane) together with weighted or unweighted lines drawn between some or all pairs of these points.

Assume, for the sake of simplicity, that Jack has only five cities, with the cost matrix shown in Fig. 1.3.1a. The network model could then be drawn as in Fig. 1.3.1b. We assume that the cost of the trip from city i to city j is the same as that from j to i, but this is not necessary.

What are we looking for in the problem? In terms of the network, the list

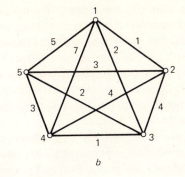

City

$$
\begin{array}{c|ccccc}
 & 1 & 2 & 3 & 4 & 5 \\
\hline
1 & - & 1 & 2 & 7 & 5 \\
2 & 1 & - & 4 & 4 & 3 \\
3 & 2 & 4 & - & 1 & 2 \\
4 & 7 & 4 & 1 & - & 3 \\
5 & 5 & 3 & 2 & 3 & - \\
\end{array}
$$

a

b

FIG. 1.3.1 A five-city traveling salesman problem.

of cities (which we previously described) defines a closed cycle starting from the base city and returning there after passing through each city exactly once. Such a cycle would correspond to a closed continuous pencil tracing along the lines of the network which passes through every point once and only once and begins and ends with the same point. We call this kind of traversal a *tour*. The cost of a tour is defined as the sum of the weights of all the traversed edges. The problem is solved if we can find a tour with the smallest cost.

In Fig. 1.3.1*b*, the traversal 1–5–3–4–2–1 is a tour with cost $5 + 2 + 1 + 4 + 1 = 13$. Is it a minimum-cost tour?

The problem which we have been considering is known in the literature as the *traveling salesman problem*, and it is something of a classic. It is one of the best known members of a class of problems that are very easy to state and model but very difficult to solve. We will return to this problem from time to time for illustrative purposes.

Design of an Algorithm

Once a problem has been clearly stated and a model has been developed, we must get down to the business of designing an algorithm for solving the problem. The choice of a design technique, which is often highly dependent on the choice of model, can greatly influence the effectiveness of a solution algorithm. Two different algorithms may be correct, but may differ tremendously in their effectiveness. Measures of effectiveness are discussed in a later section of this chapter.

Example Let us return to the traveling salesman of the previous section. The problem statement and model given earlier suggest the following algorithm.

Start by arbitrarily numbering the n cities with the integers from 1 to n, each city being given a unique integer. The base city is given the number n. Now note that every tour corresponds uniquely to a permutation of the integers $1, 2, \ldots, n-1$. In fact, each tour corresponds to a unique permutation *and* each permutation corresponds to a unique tour. Such a correspondence is called *one-to-one*. Thus, for a given permutation, we can easily trace out the corresponding tour on the network model and, at the same time, compute the cost of this tour.

We can solve the problem by generating all the permutations of the first $n-1$ positive integers. For each permutation, construct the corresponding tour and compute its cost. Proceed through the list of all permutations, saving the tour that, so far, has the least cost. If we find a tour with a lower cost, we make this new tour the standard for future comparison.

Algorithm ETS (*Exhaustive Traveling Salesman*) To solve an N-city traveling salesman problem by systematically considering all the permutations on the first N − 1 positive integers. In this way we will consider every possible tour and choose a TOUR with the least cost MIN. ETS requires as input the number of cities N and the cost matrix C.

Step 0. [Initialize] **Set** TOUR ← ∅; **and** MIN ← ∞.

Step 1. [Generate all permutations] **For** I ← 1 **to** (N − 1)! **do through** step 4 **od**; **and** STOP.

  Step 2. [Get new permutation] **Set** P ← the I*th* permutation of the integers $1, 2, \ldots, N-1$. (Note that we need a subalgorithm here.)

  Step 3. [Construct new tour] Construct the tour T(P) that corresponds to the permutation P; **and** compute the cost COST(T(P)). (Note that we need two other subalgorithms here.)

  Step 4. [Compare] **If** COST(T(P)) < MIN **then set** TOUR ← T(P); **and** MIN ← COST(T(P)) **fi**.

Algorithm ETS is a respectable first pass at a precise algorithm. It lacks some important subalgorithms and is not very close to a final coded form. These refinements will come later.

There seems to be a natural tendency for programmers to spend relatively little time in the design phase of the development of a program. The tendency is strong to want to start writing code as soon as possible. This urge should be resisted. The design phase should be carried out with much deliberation, and some consideration should be given to the two steps that precede it and the first three steps that follow it. As one might expect, the eight fundamental steps listed in Sec. 1.1 cannot be considered independently of each other. The first three, in particular, have much influence on those that follow, and the sixth and seventh steps provide valuable feedback which might force us to reconsider some of the earlier steps.

Correctness of the Algorithm

One of the more difficult, and sometimes more tedious, steps in the development of an algorithm is proving or asserting that the algorithm is correct.

Perhaps the most common procedure followed to assert that a program is correct is to run it on a variety of test cases. If the answers produced by the program can be verified against hand calculations or known values, we are tempted to conclude that the program "works." However, this technique rarely removes all doubts that there is some case for which the program will fail.

For now, we offer the following as a general guide for proving the correctness of an algorithm. Suppose that an algorithm is given in terms of a series of steps, say, step 0 through step m. Try to offer some justification for *each* step. In particular, this might involve a lemma about conditions that exist before and after the step is executed. Then try to offer some proof that the algorithm will terminate, and, in doing so, will have examined *all* the appropriate input data and produced *all* the appropriate output data.

Example Algorithm ETS is so straightforward that its correctness is easy to prove. Since every tour is examined, the tour with the minimum cost must be examined; once it is seen, it will be retained by the algorithm. It will never be discarded since this can only happen if there exists a cheaper tour to replace it. The algorithm must terminate because there are only a finite number of tours to examine. The method just used is known as "proof by exhaustion," and it is the crudest of all proof techniques.

We emphasize the fact that algorithm correctness does not necessarily imply anything about efficiency. Exhaustive algorithms are rarely very good in any sense.

Implementation

Once an algorithm has been stated, say, in terms of a sequence of steps, *and* one is convinced that it is correct, it is time to implement the algorithm, that is, to code it into a computer program.

This fundamental step can be quite hard. One reason for the difficulty is that all too often a particular step of an algorithm will be stated in a form that is not directly translatable into code. For example, one of the steps in the algorithm may be stated in such a way as to require an entire subroutine for its implementation. Another reason why implementation can be a difficult process is that before we can even begin to write code, we must design an entire system of computer data structures to represent important aspects of the model being used. To do this, we must answer such questions as the following:

What are the variables?

What are their types?

How many arrays, and of what size, are needed?

Would it be worthwhile to use linked lists?

What subroutines (possibly already canned) are needed?

What programming language should be used?

The particular implementation used can significantly affect both the memory requirements and the speed of the algorithm.

Another structured aspect of program implementation concerns top-down programming. In Sec. 2.1 we shall try to explain this concept, but for now let us simply state that top-down programming is an approach to both design and implementation which suggests that we should proceed by successively modifying the algorithm into a sequence of increasingly refined algorithms in such a way that the final version is, in fact, a computer program.

One important point should be mentioned. It is one thing to prove the correctness of a particular algorithm which has been stated in verbal form. It is another thing altogether to prove that a given computer program, which supposedly is an implementation of this algorithm, is also correct. That is, one must be *very* careful that the process of converting a proven algorithm (in verbal form) to a computer program is a "faithful" one.

We suggest that you reconsider Algorithm ETS in light of the discussion in this subsection and try to refine it in successive stages, as was suggested in this discussion, until you obtain a computer program.

Analysis and Complexity of the Algorithm

There are a number of important practical reasons for analyzing algorithms. One reason is that we need to obtain estimates or bounds on the storage or run time which our algorithm will need to successfully process a particular input. Computer time and memory are relatively scarce (and expensive) resources which are often simultaneously sought by many users. It is to everyone's advantage to avoid runs that are aborted because of an insufficient time allocation on a job card. It is also amazing how many programmers have to learn the hard way that their program simply cannot handle a given input without using literally days of computer time. One would like to predict such things with pencil and paper in order to avoid disastrous runs. A good analysis is also capable of finding bottlenecks in our programs, that is, sections of a program where most of the time is spent (see Exercise 1.3.16).

There are also important theoretical reasons for analyzing algorithms. One would like to have some quantitative standard for comparing two algorithms which claim to solve the same problem. The weaker algorithm should be improved or discarded. It is desirable to have a mechanism for filtering out the most efficient algorithms and replacing those that have been rendered obsolete. Sometimes a clear judgment on the relative efficiency of two algorithms is not possible. One might run better on the average, say, on random input data, while another runs better on specialized input data. We would like to be able to reach conclusions such as these about the relative merits of two algorithms.

It is also important to establish an absolute standard. When is a problem optimally solved? That is, when do we have an algorithm which is so good that it is *not possible*, no matter how clever we are, to make it significantly better?

Let A denote an algorithm for solving a particular class of problems. Let n denote a measure of the size of a particular problem in this class. In many of the problems in this book, n is just a scalar representing the number of vertices in a network. In general, however, n might be an array or the length of an input sequence. Define $f_A(n)$ as a *work function* that gives an upper bound on the maximum number of basic operations (additions, comparisons, etc.) that algorithm A has to perform to solve any problem of size n. We use the following criterion to judge the quality of algorithm A. Algorithm A is said to be *polynomial* if $f_A(n)$ grows no more rapidly than a polynomial in n, and *exponential* otherwise. This criterion is based on worst-case run time, but similar criteria could also be specified for average run time. The "experimental" basis for this measure of quality is that sequential or parallel machines seem to be more or less capable of digesting polynomial algorithms for large problems, but they "choke" rather quickly on exponential algorithms.

The following notation is standard in a number of mathematical disciplines, including the analysis of algorithms. A function $f(n)$ is defined to be $O[g(n)]$ and said to be of *order* $g(n)$ for large n if

$$\lim_{n \to \infty} \frac{f(n)}{g(n)} = \text{constant} \neq 0$$

This will be denoted as $f(n) = O[g(n)]$. A function $h(n)$ is defined to be $o[z(n)]$ for large n if

$$\lim_{n \to \infty} \frac{h(n)}{z(n)} = 0$$

These symbols are often verbalized as "big oh" and "little oh," respectively. Intuitively, if $f(n)$ is $O[g(n)]$, then the two functions grow at essentially the same rate as $n \to \infty$. If $f(n)$ is $o[g(n)]$, then $g(n)$ grows much more rapidly than $f(n)$.

Example

(a) The polynomial $f(n) = 2n^5 + 6n^4 + 6n^2 + 18$ is $O(n^5)$ since

$$\lim_{n \to \infty} \frac{2n^5 + 6n^4 + 6n^2 + 18}{n^5} = 2$$

It is $o(n^{5.1})$, $o(e^n)$, and $o(2^n)$. In fact, it is "little oh" of any function that grows faster than a fifth-degree polynomial.

(b) The function $f(n) = 2^n$ is $o(n!)$ since

$$\lim_{n \to \infty} \frac{2^n}{n!} = 0$$

However, 2^n is $O(2^{n+1})$ and $o(5^{n-1})$.
(c) The function $f(n) = 1000\sqrt{n}$ is $o(n)$.

Therefore, an algorithm is polynomial if $f_A(n) = O[P_k(n)]$ or $f_A(n) = o[P_k(n)]$, where $P_k(n)$ is any polynomial of any fixed degree k in the variable n. The algorithm is exponential otherwise.

Of course, we would like to obtain as precise an analysis as possible; that is, we would prefer to know $f_A(n)$ in as much detail as possible. We would understand more about the performance of algorithm A if we knew that $f_A(n) = 2.5n^2 + 3.7n - 5.2$ than if we knew only that $f_A(n) = O(n^2)$. Such detailed information about an algorithm can only be obtained from a specific implementation. The explicit coefficients of $f_A(n)$ generally depend on the implementation; the $O(n^2)$ characteristic is usually intrinsic to the algorithm, that is, independent of a wide range of implementation features.

It is also important to know just how badly behaved an exponential algorithm is. There are many important problems for which only exponential algorithms are known at the present time. The traveling salesman problem is one, and others are described elsewhere in this book. These problems need to be solved because of their practical applications. If only exponential algorithms are known, then we want to use the most efficient of these. An algorithm that takes $O(2^n)$ steps to solve a problem of size n is obviously preferable to one that takes $O(n!)$ or $O(n^n)$ steps.

Example Consider previously discussed Algorithm ETS. We can immediately conclude that the algorithm is exponential and at least $O(n!)$. In an n-city problem, Algorithm ETS asks us to enumerate exhaustively the permutations of the first $n - 1$ positive integers. There are $(n - 1)!$ of these permutations. Even if we needed only one step for each permutation (a gross underestimate—see Exercise 1.3.5), this part of the algorithm would still require $O[(n - 1)!]$ steps. Once a permutation is presented, as in step 1 of Algorithm ETS, it is possible to find the corresponding tour and its associated cost in $O(n)$ steps (see Exercise 1.3.6). Every upper bound on the total run time must then be at least $O(n!)$.

Assume that our salesman has 20 cities and that we have a phenomenal subalgorithm for step 1 of Algorithm ETS which generates a new permutation in only one step. Assume also that we have a fast machine which executes every basic step (for example, a comparison, an addition, the retrieval of a matrix element) in 10^{-7} seconds. Then, since $20! \simeq 2(10^{18})$, it would take slightly less than 70 centuries to solve our problem using Algorithm ETS.

Of course, this pretty well shatters our confidence in Algorithm ETS. In

Chap. 3 we shall see how we can get enumerative algorithms to yield respectable, but not necessarily optimal, solutions for large problems in reasonable time.

This is a good place to point out that the steps listed near the end of Sec. 1.1 should not be treated as though they are carved in stone. They are guidelines. Some steps may be performed concurrently with others; some may even be omitted. If you are given a good model, there is probably no need to develop another. Nothing is holy about the ordering of the steps. Of course, you cannot prove the correctness of an algorithm before it has been designed, but it may be better to analyze the design to some extent before implementing it. This is particularly true if you have a reason to suspect that your algorithm will be exponential (as in our example). Some analysis in the design stage may help you to see how to make the algorithm more efficient. Finally, parts of the development process may be reconsidered profitably after they were once considered finished. For example, the analysis and testing phases can provide valuable feedback to the design and implementation steps.

For a given algorithm, the derivation of a function such as a worst-case upper bound falls under the heading of "an analysis of the algorithm." It is also of interest to investigate all possible algorithms that solve the same kind of problem and to determine which of these is best relative to a given criterion. This activity goes under the heading of "computational complexity" and is very difficult.

Program Testing

Once a program has been coded, it is time to run it. As we know all too well, running is preceded by debugging. After a variety of syntactic, keypunching, and logical errors have been corrected, we finally get our program to run for a simple case (one that can be hand checked). Now what?

The program testing process should include considerably more than the above. It would be an exaggeration to say that program testing in computer science is analogous to experimentation in the natural sciences, but we think that there are some similarities. Program testing might be described as an experimental verification that the program is doing what it should. It is also an experimental attempt to ascertain the usage limits of the algorithm/program.

All of us are capable of making mistakes in our proofs and in transcribing a correct algorithm into coded form. Each of us has forgotten or did not plan for a special case of a problem. It is not enough to prove that an algorithm is correct. The final coded product must be extensively tested and verified. Minute peculiarities of your operating system might cause some part of your algorithm to be executed, for some input, in a way that you had not anticipated. The program must be verified for a broad spectrum of allowable inputs. This process can be time-consuming, tedious, and complex.

How does one choose the test input? This question cannot be given a general answer. For any algorithm the answer depends on the complexity of the program, the time and staff available for testing, the number of inputs whose correct output can be ascertained, and so forth. Usually the set of all possible inputs is astronomical and a complete testing is impractical. We must choose a variety of inputs which test every segment of code in the program. A representative sampling of the cases that we are likely to encounter in practice is a must. It is rarely possible to guarantee that a program is correct, but we can and must do enough testing to be reasonably confident that it is.

Further testing is also necessary to ascertain the performance quality of the algorithm. The kind of analysis described in the previous section is not always infallible. Simplifying assumptions made in the analysis must be experimentally verified. Many large, complicated algorithms are difficult or impossible to study mathematically. An experimental performance evaluation is especially important in such cases since it is all that is available to judge the quality of the algorithm.

Experience indicates that average performance analyses are more valuable and more difficult to obtain than best- or worst-case analyses. If a worst-case analysis is available, but not an average or expected performance analysis, it is of considerable importance to ascertain experimentally if the algorithm performs significantly better on the average than it does in the worst case.

Analytical and experimental analyses tend to complement each other. Analytical analyses can be inaccurate if major simplifying assumptions are made. These may be only "ball park" estimates. On the other hand, it may be impossible or impractical to obtain enough of an experimental sample to guarantee any statistical confidence. Experimental results, especially when randomly generated data are used, may be unknowingly biased. Both analytical and experimental evidence should be offered, whenever possible, to support performance claims.

Programs should also be tested to determine their computational limitations. Many programs work well for some input cases and poorly for others. It is desirable that the algorithm's performance "gracefully" change from good to bad as we move from inputs for which the algorithm performs well to those for which it does not. Algorithm ETS performs well for $n \leq 6$ and very badly for $n \geq 15$. Unfortunately, the transition is not gradual; the algorithm tends to perform poorly for the intermediate cases. It is desirable to use both analytical and experimental methods to characterize those input data that are either "good" or "bad." For example, suppose we have algorithm that is worst-case $O(n!)$ but has an $O(n^3)$ average performance. It would be extremely convenient if we could characterize the input to our algorithm by another parameter α and then ascertain which (n, α) combinations give rise to exponential running times and which combinations can be solved in polynomial time. If the average behavior is $O(n^3)$, clearly those inputs which require exponential time must be in the minority. If these inputs can be recognized, they can be avoided. Unfortunately, the state of the art has not yet developed to the point where we can recognize such inputs, but it is something to strive for.

Documentation

Documentation is not really the last step in the complete development of an algorithm. In particular, it does not consist of adding comment cards when you are finished with everything else. The documentation process should be interwoven with the entire development of the algorithm, and especially with the design and implementation steps.

It is hard to read someone else's raw code. The most obvious reason for documentation is to enable individuals to understand programs which they did not write. Of course, the best way to do this is to write code that is so clear that it is virtually self-documenting. For all but the simplest programs, this is not possible; and code must be supplemented by other forms of documentation. This usually takes the form of comment cards.

But this is really only the tip of the iceberg. Documentation includes every piece of information that you produce which helps to explain what is going on, that is, such things as flowcharts, records of the stages in your top-down development, supporting proofs of correctness, test results, detailed descriptions of input-output requirements and format, and so forth. A more detailed discussion of documentation can be found in Sec. 4.3. For the time being, we leave you with a golden rule: Document your programs the way you would want others to document the programs which you read.

Exercises 1.3

1.3.1 *Traveling salesman solution.* Find an optimum solution to the traveling salesman problem of Fig. 1.3.1 using Algorithm ETS of this section.

1.3.2 *Factorials* (*testing*). What is the largest positive integer N such that N! will fit exactly into one word on your local computer? Analytically predict your answer before you go to the computer. Try to be clever. What tricks might you use to squeeze larger values into the word?

1.3.3 *Encoding-decoding* (*complete development*). One elementary code is to place the letters of the alphabet into one-to-one correspondence with a scrambled version of the alphabet. For example, if the correspondence were as follows:

Alphabet: A B C D E F G H I J K L M N O P Q R S T U V W X Y Z
Code letter: M T J C Z E O K L N S U X Y A D F B W V G H I P R Q

then the word CODE would be encoded as JACZ.

Design, implement, test, and document an algorithm which will take a code as input and encode/decode arbitrary messages.

1.3.4 *Permutations (a proof).* Show that there are $n!$ permutations of the first n positive integers.

1.3.5 *Permutation generator (complete development).* Completely develop an algorithm which generates all the permutations of the first n positive integers. Would your algorithm be suitable for step 2 of Algorithm ETS?

1.3.6 *Tour construction (design).* Design a subalgorithm for the tour construction in step 3 of Algorithm ETS.

1.3.7 *Number of salesman tours (proof).* If the cost matrix C in the n-city traveling salesman problem is symmetric, that is, $c_{ij} = c_{ji}$ for all i and j, then show that there are $(n-1)!/2$ nonidentical tours. Two tours are nonidentical if they do not list exactly the same sequence of cities.

1.3.8 *Complexity algebra.*
- (a) Show $f(n) = 3.7n^2 + 100.8n + 10^6$ is $O(n^2)$ as $n \to \infty$.
- (b) Show $f(n) = 2^n/100 - 100$ is $O(2^n)$ as $n \to \infty$.
- (c) Show $n!$ is $o(n^n)$ as $n \to \infty$.
- (d) Show that 2^n grows faster than any finite-degree polynomial in n as $n \to \infty$.

1.3.9 *Traveling salesman conjecture (model/design).* Consider the cost matrix C of an n-city traveling salesman problem. If we choose n elements from C in such a way that exactly one element is chosen from each row and each column, do the lines corresponding to these elements form a tour?

1.3.10 *Roman numerals (complete development).* Develop an algorithm which converts an arbitrary positive Arabic integer into a Roman numeral and vice versa.

1.3.11 *Triangle triples (complete development).* For any 3-tuple of numbers (x, y, z), completely develop an algorithm which determines whether or not there exists a triangle T with sides x, y, and z.

*1.3.12 *Permutations (algorithm comparison).* Design and implement two different algorithms for generating a random permutation. Discuss their relative efficiencies.

*1.3.13 *Factorials (design).* Design an algorithm which will compute the value of the function $F(n) = m$, where the decimal expansion of $n!$ contains m digits.

1.3.14 *Exponential functions (complexity).* Design an algorithm which will determine how long it will take your computer to execute 2^n, n^n, and $n!$ basic operations for $n = 1, 2, 3, \ldots, 50$.

*1.3.15 *Exponential functions (complexity).* Design an algorithm for computing $G(m, n) = k$, where k is defined such that $n^{k-1} \le m! \le n^k$. Compute some values of $G(m, n)$.

L1.3.16 *Program profile* (*complexity, testing*). The profile of a program for a given input is essentially a histogram of the number of times each statement of the code is executed when the program is run.

Implement Algorithm MAX of Sec. 1.2. For N = 20, create input uniformly over the range [0, 100] using a random number generator. Construct an average profile for your program based on a sample of 50 input sets.

2 SOME BASIC TOOLS AND ALGORITHMS

There are a number of basic tools that should be part of the working knowledge of anyone who designs and analyzes algorithms. In this chapter we present some fundamental theory and algorithms from four different areas: top-down structured programming, networks, data structures, and probability and statistics. The material in these sections will be useful throughout the remainder of this text.

2.1 TOP-DOWN STRUCTURED PROGRAMMING AND PROGRAM CORRECTNESS

A mathematical function $f : X \to Y$ can be defined as a rule which assigns to every element x in some *domain* X, a corresponding (unique) value y in some *range* Y. A specific function f from a given domain X to a given range Y can be completely described in one of two ways: either by providing a table of ordered pairs $[x, f(x)]$, which indicates for every argument $x \in X$, the value of the function $f(x)$; or by providing a computational rule, or set of rules (that is, an algorithm), which enables one to compute the value $f(x)$ given the value x. This latter method is necessary when the domain of the function is either an infinite set or an extremely large finite set.

The primary purpose of an algorithm is to *correctly implement* a specification of a given function $f: X \to Y$. Stated in other words, every algorithm serves to define a function $a : X' \to Y'$ from a domain X' of allowable inputs to a range Y' of possible outputs. The algorithm is a correct implementation of the function f if $X \subseteq X'$ and $Y \subseteq Y'$, and if

$$f(x) = a(x) \qquad \text{for every } x \in X$$

A secondary purpose of an algorithm is to implement a function so that the time and effort required to compute an arbitrary value $f(x) = a(x)$ is as little as possible.

Another purpose of an algorithm, and one which has become increasingly important, is to implement a function in a manner that is easy to understand, simple to prove correct, and easy to modify if the specifications of the function change.

A major reason for this increased importance is that as algorithms become more and more complex, so do the jobs of understanding how they work, correcting them when errors are found, verifying their correctness, and correctly modifying them when necessary.   In recent years it has been observed that from 50 to 100 percent of a programmer's time is spent in problems of program correction, maintenance, and modification.   In an effort to decrease this programming effort, the computing industry has sought a more systematic approach to computer programming, that is, a methodology which could decrease the likelihood of errors in computer programs and increase their clarity and modifiability.

Perhaps the most notable methodology introduced to date is called *top-down structured programming*.   In this section we introduce the basic ideas of this methodology and illustrate it with an example.

Structured Programming

We begin our explanation of structured programming by defining a flowchart.   A *flowchart* is a directed network having three kinds of vertices, which are illustrated in Fig. 2.1.1.

A *function vertex* is used to represent a function $f: X \to Y$.   A *predicate vertex* is used to represent a function (or predicate) $p: X \to \{T, F\}$, that is, a Boolean expression, which passes control along one of two branches.   A *collecting vertex* represents the passage of control from one of two incoming branches to one outgoing branch.

A *structured* flowchart is a flowchart which can be expressed as a composition of the four primitive flowcharts illustrated in Fig. 2.1.2.   It is a relatively straightforward matter to show that any computer program can be "represented" by a flowchart.   It is not at all obvious, but has been shown by Böhm and Jacopini, that any flowchart can in turn be represented by a structured flowchart.   An immediate

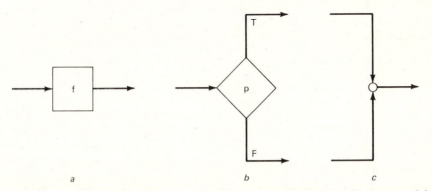

FIG. 2.1.1   Types of vertices in a flowchart: (*a*) function vertex, (*b*) predicate vertex, (*c*) collecting vertex.

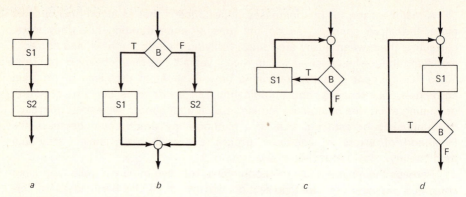

FIG. 2.1.2 The four primitives of a structured flowchart.

corollary of this result is that the four primitive flowcharts of Fig. 2.1.2 are sufficient to design any algorithm.

When a structured flowchart is used to represent a computer program, B is interpreted as a Boolean expression, and S1, S2 are interpreted as program statements (or procedures).

The flowcharts of Fig. 2.1.2a to d are referred to as *program control structures*. Figure 2.1.2a is called *composition* and is written as **do** S1; S2 **od** (or simply as S1; S2). Figure 2.1.2b is called *selection* (or *alternation*) and is written as **if** B **then** S1 **else** S2 **fi** (the **fi** is optional and serves to complete the **if**). The flowcharts of Fig. 2.1.2c and d are called *iteration* (or *repetition*) and are written, respectively, as **while** B **do** S1 **od** and **do** S1 **while** B **od** (the **od** is also optional).

We should point out that the often used, simpler statement, **if** B **then** S1, whose flowchart is given in Fig. 2.1.3, is a special case of the **if-then-else** statement.

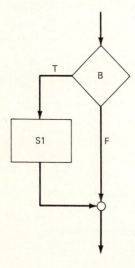

FIG. 2.1.3 Flowchart for the statement **if** B **then** S1.

It is important to observe that each of these four program control structures has a single entry branch and a single exit branch. Therefore, any flowchart composed of these primitives will also have a single entry and a single exit. Figure 2.1.4 illustrates several examples of structured flowcharts built up from these primitives; these flowcharts can be described linguistically as follows:

(*a*)
> **if** B **then do** S1; S2 **od**
> **else if** C **then** S3
> **else** S4 **fi fi**

(*b*)
> **if** B **then if** C **then do** S1; S2 **od**
> **else while** D **do** S3 **od fi**
> **else do** S4; S5; S6 **od fi**

Notice the complete absence of **goto**'s in the preceding flowcharts.

Strictly speaking, structured programming refers to the process of designing algorithms in terms of structured flowcharts. More generally, however, structured programming permits a wider variety of primitive control structures than those of Böhm and Jacopini (that is, Fig. 2.1.2*a* to *d*). The reason for this is that although these control structures are sufficient to build any computer program, they do not necessarily build them in either the simplest or most natural way. Several examples will illustrate this.

The first example (see Fig. 2.1.5) corresponds to the situation that is handled in

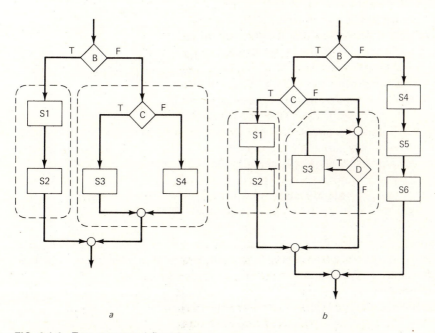

a

b

FIG. 2.1.4 Two structured flowcharts.

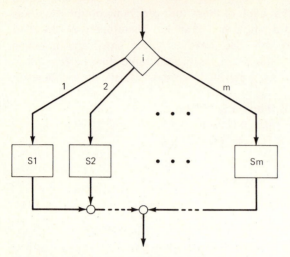

FIG. 2.1.5 Flowchart for a **case** statement.

Fortran by the COMPUTED GO TO statement. This flowchart can be expressed linguistically as

case i **of** S1; S2; . . . ; Sm **fo**

which is equivalent in (less natural) terms to

if i = 1 **then** S1 **else**
if i = 2 **then** S2 **else**

.
.

if i = m **then** Sm **fi** . . . **fi fi**†

A second example (see Fig. 2.1.6) corresponds to the situation where one needs to abnormally terminate an iteration, or DO loop, by providing an exit branch. One possible linguistic statement of the flowchart in Fig. 2.1.6 is

while B **do** S1; **if** C **then** S2
else goto OUT **fi od**

Although the purer forms of structured programming do not permit **goto** statements, flowcharts which use **goto** statements carefully can still retain much of the single-entry/single-exit character of structured flowcharts.

Another example of a simple, unstructured flowchart which occurs naturally in programming is given in Fig. 2.1.7a. One way of structuring this flowchart is given

---

†Strictly speaking, if i is not equal to any of 1, 2, . . . , m, this statement is bypassed; Fig. 2.1.5 does not reflect this.

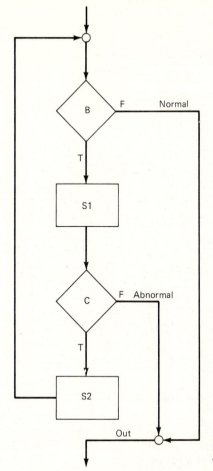

FIG. 2.1.6 Flowchart for an abnormal termination of an iteration.

in Fig. 2.1.7b, although the result is not particularly natural. Notice that a linguistic statement of the unstructured flowchart in Fig. 2.1.7a requires the use of a **goto** statement. For example,

$$k\text{: S1; }\textbf{if } B \textbf{ then } S2; \textbf{ goto } k \textbf{ fi}$$

whereas a linguistic statement of the structured flowchart in Fig. 2.1.7b does not. For example,

$$\textbf{do } S1; \textbf{ while } B \textbf{ do } S2; S1 \textbf{ od od}$$

Loosely speaking, structured programming refers to the process of designing algorithms in terms of "quasistructured" flowcharts, where the primitive control structures are preferably those of Böhm and Jacopini. However, others of a "simple type" are allowed, provided they have the single-entry/single-exit property.

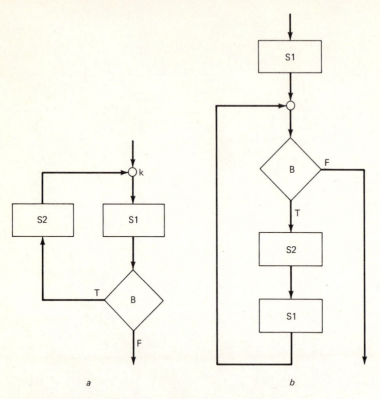

FIG. 2.1.7 (*a*) An unstructured flowchart; (*b*) an equivalent structured flowchart.

Top-down Programming and Program Correctness

As we mentioned in Sec. 1.3, top-down programming refers to the process of stepwise refinement of an algorithm into successively smaller pieces until a point is reached from which code can easily be written. Figure 2.1.8 illustrates this process using the flowchart of Fig. 2.1.4*b*.

Top-down structured programming refers to the top-down process restricted to the use of structured flowcharts. The idea is simple. Suppose one is trying to design an algorithm for a particular function *f*. Suppose further that it can be proved that *f* equals the composition of two other (presumably simpler) functions *g* and *h*—that is, $f(x) = h(g(x))$—as illustrated in Fig. 2.1.9. Then the problem of designing an algorithm for *f* reduces to the problems of designing algorithms for *g* and *h*.

Furthermore assume that it can be proved that the function *g* equals some function *i* if a given parameter *x* is nonnegative, or equals some other function *j* if *x* is negative. Then an algorithm for computing *g* can be expressed as an **if-then-else** (see Fig. 2.1.10). Therefore, if algorithms for the functions *i* and *j* can be designed, a correct algorithm for function *g* can be designed automatically.

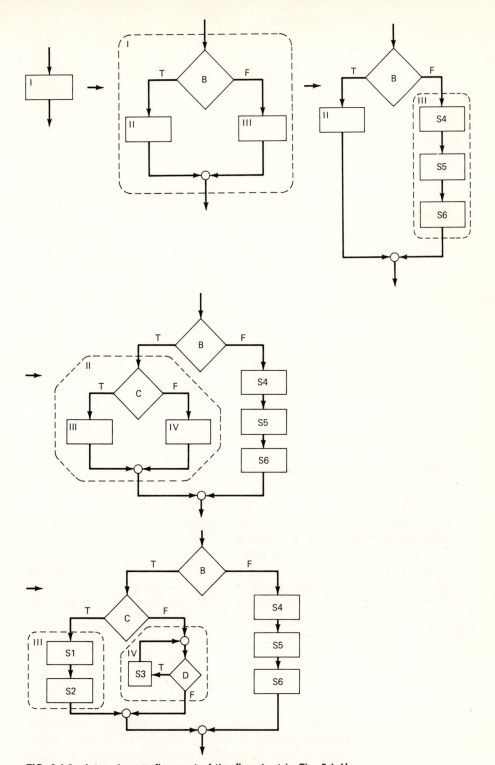

FIG. 2.1.8 A top-down refinement of the flowchart in Fig. 2.1.4*b*.

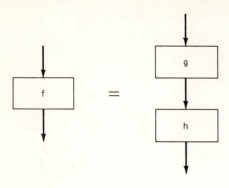

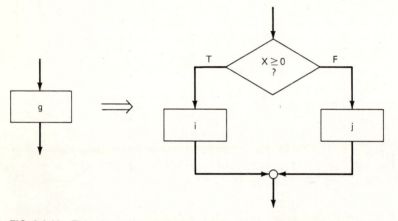

FIG. 2.1.9 The expression of a function f as a composition of functions g and h.

FIG. 2.1.10 The expression of the function g using an **if-then-else** predicate.

Algorithms designed in such a top-down fashion tend to have correctness built into them in small steps as they are developed. For this reason, they tend to have fewer errors and are easier to prove correct.

In top-down structured programming one asks, at every step of the refinement process, whether the (subfunction) function currently under design consideration can be expressed as a composition of two (or more) other functions—that is, a **do** S1; S2 **od**, an **if-then-else** function, a **do-while**, or **while-do** function. A specific example will help clarify these ideas.

The Knight's Tour

In the game of chess, a knight can move from a given square (or position) to one of at most eight other positions, as indicated in Fig. 2.1.11. Since a knight cannot move off the chessboard, it cannot move to eight new positions from every

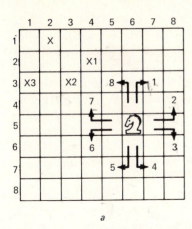

New position from position (I, J)

1 (I − 2, J + 1)

2 (I − 1, J + 2)

3 (I + 1, J + 2)

4 (I + 2, J + 1)

5 (I + 2, J − 1)

6 (I + 1, J − 2)

7 (I − 1, J − 2)

8 (I − 2, J − 1)

a   b

FIG. 2.1.11 The possible moves of a knight.

position. For example, from position X = (1, 2) it can only reach in one move the positions X1, X2, X3 indicated in Fig. 2.1.11a.

Consider the following question: Is it possible for a knight to start on some square of the chessboard and make a sequence of 63 moves in such a way that it visits every square exactly once? Such a traversal is called a *knight's tour*.

Lacking any mathematical theory which can answer this question quickly the only recourse available would seem to involve enumerating all possible walks of a knight on a chessboard. But surely the number of such walks is combinatorially prohibitive.

Perhaps we could use a computer to cut through this combinatorial explosion and find a knight's tour. Let us therefore design an algorithm, using some intuitive procedure, which can construct a series of walks by a knight on a chessboard, and hope that a knight's tour will emerge.

Consider an arbitrary walk by the knight from an arbitrary square, (5, 6) for example (see Fig. 2.1.12); an integer N indicates the N*th* square visited in the

	1	2	3	4	5	6	7	8
1	22	19	24	17	14	5	10	7
2	25	16	21	32	11	8	13	4
3	20	23	18	15		3	6	9
4	29	26	31		33	12		2
5	40	37	28	35	44	1		
6	27	30	39			34		
7	38	41	36	45		43		
8		46		42				

FIG. 2.1.12 An arbitrary walk by a knight from position (5, 6).

walk. It is clear in this example that after the forty-fifth move, to position (8, 2), the knight cannot move without either going off the board or visiting a square for the second time. Perhaps a more systematic approach can produce a longer walk.

Consider the following simple strategy. Start at an arbitrary square. From a given square, attempt to move first to position 1, as indicated in Fig. 2.1.11*b* (that is, up 2 and to the right 1). If we cannot do this, try to move to position 2; failing this, position 3, etc., in a clockwise fashion. If we ever reach a position from which it is not possible to move to any of these eight positions without either moving off the board or revisiting a square, then the walk will stop and we will record (or print out) the results.

With this much in mind, let us begin the top-down design of such an algorithm. Start with the single statement: Create a possible knight's tour (Fig. 2.1.13*a*). This will involve constructing a walk and then printing the result (Fig. 2.1.13*b*). Constructing a walk breaks down into selecting an initial position and then constructing a walk from that position (Fig. 2.1.13*c*).

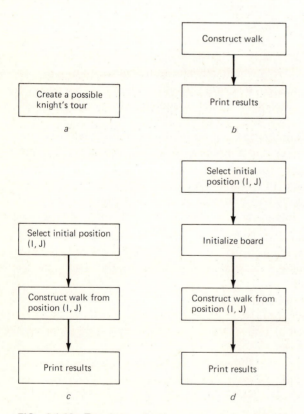

FIG. 2.1.13 Top-down development of a possible knight's tour algorithm.

99	99	99	99	99	99	99	99	99	99	99	99
99	99	99	99	99	99	99	99	99	99	99	99
99	99	0	0	0	0	0	0	0	0	99	99
99	99	0	0	0	0	0	0	0	0	99	99
99	99	0	0	0	0	0	0	0	0	99	99
99	99	0	0	0	0	0	0	0	0	99	99
99	99	0	0	0	0	0	0	0	0	99	99
99	99	0	0	0	0	0	0	0	0	99	99
99	99	0	0	0	0	0	0	0	0	99	99
99	99	0	0	0	0	0	0	0	0	99	99
99	99	99	99	99	99	99	99	99	99	99	99
99	99	99	99	99	99	99	99	99	99	99	99

FIG. 2.1.14 Initial board configuration.

At this point we have a fair idea as to how to select a starting position, for example, by reading in two integers (I, J) between 1 and 8. We can also see that printing the results will involve printing the integers stored in an array—call it BOARD(I, J)—corresponding to the chessboard. Thus, we should concentrate more on how to construct the walk from position (I, J).

The fact that integers are stored in the array BOARD(I, J) suggests the need to initialize all elements in the array to 0 (Fig. 2.1.13d). A move into the square at position (I, J) is then possible if BOARD(I, J) = 0. Furthermore, a move off the board can be detected if either I or J lie outside the range of integers between 1 and 8.

Moving off the board can also be detected by another scheme (see Fig. 2.1.14). Create two additional rows around the array BOARD and store an initial value, say, 99, in each new square. An attempt to move off the board can then be detected by the nonzero value.

Having settled the matter of initializing the array BOARD, consider again the problem of constructing a tour from an arbitrary position (I, J). We must try to break this step into a sequence of smaller steps, an **if-then-else**, a **do-while**, or a **while-do**.

One can sense that there is a basic iteration involved here in which an index, say K, runs through each of the eight possible positions which can be reached from position (I, J). The walk stops whenever K > 8. This suggests the breakdown in Fig. 2.1.15a.

In attempting to move to a new position from (I, J), one of two things can happen: either it is possible, in which case we change the value of (I, J) to the new

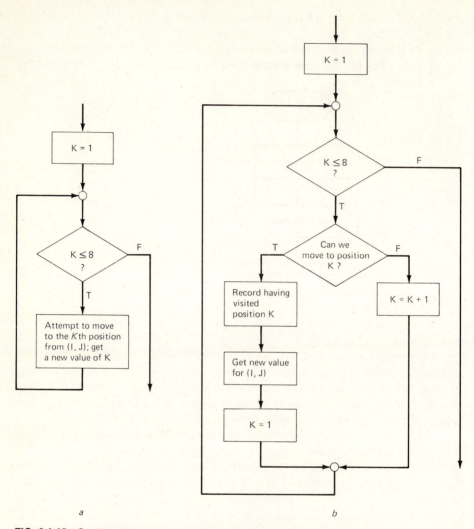

a

b

FIG. 2.1.15 Continued top-down development of knight's tour algorithm.

K	IMOVE	JMOVE
1	−2	+1
2	−1	+2
3	+1	+2
4	+2	+1
5	+2	−1
6	+1	−2
7	−1	−2
8	−2	−1

FIG. 2.1.16 Tables of changes in I and J required to reach position K.

position and reset K to 1; or it is not possible, in which case we increment K to K + 1 (see Fig. 2.1.15*b*).

There remains the problem of determining which square is in position K from square (I, J).   For this purpose a table is created (Fig. 2.1.16) which indicates the

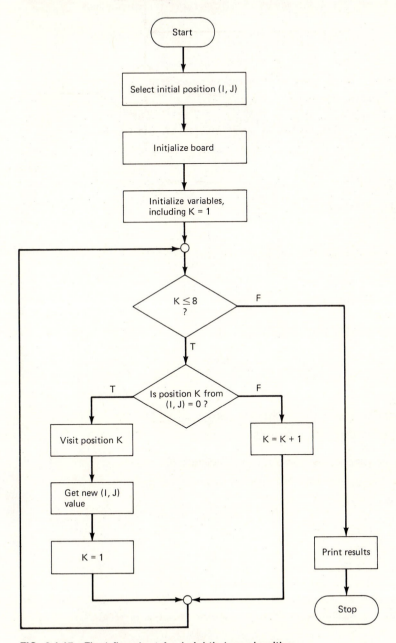

FIG. 2.1.17   Final flowchart for knight's tour algorithm.

```
C       PROGRAM KNIGHT (OUTPUT,INPUT,TAPE5=INPUT,TAPF6=OUTPUT)
C       THIS PROGRAM CONSTRUCTS A TOUR OF A KNIGHT ON A CHESSBOARD
C       USING A CLOCKWISE STRATEGY FOR MOVING TO A NEW POSITION, WHERE THE
C       INITIAL POSITION IS READ IN.
C
C       VARIABLE        DESCRIPTION
C
C       BOARD(I,J)      =N MEANS THAT THE SQUARE IN ROW I, COLUMN J
C                       WAS THE N-TH SQUARE VISITED ON THE KNIGHTS TOUR.
C                       =0 MEANS THAT THE SQUARE WAS NEVER VISITED.
C                       =99 MEANS THAT THE SQUARE IS OFF THE BORDER OF
C                       THE BOARD AND IS USED TO PREVENT THE KNIGHT FROM
C                       MOVING OFF THE BOARD.
C
C       IMOVE(K)        THE K-TH POSITION, 1 .LE. K .LE. 8 TO WHICH THE
C       JMOVE(K)        KNIGHT CAN MOVF FROM A GIVEN SQUARE.
C
C       I,J             THE CURRENT POSITION OF THE KNIGHT.
C
C       INEXT,JNEXT     A POSSIBLE NEXT SQUARE TO BE VISITED.
C
        INTEGER BOARD(12,12),IMOVE(8),JMOVE(8)
        DATA IMOVE(1),IMOVE(2),IMOVE(3),IMOVE(4),IMOVE(5),IMOVE(6),
       + IMOVE(7),IMOVE(8)/-2,-1,1,2,2,1,-1,-2/
        DATA JMOVE(1),JMOVE(2),JMOVE(3),JMOVE(4),JMOVE(5),JMOVE(6),
       + JMOVE(7),JMOVE(8)/1,2,2,1,-1,-2,-2,-1/
C
C       SELECT INITIAL POSITION
C
        READ(5,1000) IINIT,JINIT
1000    FORMAT(2I2)
C
C       INITIALIZE BOARD
C
        DO 200 I = 1,12
            DO 100 J = 1,12
                BOARD(I,J) = 0
                IF ( I .LT. 3 .OR. I .GT. 10 .OR.
       +             J .LT. 3 .OR. J .GT. 10 ) BOARD(I,J) = 99
100         CONTINUE
200     CONTINUE
C
C       INITIALIZE VARIABLES.
C
        K = 1
        BOARD(IINIT,JINIT) = 1
        I = IINIT
        J = JINIT
        N = 2
C
C       CHECK IF TOUR IS ENDED.
C
300     IF ( K .GT. 8 ) GOTO 500
C
C           CHECK IF A MOVE CAN BE MADE TO POSITION K.
C
        INEXT = I+IMOVE(K)
        JNEXT = J+JMOVE(K)
C
        IF ( BOARD(INEXT,JNEXT) .NE. 0 ) GOTO 400
C
C           THEN (VISIT NEW POSITION AND GET NEW (I,J) VALUE)
C
            BOARD(INEXT,JNEXT) = N
            N = N+1
            J = JNEXT
            I = INEXT
            K = 1
            GOTO 300
C
C           ELSE (TRY NEXT POSITION)
C
400         K = K+1
            GOTO 300
C
C           TOUR HAS ENDED. PRINT BOARD AND NUMBER OF MOVES IN TOUR.
C
500     N = N-1
        WRITE(6,2000)((BOARD(I,J),J=3,10),I=3,10),N
2000    FORMAT(9H1BOARD IS,//,8(8I10/),//,11H THERE WERE,I5,5HMOVES)
        STOP
        END
```

FIG. 2.1.18 A Fortran implementation of the knight's tour algorithm.

changes in value of I and J required to reach position K. At this point we can complete our final *structured* flowchart, which is shown in Fig. 2.1.17.

A Fortran implementation of this algorithm follows (Fig. 2.1.18). We leave it as exercises to code this algorithm, to see if it actually finds a knight's tour, or to modify the algorithm in order to find a knight's tour by some other strategy. We assure you that it can be done!

Top-down Structured Programming: Additional Considerations

We do not mean to suggest that the subject of top-down structured programming is as simple as we have described it. It involves a variety of additional aspects, one of which is the motto "Simplify your control structures." Other aspects include appropriate documentation, indentation of program statements, and breaking a program into manageable pieces.

It is recommended, for example, that program modules be limited to one or two pages of printer output. A page is a meaningful unit which can be kept in the mind at one time, and which minimizes the necessity of having to turn a page to follow an arbitrary jump in a program.

It is to be expected that the effort required to design a top-down structured program will be greater than that required to obtain an unstructured program. However, experience shows that the rewards outweigh this additional investment of time. Structured programs are usually easier to read and understand since they can be read from top to bottom without having to scan backward or jump far ahead. The primary reason for this is that the overall control structure of a structured program is a *tree* rather than a network with many cycles. For example, in Fig. 2.1.19 we present the trees which describe the control structures

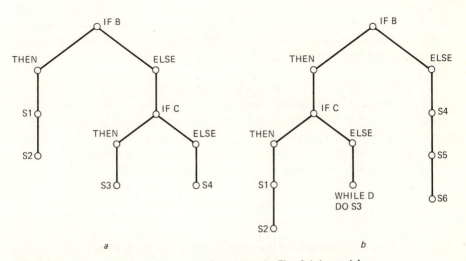

FIG. 2.1.19 The control structures for flowcharts in Fig. 2.1.4*a* and *b*.

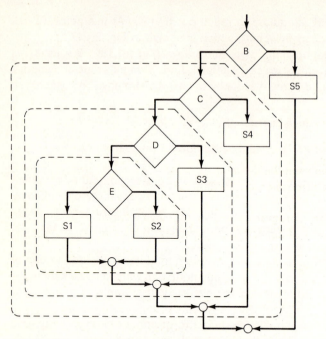

FIG. 2.1.20 A structured flowchart nested three deep.

of the flowcharts of Fig. 2.1.4*a* and *b*. This observation has caused some people to refer to these as *tree-structured* programs.

Before concluding this discussion of top-down structured programming, we should offer two words of caution. First, this approach to algorithm design does not guarantee that errors will not be made. Experience shows, for example, that when control structures are nested three deep or more, the likelihood of making an error increases significantly. Figure 2.1.20 provides an example of a structured flowchart nested three deep. A similar situation exists when modules become too long.

A second word of caution stems from the term "**goto**-less programming," which has been used to describe structured programming. Whatever structured programming is, it is neither the method of programming which forbids the use of **goto** statements, nor the process of taking an unstructured program and stripping it of its **goto** statements. In addition to failing to produce a structured program, these processes are likely to make a program less transparent.

Exercises 2.1

2.1.1 Does PROGRAM KNIGHT find a knight's tour from an arbitrary starting position? From any starting position?

2.1.2 Develop the following heuristic for the knight's tour problem. Start at an arbitrary square of the chessboard and move to a square from which the smallest (largest?) number of squares can be reached in the following move. Continue this procedure until it is impossible to move or until a knight's tour is found.

2.1.3 Does the heuristic in Exercise 2.1.2 find a knight's tour from an arbitrary starting position?

2.1.4 Distinguish between the concept of "program correctness" as used in this section and the discussion of algorithm correctness in Sec. 1.3.

2.1.5 Review whatever programming languages you are familiar with, and rank them on the basis of suitability for structured programming.

*L**2.1.6** Reconsider selected problems from the exercise set in Chap. 1 which involve writing programs. Rework these algorithms in a top-down structured fashion. Compare and contrast the old and new versions of these programs. From this experience, discuss the advantages and disadvantages of the top-down structured approach to programming.

2.2 NETWORKS[1]

The fact that networks are among the most useful of mathematical tools is indicated by the many diverse areas in which they have been applied; these include chemistry, physics, civil and electrical engineering, operations research, psychology, sociology, linguistics, and many areas within mathematics (including numerical analysis, matrix theory, group theory, topology, discrete probabilistic processes, game theory, and combinatorics). Furthermore, networks, and in particular trees, are probably the most commonly used mathematical structures in computer science. Networks and trees are used in the study of data structures, compiling, programming languages, operating systems, computation theory, sorting, searching, and artificial intelligence. Figures 2.2.1 and 2.2.2 illustrate several examples of the use of networks as models. In this section we shall present the fundamentals of this theory, discuss various means of representing a network in a computer, and formulate several algorithms for determining elementary properties of networks.

---

[1]There is some disagreement in the computer science world as to whether "graph" or "network" is the more common term. We have chosen to use "network" since it appears to be the term used most often in applications.

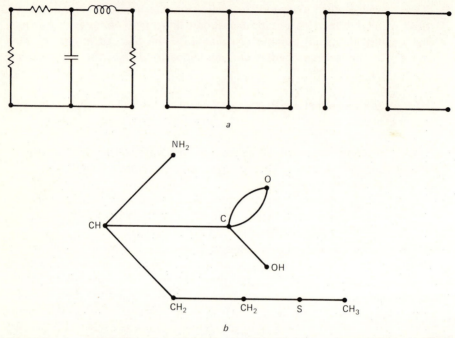

FIG. 2.2.1 (*a*) Spanning trees and electrical networks; (*b*) representation of organic compounds: methionine (without H atoms).

Fundamentals

A *network* $G = (V, E)$ consists of a finite set $V = V(G)$ of $M \geq 1$ *vertices* together with a finite set $E = E(G)$ of $N \geq 0$ unordered pairs (u, v) of distinct vertices, which are called the *edges* of G. The network $G_1 = (V_1, E_1)$ in Fig. 2.2.3*a* consists of seven vertices, $V_1 = \{t, u, v, w, x, y, z\}$, and seven edges, $E_1 = \{(u, v), (v, w), (w, x), (w, z), (z, v), (v, x), (w, y)\}$.

It is important to understand that *a network can be drawn in many different ways*; for example, the networks shown in Fig. 2.2.3*b* and *c* are the same as that shown in Fig. 2.2.3*a*. This follows from the definition of a network (convince yourself). The problem of deciding whether or not two drawings represent the same network will be considered in more detail at the end of this section.

Two vertices *u* and *v* are *adjacent* if there is an edge (u, v) in G; otherwise *u* and *v* are *independent*. Edge (u, v) is also said to be *incident* to vertices *u* and *v*.

Notice that we have said that edges consist of unordered pairs of distinct vertices. Thus, edges are *undirected* in the sense that (u, v) and (v, u) are considered to be the same. Furthermore, edges of the form (u, u), which are called *loops*, are not allowed. We also do not allow *multiedges* in a network, that is, the occurrence of two or more copies of a given edge. When multiedges are

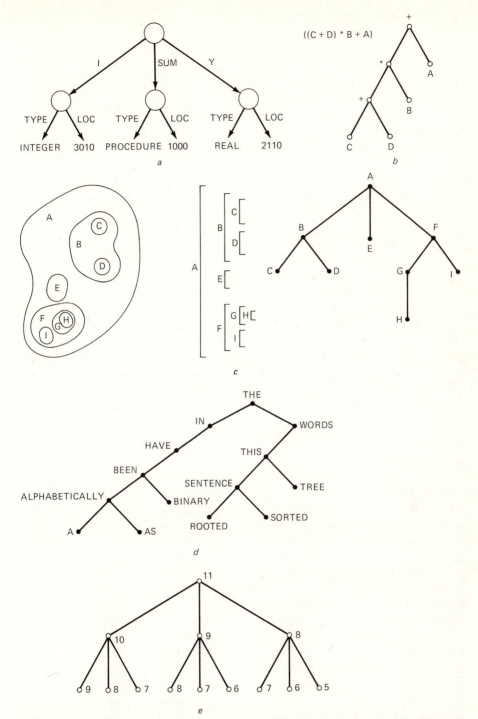

FIG. 2.2.2 Some applications of trees in computer science: (*a*) symbol tables; (*b*) arithmetic expressions; (*c*) subsets of sets and nested structures; (*d*) sort trees; (*e*) game trees: partial game tree of Nim.

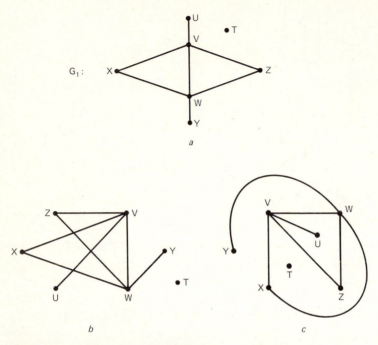

FIG. 2.2.3 An undirected network drawn three ways.

considered in a particular application, the network is called a *multinetwork* (see Fig. 2.2.4).

If we change the definition so that a network consists of a finite set of vertices together with a set of *ordered* pairs $[u, v]$ of distinct vertices, we define a *directed network*; see Fig. 2.2.5, in which $V(G_3) = \{u, v, w, x, y, z\}$ and $E(G_3) = \{[u, v], [v, w], [v, x], [x, w], [w, y], [w, z], [z, v]\}$. When considering directed networks $G = (V, E)$, we usually refer to the elements of V as *nodes* and the elements of E as *arcs*.

If $[u, v]$ is an arc in a directed network, we say that *u is adjacent to v* and *v is adjacent from u*.

In many applications it is desirable to weight the edges or arcs of a network in order to model quantities such as time, distance, or cost. A *weighted network* is one whose edges or arcs have been assigned real numbers.

The *neighborhood of a vertex v*, $N(v)$, consists of the set of vertices adjacent to v—that is, $N(v) = \{u | (u, v) \in E\}$. Thus the neighborhood of vertex v in Fig. 2.2.3a consists of vertices u, x, w, and z. The *degree of a vertex v*, denoted d_v or $\deg(v)$, equals the number of vertices in $N(v)$—that is, $d_v = \deg(v) = |N(v)|$. Thus, if the vertices of G_1 in Fig. 2.2.3 are ordered w, v, x, z, u, y, t, their corresponding degrees are 4, 4, 2, 2, 1, 1, 0—that is, $d_w = 4$, $d_v = 4$, $d_x = 2$, etc.

A vertex v is an *end-vertex* if $\deg(v) = 1$; and if $\deg(v) = 0$, v is said to be *isolated*. In Fig. 2.2.3a, vertices u and y are end-vertices and vertex t is isolated.

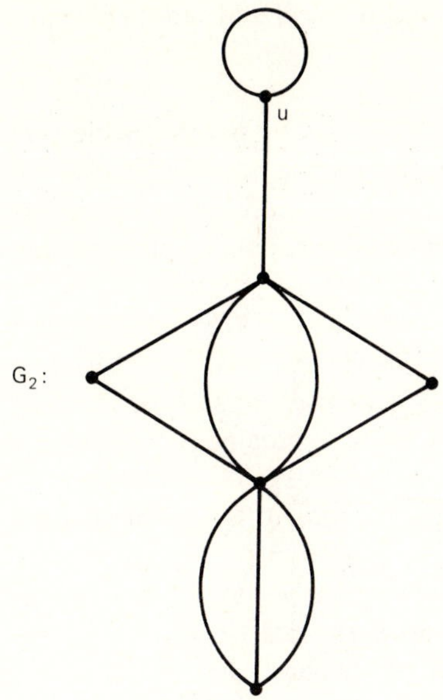

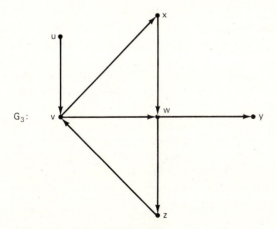

G_2:

FIG. 2.2.4 A multinetwork with a loop at *u*.

G_3:

FIG. 2.2.5 A directed network.

Theorem 2.2.1 Let G be a network having M vertices $v_1, v_2, \ldots, v_M$ and N edges. Then

$$\sum_{i=1}^{M} d_i = 2N$$

Proof The theorem follows immediately from the observation that each edge contributes 1 to the degree of each of its two vertices, therefore contributing 2 to the sum of the degrees of all vertices.

Corollary 2.2.1 In any network G the number of vertices of odd degree is even.

The proof of this corollary is left as an exercise.

As an application of Corollary 2.2.1, consider a group of k persons which we shall represent by k vertices $V = \{v_1, v_2, \dots, v_k\}$. If two people v_i and v_j know each other, let us say that there is an edge (v_i, v_j) between them. Corollary 2.2.1 tells us that in any group the number of people who know an odd number of other people is even.

A network $G' = (V', E')$ is a *subnetwork* of a network $G = (V, E)$ if $V' \subseteq V$ and $E' \subseteq E$. If $V' = V$ then we say that G' is a *spanning subnetwork* of G. If $v \in V$, then $G - v$ denotes the subnetwork whose vertices are $V - \{v\}$ and whose edges consist of all edges in E that are not incident to v; that is, $G - v$ is obtained by deleting v and all its incident edges. Similarly, for an edge $e = (u, v) \in E$, $G - e$ denotes the subnetwork obtained by removing e, but not u and v, from G; $G + e$ denotes the network obtained by adding e to G.

A *walk* in a network $G = (V, E)$ from a vertex u_1 to a vertex u_n is a (finite) sequence of vertices $W = u_1, u_2, \dots, u_n$ with the property that $(u_i, u_{i+1}) \in E(G)$ for every $1 \le i \le n - 1$; W is *closed* if $u_1 = u_n$, but otherwise it is *open*. A walk is a *path* if no vertex (and therefore no edge) appears more than once in W. A *cycle* is a closed walk $u_1, u_2, \dots, u_n, u_1$ for which $u_i \ne u_j$ if $i \ne j$. Figure 2.2.6 illustrates these terms.

A network G is *connected* if and only if for any two vertices u and v of G there exists a path from u to v; otherwise G is said to be *disconnected*. In a disconnected network G, we refer to the maximal connected subnetworks as the *components* of G.

Some connected networks can be disconnected by the removal of a single vertex or edge. A vertex v is said to be a *cut-vertex* of a network G if $G - v$ has

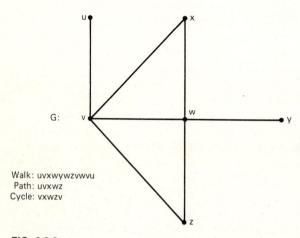

Walk: uvxwywzvwvu
Path: uvxwz
Cycle: vxwzv

FIG. 2.2.6

more components than G. An edge is a *bridge* of G if G − e has more components than G. In Fig. 2.2.6, w is a cut-vertex and (w, y) is a bridge.

Theorem 2.2.2 An edge e of a connected network G is a bridge if and only if there exist two vertices v_1 and v_2 such that e is on every path from v_1 to v_2.

The proof of this theorem is very simple and is left as an exercise. Theorem 2.2.2 provides a characterization of bridges that is used in the proof of Theorem 2.2.3.

Theorem 2.2.3 An edge e of a network G is a bridge if and only if e is not on a cycle of G.

Proof Let G′ be the component of G containing edge $e = (u, v)$. Assume that e is not on a cycle of G and is not a bridge. Then since G′ − e is connected, there must be a path P from u to v in G′ − e. However, e and P together produce a cycle in G′ containing e, which is a contradiction.

Conversely, let $e = (u, v)$ be an edge which lies on a cycle C of G′. Let v_1 and v_2 be arbitrary distinct vertices of G′. If e is not on a path P_1 from v_1 to v_2, then P_1 is also a path from v_1 to v_2 in G′ − e. If e is on a path P_2 from v_1 to v_2, then a walk from v_1 to v_2 can be constructed in G′ − e by replacing e by the remainder of cycle C. Since every walk from v_1 to v_2 contains a path from v_1 to v_2, there is a path from v_1 to v_2 in G′ − e. Since v_1 and v_2 are arbitrary, e cannot be a bridge.

Representations of Networks

A network G = (V, E) can be completely specified by simply listing the sets V and E. However, for most purposes this method of representing a network provides little insight into various properties that it may or may not possess.

We can also represent a network by drawing a (somewhat arbitrary) picture. Although a visual representation can be useful in gaining insights into properties of a given network, it becomes impractical for large networks and is of little use in computer applications.

There are a variety of techniques for representing a network in a computer. No single method is better than any other; the best representation depends on the problem to be solved. Caution should be exercised in this regard since the particular representation used can noticeably affect the speed and efficiency of an algorithm.

The adjacency matrix Any network G = (V, E) having M vertices can be represented by an M × M matrix, provided the vertices of G are given some (arbitrary) labeling. If the vertices of G are labeled $v_1, v_2, \ldots, v_M$, then the

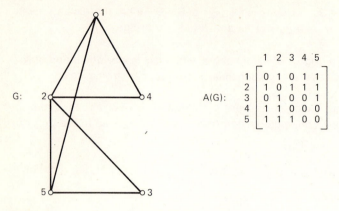

FIG. 2.2.7 An adjacency matrix representation.

adjacency matrix A(G) is defined as follows:

$$A(G) = [a_{ij}]$$

where $a_{ij} = 1$ if v_i is adjacent to v_j†
    $a_{ij} = 0$ otherwise

Figure 2.2.7 illustrates a network and its adjacency matrix. Note that for an undirected network G, A(G) will always be a symmetric (0, 1) matrix, with 0s on the diagonal. Note also that the degree of vertex v_i equals the number of 1s in either the *i*th row or the *i*th column of A(G).

The incidence matrix A second method for representing a network involves the incidence matrix I(G). If the vertices of G are labeled (arbitrarily) $v_1, v_2, \ldots, v_M$, and the edges are labeled $e_1, e_2, \ldots, e_N$, then the M × N *incidence matrix* is defined as follows:

$$I(G) = [b_{ij}]$$

where $b_{ij} = 1$ if v_i is incident to e_j
    $b_{ij} = 0$ otherwise

Figure 2.2.8 contains the incidence matrix I(G) of the network G in Fig. 2.2.7.

Note that every column in I(G) contains exactly two 1s and that no two columns are identical. Also note that the number of 1s in the *i*th row equals the degree d_i of v_i in G. The incidence matrix is useful for solving a variety of network problems involving cycles. On the other hand, the incidence matrix requires more memory (M × N, that is, on the order of M^3 words) and uses it more inefficiently, insofar as (M − 2) × N of these words of memory have a 0 stored in them.

---

†If G is a weighted network, a_{ij} equals the weight of the edge between vertices *i* and *j*.

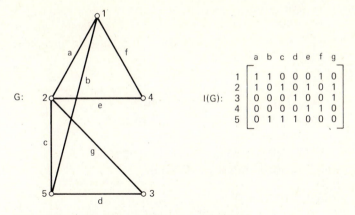

FIG. 2.2.8 An incidence matrix representation.

Adjacency vectors Instead of representing networks by (0, 1) matrices, we can use a matrix in which the entries correspond directly to the labels $v_1, v_2, \ldots, v_M$, given the vertices of G. In such a matrix the ith row contains a vector of all vertices adjacent to v_j. The order of the elements in such a vector, which is called an *adjacency vector*, is usually determined by the order in which the edges of G are presented (for example, as input to a computer program). In Fig. 2.2.9 we present a network G, a random listing of the edges of G, and an adjacency vector representation of G. The size of a matrix containing adjacency vectors need only be $M \times D$, where D is the maximum degree of a vertex in G.

Adjacency vectors are a particularly good means for representing a network when the problem can be solved by making a small number of passes over every edge of G.

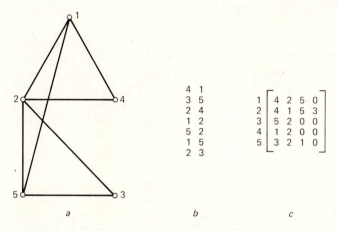

FIG. 2.2.9 An adjacency vector representation.

The following is a segment of Fortran code which can be used (subject to minor modifications in the READ statement) to create the adjacency vector representation of the network in Fig. 2.2.9a, given the edges in the order indicated in Fig. 2.2.9b.

```
      C
      C        WE ASSUME THAT ARRAYS NETW(I,J) AND
      C        DEGREE(I) ARE INITIALIZED TO ZERO
      C
      C        READ IN THE NUMBER M OF VERTICES
      C        AND THE NUMBER N OF EDGES
      C
               READ (    ) M,N
      C
      C        READ IN THE EDGES (U,V) OF G
      C
               DO 1  K = 1,N
                  READ (    ) U,V
                  DEGREE(U) = DEGREE(U) + 1
                  NETW(U,DEGREE(U)) = V
                  DEGREE(V) = DEGREE(V) + 1
                  NETW(V,DEGREE(V)) = U
      1        CONTINUE
                       .
                       .
                       .
```

Another useful network representation, in terms of *adjacency lists*, is considered in Sec. 2.3.

Let us use some of the ideas we have seen so far to develop an algorithm for determining if a network is connected and to identify its components if it is not. Such an algorithm can be an important subroutine in more complicated procedures.

The idea behind algorithm CONNECT is quite simple. Intuitively, we would like to shrink a component into a single vertex. This can be done by a sequential reduction process in which all vertices adjacent to a given vertex are "fused" with it. A vertex v is *fused* with an adjacent vertex u by deleting edge (v, u) and identifying v with u. The single resulting vertex, denoted as u, is adjacent to every vertex that was adjacent to u and/or v before fusion. Figure 2.2.10 illustrates this operation.

The procedure will consist of choosing an initial vertex v_0 and fusing an adjacent vertex with it. This is then repeated until v_0 has no remaining adjacent vertices. At this point the reduced network will either consist of the single vertex v_0, in which case the original network G was connected, or we shall have identified one of the components of G. In the latter case, a new initial vertex is chosen and the procedure is repeated. All the components can be identified in this way.

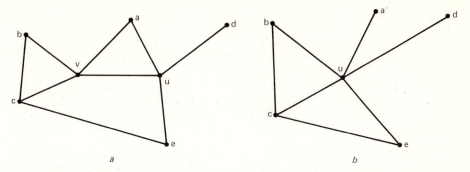

FIG. 2.2.10 Reduction process (*a*) before and (*b*) after fusion of *v* with *u*.

Algorithm CONNECT To determine the connected components of an arbitrary network G. Variable C counts the number of components.

Step 0. [Initialize] **Set** $H \leftarrow G$; **and** $C \leftarrow 0$.

Step 1. [Generate next component] **While** $H \neq \emptyset$ **do through** step 5 **od**; **and** STOP.

   Step 2. [Select vertex V_0 in H] **Set** $V_0 \leftarrow$ an arbitrary vertex in H.

   Step 3. [Fuse vertices with V_0] **While** V_0 is adjacent to at least one vertex U in H **do** step 4 **od**.

      Step 4. [Fusion] Let U be a vertex adjacent to V_0 in H. **Set** $H \leftarrow$ resulting network after U has been fused with V_0. (A record should be kept of all vertices fused with V_0 in this loop. For simplicity, we omit this bookkeeping task here.)

   Step 5. [Remove V_0] **Set** $H \leftarrow H - V_0$; **and** $C \leftarrow C + 1$.

A flowchart for Algorithm CONNECT is given in Fig. 2.2.11. The proof, implementation, and analysis of this algorithm are left as exercises.

Trees

A *tree* is an undirected, connected network that has no cycles. Any network without cycles is a *forest*, the connected components of which are trees. Figure 2.2.12 illustrates all the distinct trees with six vertices. The entire figure can be considered a forest with 36 vertices and 6 components.

A directed network is a tree if and only if it is a tree with its arcs taken as undirected edges. An *acyclic* directed network has no directed cycles. The directed network in Fig. 2.2.13 is acyclic but is not a tree. The following theorem provides several different characterizations of trees.

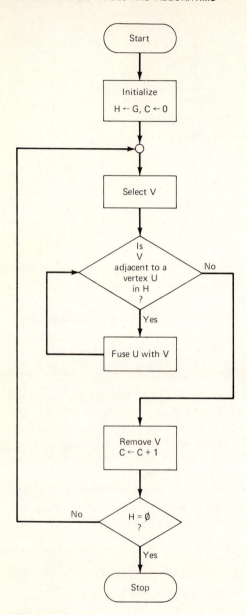

FIG. 2.2.11 Flowchart for Algorithm CONNECT.

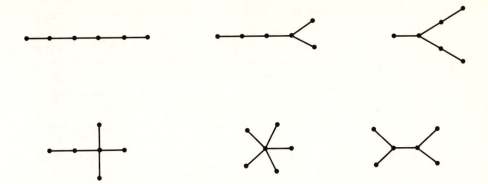

FIG. 2.2.12 All distinct trees with six vertices.

Theorem 2.2.4 Let T be a network with $M \geq 2$ vertices. Then the following statements are equivalent (that is, if any one is true, then all are true):

- (a) T is a tree. That is, T is connected and has no cycles.
- (b) T has $M - 1$ edges and no cycles.
- (c) T has $M - 1$ edges and is connected.
- (d) T is connected, and every edge is a bridge.
- (e) Any two vertices of T are joined by a unique path.
- (f) T has no cycles, but the addition of any new edge creates exactly one cycle.

Proof Statement a implies statement b. Since T contains no cycles, the removal of any edge disconnects T into two trees. This follows from the fact that an edge is a bridge if and only if it is not contained in any cycle (Theorem 2.2.3). By induction on M, it is easy to show that the number of edges in each

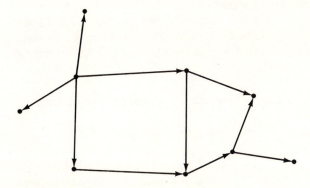

FIG. 2.2.13 An acyclic directed network.

of these two trees is one fewer than the number of vertices. Statement *b* thus follows.

Statement *b* implies statement *c*. If T is not connected, each component of T is connected and has no cycles. Thus, by statement *b*, the number of vertices in each component exceeds the number of edges by 1. It then follows that the total number of vertices in T is at least two greater than the total number of edges, thereby contradicting the hypothesis *b*.

Statement *c* implies statement *d*. We first prove the following lemma.

Lemma If G has M vertices, N edges, and K components, then $M - K \leq N$.

Proof We induct on the number of edges. The result is immediate for $N = 1$. Let G contain as few edges as possible, say, N_0. The removal of any edge of G must then increase K by one, leaving a network with M vertices, $K + 1$ components, and $N_0 - 1$ edges. It follows from the induction hypothesis that $N_0 - 1 \geq M - (K + 1)$, that is, $N_0 \geq M - K$. This proves the lemma since $N > N_0$.

Statement *d* then follows by contradiction from statement *c* and the lemma, since $K = 1$ and the removal of any edge leaves $M - 2$ edges and M vertices.

Statement *d* implies statement *e*. Each pair of vertices is joined by at least one path since T is connected. If every pair of vertices is joined by two or more distinct paths, then any two such paths form a cycle; thus we have a contradiction, since no edge on such a cycle can be a bridge by Theorem 2.2.3.

Statement *e* implies statement *f*. If T contained a cycle, then any two vertices in the cycle would be connected by at least two paths. If edge I is added to T, then two paths [edge I and the unique path given by statement *e*] will exist in T + I between the end-vertices of I. This is the only cycle in T + I because any other cycle would also have to contain edge I. This would then imply the existence of two vertices in T between which there exist at least two distinct paths—a contradiction to statement *e*.

Statement *f* implies statement *a*. Assume T is not connected. If we add an edge to T that joins vertices in two components, no cycle can be created; this contradicts statement *f*. Thus, T must be connected, and Theorem 2.2.4 is proved.

Corollary 2.2.4 Every tree with $M \geq 2$ vertices has at least two end-vertices.

Proof The corollary follows directly from Theorems 2.2.1 and 2.2.4.

A tree with one vertex that is distinguished from the others is called a *rooted tree*; the distinguished vertex is called the *root* of the tree. Usually, rooted trees are drawn with the root at the top level and the other vertices below it, at levels equal to their distance from the root. This is illustrated in Fig. 2.2.14a. We shall assume that every rooted tree has at least three vertices. The maximum level of any vertex in a rooted tree is known as the *height* of the tree.

One special class of rooted trees, known as *rooted binary trees*, are among the most widely used mathematical structures in computer science, and they will appear often in this book. A rooted binary tree is a rooted tree where the root has degree 2, and all the other vertices have degree 1 or 3. One such tree is illustrated in Fig. 2.2.14b.

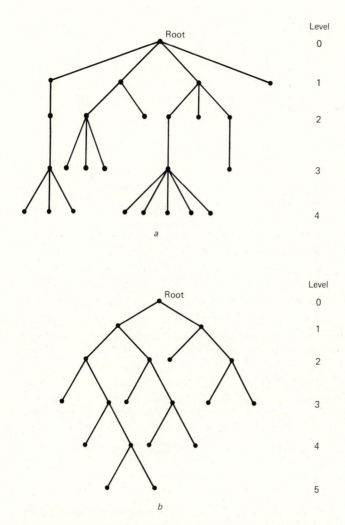

FIG. 2.2.14   (a) A rooted tree with height 4; (b) a rooted binary tree with height 5.

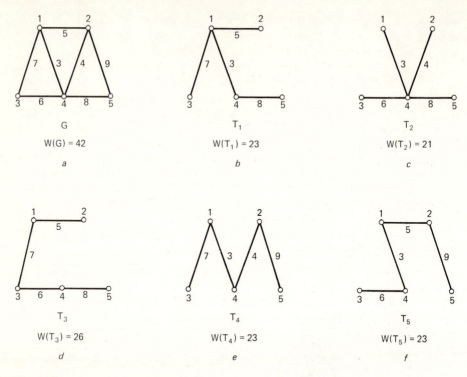

FIG. 2.2.15 A weighted network and several of its spanning trees.

Theorem 2.2.5 Let T be a rooted binary tree with M vertices, height L, and Q end-vertices. Then

(a)   M is odd.

(b) $Q = \dfrac{M+1}{2}$

(c) $M \leq \displaystyle\sum_{i=0}^{L} 2^i$

(d)
$$\lceil \log_2(M+1) - 1 \rceil \leq L \leq \frac{M-1}{2}$$

The proof of Theorem 2.2.5 is left as an exercise.

A *spanning tree* of a network G is a spanning subnetwork that is a tree. Figure 2.2.15 illustrates a weighted network G and several of its spanning trees together with their weights. How many spanning trees does the network have? It is easy to demonstrate the following.

Theorem 2.2.6 A network G is connected if and only if it contains a spanning tree.

Isomorphism

We conclude this section with a brief discussion of the following important problem: If there are two network representations before us, how can we tell whether or not they describe the same network?

It is clearly necessary to define what is meant when we say that "two networks are the same." Two networks G and G' are *isomorphic* if there exists a one-to-one correspondence between the vertices of G and G' such that two vertices u and v are adjacent in G if and only if their corresponding vertices are adjacent in G'. Stated more formally, $G = (V, E)$ is isomorphic to $G' = (V', E')$—written $G \cong G'$—if there exists a one-to-one function h from V onto V' which satisfies the property that $(u, v) \in E$ if and only if $(h(u), h(v)) \in E'$.

The problem of determining whether or not two networks are isomorphic is a deceptively difficult one. For arbitrary networks, the only known algorithms which guarantee a correct answer to the isomorphism question are exponential.

Actually, the problem is not even easy for small networks. All three networks in Fig. 2.2.16 are isomorphic. If this appears obvious, try to decide which (if any) of the graphs in Fig. 2.2.17 are isomorphic.

Given that the isomorphism problem is particularly difficult, what can be done with it? Although it may not be possible to develop a worst-case polynomial isomorphism algorithm, we should be able to develop something useful.

We shall start with a fairly obvious observation. It follows from the definition that if networks G and G' are isomorphic and an isomorphism h is found, then any vertex v_i having degree d_i in G must map onto a vertex $v'_i = h(v_i)$ in G' having the same degree.

What if we attempt to turn this observation into an exhaustive trial-and-error procedure? Consider, for example, two networks G and G': each has 10 vertices, and each vertex is of degree 3. Any possible one-to-one function h from V onto V' will satisfy the above-mentioned degree condition; there are 10! such functions. Thus, in order to decide if G and G' are isomorphic, we might have to

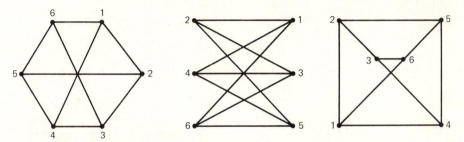

FIG. 2.2.16 Three isomorphic networks.

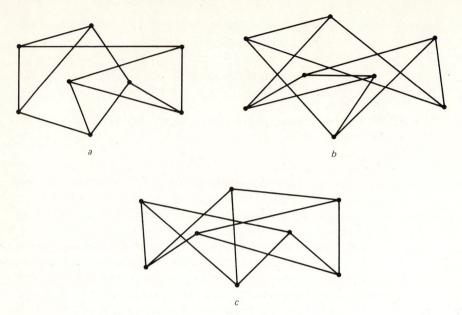

FIG. 2.2.17

try each of 10! possible functions to see if one exists which satisfies the isomorphism condition.

In the face of this combinatorial explosion, researchers have tended to forego the search for an efficient isomorphism algorithm in favor of simple procedures which seem to perform well in most cases. Researchers have also preferred isomorphism algorithms which perform well on special classes of networks that appear in certain applications.

An *invariant* of a network G is a parameter that has the same value for all networks that are isomorphic to G. Some obvious invariants include:

1 The number of vertices
2 The number of edges
3 The number of components
4 The *degree sequence*, that is, a listing of all the vertex degrees in descending order

In the context of this book, a *heuristic* algorithm has the following two properties:

1 It will usually find good, although not necessarily optimum, solutions.
2 It is faster and easier to implement than any known exact algorithm (that is, one which guarantees an optimum solution).

A more complete discussion of such algorithms can be found in Sec. 3.2. Heuristics for the isomorphism problem generally operate by trying to show that the two networks under consideration are *not* isomorphic. This is done by listing an assortment of invariants, the order of which is determined by the complexity of computing the invariants. The two networks are then checked, one parameter at a time, to see if they have the same values. As soon as two values of an invariant differ, we conclude that the networks *are not* isomorphic.

Unfortunately, no set of invariants is known which will enable such a procedure to determine that the two networks *are* isomorphic in polynomial time. Such a set, if one is ever found, is known as a *coding* of a network. Essentially, a heuristic algorithm of the type being discussed here amounts to matching incomplete codings of two networks. Of course, the consideration of a larger number of invariants increases the likelihood of isomorphism should they all agree in value, but no guarantee can be made in general. For example, the 2 five-vertex networks shown in Fig. 2.2.18 match all four of the invariants listed above, but they are not isomorphic.

Let us now consider an example of a somewhat complicated heuristic involving the adjacency matrix A(G). The adjacency matrix itself is not an invariant, although if G_1 and G_2 are isomorphic then some rearrangement of the rows and columns of $A(G_1)$ will yield $A(G_2)$. If G_1 and G_2 have M vertices, a search for the correct sequence of row and column interchanges is worst-case $O(M!)$. However, the following polynomial procedure seems to work quite well in weeding out nonisomorphic networks.

Compute $A^2(G_i)$ for $i = 1, 2$. Now reorder the rows and columns of $A^2(G_1)$ and $A^2(G_2)$ so that the elements of the main diagonal appear in descending order. If G_1 and G_2 are isomorphic and all the diagonal elements are distinct, then this reordering must produce identical matrices. If not, the two networks cannot be isomorphic. If they are identical, additional tests can be made using $A^3(G_i)$, $A^4(G_i), \ldots, A^k(G_i)$, for $i = 1, 2$. The value of k is determined by one's computing budget. If all of these matrices match, the evidence is strong, but not necessarily conclusive, that G_1 and G_2 are isomorphic. We shall refer to this procedure as the

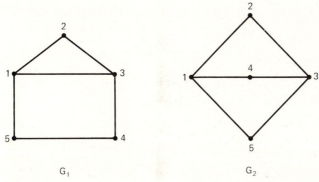

G_1 G_2

FIG. 2.2.18

$$
A(G_1) = \begin{array}{c|ccccc} & 1 & 2 & 3 & 4 & 5 \\ \hline 1 & 0 & 1 & 1 & 0 & 1 \\ 2 & 1 & 0 & 1 & 0 & 0 \\ 3 & 1 & 1 & 0 & 1 & 0 \\ 4 & 0 & 0 & 1 & 0 & 1 \\ 5 & 1 & 0 & 0 & 1 & 0 \end{array}
\qquad
A(G_2) = \begin{array}{c|ccccc} & 1 & 2 & 3 & 4 & 5 \\ \hline 1 & 0 & 1 & 0 & 1 & 1 \\ 2 & 1 & 0 & 1 & 0 & 0 \\ 3 & 0 & 1 & 0 & 1 & 1 \\ 4 & 1 & 0 & 1 & 0 & 0 \\ 5 & 1 & 0 & 1 & 0 & 0 \end{array}
$$

$$
A^2(G_1) = \begin{array}{c|ccccc} & 1 & 2 & 3 & 4 & 5 \\ \hline 1 & 3 & 1 & 1 & 2 & 0 \\ 2 & 1 & 2 & 1 & 1 & 1 \\ 3 & 1 & 1 & 3 & 0 & 2 \\ 4 & 2 & 1 & 0 & 2 & 0 \\ 5 & 0 & 1 & 2 & 0 & 2 \end{array}
\qquad
A^2(G_2) = \begin{array}{c|ccccc} & 1 & 2 & 3 & 4 & 5 \\ \hline 1 & 3 & 0 & 3 & 0 & 0 \\ 2 & 0 & 2 & 0 & 2 & 2 \\ 3 & 3 & 0 & 3 & 0 & 0 \\ 4 & 0 & 2 & 0 & 2 & 2 \\ 5 & 0 & 2 & 0 & 2 & 2 \end{array}
$$

$$
\text{Reordered } A^2(G_1) = \begin{array}{c|ccccc} & 1 & 2 & 3 & 4 & 5 \\ \hline 1 & 3 & 1 & 1 & 2 & 0 \\ 2 & 1 & 3 & 1 & 0 & 2 \\ 3 & 1 & 1 & 2 & 1 & 1 \\ 4 & 2 & 0 & 1 & 2 & 0 \\ 5 & 0 & 2 & 1 & 0 & 2 \end{array}
\qquad
\text{Reordered } A^2(G_2) = \begin{array}{c|ccccc} & 1 & 2 & 3 & 4 & 5 \\ \hline 1 & 3 & 3 & 0 & 0 & 0 \\ 2 & 3 & 3 & 0 & 0 & 0 \\ 3 & 0 & 0 & 2 & 2 & 2 \\ 4 & 0 & 0 & 2 & 2 & 2 \\ 5 & 0 & 0 & 2 & 2 & 2 \end{array}
$$

$$
A^3(G_1) = \begin{array}{c|ccccc} & 1 & 2 & 3 & 4 & 5 \\ \hline 1 & 15 & & & & \\ 2 & & 8 & & & \\ 3 & & & 15 & & \\ 4 & & & & 9 & \\ 5 & & & & & 9 \end{array}
\qquad
A^3(G_2) = \begin{array}{c|ccccc} & 1 & 2 & 3 & 4 & 5 \\ \hline 1 & 18 & & & & \\ 2 & & 12 & & & \\ 3 & & & 18 & & \\ 4 & & & & 12 & \\ 5 & & & & & 12 \end{array}
$$

FIG. 2.2.19

APM (adjacency powers matching) technique. A complete specification of an algorithm using the APM technique, and some other questions on this method, are left as exercises. Exercise 2.2.25 gives an important theoretical interpretation of the elements in the powers of the adjacency matrix.

The APM technique is illustrated in Fig. 2.2.19 using the two networks in Fig. 2.2.18. The fact that G_1 and G_2 are not isomorphic is clear rather early at two places: (1) the reordered $A^2(G_i)$ do not match in the off-diagonal elements; and (2) the diagonal elements of $A^3(G_i)$ are not the same. For both $A^2(G_1)$ and $A^2(G_2)$, the reordering is accomplished by interchanging columns and rows 2 and 3. Note how the elements at the intersections of row-column pairs have been moved.

Exercises 2.2

2.2.1 Draw all the nonisomorphic networks with five vertices. There are 34.

2.2.2 Draw all the nonisomorphic trees with eight vertices. There are 23.

2.2.3 Prove Theorem 2.2.1 using mathematical induction.

2.2.4 Prove Corollary 2.2.1.

2.2.5 *Algorithm* CONNECT (*correctness*). Verify the correctness of Algorithm CONNECT.

*L2.2.6 *Algorithm* CONNECT (*implementation, testing*). Implement and test Algorithm CONNECT. One interesting way to implement the fusion operation involves the adjacency matrix and the binary-OR operation (see Appendix B). To fuse vertex v_j with v_i, simply add row $R(j)$ corresponding to v_j to that of v_i using the binary-OR form of addition. Now add column $C(j)$ to column $C(i)$, and zero the diagonal element in row R(i). After deleting R(j) and C(j), the resulting matrix will represent the network after fusion.

2.2.7 *Algorithm* CONNECT (*analysis*). Using the implementation from Exercise 2.2.6, analyze the complexity of Algorithm CONNECT.

2.2.8 *Algorithm* TREETEST (*design*). Use Algorithm CONNECT to design Algorithm TREETEST, which determines whether or not a given network is a tree.

2.2.9 *Cut-vertices and bridges* (*proofs*). Prove the following two characterization theorems.

> **Theorem** A vertex v of a connected network G is a cut-vertex if and only if there exist two vertices v_1 and v_2, with v_1, v_2, and v all distinct, such that v is on every path from v_1 to v_2.
>
> **Theorem 2.2.2** An edge e of a connected network G is a bridge if and only if there exist two vertices v_1 and v_2 such that e is on every path from v_1 to v_2.

L**2.2.10** *Representation conversion* (*design, implementation*). Design and implement an algorithm which converts an adjacency matrix representation to an incidence matrix representation, and vice versa.

*__2.2.11__ *Bipartite networks* (*proof*). A network G $= (V, E)$ is called *bipartite* if V can be decomposed into two disjoint subsets V_1 and V_2 such that every edge in E joins a vertex in V_1 to a vertex in V_2. Prove that a network is bipartite if and only if every cycle contains an even number of edges.

2.2.12 *Complete bipartite networks.* A bipartite network (see definition in Exercise 2.2.11) is called *complete* if for every $u \in V_1$ and $v \in V_2$, $(u, v) \in V$. Let $K_{m,n}$ denote the unique complete bipartite network with $|V_1| = m$ and $|V_2| = n$. Derive an expression for the number of edges in $K_{m,n}$.

2.2.13 Draw two nonisomorphic networks with six vertices which have the same degree sequence.

*__2.2.14__ How could the characteristic vector representation for sets (see Appendix B) be used to save storage in the representation of networks? What are some of the limitations of your ideas?

2.2.15 *Complete networks.* A network with M vertices is called *complete*, and denoted K_M, if every pair of vertices is adjacent. These networks were used to model the traveling salesman. Show, in two different ways, that the number of edges in K_M is given by

$$\binom{M}{2} = \frac{M(M-1)}{2}$$

2.2.16 Redraw K_5 and $K_{3,3}$ (see Exercises 2.2.12 and 2.2.15) so that each has only one edge crossing, that is, only one crossing at a point that is not a vertex of the network.

*L2.2.17 *Algorithm* CUTVERT (*complete development*). Completely develop an algorithm which finds all the cut-vertices in a given network.

**2.2.18 *Realizable degree sequences* (*proof*). A nonincreasing sequence of positive integers is said to be *realizable* if there exists a network which has that sequence as its degree sequence. Prove that a sequence $d_1, d_2, \ldots, d_M$ (with $d_1 \geq d_2 \geq \cdots \geq d_M \geq 0$) is realizable if and only if the sequence $d_2 - 1$, $d_3 - 1, \ldots, d_{d_1+1}, d_{d_1+2}, \ldots, d_M$ is realizable.

**2.2.19 *Algorithm* REALIZE (*design*). Design an algorithm based on the theorem of Exercise 2.2.18 which determines whether or not a finite sequence of positive integers is realizable.

*2.2.20 Which of the networks in Fig. 2.2.17 are isomorphic?

**L2.2.21 *APM technique* (*design, implementation*). Design and implement a subroutine for the APM technique. What do you do when two or more of the diagonal elements have the same value?

**L2.2.22 *Isomorphism heuristic* (*design, implementation, testing*). Design, implement, and test a heuristic algorithm for testing isomorphism. Limit your attention to networks with no more than 12 vertices.

*2.2.23 *Invariants*. Try to list 10 or more network invariants.

*2.2.24 Prove Theorem 2.2.5.

**2.2.25 Prove the following theorem. If A is the adjacency matrix of an unweighted network G with $V(G) = \{v_1, v_2, \ldots, v_M\}$, then the (i, j) element of A^n, $n \geq 1$, is the number of different walks from v_i to v_j of length n in G (assume each edge has unit length).

2.2.26 Prove Theorem 2.2.6.

2.3 SOME DATA STRUCTURES

We suggested in Chap. 1 that the choice of data structures can significantly influence the speed and efficiency of an implementation of an algorithm. In this section we shall present several data structures (linked lists, pushdown stores, and queues) and procedures for handling them that frequently prove useful.

Consider the advantages and disadvantages of using arrays. Among the advantages are:

1 Arrays are helpful in organizing sets of data into meaningful groups.
2 Array names with subscripts minimize the need for keeping track of many data items with different names.
3 The use of subscripts allows for (seemingly) instant and automatic access to any element in an array.

	CS 100			CS 100
	1	ADAMS		1	ADAMS
	2	BUCHANAN		2	BUCHANAN
DROP	3	GRANT		3	HARRISON
	4	HARRISON		4	JACKSON
	5	JACKSON	ADD	5	JEFFERSON
	6	KENNEDY		6	KENNEDY
	7	LINCOLN		7	LINCOLN
DROP	8	ROOSEVELT		8	TRUMAN
	9	TRUMAN		9	WASHINGTON
	10	WASHINGTON		

a   b

FIG. 2.3.1 Rearranging a linear list.

4 Subscripting also allows, via DO- or FOR-loops, for automatic, fast, and efficient processing of all data or selected subsets of data stored in arrays. Such processing includes initializing, searching, storing, and updating.

The disadvantages of arrays are not so apparent. Arrays are best-suited for data whose values do not change, whose order is not important, or whose order is important but does not change. If the order of the elements in an array is subject to change, then it is time-consuming to have to rearrange the elements every time the order changes.

Consider, for example, an N-element array CS100(N) which contains the alphabetized names of students currently enrolled in computer programming course CS100 (see Fig. 2.3.1a). If students GRANT and ROOSEVELT drop the course and a new student JEFFERSON adds in, then we would want to form the updated class roll shown in Fig. 2.3.1b. Consider the difficulty and cost involved in writing and running a program that could rearrange the array CS100 subject to such changes. A linked list, on the other hand, is a data structure which requires additional memory but allows such changes to be made easily.

Linked Lists

In Fig. 2.3.2a we have changed CS100 from a one-dimensional to a two-dimensional array CS100L. Column 1 of CS100L still contains the names of the students enrolled in the course CS100, although, as Fig. 2.3.2b indicates, it is no longer important that these names appear in alphabetical order. Column 2 of

CS100L	INFO 1	LINK 2
1	ADAMS	2
2	BUCHANAN	3
DROP 3	GRANT	4
4	HARRISON	5
5	JACKSON	6
6	KENNEDY	7
7	LINCOLN	8
DROP 8	ROOSEVELT	9
9	TRUMAN	10
10	WASHINGTON	0
11		

a

CS100L	INFO 1	LINK 2	
1	ADAMS	2	
2	BUCHANAN	4	*
3	GRANT	4	
4	HARRISON	5	
5	JACKSON	11	*
6	KENNEDY	7	
7	LINCOLN	9	*
8	ROOSEVELT	9	
9	TRUMAN	10	
10	WASHINGTON	0	
ADD 11	JEFFERSON	6	*

b

FIG. 2.3.2 Rearranging a linked list.

CS100L contains nonnegative integers, called *links* or *pointers*, the value of which is the row of the array containing the name of the next person (in alphabetical order) in the current list. We have marked with an asterisk (*) those pointers whose values are changed by dropping GRANT and ROOSEVELT and adding JEFFERSON. Notice that in Fig. 2.3.2b:

ADAMS points to BUCHANAN [CS100L(1, 2) = 2 and CS100L(2, 1) = BUCHANAN].

BUCHANAN points to HARRISON [CS100L(2, 2) = 4 and CS100L(4, 1) = HARRISON].

JACKSON points to JEFFERSON.

JEFFERSON points to KENNEDY, and so forth.

The $N \times 2$ array CS100L(I, J) functions as a linear linked list. A *linear linked list* is a finite collection of pairs, each consisting of an information part (INFO) and a pointer part (LINK). Each pair is called a *cell*. If the desired order of the cells is $c_{i_1}, c_{i_2}, \ldots, c_{i_n}$, then $\text{LINK}(i_j) = i_{j+1}$, for $j = 1, \ldots, n - 1$, and $\text{LINK}(i_n) = 0$, indicating the end of the list.

Figure 2.3.3a shows the standard diagram of a linear linked list; Fig. 2.3.3b shows the diagram of the linked list of Fig. 2.3.2b. Notice that GRANT and ROOSEVELT do not appear in the list in Fig. 2.3.3b, although they still appear as shaded elements in Fig. 2.3.2b. Implementations of linked lists also involve the

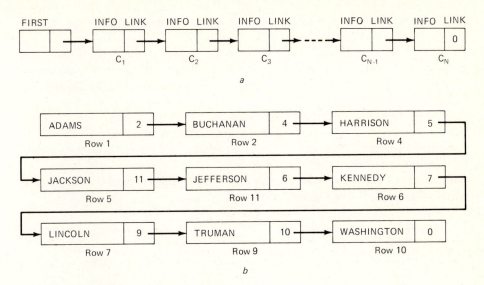

FIG. 2.3.3 Diagrams of linear linked lists.

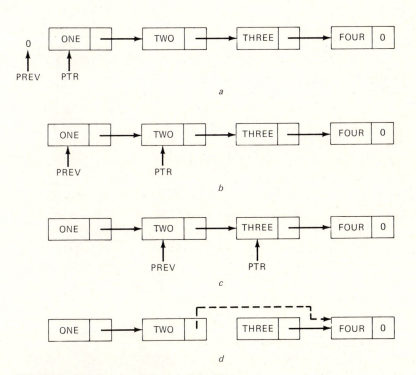

FIG. 2.3.4 Deleting a cell from a linked list.

use of a variable FIRST (or HEAD), the value of which is the location of the first cell in the list (see Fig. 2.3.3a).

As we indicated above, one of the primary advantages of a linked list is that items can be deleted or added easily. We next present two algorithms that can be used to implement the modifications required in transforming Fig. 2.3.2a into Fig. 2.3.2b.

The first algorithm will delete a given element from a linked list. This process is illustrated in Fig. 2.3.4, where we search for the cell c_i with INFO(i) = THREE by moving the pointers PREV and PTR until we find it. We then change the value of LINK in the cell designated by PREV to equal the value of LINK in the cell designated by PTR. A flowchart (Fig. 2.3.5), a formal statement, and an implementation (Fig. 2.3.6) of this algorithm follow.

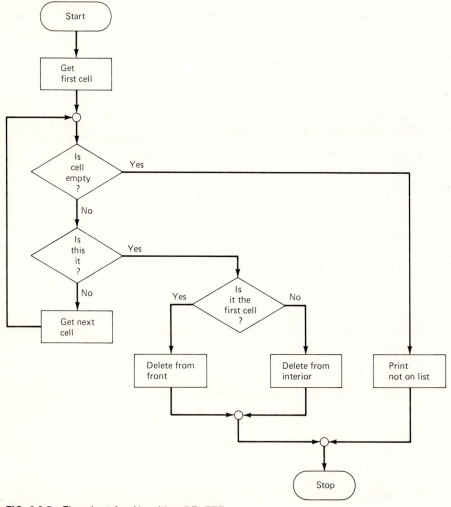

FIG. 2.3.5 Flowchart for Algorithm DELETE.

```
      SUBROUTINE DELETE (FIRST,INFO,LINK,VALUE)
      INTEGER INFO(500),LINK(500),FIRST,VALUE,PREV,PTR
C
C         GET FIRST CELL.
C
      PTR = FIRST
      PREV = 0
C
C         CHECK IF CELL IS EMPTY.
C
    5 IF ( PTR .NE. 0 ) GOTO 20
C
C         THEN
C
   10     WRITE(6,1000)
 1000     FORMAT(18H VALUE NOT ON LIST)
          RETURN
C
C         CHECK IF THIS CELL IS IT.
C
   20 IF ( INFO(PTR) .NE. VALUE ) GOTO 60
C
C         THEN (IS IT THE FIRST CELL)
C
   30     IF ( PREV .NE. 0 ) GOTO 50
C
C             THEN (DELETE FROM FRONT)
C
   40         FIRST = LINK(PTR)
              RETURN
C
C         ELSE (DELETE FROM INTERIOR)
C
   50         LINK(PREV) = LINK(PTR)
              RETURN
C
C         GET NEXT CELL.
C
   60 PREV = PTR
      PTR = LINK(PTR)
      GOTO 5
C
      END
```

FIG. 2.3.6 An implementation of Algorithm DELETE.

Algorithm DELETE   To delete a cell c_i with $INFO(i) = VALUE$ from a linked list, the first cell of which is given by FIRST.

Step 1. [Get FIRST cell] **Set** PTR ← FIRST; PREV ← 0.

Step 2. [Is cell empty?] **While** PTR ≠ 0 **do** step 3 **od**.

    Step 3. [Is this it?] **If** INFO(PTR) = VALUE

        then [is it the first cell?]

            if PREV = 0 **then** [delete from front]

                set FIRST ← LINK(PTR); **and** STOP

            else [delete from interior]

                set LINK(PREV) ← LINK(PTR);

                and STOP **fi**

        else [get next cell]

            set PREV ← PTR; PTR ← LINK(PTR) **fi**.

Step 4. [Not on list] PRINT "VALUE NOT ON LIST"; **and** STOP.

The next algorithm will insert a new cell into a linked list. Assume that the INFO contents of the cells in the list are arranged in increasing order. This algorithm is similar to Algorithm DELETE in that two pointers, PREV and PTR, are used to perform the insertion operation.

Figure 2.3.7 illustrates the insertion process, in which we assume

ONE < TWO < THREE < FOUR

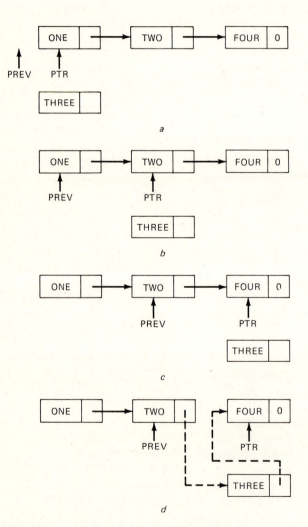

FIG. 2.3.7 Inserting a cell into a linked list.

Figures 2.3.8 and 2.3.9 present a flowchart and an implementation of the following algorithm.

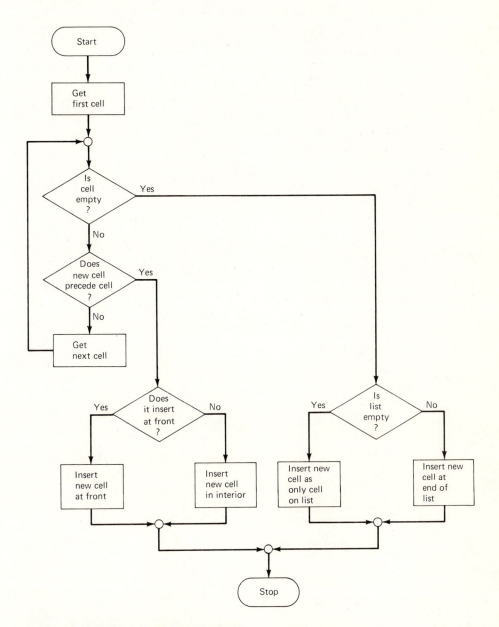

FIG. 2.3.8 Flowchart for Algorithm INSERT.

```
          SUBROUTINE INSERT (FIRST,INFO,LINK,ROW,VALUE)
          INTEGER INFO(500),LINK(500),FIRST,ROW,VALUE,PREV,PTR
C
C         GET FIRST CELL.
C
          PTP = FIRST
          PREV = 0
C
C         CHECK IF CELL IS EMPTY.
C
    5     IF ( PTR .NE. 0 ) GOTO 40
C
C         THEN (IS LIST EMPTY)
C
   10         IF ( PREV .NE. 0 ) GOTO 30
C
C             THEN (INSERT NEW CELL AS ONLY CELL ON LIST)
C
   20             FIRST = ROW
                  LINK(ROW) = 0
                  RETURN
C
C             ELSE (INSERT NEW CELL AT END OF LIST)
C
   30             LINK(PREV) = ROW
                  LINK(ROW) = 0
                  RETURN
C
C         CHECK IF NEW CELL PRECEDES CELL.
C
   40     IF ( VALUE .GT. INFO(PTR) ) GOTO 80
C
C         THEN (DOES IT INSERT AT FRONT)
C
   50     IF ( PREV .NE. 0 ) GOTO 70
C
C             THEN (INSERT NEW CELL AT FRONT)
C
   60             FIRST = ROW
                  LINK(ROW) = PTR
                  RETURN
C
C             ELSE (INSERT NEW CELL IN INTERIOR)
C
   70             LINK(PREV) = ROW
                  LINK(ROW) = PTR
                  RETURN
C
C         GET NEXT CELL.
C
   80     PREV = PTR
          PTR = LINK(PTR)
          GOTO 5
C
          END
```

FIG. 2.3.9 An implementation of Algorithm INSERT.

Algorithm INSERT   To insert a new cell ROW, with INFO(ROW) = VALUE, into an ordered linked list, the first cell of which is given by FIRST.

Step 1. [Get FIRST cell] **Set** PTR ← FIRST; PREV ← 0.

Step 2. [Is cell empty?] **While** PTR ≠ 0 **do** step 3 **od**.

   Step 3. [Does new cell precede cell?] **If** VALUE ≤ INFO(PTR)

     then [does it insert at front?]

       if PREV = 0 **then** [insert new cell at front]

           set FIRST ← ROW; LINK(ROW)

            ← PTR; **and** STOP

         else [insert new cell in interior]

           set LINK(PREV) ← ROW; LINK(ROW)

            ← PTR; **and** STOP **fi**

     else [get next cell] **set** PREV ← PTR; PTR ← LINK(PTR) **fi**.

Step 4. [Is list empty?] **If** PREV = 0

   then [insert new cell as only cell on list]

     set FIRST ← ROW; LINK(ROW) ← 0; **and** STOP

   else [insert new cell at end of list]

     set LINK(PREV) ← ROW; LINK(ROW) ← 0; **and** STOP **fi**.

Adjacency Lists

An efficient means of representing a network $G = (V, E)$ uses linked lists of adjacencies.   This representation strongly resembles adjacency vectors (see Sec. 2.2), but it generally uses less memory.   Figure 2.3.10c shows a linked list representation of the network G in Fig. 2.3.10a.   This representation depends both on the labeling given the vertices $v_1, v_2, \ldots, v_M$ and on the order in which the edges of G are input (a random ordering of the edges is presented in Fig. 2.3.10b).

In order to determine which vertices are adjacent to a given vertex in a linked list representation, we must follow the pointers in the column marked NEXT.   For example, to find the vertices adjacent to vertex 3, we find that NEXT(3) = 12.   Looking in the twelfth row, we see that ADJ(12) = 4, that is, 3 is adjacent to 4.   We also see that NEXT(12) = 7.   Since ADJ(7) = 1, 3 is also adjacent to 1.   Finally, since NEXT(7) = 0, 3 is not adjacent to any other vertices.

This representation requires $2(M + 2N)$ words of memory, where M is the number of vertices and N is the number of edges in G.   Notice that 2M of these words [ADJ(1), . . . , ADJ(M) and the M words for which NEXT(I) = 0] have a 0 stored in them.   However, the first M words of the array ADJ could be used to store useful information about the vertices $v_1, v_2, \ldots, v_M$.   For example, they could be used to store the values of the degrees d_i of v_i.

Figure 2.3.11 is a segment of Fortran code which can be used to create the adjacency lists in Fig. 2.3.10c, given the edges in the order indicated in Fig. 2.3.10b.

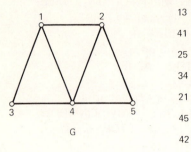

13
41
25
34
21
45
42

	ADJ	NEXT
1		15
2		19
3		12
4		18
5		17
6	3	0
7	1	0
8	1	0
9	4	6
10	5	0
11	2	0
12	4	7
13	3	8
14	1	10
15	2	9
16	5	13
17	4	11
18	2	16
19	4	14
20		
21		

a   b   c

FIG. 2.3.10 A linked list representation of a network.

Pushdown Lists and Stacks

We have seen that (linear) linked lists are effective data structures for modeling situations in which ordered arrays of data items are subject to change. This is particularly true when the changes are primarily those of inserting or deleting elements in the middle of arrays. If modifications take place only at the front or the end, linked lists are no longer necessary and simple linear (one-dimensional) arrays will again suffice.

As an example of this, consider the following problem. All programming language compilers are required to decide, for an arbitrary expression, whether or not it is well-formed. Part of this requirement involves the determination of

```
        DO 1 I = 1,100
            ADJ(I) = 0
            NEXT(I) = 0
    1   CONTINUE
C
C           READ IN THE NUMBER OF VERTICES P
C
        READ(5,1000)P
1000    FORMAT(2I3)
C
        I = P+1
C
C           READ IN THE EDGES (M,N) OF G.
C
100     READ(5,1000)M,N
C
C           IF M IS NEGATIVE, THERE ARE NO MORE EDGES
C
        IF ( M .LT. 0 ) GOTO 200
C
        ADJ(I) = N
        NEXT(I) = NEXT(M)
        NEXT(M) = I
        I = I+1
        ADJ(I) = M
        NEXT(I) = NEXT(N)
        NEXT(N) = I
        I = I+1
C
C           READ IN ANOTHER EDGE
C
        GOTO 100
C
C           CONTINUE THE PROGRAM
200     •
        •
        •
```

FIG. 2.3.11 A code segment to create a linked list representation of a network.

whether or not the parentheses in the expression are properly nested and placed. For example,

$$(\quad)\ ((\quad)\ (\quad))$$

represents a proper sequence of parentheses, but

$$(\quad)\ (((\quad)\ (\quad))$$

does not (it has one too many left parentheses). In a more general mathematical setting, one typically will see brackets [ ] and braces { } in an arithmetic expression.

Suppose you are asked to design an algorithm for deciding if an arbitrary sequence of parentheses, brackets, and braces is well-formed. What do we mean by well-formed? The standard definition is as follows:

1 The sequences ( ), [ ], and { } are well-formed.

2 If sequence x is well-formed, so are (x), $[x]$ and $\{x\}$.

3 If sequences x and y are well-formed, so is xy.

4 Nothing is well-formed unless its being so follows from a finite sequence of applications of 1, 2, and 3.

This definition defines well-formed sequences by a constructive process. For example, the following are all well-formed:

Item	Sequence	Formed by rule
a	( )	1
b	[( )]	2 and a
c	{[( )]}	2 and b
d	{[( )]}{ }	1, 3, and c
e	({[( )]}{ })	2 and d
f	[ ]({[( )]}{ })	1, 3, and e
g	{[ ]({[( )]}{ })}	2 and f

A standard technique for deciding if expressions such as these are well-formed involves the use of a *pushdown store*, which is a one-way infinite sequence of words of memory, as depicted in Fig. 2.3.12.

A data item is stored in a pushdown memory by placing it on the TOP, thereby shoving down (by one word) all other words on the pushdown store (in exactly the same manner as placing a tray on a pushdown stack of trays in a cafeteria line). Data items are retrieved from a pushdown store only by removing them one at a time from the TOP, thereby popping up data items stored beneath the TOP.

We are not allowed to remove data items from the interior of a pushdown store. (We usually do not remove the twentieth tray from the TOP in a cafeteria stack of trays.) The term "pushdown stack" is given to a pushdown store in which we are allowed to read items below the TOP, but not to change the values or to add new items below the TOP.

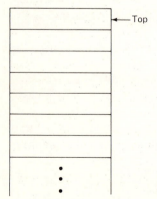

FIG. 2.3.12 Diagram of a pushdown store.

Let us illustrate how a pushdown store makes it easy to decide if a sequence like $g = \{[\quad] (\{\quad [(\quad)]\}\{\quad \})\}$ is well-formed. The elements of g will be denoted $x_1 x_2 \cdots x_n$, where each x_i is one of $\{, \}, (,), [,$ or $]$. We refer to $\{, (,$ and $[$ as LEFT symbols; we say that x_i is a *left mate* of x_j if $x_i = [$ and $x_j =]$, or $x_i = ($ and $x_j =)$, or $x_i = \{$ and $x_j = \}$.

Algorithm WELL-FORMED   To determine if an arbitrary sequence of symbols $x_1 x_2 \cdots x_N$, where each x_i is one of $\{, \}, (,), [,$ or $]$, is well-formed.

Step 0. [Initialize] **Set** TOP $\leftarrow 0$; I $\leftarrow 1$.

Step 1. [Read the sequence from left to right]

   While I $\leq$ N **do through** step 3 **od.**

   Step 2. [Push a LEFT symbol down] **If** x_i is a LEFT symbol

   then put x_i on top of the pushdown

   else [pop a symbol off] **if** TOP is a left mate of x_i

   then pop the element TOP off the store

   else PRINT "NOT WELL-FORMED";

   and STOP **fi fi.**

   Step 3. [Read next symbol] **Set** I $\leftarrow$ I $+ 1$.

Step 4. [Is store empty?] **If** TOP $= 0$ **then** PRINT "WELL-FORMED";

   else PRINT "NOT WELL-FORMED" **fi**;

   and STOP.

We next apply Algorithm WELL-FORMED to the sequence

$$g = \{\ [\quad]\ (\ \{\ [\ (\quad)\ ]\ \}\ \{\ \}\ )\ \}$$
$$\text{1 2} \quad \text{3 4 5 6 7} \quad \text{8 9 10 11 12 13 14}$$

Figure 2.3.13 shows the successive contents of the pushdown store as the elements of g are read from left to right. The integer value above the I*th* pushdown store configuration indicates that the $x_i th$ symbol is currently being read.

To implement a pushdown store in Fortran, we use a one-dimensional array called STORE [dimensioned as STORE(M)] and an integer variable called TOP. Whenever we want to place an item X(I) on top of the pushdown, we simply execute the following instructions:

```
            TOP = TOP + 1
            IF (TOP .GT. M) GO TO 100

                STORE(TOP) = X(I)
                GO TO 200

      100     PRINT "PUSHDOWN OVERFLOW"
      200     CONTINUE
                    ⋮
```

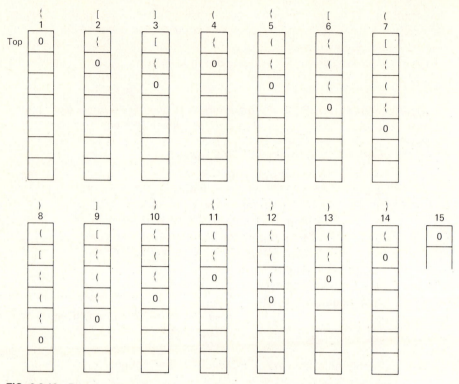

FIG. 2.3.13 Pushdown configurations produced by Algorithm WELL-FORMED.

Then, in order to pop an element off the top, we execute the following:

IF (TOP .EQ. 0) GO TO 300

$X(I) = STORE(TOP)$
$TOP = TOP - 1$
GO TO 400

300 PRINT "PUSHDOWN IS EMPTY"
400 CONTINUE

    .
    .
    .

Queues

In a pushdown store, items are inserted and deleted only at the TOP. In a *queue*, items are inserted at one end and deleted at the other. We usually refer to the ends as the FRONT and the REAR. The term "queue" is used because these data structures often model waiting lines, for example, people waiting at a box office, cars waiting at a stoplight, or jobs waiting in a queue in an operating system.

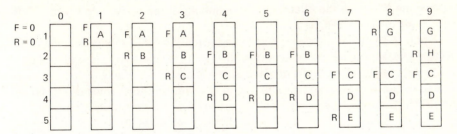

FIG. 2.3.14 An implementation of a queue using a linear array.

A queue is typically modeled using a linear array [for example, QUEUE(500)] and two integer variables FRONT and REAR which point to the items at the front and rear of the queue, respectively. At first, REAR ≥ FRONT, but when over 500 elements have been added to the queue it is likely that some entries have been deleted from the front. If so, instead of overflowing the array, we reset REAR = 1

```
        SUBROUTINE QADD (QUEUE,N,FRONT,REAR,VALUE)
        INTEGER QUEUE(N),FRONT,REAR,VALUE
C
C            CHECK IF QUEUE IS EMPTY.
C
        IF ( REAR .NE. 0 ) GOTO 20
C
C       THEN (ADD FIRST ELEMENT TO QUEUE)
C
   10        FRONT = 1
             REAR = 1
             QUEUE(1) = VALUE
             RETURN
C
C            CHECK IF REAR IS EQUAL TO N.
C
   20   IF ( REAR .NE. N ) GOTO 40
C
C       THEN (RESET REAR TO 0)
C
   30   REAR = 0
C
C            MOVE REAR
C
   40   REAR = REAR+1
C
C            CHECK IF QUEUE IS FULL.
C
     IF ( REAR .NE. FRONT ) GOTO 60
C
C       THEN
C
   50        WRITE(6,1000)
 1000        FORMAT(14H QUEUE IS FULL)
             REAR = REAR-1
        IF ( REAR .EQ. 0 ) REAR = N
             RETURN
C
C       ELSE (ADD TO REAR)
C
   60        QUEUE(REAR) = VALUE
             RETURN
        END
```

FIG. 2.3.15 Subroutine to add an element to a queue.

and resume filling up the queue at the beginning of the array. However, REAR must never overtake FRONT.

Figure 2.3.14 illustrates what is called a *single-queue / single-server situation*. In this example, the queue has capacity 5, individuals are labeled A to H, and it takes 3 time units for a person at the front of the queue to be served, after which the person leaves the queue. At time $T = 0$ the queue is empty and the values of FRONT(F) and REAR(R) are both zero. At $T = 1$, A arrives, waits 3 time units, and leaves at $T = 4$. Individuals B, C, D, E, G, and H arrive at times 2, 3, 4, 7, 8, and 9, respectively. C waits 4 units before moving to the front of the queue and leaves at $T = 10$. When G arrives, at $T = 8$, the rear of the queue is at position 5 of the array. At this point we place G in position 1 of the queue and set $R = 1$. When H arrives at $T = 9$ we set $R = 2$, and the queue is completely filled. Now the rear has caught up with the front, and no further additions are possible until C leaves.

Subroutine QADD (Fig. 2.3.15) adds an element VALUE to the REAR of a queue. Assume that if the queue is empty, then FRONT = REAR = 0. The process of deleting an element from a queue is similar. Subroutine QDELET (Fig. 2.3.16) does the job; if the last item in the queue is being deleted, it resets FRONT = REAR = 0. Queues will be reconsidered from the standpoint of simulation in Sec. 3.6.

```
      SUBROUTINE QDELET (QUEUE,N,FRONT,REAR,VALUE)
      INTEGER QUEUE(N),FRONT,REAR,VALUE
C
C         CHECK IF QUEUE IS EMPTY.
C
      IF ( REAR .NE. 0 ) GOTO 20
C
C     THEN
C
   10       WRITE(6,1000)
 1000       FORMAT(15H QUEUE IS EMPTY)
            RETURN
C
C         CHECK IF THERE IS ONLY ONE LEFT IN QUEUE.
C
   20 IF ( FRONT .NE. REAR ) GOTO 40
C
C     THEN (RESET QUEUE TO EMPTY)
C
   30       VALUE = QUEUE(FRONT)
            REAR = 0
            RETURN
C
C         DELETE FROM QUEUE AND MOVE FRONT
C
   40 VALUE = QUEUE(FRONT)
      FRONT = FRONT+1
C
C         CHECK IF FRONT HAS EXCEEDED N.  IF SO RESET TO 1.
C
      IF ( FRONT .GT. N ) FRONT = 1
      RETURN
C
      END
```

FIG. 2.3.16 Subroutine to delete an element from a queue.

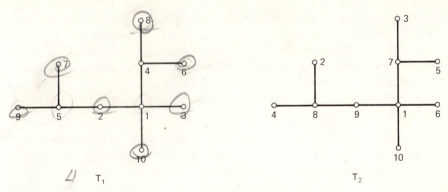

FIG. 2.3.17 A recursive tree T_1 and a nonrecursive tree T_2.

Trees

Linear arrays can also be used to represent certain trees very compactly. Let T be a tree with M vertices in which the vertices are labeled with the integers $1, 2, \ldots, M$. The tree T is said to be *recursively labeled* (or *recursive*) if every vertex with label greater than 1 is adjacent to exactly one vertex with a smaller label. Figure 2.3.17 presents an example of a recursive tree T_1 and a nonrecursive tree T_2.

The following linear array TREE shows how compactly the recursive tree T_1 can be represented; TREE(I) = J denotes that vertex I is adjacent to vertex J.

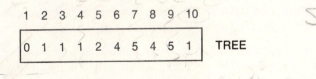

1	2	3	4	5	6	7	8	9	10	
0	1	1	1	2	4	5	4	5	1	TREE

Exercises 2.3

2.3.1 What data structure would you use for each of the following data sets: (a) a seating plan; (b) a table for showing average height as a function of weight, sex, and age; (c) the set of all subsets of M items; (d) a deck of cards; (e) a set of k people and the relation X knows Y; (f) a checker game; (g) pi ($\pi = 3.14159\ldots$); (h) an organization hierarchy; (i) a set of observations on a single random variable? Note that you might have to specify some additional information (for example, potential use of the data, desired accuracy of π) before you can answer this question for some of these data sets.

2.3.2 *Large integers.* Write a program that will compute very large integers, that is, integers which overflow your word size. More specifically, you might try to compute a large Fibonacci number or value of a factorial.

L2.3.3 *Railroad yard.* Design and computerize the operation of a small railroad classification yard. Trains will come in according to some schedule. The cars on the incoming trains will be redistributed and re-formed into outgoing trains which will leave for various destinations determined by another schedule. Empty cars, which belong to other railroads, may also be brought in. These have to be collected and periodically returned to the owner companies.

2.3.4 Discuss some advantages and disadvantages of using linked linear lists versus sequential linear lists. Give special attention to questions of storage volume, insertion, deletion, and accessing.

2.3.5 Write two subroutines which will (*a*) delete and (*b*) insert an element into a well-ordered array CS100(N). Compare their speed and efficiency with subroutines DELETE and INSERT for linked lists.

2.3.6 Write subroutines which will (*a*) add an element to the front of a linked list, (*b*) add an element to the end of a linked list, and (*c*) print out the contents of all cells in a linked list.

2.3.7 *Permutations (stacks).* Let the integers 1, 2, 3, 4 arrive in natural order on the input stream of a stack. By considering all possible sequences of stacking and unstacking operations, decide which of the 24 possible permutations are obtainable as an output stream. For example, the permutation 2314 is obtainable from the sequence: push down 1, push down 2, pop off 2, push down 3, pop off 3, pop off 1, push down 4, pop off 4.

2.3.8 *Permutations (deques).* A *deque* (double-ended queue) is a linear list for which all insertions, deletions, and accesses can be made at *either* end of the list. Rework Exercise 2.3.7 for a deque.

2.3.9 *Simulation (queues).* Write a program which simulates a waiting line with a capacity of 10 people in which 2 time units are required to service a customer and delete him or her from the FRONT. The probability of a single new arrival in 1 time unit is p, where $0 < p < 1$. We never have two or more arrivals during a time unit. Observe queue overflow as a function of p.

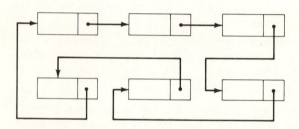

FIG. 2.3.18

2.3.10 *Circular linked lists.* Figure 2.3.18 illustrates a circular linked list. Can you think of any uses for such a data structure? You might implement one of your ideas.

2.3.11 *Linked list manipulation.* Design algorithms which do the following for singly linked lists:

      (*a*) Converts a linked list into a circular linked list (see Exercise 2.3.10).

      (*b*) Merges two lists, each with INFO cells arranged in alphabetical order, into a single list.

      (*c*) Converts a linked list into a sequential list (ordinary one-dimensional array).

2.3.12 *Packed decimal representation.* Find out what is meant by a "packed decimal representation of integers" [see Page and Wilson (1973), p. 37). What are some of the advantages and disadvantages of this representation?

*L**2.3.13** *Check.* Write a program that will read in a state of a game of chess and ascertain whether or not one of the kings is in check. You might further determine if a check is a checkmate.

2.3.14 *Stack overflow.* We have to try to fit two pushdown stacks into a single fixed block of storage which is arranged as a consecutive interval of addresses. How might we arrange our stacks so as to minimize potential overflow problems?

**L2.3.15 *Crossword puzzles.* Write a crossword puzzle generating program. Assume an input of a 6×6 pattern (an arrangement of blank and filled squares) and a list of words with six or fewer letters. The output should be an arrangement of these words which forms a legitimate English-language crossword puzzle or a statement that no such arrangement is possible.

*2.3.16** *Recursive trees.* Design an algorithm for constructing the unique path in a recursive tree T between arbitrarily given vertices u and v using the compact linear representation of Fig. 2.3.17. *Hint*: An algorithm can be constructed which makes one pass over this representation, moving right to left.

2.4 ELEMENTARY NOTIONS FROM PROBABILITY AND STATISTICS

A large number of important problems involve some degree of uncertainty. Quantities of interest will not be predictable in advance but will exhibit an inherent randomness that must be incorporated into any useful model. Models of this sort are called *probabilistic*.

This section is concerned with topics from the theories of probability and statistics.   Some of the applications of this knowledge to the design and analysis of algorithms are briefly described below:

1   *Analysis of the average performance of an algorithm.*   Assume that we have an algorithm (Algorithm S) for scheduling jobs on a computing facility in some optimal way.   Important factors that determine the run time of the algorithm are the number N and the types of jobs waiting to be scheduled.   If all the jobs are of a simple type, Algorithm S can construct a schedule in O(N) time.   However, if all the jobs are of a very complicated type, then Algorithm S requires $O(N^4)$ time.   Assume there are 12 different types of jobs between these two extremes, and that most job loads contain a mixture of several types.   How good is the algorithm?   In order to answer this question, we need to know what an average set of jobs looks like.   Then we must decide how well the algorithm performs on the average.   All this implies some precise definition of "average."   Perhaps the worst-case $O(N^4)$ is unacceptably slow for the operating system; for example, the whole system might find itself doing nothing but waiting for the $O(N^4)$ subroutine to come up with a schedule.   If the worst-case behavior occurs infrequently and the average performance of the algorithm is $O(N^{3/2})$, it may be possible to use Algorithm S in the operating system.   On the other hand, if the average behavior is $O(N^4)$, we may be forced to use a fast, greedy, heuristic algorithm which cannot guarantee optimal schedules.   This example is representative of a number of important questions which arise in the analysis of algorithms.

2   *Simulation.*   One of the most important uses of a computer is to provide a vehicle for conducting controlled experiments on complicated real systems at relatively low cost and over brief time intervals.   This is done using an algorithm that models and simulates the real system.   In many ways, this is a design and analysis technique of last resort.   Simulation models are generally used for problems that are hopelessly beyond our analytic powers, and which usually combine large size and uncertainty.   Virtually all serious simulation models are probabilistic.

3   *Computational statistics.*   The computer is often used to process and analyze statistical information.   Algorithms must be designed and analyzed to perform statistical computations accurately and efficiently.

4   *Decision-making algorithms.*   The computer is becoming increasingly popular in the world of business and government as a decision-making aid.   Basically all the problems in this applications area involve decision making under uncertainty.

For example, consider the following problem.   A state government is currently supporting a number of administrative and service agencies.   In the face of a drastic budget cut, a number of these agencies will have to be eliminated or cut back.   An immense quantity of data relating to the past, present, and future activities of these agencies is available.   How are these decisions to be made?   One of the most promising quantitative methods for dealing with such problems is known as *Bayesian statistical decision theory*. Unfortunately, this theory is badly in need of good computational algorithms. Its usefulness is currently restricted to relatively simple problems.

5 *Random number generation.* Most of the preceding applications of probability and statistics require a means of introducing uncertainty into data. If possible, we would like to do this by some mechanism internal to the computer itself, thus avoiding time-consuming and expensive external activity. The design and analysis of good algorithms for generating random data is a significant problem in its own right.

Multiprocessor System

Let us start with a simple problem. A multiprocessor system with five identical processing units is available. A large, complicated program is to be run on this system. The program requires three of the five processors and cannot be loaded unless three processors are available. What is the probability that we will be able to load the program when we are ready to run it?

Every probability model is formulated in terms of an experiment. An *experiment* is any well-defined action. In the example, the experiment consists of checking the multiprocessor system to see how many processors are available. With each experiment we can associate a set of *outcomes*. Label the five processors in the example with the integers 1 through 5. One possible outcome of this experiment could then be denoted by the 5-tuple $(1, 0, 1, 0, 0)$, which represents the state with processors 1 and 3 busy and processors 2, 4, and 5 available. If the system is in this state when we are ready to load, then the program will be accepted. The set of all possible outcomes is known as the *sample space* of the experiment. Using the 5-tuple representation, we see that there are 2^5 elements in the sample space of our multiprocessor experiment. They are listed explicitly below:

$$s_1 = (0, 0, 0, 0, 0) \qquad s_{12} = (0, 1, 0, 1, 0) \qquad s_{23} = (1, 0, 1, 1, 0)$$
$$s_2 = (1, 0, 0, 0, 0) \qquad s_{13} = (0, 1, 0, 0, 1) \qquad s_{24} = (1, 1, 0, 0, 1)$$
$$s_3 = (0, 1, 0, 0, 0) \qquad s_{14} = (0, 0, 1, 1, 0) \qquad s_{25} = (1, 1, 0, 1, 0)$$
$$s_4 = (0, 0, 1, 0, 0) \qquad s_{15} = (0, 0, 1, 0, 1) \qquad s_{26} = (1, 1, 1, 0, 0)$$
$$s_5 = (0, 0, 0, 1, 0) \qquad s_{16} = (0, 0, 0, 1, 1) \qquad s_{27} = (0, 1, 1, 1, 1)$$
$$s_6 = (0, 0, 0, 0, 1) \qquad s_{17} = (0, 0, 1, 1, 1) \qquad s_{28} = (1, 0, 1, 1, 1)$$
$$s_7 = (1, 1, 0, 0, 0) \qquad s_{18} = (0, 1, 0, 1, 1) \qquad s_{29} = (1, 1, 0, 1, 1)$$
$$s_8 = (1, 0, 1, 0, 0) \qquad s_{19} = (0, 1, 1, 0, 1) \qquad s_{30} = (1, 1, 1, 0, 1)$$
$$s_9 = (1, 0, 0, 1, 0) \qquad s_{20} = (0, 1, 1, 1, 0) \qquad s_{31} = (1, 1, 1, 1, 0)$$
$$s_{10} = (1, 0, 0, 0, 1) \qquad s_{21} = (1, 0, 0, 1, 1) \qquad s_{32} = (1, 1, 1, 1, 1)$$
$$s_{11} = (0, 1, 1, 0, 0) \qquad s_{22} = (1, 0, 1, 0, 1)$$

Let $S = \{s_1, s_2, s_3, \ldots\}$ be the sample space of an experiment. For the time being we assume that S contains a finite or countably infinite number of elements. An *event* is any subset of the sample space. Usually, an event is expressed in verbal form in terms of the experiment and then translated into a subset of S. For example, consider the event: At least four processors are being used. In terms of S, this event consists of all the outcomes which represent states of the system with four or five processors in use. That is,

$$E = \{(0, 1, 1, 1, 1), (1, 0, 1, 1, 1), (1, 1, 0, 1, 1), (1, 1, 1, 0, 1), (1, 1, 1, 1, 0),$$

$$(1, 1, 1, 1, 1)\}$$

$$= \{s_{27}, s_{28}, s_{29}, s_{30}, s_{31}, s_{32}\}$$

A single performance of an experiment is known as a *trial*. Let E be an event defined on a sample space S. If the outcome of a trial of the experiment is in E, then we say that event E has *occurred*. Only one outcome s in S can occur on any trial. However, every event that includes s will occur.

Events can be formed from other events using the standard set operations of union, intersection, and complementation. If

$$E_1 = \text{event that at least four processors are being used}$$

and $\quad E_2 = \text{event that at most four processors are being used}$

then $\quad E_3 = E_1 \cap E_2 = \text{event that exactly four processors are being used}$

$$= \{(0, 1, 1, 1, 1), (1, 0, 1, 1, 1), (1, 1, 0, 1, 1), (1, 1, 1, 0, 1),$$

$$(1, 1, 1, 1, 0)\}$$

$$= \{s_{27}, s_{28}, s_{29}, s_{30}, s_{31}\}$$

Verbally, $\cap$ should be read as *and*, $\cup$ as *or*, and complementation as *not*.

If E_1 and E_2 are any two *disjoint events* (that is, $E_1 \cap E_2 = \emptyset$), they are called *mutually exclusive*. If E_1 and E_2 are mutually exclusive, it is not possible for both events to occur on the same trial. In the current example, if

$$E_1 = \text{event that processor 1 is busy}$$

and $\quad E_2 = \text{event that processor 1 is available}$

then $E_1 \cap E_2 = \emptyset$. Check this by explicitly listing the elements of E_1 and E_2.

We are now ready to start talking about probability. Let us first try to formulate the standard intuitive concept of probability in terms of our new vocabulary. We are interested in the probability that a given event will happen as a result of an experiment $\mathscr{E}$. Experiment $\mathscr{E}$ is repeated N times, where N is a large number. Each trial produces an outcome in S. The outcome is either in E, in which case this event has occurred, or it is not. Assume E has occurred on n of the N trials. We would then be inclined to define the *probability of event E* as

$$P(E) = \frac{n}{N}$$

This number can be interpreted as the fraction of time event E will occur when experiment $\mathscr{E}$ is performed. This is the essence of the *frequency interpretation of probability.*

It is important to realize that the frequency interpretation is not an essential part of probability *theory* even though it is very popular and useful in *practice.* Probability theory has a formal, axiomatic foundation which should not be dismissed as a useless abstraction of pure mathematics. *The axiomatic theory defines all the computational rules that are used to calculate probability.* As we shall see, this theory is fundamentally deficient, and the frequency interpretation provides one possible way of dealing with this deficiency.

Let S be a sample space for an experiment $\mathscr{E}$. Let P be a *probability measure* associated with S which assigns to *certain* events $E \subseteq S$ a real number $P(E)$, which is called the *probability of event E.* These probabilities must satisfy three basic rules (called *axioms*):

I $\qquad\qquad\qquad P(E) \geq 0 \qquad$ for any $E \subseteq S$

II $\qquad\qquad\qquad P(S) = 1$

III $\qquad P(E_1 \cup E_2) = P(E_1) + P(E_2) \qquad$ if E_1 and E_2 are mutually exclusive, that is, if $E_1 \cap E_2 = \emptyset$

Once these "certain" events are assigned probabilities consistent with these axioms, then it is possible (in principle) to compute the probability of any other event defined on S from these assignments and the three axioms.

Perhaps the most difficult aspect of constructing probabilistic models is the assignment of probabilities to those certain events. The general theory does not tell us how to look at a specific problem and decide which events to use and what numbers to assign to these events. These choices are left entirely to the analyst. Assignments based on experimentation and the frequency interpretation are common. Another commonly used scheme is called the *equally likely distribution*, which is described in the next paragraph. It is very important to understand that these modeling choices can (and do!) strongly affect the usefulness of the model. The *theory* is neutral; it will make predictions regardless of these assignments! However, these predictions will be misleading and not reflect the behavior of the "real-world" problem being modeled if these assignments are inaccurate.

Let us return to the multiprocessor problem. Assume that solid experimental evidence indicates that each of the 32 states in sample space S is equally likely to be the actual state of the system (outcome) on any trial. Thus, at the start of any trial, we have no reason to prefer any state over any other. Note that *all* 32 elements in S are mutually exclusive.[1]   Using induction and axioms II and III, it is easy to show (do it!) that

$$P(S) = P(s_1) + P(s_2) + \cdots + P(s_{31}) + P(s_{32}) = 1\dagger$$

Since each state is equally likely,

$$P(s_1) = P(s_2) = \cdots = P(s_{32}) = \tfrac{1}{32}$$

We have now made our basic assignments.

It is time to *solve* the multiprocessor problem.   What is the probability that we will be able to load the program when we are ready to run it?   The event of interest is

$$E = \text{three or more processors are available}$$

In terms of the elements of S,

$$E = \{s_1, s_2, \ldots, s_{15}, s_{16}\}$$

Then
$$P(E) = P(s_1 \cup s_2 \cup s_3 \cup \cdots \cup s_{15} \cup s_{16})$$
$$= P(s_1) + P(s_2) + \cdots + P(s_{16})$$
$$= \tfrac{1}{32} + \tfrac{1}{32} + \cdots + \tfrac{1}{32} = \tfrac{16}{32} = \tfrac{1}{2}$$

Thus, we expect to be able to load half the time using the *equally likely model and the frequency interpretation of the final result*.   If the system is one that is heavily used, and more probability was assigned to $s_{27}, s_{28}, \ldots, s_{32}$ and less to $s_1, s_2, \ldots, s_6$, then the theory would have predicted a smaller chance of success.

It is a good idea to approach probability problems using the basic solution procedure employed in the example.   Let us summarize it.

1   *Identify the sample space S.*   In this book, S will often contain a finite number of elements.   Try to choose S so that all its elements are *mutually exclusive* and *collectively exhaustive*—that is, no two elements can occur simultaneously and one element must occur on any trial.[2]

2   *Assignment of probabilities.*   Assign probabilities to the elements in S.   This assignment must be consistent with axioms I, II, and III.   Sample space S should consist of a finite number of mutually exclusive and collectively exhaustive elements.   Probabilities should then be assigned to the elements in S such that the sum of all the assignments adds to 1.   (Why should they add to 1?)

[1]Be   sure   you   understand   that $s_{17} \cap s_{18} = (0, 0, 1, 1, 1) \cap (0, 1, 0, 1, 1) = \emptyset$,   not $(0, 0, 0, 1, 1)$.   These 5-tuples are not characteristic vectors (see Appendix B); remember their interpretation.
†Note that $S = s_1 \cup s_2 \cup s_3 \cup \cdots \cup s_{31} \cup s_{32}$.
[2]More formally, a set of subsets $A_1, \ldots, A_n$ of S is mutually exclusive and collectively exhaustive if $A_i \cap A_j = \emptyset$ for any $i \neq j$, and $\cup_{i=1}^{n} A_i = S$.

3 *Identify the solution events.*   Translate the desired solution into events on S.
4 *Compute desired probabilities.*   Using computational rules (axioms I, II, III, and others to be developed in the exercises), calculate the desired probabilities.

Although the derivation of most of the computational formulas will be left as exercises, there is one that is so important that it must be discussed in considerable detail.   This is known as the *conditional probability formula.*   Let E and F be two events defined on a sample space S, and let $P(E)$ and $P(F)$ be the probabilities associated with these events.   Let $P(E|F)$ denote the probability of event E *given* that event F has occurred.   Usually, $P(E) \neq P(E|F)$.   *Once we know that F has occurred, the computation of the probability of E is no longer based on the whole space S; now we need only consider those elements of S which imply the occurrence of F.*   All this is done for us automatically by the formula

$$P(E|F) = \frac{P(E \cap F)}{P(F)} \qquad \text{(defined only if } P(F) \neq 0\text{)}$$

Let us verify the conditional probability formula in the multiprocessor example.   We continue to assume the equally likely distribution.   Suppose that on the way to the computer room to submit the program, we pass a friend who tells us that she just put her own program on processor 1 and that it will run for a long time.   She tells us nothing about the status of any of the other four processors.   *Now* what is the probability that we will be able to load the program?   Let

E = event that we will load, that is, that three or more processors are available

F = event that processor 1 is in use

Given event F, we know that the system must be in one of the following 16 states: s_2, s_7–s_{10}, s_{21}–s_{26}, s_{28}–s_{32}.   Each of *these* 16 states is *still* equally likely—that is, we have no reason to prefer one over any of the others.   Therefore, the probability that any particular outcome in this set will occur in the forthcoming trial is $\frac{1}{16}$, that is, $P(s_i|F) = \frac{1}{16}$ for $i = 2$, 7–10, 21–26, and 28–32.   In this reduced sample space, outcomes s_2, s_7, s_8, s_9, and s_{10} imply the occurrence of E.   Thus, by axiom III

$$P(E|F) = P(s_2|F) + P(s_7|F) + P(s_8|F) + P(s_9|F) + P(s_{10}|F)$$
$$= \tfrac{5}{16}$$

In order to use the conditional probability formula directly, we use the full sample space S.   Then

$$E = \{s_1, s_2, \ldots, s_{16}\}$$
$$F = \{s_2, s_7\text{–}s_{10}, s_{21}\text{–}s_{26}, s_{28}\text{–}s_{32}\}$$

$$E \cap F = \{s_2, s_7, s_8, s_9, s_{10}\}$$

$$P(E \cap F) = P(s_2) + P(s_7) + P(s_8) + P(s_9) + P(s_{10}) \qquad \text{(axiom III)}$$

$$= \tfrac{5}{32}$$

$$P(F) = P(s_2) + P(s_7) + \cdots + P(s_{10}) + P(s_{21}) + \cdots + P(s_{26}) + P(s_{28})$$

$$+ \cdots + P(s_{32}) \qquad \text{(axiom III)}$$

$$= \tfrac{16}{32}$$

and $\qquad P(E|F) = \dfrac{P(E \cap F)}{P(F)} = \dfrac{\frac{5}{32}}{\frac{16}{32}} = \tfrac{5}{16}$

What if the occurrence of F has no bearing whatever on the likelihood of E? Then it follows that

$$P(E) = P(E|F)$$

But $\qquad P(E|F) = \dfrac{P(E \cap F)}{P(F)}$

so $\qquad P(E) = \dfrac{P(E \cap F)}{P(F)} \qquad \text{or} \qquad P(E \cap F) = P(E)P(F)$

If events E and F are such that the probability of both occurring is equal to the product of their separate probabilities of occurrence, these events are said to be *independent*. This formula is readily extended to the case of three or more mutually independent events; that is, if sets $A_1, \ldots, A_n$ are such that

$$P(A_i \cap A_j) = P(A_i)P(A_j) \qquad \text{for any } i \neq j$$

then $\qquad P(A_1 \cap A_2 \cap \cdots \cap A_n) = P(A_1)P(A_2) \cdots P(A_n)$

In most problems, it is possible to identify one or more real-valued quantities which provide information more conveniently and compactly than explicit descriptions of events. For example, the integer-valued function

$$X = \text{the number of free processors}$$

tells us everything we want to know in our multiprocessor experiment. The desired final probability can be expressed as $P(X \geq 3)$ equals the probability that X has a value greater than or equal to 3. Observe that X is actually a *function*, whose domain is the sample space S and whose range is the set $\{0, 1, 2, 3, 4, 5\}$. Any such *function* from the sample space (and its assigned probability measure) of a problem to a set of real numbers is called a *random variable*. Virtually all serious probabilistic computations are done in terms of random variables.

An allocation of probability to the range of a random variable is called a *distribution.* In our multiprocessor example, assuming the equally likely assignment on the elements of S, we find that

$$P(X = 0) = \tfrac{1}{32}$$
$$P(X = 1) = \tfrac{5}{32}$$
$$P(X = 2) = \tfrac{10}{32}$$
$$P(X = 3) = \tfrac{10}{32}$$
$$P(X = 4) = \tfrac{5}{32}$$
$$P(X = 5) = \tfrac{1}{32}$$

To see how these values are computed, consider

$$P(X = 4) = P \text{ (there are exactly four free processors)}$$
$$= P(s_2 \cup s_3 \cup s_4 \cup s_5 \cup s_6)$$
$$= P(s_2) + P(s_3) + P(s_4) + P(s_5) + P(s_6)$$
$$= \tfrac{1}{32} + \tfrac{1}{32} + \tfrac{1}{32} + \tfrac{1}{32} + \tfrac{1}{32}$$
$$= \tfrac{5}{32}$$

A random variable whose range consists of a countable number of possible values is called *discrete.* If a random variable Y must assume one of the values $y_1, y_2, \ldots$, then

$$P(Y = y_i) > 0 \qquad i = 1, 2, \ldots$$
$$P(Y = y) = 0 \qquad \text{for all other values of } y$$

Discrete distributions of this form are called *probability mass functions.* Since Y must take on one of the values y_i in the experiment, the mass function must satisfy the relation

$$\sum_i P(Y = y_i) = 1$$

That is, there is probability 1 (certainty) that Y will equal one of its allowed values (note that it cannot equal more than one simultaneously).   It is easy to verify that the probability mass function of random variable X in the last paragraph satisfies this relation.

The *expected value*, or *average value*, or *mean*, of a random variable Y is defined as

$$E[Y] = \sum_i y_i P(Y = y_i)$$

In terms of the frequency interpretation of probability, the mean is the average value of the random variable observed over a large number of trials. In our example,

$$E[X] = \tfrac{1}{32}(0) + \tfrac{5}{32}(1) + \tfrac{10}{32}(2) + \tfrac{10}{32}(3) + \tfrac{5}{32}(4) + \tfrac{1}{32}(5)$$

$$= \tfrac{80}{32} = 2.5$$

Note that the mean is not necessarily in the range of the random variable. Any function of a random variable $G(Y)$ is also a random variable (why?), with expected value given by

$$E[G(Y)] = \sum_i G(y_i)P(Y = y_i)\dagger \qquad (1)$$

Once again, let random variable X denote the number of free processors. If random variable G equals our processor deficiency, that is, the number by which we fall short of being able to run our program, then

$$G(X) = \begin{cases} 3 & \text{if } X = 0 \\ 2 & \text{if } X = 1 \\ 1 & \text{if } X = 2 \\ 0 & \text{if } X \geqslant 3 \end{cases}$$

Using Eq. (1),

$$E[G(X)] = 3[P(G = 3)] + 2[P(G = 2)] + 1[P(G = 1)] + 0[P(G = 0)]$$

$$= 3[P(X = 0)] + 2[P(X = 1)] + 1[P(X = 2)] + 0[P(X \geqslant 3)]$$

$$= 3(\tfrac{1}{32}) + 2(\tfrac{5}{32}) + 1(\tfrac{10}{32}) = \tfrac{23}{32}$$

The usefulness of the expected value is increased when the actual value taken on by the random variable is unlikely to deviate much from the mean. One measure of this deviation is known as the *variance* of the random variable. Let Y be a random variable with mean $\mu = E[Y]$. Then the variance of Y, denoted var$[Y]$, is defined as

$$\text{var}[Y] = E[(Y - \mu)^2] = \sum_i (y_i - \mu)^2 P(Y = y_i) \qquad (2)$$

where we have used the formula for the expected value of a function of a random variable. The *standard deviation* of a random variable is defined as

$$\sigma[Y] = \sqrt{\text{var}[Y]}$$

†This is often called the "law of the unconscious statistician" because it is often essentially presented as a definition (as we have done) by "unconscious" statisticians who forget that this formula can be derived.

For the random variable X in the multiprocessor example,

$$\text{var}[X] = (0 - 2.5)^2(\tfrac{1}{32}) + (1 - 2.5)^2(\tfrac{5}{32}) + (2 - 2.5)^2(\tfrac{10}{32})$$

$$+ (3 - 2.5)^2(\tfrac{10}{32}) + (4 - 2.5)^2(\tfrac{5}{32}) + (5 - 2.5)^2(\tfrac{1}{32})$$

$$= \tfrac{40}{32} = 1.25$$

and $$\sigma[X] = 1.12$$

Straight Insertion Sort

We conclude this section with an expected, or average, performance analysis of a simple sorting algorithm.

Straight insertion sort takes a list of unordered positive integers (usually called *keys*) and sorts them into ascending order. This is done in much the same way that many card players order the cards in their hand by picking them up one at a time. The general procedure is illustrated with the following unsorted list of eight integers.

$$27 \quad 412 \quad 71 \quad 81 \quad 59 \quad 14 \quad 273 \quad 87$$

A sorted list is created (it is initially empty), and at each iteration the top number on the unsorted list is removed and put into its proper place in the sorted list. This is done by moving along the sorted list, from the smallest to the largest number, until the correct place for the new number is located—that is, until all sorted numbers with smaller values come before it and all those with larger values come after it. The following sequence of lists shows how this is done.

Iteration 0	Unsorted	412	71	81	59	14	273	87	
	Sorted	27							
Iteration 1	Unsorted	*412*	71	81	59	14	273	87	
	Sorted	27	*412*						
Iteration 2	Unsorted	*71*	81	59	14	273	87		
	Sorted	27	*71*	412					
Iteration 3	Unsorted	*81*	59	14	273	87			
	Sorted	27	71	*81*	412				
Iteration 4	Unsorted	*59*	14	273	87				
	Sorted	27	*59*	71	81	412			
Iteration 5	Unsorted	*14*	273	87					
	Sorted	*14*	27	59	71	81	412		
Iteration 6	Unsorted	*273*	87						
	Sorted	14	27	59	71	81	*273*	412	
Iteration 7	Unsorted	*87*							
	Sorted	14	27	59	71	81	*87*	273	412

The following algorithm avoids keeping two lists and rearranges the numbers in place.

Algorithm SIS (*Straight Insertion Sort*)   To sort, in place, a sequence of integers I(1), I(2), . . . , I(N) into ascending order.

Step 1. [Basic iteration] **For** J ← 2 **to** N **do through** step 4 **od**; **and** STOP.

   Step 2. [Take next integer] **Set** K ← I(J); **and** L ← J − 1.

   Step 3. [Compare with sorted integers] **While** K < I(L) AND L ≥ 1
      do set I(L + 1) ← I(L); **and** L ← L − 1 **od**.

   Step 4. [Insert] **Set** I(L + 1) ← K.

A flowchart for Algorithm SIS is given in Fig. 2.4.1.

We shall now estimate the average number of comparisons needed to sort random data using straight insertion sort. It will be left as an exercise to determine the maximum and minimum numbers of comparisons needed.

Let N be the number of keys to be sorted. Consider the ith pass through the loop at step 1. At the *beginning* of this pass, the first i keys of the unsorted list have been ordered correctly, and we are now about to insert the $(i + 1)$st key into the list of i sorted keys. There are $i − 1$ "slots" between the currently sorted keys and two more positions at the end of this list, giving a total of $i + 1$ possible positions where the next key could be inserted. Assume that the new key is equally likely, with probability $1/(i + 1)$, to be inserted into any one of these slots. Let X_i be a random variable which equals the number of comparisons needed to place key $i + 1$ into its correct position on this pass. Then

$$E[X_i] = 1\left(\frac{1}{i+1}\right) + 2\left(\frac{1}{i+1}\right) + 3\left(\frac{1}{i+1}\right) + \cdots + \frac{i}{i+1} + \frac{i}{i+1}$$

$$= \frac{1}{i+1}[1 + 2 + 3 + \cdots + (i-1) + i + i]$$

$$= \frac{1}{i+1}\frac{i(i+1)}{2} + \frac{i}{i+1} \qquad \text{(using Gauss' formula)}$$

$$= \frac{i}{2} + \frac{i}{i+1}$$

Observe that only i comparisons are made if the correct position is at the far end. Since there are N keys, there are N − 1 iterations of the loop at step 1. If random variable Y denotes the total number of comparisons in the sort, then

$$Y = X_1 + X_2 + \cdots + X_{N-1}$$

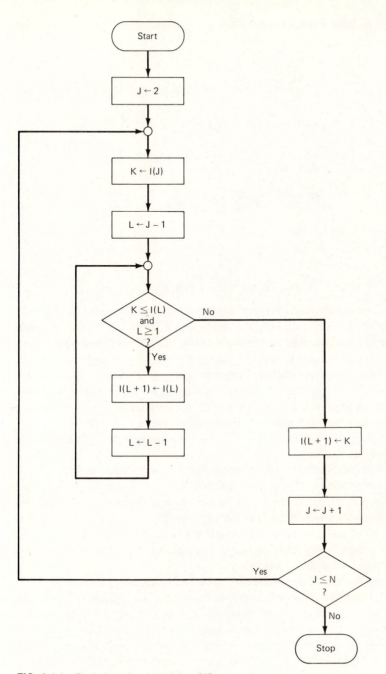

FIG. 2.4.1 Flowchart for Algorithm SIS.

Using the result of Exercise 2.4.11, we have

$$E[Y] = E[X_1] + E[X_2] + \cdots + E[X_{N-1}]$$

$$= \left(\frac{1}{2} + \frac{1}{2}\right) + \left(\frac{2}{2} + \frac{2}{3}\right) + \cdots + \left(\frac{N-1}{2} + \frac{N-1}{N}\right)$$

$$= \tfrac{1}{2}[1 + 2 + \cdots + (N-1)] + \left[\frac{1}{2} + \frac{2}{3} + \cdots + \frac{N-1}{N}\right]$$

$$= \frac{1}{2}\sum_{i=1}^{N-1} i + \sum_{i=1}^{N-1} \frac{i}{i+1}$$

$$= \frac{1}{2}\frac{N(N-1)}{2} + N - \sum_{i=1}^{N} \frac{1}{i} \qquad \text{(see Exercise 2.4.10)}$$

$$= \frac{N^2}{4} + \frac{3N}{4} - H_N$$

where $H_N = \sum_{i=1}^{N} \frac{1}{i}$ is known as the N*th harmonic number.*[1]

Thus the average number of comparisons needed by Algorithm SIS to sort N keys is roughly $N^2/4$, and the average complexity is $O(N^2)$. A similar analysis reveals that the average number of times the move $I(L+1) \leftarrow I(L)$ is made is also $O(N^2)$.

Algorithm SIS is not a very good sorting algorithm even though it is one of the simplest and easiest to implement. More sophisticated sorting algorithms, whose average or worst-case complexity is $O(N \log N)$, will be studied in Sec. 5.1.

The straight insertion sort example illustrates a simple and theoretical probabilistic complexity analysis. A number of similar analyses are scattered throughout the remainder of this book.

To illustrate a basic distinction between probability and statistics, we shall use our expected performance analysis of Algorithm SIS. Specifically, from a given or assumed distribution of the elements to be sorted, we computed the expected number of comparisons that are made in sorting N keys. This was done using the definitions and computational rules from the theory of probability. Thus, a *given distribution* was used to *predict the behavior* of the algorithm. This type of analysis characterizes most probabilistic models.

In many ways, statistical problems are "reversed" probability problems. The *behavior of the system is observed*, and one tries to *draw inferences about the underlying unknown distributions* of random variables that describe system activity. Define a random variable Y which equals, for any random sequence of N integers, the number of comparisons required by Algorithm SIS to sort the sequence. Every application of Algorithm SIS to a random sequence of integers therefore produces a *sample* of Y. Although we do not know the underlying

[1]As $N \rightarrow \infty$, H_N is roughly equal to $\log_e N + 0.577 + O(1/N)$.

distribution of Y, we could take a number of samples, compute the average $\bar{Y}$ of these experimental numbers, and use $\bar{Y}$ as an *estimator* of the mean of Y (that is, use $\bar{Y}$ to approximate $E[Y]$). Thus, observed values are used to make a statement about the random variable.

It is not possible to make general statements about which form of analysis is better. They should be used to complement each other. In our example, an assumption was made about the distribution before we could probabilistically compute $E[Y]$. That is, we assumed that the $(i + 1)$st key was equally likely to be placed in any of the positions at the ends or between the sorted list of i elements. Is this assumption true for "real" data? On the other hand, the statistical estimate of $E[Y]$ might be poor because the observed sample was "unrepresentative" in some sense. If we are dealt a sample hand of four cards, and they are all aces, do we conclude that the whole deck contains nothing but aces? If we do both forms of analysis—compare the statistical estimator $\bar{Y}$ with the derived value of $E[Y]$—and the values are close, there is reason to believe that we understand the average performance of the algorithm. If they differ widely, there is cause to worry.

Let us continue our discussion of estimators and the statistical analysis of algorithms in slightly more general terms. We are interested in the expected or average performance of some algorithm A on the set of possible inputs D. Set D is very large and algorithm A is rather complicated. Consider the execution of some randomly chosen input from D on A as an experiment that defines a random variable T, the run time of A. The distribution of T is unknown. For our purposes, it is not necessary to estimate statistically the entire distribution of T. It will be sufficient to estimate the values of certain properties of the distribution, namely, the mean and the variance.

The general procedure for estimating a property θ of a distribution is as follows. Take a number of observations $(X_1, X_2, \ldots, X_n)$ of the random variable X of interest. Form a function $F(X_1, X_2, \ldots, X_n)$ whose domain is the set of observations and whose range is the set of possible values of property θ. Such a function is called an *estimator of* θ, and is itself a random variable (why?).

How do we choose a specific function to use as an estimator? Since there are many possible choices, some criteria should be provided to guide the selection of a good estimator. The most intuitively obvious criteria is to choose an estimator function F whose own distribution[1] is highly concentrated around the true value of θ. We shall consider three specific characteristics of good estimators which reflect this intuitive requirement.

A random variable F is an *unbiased* estimator of θ if $E[F] = \theta$. There are very simple unbiased estimators for the mean and variance of any random variable. The estimator

$$\bar{X}(X_1, \ldots, X_n) = \frac{1}{n} \sum_{i=1}^{n} X_i$$

[1] Remember, F is a random variable!

is an unbiased estimator of the mean $E[X]$. This follows from

$$E[\bar{X}] = E\left[\frac{1}{n}\sum_{i=1}^{n} X_i\right]$$

$$= \frac{1}{n}\sum_{i=1}^{n} E[X_i] \qquad \text{(see Exercise 2.4.11)}$$

$$= \frac{1}{n}n(E[X]) \qquad \text{(why?)}$$

$$= E[X]$$

Since var $[X]$ is defined in terms of $E[X]$ (see Eq. (2) and Exercise 2.4.12), the estimator chosen for var $[X]$ will depend on whether $E[X]$ is known or must be estimated. If $E[X]$ is known, then the estimator

$$G(X_1, \ldots, X_n) = \frac{1}{n}\sum_{i=1}^{n} (X_i - E[X])^2$$

suggests itself from the definition of var $[X]$. That G is unbiased is readily established.

$$E[G] = E\left[\frac{1}{n}\sum_{i=1}^{n} (X_i - E[X])^2\right]$$

$$= \frac{1}{n}\sum_{i=1}^{n} E[(X_i - E[X])^2]$$

$$= \frac{1}{n}\sum_{i=1}^{n} (E[X_i^2] - 2E[X_i]E[X] + (E[X])^2)$$

$$= \frac{1}{n}nE[X^2] - n(E[X])^2$$

$$= \text{var}\,[X]$$

using the results of Exercise 2.4.12. If $E[X]$ is not known, as is usually the case, then the estimator

$$S^2(X_1, \ldots, X_n) = \frac{1}{n-1}\sum_{i=1}^{n} (X_i - \bar{X})^2$$

is an unbiased estimator of var $[X]$. The proof of this is left as an exercise.

A *consistent* estimator $G(X_1, \ldots, X_n)$ of a property θ is one whose value will be arbitrarily close to θ with probability approaching 1 as $n \to \infty$. More formally, $G(X_1, \ldots, X_n)$ is a consistent estimator for θ if

$$\lim_{n \to \infty} P\{|G(X_1, \ldots, X_n) - \theta| < \epsilon\} = 1 \qquad \text{for every } \epsilon > 0$$

The consistency characteristic reflects the intuitive feeling that larger samples should be more reliable. This intuitive feeling is mathematically justified by one of the most important results in probability theory.

Theorem 2.4.1 (*the weak law of large numbers*) Let $X_1, \ldots, X_n$ be independent random variables with (a) $E[X_i] = m$, and (b) var $[X_i] = q^2$ for $i = 1, 2, \ldots, n$. If $\bar{X}$ is defined as

$$\bar{X}(X_1, \ldots, X_n) = \frac{1}{n} \sum_{i=1}^{n} X_i$$

then for any $\epsilon > 0$,

$$\lim_{n \to \infty} P\{|\bar{X} - m| < \epsilon\} = 1$$

A stronger version of this theorem permits the finite variance condition (b) to be dropped. One immediate consequence of the law of large numbers is that $\bar{X}$ is a consistent estimator of the mean of any random variable.

A *minimum-variance unbiased estimator* is one whose variance is least among all unbiased estimators, or perhaps among all unbiased estimators of a certain kind. The variance can often be considered to be a measure of the precision of an estimator. The smaller the variance, the better are the chances that the value of the estimator will be close to the property it estimates. Thus, small variance is a desirable characteristic of an estimator.

Example The run time of a dynamically executing algorithm is measured on two system clocks. The first clock gives a reading of T_1, the second records a value T_2. Both clocks suffer inaccuracies due to system noise. However, the noise is such that each clock is just as likely to give too low a reading as it is to give too high a reading by the same magnitude. Therefore,

$$E[T_1] = E[T_2] = T = \text{true run time}$$

Thus both clocks are unbiased, but their known precisions are not the same—that is,

$$\text{var}[T_1] \neq \text{var}[T_2]$$

Let us assume that var $[T_1] < $ var $[T_2]$.

Should T_1 or T_2 be used to estimate T? Why not use both in some sort of weighted average? Accordingly, let

$$H(T_1, T_2) = sT_1 + (1 - s)T_2$$

for some constant $0 \leq s \leq 1$ which has yet to be determined. Clearly, the estimator $H(T_1, T_2)$ is unbiased since

$$E[H] = sE[T_1] + (1 - s)E[T_2] \qquad \text{(see Exercise 2.4.11)}$$

$$= sT + (1 - s)T = T$$

The constant s will be chosen so as to give us the estimator with the smallest possible variance from among all possible estimators which are in the form of a simple weighted average of T_1 and T_2.

To find the value of s which minimizes var $[H]$, we proceed as follows, using a standard technique from calculus.

$$\text{var } [H] = s^2 \text{ var } [T_1] + (1-s)^2 \text{ var } [T_2] \qquad \text{(see Exercise 2.4.13)}$$

$$\frac{d}{ds} \text{ var } [H] = 2s \text{ var } [T_1] + (-2+2s) \text{ var } [T_2] = 0$$

$$\text{var } [T_2] = s \text{ var } [T_1] + s \text{ var } [T_2]$$

$$s = \frac{\text{var } [T_2]}{\text{var } [T_1] + \text{var } [T_2]}$$

It is not difficult to check that this value of s actually minimizes var $[H]$.

Is it surprising that we do not take $s = 1$—that is, that we do not use T_1 alone to estimate T? After all, var $[T_1] < $ var $[T_2]$, and therefore the first clock has greater precision than the second. This ignores the important fact that T_2 is also an unbiased estimator, and its value provides information about the run time T. Of course, the more precise clock should be weighted more heavily. Is that the case with our choice of s? If var $[T_1] = $ var $[T_2]$, does our choice of s weight the two clocks equally?

Exercises 2.4

2.4.1 Rework the entire multiprocessor problem for the case of a six-processor system and a program that needs four processors. Use the equally likely distribution again. Compute $E[X]$ and var $[X]$, where random variable X equals the number of free processors.

2.4.2 What is the probability of obtaining exactly 7 heads in 12 tosses of a fair coin?

2.4.3 In the multiprocessor problem, let $G(X) = X^2$, where X is the random variable whose probability mass function is given on page 83. Compute $E[G]$ and var $[G]$.

2.4.4 *Straight insertion sort (analysis).* What are the maximum and minimum possible numbers of comparisons needed by Algorithm SIS to sort N keys?

2.4.5 If all possible orderings of N keys are equally likely, what is the probability that the keys will already be sorted when they are input into Algorithm SIS?

2.4.6 A gambler believes that he has a first-rate roulette strategy. He watches the occurrence of red and black. If five red (black) numbers appear consecutively, he will bet $10 on black (red) at the next spin of the wheel. His reasoning is that there is a very small probability of having six reds (or blacks) in a row. Analyze this strategy.

2.4.7 If E is any event defined on any sample space S, show that $P(E) \le 1$.

*__2.4.8__ If E and F are any two events, show that

$$P(E \cup F) = P(E) + P(F) - P(E \cap F)$$

2.4.9 Show that $P(\emptyset) = 0$, where $\emptyset$ is the null set.

2.4.10 Prove the identity

$$\sum_{i=1}^{N-1} \frac{i}{i+1} = N - \sum_{i=1}^{N} \frac{1}{i}$$

This identity was used in the analysis of Algorithm SIS.

*__2.4.11__ If $X_1, \ldots, X_n$ are random variables with *joint* mass function $P(x_1, x_2, \ldots, x_n) = P(X_1 = x_1, X_2 = x_2, \ldots, \text{and } X_n = x_n)$, and if $a_1, \ldots, a_n$ are arbitrary constants, show that

$$E[a_1 X_1 + a_2 X_2 + \cdots + a_n X_n] = a_1 E[X_1] + a_2 E[X_2] + \cdots + a_n E[X_n]$$

2.4.12 If X is any discrete random variable, show that

$$\text{var}[X] = E[X^2] - (E[X])^2$$

2.4.13 For any random variable X and constant a, show that

$$\text{var}[aX] = a^2 \text{var}[X]$$

*__2.4.14__ Two airplanes are flying from city X to city Y. The first has two engines but can fly on one in an emergency. The second has four engines but can fly on two in an emergency. All six engines are identical, and each has a probability p of failure during the flight. Assume the performance of any engine does not depend on that of any other. Which plane would you prefer to take? Consider all values of p in the range $0 < p < 1$.

2.4.15 Four fair dice are rolled. What is the probability that no 5 appears?

2.4.16 Let S be a sample space, and let $\{F_1, \ldots, F_n\}$ be a set of events that are mutually exclusive and collectively exhaustive on S. If E is any event, show that

$$E = \bigcup_{i=1}^{n} (E \cap F_i)$$

2.4.17 Using the result of Exercise 2.4.16, show that

$$P(E) = \sum_{i=1}^{n} P(E|F_i) P(F_i)$$

*2.4.18 Reconsider Algorithm MAX of Sec. 1.2. Assume every ordering of the N numbers is equally likely. Let random variable Y denote the position of the largest number. Compute $E[Y]$ and var $[Y]$.

*2.4.19 What is the probability that a randomly selected tour in an N-city traveling salesman problem will be optimum? What assumptions are you making to obtain your answer?

*2.4.20 *Independent random variables.* Two random variables X_1 and X_2 are *independent* if

$$P(X_1 \le a \text{ and } X_2 \le b) = P(X_1 \le a) P(X_2 \le b) \qquad \text{for all } a \text{ and } b$$

Show that if X_1 and X_2 are independent then

$$E[X_1 X_2] = E[X_1] E[X_2]$$

**2.4.21 *Algorithm SIS (analysis).* As in the discussion of straight insertion sort, let random variable Y equal the number of comparisons needed to sort N keys using Algorithm SIS. Compute var $[Y]$. Assume all the X_i are independent random variables.

*2.4.22 *Binomial distribution.* Consider n trials of an experiment in which there is a probability p of "success." Let random variable X record the number of successes in the n trials. Assume that the outcome on any trial does not influence the outcome of any other trial. Show that the probability mass function of X is given by

$$P(X = k) = \binom{n}{k} p^k (1 - p)^{n-k} \qquad k = 0, 1, \ldots, n$$

Compute $E[X]$ and var $[X]$.

*2.4.23 Let G be a network with N vertices whose edges are chosen at random according to the following scheme. For every pair of vertices i and j, edge (i, j) is present in G with probability p, independent of i and j, and absent with probability $1 - p$. What is the expected number of edges in G? Networks generated in this way are known as *p-random networks.*

*2.4.24 *Geometric distribution.* On any trial of an experiment, let the probability of success be p. Each trial is independent of every other trial. We are prepared to conduct as many trials as necessary until we have our first success. Let random variable X equal the number of trials up to and including the one where we achieve our first success. What is the probability mass function for X? Calculate $E[X]$ and var$[X]$.

2.4.25 *Straight insertion sort (complexity, testing).* Implement Algorithm SIS as a computer program. Randomly generate (how?) sets of N = 20 unsorted keys and observe the number of comparisons needed to sort each set. Let $\bar{Y}$ be the average of these observations. Compare $\bar{Y}$ with $E[Y]$ in the discussion of a straight insertion sort.

*2.4.26 Show that the estimator

$$s^2(X_1, \ldots, X_n) = \frac{1}{n-1} \sum_{i=1}^{n} (X_i - \bar{X})^2$$

is an unbiased estimator of var[X].

2.4.27 Verify that our choice of s in the example at the end of Sec. 2.4 actually minimizes var[H].

3 ALGORITHM DESIGN METHODS

There are a number of basic techniques and ideas that should be part of the working knowledge of anyone who designs algorithms. We have all had the (often painful) experience of confronting a difficult problem for the first time and asking the question: How do we get started? One way of proceeding is to review our repertory of general algorithmic methods to see if a solution to our problem might be formulated in terms of one of them. The objective of this chapter is to develop and illustrate several fundamental algorithm design and problem-solving techniques.

Section 3.1 contains brief descriptions of three basic problem-solving methods. In some form, at least one of these methods lies behind many of the procedures and algorithms in the remainder of this book. Two general techniques for handling large combinatorial problems—backtracking and branch and bound—are studied in Secs. 3.3 and 3.4. Recursion, a design tool which can greatly simplify the logical structure of many algorithms, is presented in Sec. 3.5. Sections 3.2 and 3.6 study two commonly used "real-life" techniques: heuristics and simulation. Perhaps more large, sophisticated applications programs use these two methods than all others combined.

3.1 SUBGOALS, HILL CLIMBING, AND WORKING BACKWARD

How do we design a good algorithm? How do we get started? We have all had the frustrating experience of staring at a problem, with no idea of what to do. This section briefly describes three general problem-solving methods which have been found useful in designing algorithms.

The first method involves the reduction of a difficult problem into a sequence of simpler problems. Of course, we hope that the simpler problems are more tractable than the original problem; we also hope that the solutions to the simpler problems can be organized into a solution for the original problem. We call this a *subgoals method*.

This method sounds very reasonable. But like most general problem-solving or algorithm design techniques, it is not always easy to carry out on a specific problem. The judicious choice of subproblems is more of an art than a science. Moreover, there is no general set of rules for identifying problems which can be solved by this approach. For any particular problem, start by asking questions. Subgoals can often be identified from answers to the following:

1 Can we solve part of the problem? Is it possible to ignore some conditions and solve the rest of the problem?
2 Can we solve the problem for special cases? Is it possible to design an algorithm which yields a solution that satisfies all the conditions of the problem, but whose inputs are restricted to a subset of all inputs?
3 Is there something about the problem which we do not fully understand? If we strive for a deeper understanding of some feature of the problem, can we learn something that may help us to start moving toward a solution?
4 Have we seen a similar problem whose solution is known? Could this solution be modified to solve the problem? Is it possible that the problem is equivalent to a known unsolved problem?

Virtually all attempts to solve the network isomorphism problem (see Sec. 2.2) involve the subgoals method in one way or another. This is especially true of attempts which try to solve the problem by finding a (complete) set of invariants of a network such that two networks are isomorphic if and only if the values of the invariants in the set are the same for both networks. The isomorphism algorithm in Sec. 2.2 can be viewed as one that looks at a sequence of subgoals.

A second method for designing algorithms is known as *hill climbing*. A hill-climbing algorithm starts by making an initial guess or computing an initial solution to the problem. It then proceeds to move "uphill" from the initial solution toward better solutions as quickly as possible. When a point is reached in the algorithm where it is no longer possible to move uphill, the algorithm stops. Unfortunately, one cannot always guarantee that the final solution produced by a hill-climbing algorithm will be optimal. This "defect" often limits the applicability of the hill-climbing method.

Hill climbing takes its name in part from algorithms for finding the maxima of functions of several variables. Suppose $f(x, y)$ is a function of the variables x and y, and the problem is to find the maximum value of f. The function f can be represented by a surface (having hills and valleys) above the xy plane, as in Fig. 3.1.1. A hill-climbing algorithm might start at an arbitrary point z_0 on this surface and work its way uphill to the peak at z_1. This value is a "local" maximum rather than a "global" one, and the hill-climbing method fails to produce an optimum solution.

Generally, hill-climbing methods are "greedy." They have a certain goal in mind, and they try to do whatever they can, whenever they can, to get closer to that goal. This tends to make them a bit shortsighted.

As our example illustrates, hill-climbing algorithms may be useful if we are willing to settle for a fast, approximate solution. This matter will be explored further in Sec. 3.2.

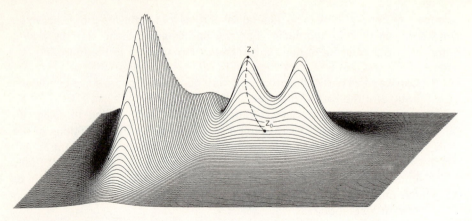

FIG. 3.1.1 Hill climbing to a local maximum.

The third technique to be considered in this section is known as *working backward*—that is, start at the goal or solution and work backward toward the initial statement of the problem.   Then, if these steps are reversible, work forward from the problem statement to the solution.   Most of us have done this while solving the maze puzzles that appear in the Sunday comic section of the newspaper.

Let us try to use all three methods of this section in a fairly difficult example.

The Jeep Problem

We would like to advance a jeep across a 1000-mile desert using a minimum of fuel.   The jeep has a fuel capacity of 500 gallons, which it uses at the uniform rate of 1 gallon per mile.   The initial position has an unlimited reservoir of fuel.   Since there are no fuel depots in the desert, we must use the vehicle to set up and stock its own storage points from its tank.   Where do we set up these storage points?   And how much fuel should be left at each?

Let us approach this problem by working backward.   How far back can we start with exactly k full loads of fuel and be able to make it to the end of the desert?   We will ask this question for $k = 1, 2, 3, \ldots$ until we find an integer n such that n full loads will enable us to cross the entire 1000-mile desert.

For $k = 1$, the answer is 500 miles, as shown in Fig. 3.1.2.   We can fill the vehicle at point B and cross the remaining 500 miles of desert.   Clearly, this is as far back as we can possibly start with exactly 500 gallons of fuel.

We have set ourselves a subgoal.   We could not readily solve the original problem.   We do not ask the question: How much fuel does the vehicle need to travel a given distance?   Rather, we ask the easier, but related, question: How far can it travel on a given amount of fuel?   A candidate answer to the first question is available when the answer to the second is at least 1000 miles.

Suppose $k = 2$—that is, two loads (1000 gallons) are available. This case will be handled by building on the result for $k = 1$. The situation is illustrated in Fig. 3.1.2. What is the maximum value of x_1 such that if we start with 1000 gallons at $500 - x_1$, it will be possible to move enough fuel to B to enable the trip to be completed as in the $k = 1$ case?

One way to determine a reasonable value of x_1 is as follows. Load up at position $500 - x_1$, travel x_1 miles to B, and drop off everything in the tank except x_1 gallons, which we use to return to position $500 - x_1$. At this point we are empty. Now pick up the second full load, travel x_1 miles to B, fill up at B with the fuel that was dropped off there, leave B with a full tank, and drive to C. The total number of miles traveled consists of three segments of x_1 miles and one segment BC of 500 miles. To make x_1 as large as possible, we use every drop of fuel. Therefore, x_1 is found from

$$3x_1 + 500 = 1000 \qquad \text{(gallons)}$$

with the solution $x_1 = \frac{500}{3}$. Thus, two loads (1000 gallons) enable us to cover

$$D_2 = 500 + x_1 = 500(1 + \tfrac{1}{3}) \text{ miles}$$

Notice that the basic argument is shortsighted and greedy. When k loads of fuel are available, we simply try to move back as far as possible from the position we found for $k - 1$ loads.

Consider $k = 3$. Where can we start with 1500 gallons so that the vehicle can move 1000 gallons to position $500 - x_1$? Returning to Fig. 3.1.2, we seek the largest value of x_2 such that starting with 1500 gallons at $500 - x_1 - x_2$, we can move

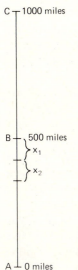

FIG. 3.1.2 The jeep problem: cross the desert from A to C.

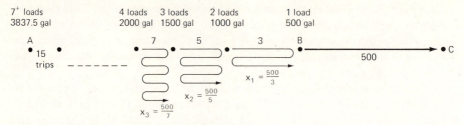

FIG. 3.1.3 Outline of solution to the jeep problem.

1000 gallons to $500 - x_1$. We start at $500 - x_1 - x_2$, move up to $500 - x_1$, drop off all but x_2 gallons, and return to position $500 - x_1 - x_2$ empty. If we repeat this, we will have used $4x_2$ gallons in transport and deposited $1000 - 4x_2$ gallons at $500 - x_1$. Now there are exactly 500 gallons left at $500 - x_1 - x_2$. Load up the last 500 gallons and drive to $500 - x_1$, using x_2 gallons in the process.

We are now at $500 - x_1$, having used $5x_2$ gallons in transporting fuel. The amount of fuel stored here is $1500 - 5x_2$ gallons. This must equal 1000; that is, $x_2 = \frac{500}{5}$. We then conclude that 1500 gallons can get us

$$D_3 = 500 + x_1 + x_2 = 500(1 + \tfrac{1}{3} + \tfrac{1}{5}) \text{ miles}$$

Continuing to work backward in an inductive fashion, we find that n loads enable our vehicle to travel D_n miles, where

$$D_n = 500 \left(\frac{1}{1} + \frac{1}{3} + \frac{1}{5} + \cdots + \frac{1}{2n-1} \right)$$

We want the smallest value of n such that $D_n \geq 1000$. A simple computation shows that for $n = 7$, $D_7 = 977.5$ miles; that is, seven loads, or 3500 gallons, will enable us to travel 977.5 miles. An eighth load would be more than we need to move 3500 gallons from position A to a point 22.5 miles $(1000 - 977.5)$ past A. You should be able to show that 337.5 gallons can be used to transport 3500 gallons to the 22.5-mile point. This gives a total fuel expenditure of 3837.5 gallons to move the vehicle across the desert from A to C.

The fuel transport algorithm can now be given as follows. Start at A with 3837.5 gallons. There is just enough fuel here to shuttle 3500 gallons to the 22.5-mile point, where we find ourselves with an empty tank and seven loads of fuel. There is enough fuel here to shuttle 3000 gallons to a position $22.5 + \frac{500}{13}$ miles from A, where we find ourselves with an empty tank. The next shuttle gets us to a position $22.5 + \frac{500}{13} + \frac{500}{11}$ miles from A with an empty tank and 2500 gallons.

Continuing in this way, we work forward over our backward analysis. We soon find ourselves at the $500(1 - \frac{1}{3}) = \frac{1000}{3}$-mile point with 1000 gallons. We then shuttle 500 gallons to B, where we fill up and travel to C without stopping. Figure 3.1.3 illustrates the travel pattern.

For those of you familiar with infinite series, note that the series for D_n is the nth partial sum of the odd harmonic series. Since this series diverges, our algorithm could be extended to enable us to cross any desert. How could this algorithm be modified to leave enough fuel along the desert for a return trip back to A?

You might be wondering if there is a way to travel the 1000 miles using less than 3837.5 gallons. There is not. The proof of this fact is fairly difficult. However, a good plausibility argument can be given as follows. We are obviously doing as well as we can for $k = 1$. For $k = 2$, we use our $k = 1$ plan, and then use the second load of fuel to get ourselves as far as possible from B. For k loads, the basic assumption is that we know how to do as well as possible with $k - 1$ loads, and we move back as far as we can with the kth load.

In one way or another, the next four sections are based on the three general methods discussed here. In fact, these methods are used regularly throughout the book even though we shall not explicitly note every such occurrence.

Exercises 3.1

3.1.1 *Coin weighing* (*hill climbing*). You have 25 gold coins. All of them have the same weight, with the exception of one defective coin that weighs less than the others. Design an algorithm which will locate the defect in three weighings. What is the maximum number of coins for which you can guarantee to find the defect in no more than three weighings on a balance scale?

3.1.2 *Uncalibrated containers* (*working backward*). You have a 5-gallon and a 3-gallon container, neither of which is calibrated. The objective is to obtain exactly 4 gallons of liquid. Design an algorithm for doing this. Assume that a very large reservoir of liquid is available.

*3.1.3 *Paper-cutting problem* (*subgoals*). Figure 3.1.4 shows the form of a Greek cross, which is composed of five identical squares. By making only two straightline cuts, cut the cross so that the resulting pieces can be fitted together to form a rectangle whose length is twice its width.

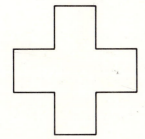

FIG. 3.1.4 The Greek cross.

3.1.4 *Partitioning a circle* (*hill climbing*). What is the maximum number of regions into which a circle can be partitioned using four straight lines?

3.1.5 *Decimal-octal-binary conversion* (*subgoals*). Design and implement an algorithm for converting decimal to binary numbers, and vice versa. Use conversion to octal numbers as a subgoal.

3.1.6 *Game* (*working backward*). Three people play a game in which one wins and the other two lose. Each loser gives the winner an amount of money equal to the winner's holdings at the beginning of the game. After three games have been played, each player has won one game and player 1 has $4, player 2 has $20, and player 3 has $6. What were their original holdings?

*L3.1.7 *Magic squares* (*problem setup and solution*). A magic square of size n is an $n \times n$ array containing the first n^2 positive integers. These integers are arranged so that the sum of all the entries in each row, column, and along the two main diagonals is equal to some common value C.

    (*a*) Set up an algebraic model whose solution will give you a magic square for $n = 3$. Try to solve the resulting set of equations without using a computer.

    (*b*) Design an algorithm for finding a magic square for $n = 3$ and $n = 4$. This procedure need not be based on your algebraic model. Implement, test, and analyze your algorithm on a computer. Is it useful for larger values of n?

*3.1.8 *Towers of Hanoi* (*working backward, subgoals*). Figure 3.1.5 illustrates an ancient game, known as the Towers of Hanoi. The game starts with n rings, each of different diameter, arranged by increasing diameter on one of three pegs. The objective is to transfer the rings, one at a time, until they are ultimately stacked in the same order on another peg. At no time are you permitted to place a ring on top of one with a smaller diameter. Design an algorithm which does this in $2^n - 1$ moves, where a move is the transfer of a ring from one peg to another. The pegs are effectively pushdown stores, and only the top ring on a pile can be moved.

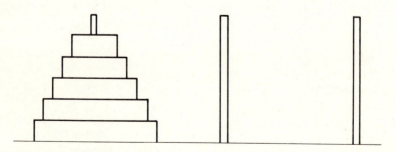

FIG. 3.1.5 Towers of Hanoi.

3.1.9 *Cannibals and missionaries.* The following problem is a classic, and any of the three basic methods discussed in this section can be used to solve it. Three missionaries and three cannibals are on one side of a river with a boat that can carry two people. They all want to cross the river. At no time can we permit a group of missionaries to be on the same side with a larger group of cannibals. Design a procedure that enables all six people to cross the river.

3.2 HEURISTICS

A *heuristic algorithm,* or *heuristic,* is defined as having the following properties:

1 It will usually find good, although not necessarily optimum, solutions.
2 It is faster and easier to implement than any known exact algorithm (one which guarantees an optimum solution).

The definitions of "good" and "usually," as used in property 1, will vary from problem to problem. For example, if we have a problem for which all known exact algorithms require years of computer time, then we might be willing to accept any nontrivial approximate solution that can be obtained in a reasonable amount of time. On the other hand, given a fast, near-optimum solution to a problem, we might not settle for anything less than an exact solution.

Although there is no real format into which we can place heuristic algorithms, quite a few are based on either the subgoals or the hill-climbing method. One general approach to the design of a heuristic is to list all the requirements of an exact solution and to divide these requirements into two classes—for example,

1 Those that are easy to satisfy
2 Those that are not so easy to satisfy

or

1 Those which must be satisfied
2 Those which we would be willing to compromise

The design objective then is to construct an algorithm that guarantees the requirements in class 1 but not necessarily those in class 2. This does not mean to imply that no effort is made to satisfy the class 2 requirements; it merely means that no guarantee can be made.

Often very good algorithms have to be considered as heuristics. For example, suppose we have designed a fast algorithm which seems to work on all test problems, but we cannot *prove* that the algorithm is correct. Until such a proof is given, the algorithm must be considered a heuristic.

As an example of this, consider the following "greedy" algorithm for solving the traveling salesman problem of Sec. 1.3.

Algorithm GTS (*Greedy Traveling Salesman*)   To construct a candidate least-cost tour TOUR, which has a cost COST, for an N-city traveling salesman problem with cost matrix C, starting at vertex U.

Step 0. [Initialize] **Set** TOUR ← Ø; COST ← 0; V ← U; label U "used" and all other vertices "unused".   (Vertex V is the present position in the network.)

Step 1. [Visit all cities] **For** K ← 1 **to** N − 1 **do** step 2 **od**.

   Step 2. [Choose next edge] Let (V, W) be a least costly edge from V to any unused vertex W;   **set**   TOUR ← TOUR + (V, W); COST ← COST + C(V, W); label W "used"; **and set** V ← W.

Step 3. [Complete tour] **Set** TOUR ← TOUR + (V, 1); COST ← COST + C(V, 1); **and** STOP.

Figure 3.2.1*a* shows the network of Fig. 1.2; Fig. 3.2.1*b* through *f* illustrate the construction of the traveling salesman tour produced by Algorithm GTS *starting at vertex 1*; a used vertex is indicated by a solid square and an unused vertex by a circle.

Algorithm GTS produces a tour of cost 14; in Chap. 1 we found a tour of cost 13.   Algorithm GTS clearly does not always find a minimum-cost tour.

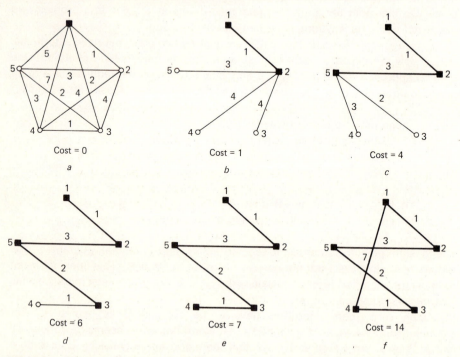

FIG. 3.2.1 Illustration of Algorithm GTS.

Greedy algorithms are usually very fast and intuitively appealing, but, as we have seen, they do not always work. We were lucky here, and we could easily find a counterexample for Algorithm GTS. However, it is not always this simple to show that a greedy algorithm does not work. Clearly, if we have a greedy algorithm that we *think* works all the time, we have an obligation to *prove* that it does.

Algorithm GTS is based on the hill-climbing idea. The goal is to find a minimum-cost tour. The problem is reduced to the set of subgoals of finding at each step the cheapest city to visit next. The algorithm does not plan ahead; the current choice is made without regard to succeeding choices.

An optimum solution to a traveling salesman problem has two basic properties:

1 It consists of a set of edges which together constitute a tour.
2 No other tour costs less than it does.

Algorithm GTS regards property 1 as a "must" or "easy" requirement, and it regards property 2 as a "difficult" one which can be compromised.

The five-city example of Fig. 3.2.1 readily establishes that Algorithm GTS does not guarantee property 2. However, step 2 does make some effort to keep down the cost of tour T.

Algorithm GTS is certainly easy to program, but is it fast? For an arbitrary n-city traveling salesman problem, it takes $O(n^2)$ operations to read in or generate the cost matrix C. A lower bound for the complexity of *any* algorithm which claims to produce a nontrivial candidate solution to this problem is therefore $O(n^2)$. It is not difficult to verify that any reasonable implementation of steps 1 to 3 requires no more than $O(n^2)$ operations. Therefore, Algorithm GTS is as fast as possible.

Algorithm GTS seems to be a candidate for a good heuristic. Of course, the adjective "good" is relative. Since Algorithm ETS (exhaustive traveling salesman) is pitifully inefficient (see Sec. 1.3), "good" might simply refer to the fact that Algorithm GTS is the best we have for reasonably large values of n.

The quality of Algorithm GTS can be improved substantially with a simple modification. The worst feature about the algorithm is that its greed to pick up very cheap edges at the early and middle executions of step 1 can force it to choose very expensive edges in the last few executions. One way to protect ourselves against this is to execute the algorithm for each of $p \le n$ different, randomly chosen, initial cities. Another modification might be to repeat the algorithm for the same initial city but start with the second cheapest edge, and then perhaps go back to using the cheapest edges from succeeding vertices. Other variations are also possible. One would then choose the smallest of the tours. Or better: retain only the cheapest tour found so far, and abort the construction of any partially completed tour whose partial cost exceeds that of the current cheapest tour. Of course, the modified algorithm, which we will call GTS2, may have complexity as high as $O(pn^2)$.

Algorithm GTS2 (*Greedy Traveling Salesman, version 2*)   To generate tours from $1 \le P \le N$ distinct initial cities for N-city traveling salesman problems.   The P tours are generated sequentially, and only the best tour found so far is retained.   The algorithm requires as input values for N, P, a cost matrix C, and P initial cities $\{V_1, V_2, \ldots, V_P\}$.

Step 0. [Initialize] **Set** K ← 0; COST ← ∞; **and** BEST ← ∅.   (Variable K counts the number of initial cities used so far; BEST retains the best tour found so far, which has cost COST.)

Step 1. [Start new tour] **Do through** step 3 **while** K < P **od**; **and** STOP.

Step 2. [Generate new tour] **Set** K ← K + 1; **and** CALL GTS(V_K).   (The statement CALL GTS(V_K) causes Algorithm GTS to generate a tour with city V_K as the initial city.   A tour T(K) with cost C(K) is returned.)

Step 3. [Update best tour] **If** C(K) < COST **then set** BEST ← T(K); **and** COST ← C(K) **fi**.

The implementation of Algorithm GTS2, with Algorithm GTS as a subalgorithm, is straightforward.   Algorithm GTS2 should pass the current value of COST to Algorithm GTS.   If, during the execution of the subroutine, the cost of the partially completed tour is greater than or equal to COST, the value C(K) = ∞ should be returned.

What happens when we apply Algorithm GTS2 to the five-city problem in Fig. 3.2.2?   Use $p = 3$, with the three odd-numbered vertices as initial cities.

Starting with vertex 1, we find the following edges:

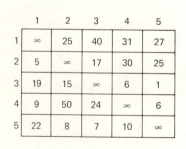

	1	2	3	4	5
1	∞	25	40	31	27
2	5	∞	17	30	25
3	19	15	∞	6	1
4	9	50	24	∞	6
5	22	8	7	10	∞

a

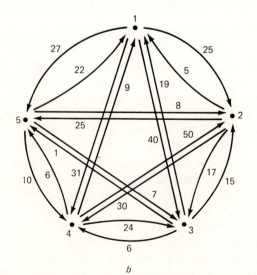

b

FIG. 3.2.2 Illustration of Algorithm GTS2.

(1,2) with cost 25

(2,3) with cost 17 [note that (2,1) gives an unwanted subtour]

(3,5) with cost 1

(5,4) with cost 10 (this edge is forced upon us as the only available edge at this stage)

(4,1) with cost 9

This gives us a tour with a total cost of 62.

Starting with vertex 3, we find the following edges:

(3,5) with cost 1

(5,2) with cost 8, [note that (5,3) gives us an unwanted subtour]

(2,1) with cost 5

(1,4) with cost 31

(4,3) with cost 24

The total cost of this tour is 69.

Finally, starting with vertex 5 we find:

(5,3) with cost 7

(3,4) with cost 6

(4,1) with cost 9

(1,2) with cost 25

(2,5) with cost 25

The total cost here is 72.

This small example illustrates how the repeated application of a heuristic, with certain modifications at each application, can compensate for some of its weaknesses. It is somewhat like sampling for the mean of a random variable. The larger the sample, the more information we have and the better the estimate. However, there is no theoretical result similar to the law of large numbers which guarantees convergence to the correct value.

The remainder of this section will be spent illustrating some extremely simple, but surprisingly effective, heuristics.

Suppose that we have a set of n identical processors denoted by $P_1, \ldots, P_n$. There are m independent jobs $J_1, \ldots, J_m$ which we would like to have processed. The processors can run simultaneously, and any job can be run on any processor. Once a job is loaded on a processor, it stays there until it is finished. Job J_i has a known run time t_i, $i = 1, \ldots, m$. Our objective is to schedule the jobs so that the entire set of jobs is completed as quickly as possible. Let us construct a model before we do anything else.

How does this system of processors and jobs operate? What is a schedule? A schedule will simply be an ordering L of the jobs. The system operates by having the next free processor take the next job on the list. If two or more processors become free at the same time, the processor with the smallest subscript will be assigned the next job on the list. Assume that the time required to set up a job is zero. A processor will run a job until it is complete, and then it will get another job if one is available.

Assume that we have three processors and six jobs with $t_1 = 2$, $t_2 = 5$, $t_3 = 8$, $t_4 = 1$, $t_5 = 5$, and $t_6 = 1$. Consider the schedule $L = (J_2, J_5, J_1, J_4, J_6, J_3)$. At time $T = 0$, P_1 starts executing J_2, P_2 starts J_5, and P_3 starts J_1. Processor P_3 finishes J_1 at $T = 2$ and then starts job J_4, while P_1 and P_2 are still working on the first jobs. At $T = 3$, P_3 is again finished and starts J_6, which it completes at $T = 4$. It then starts the last job J_3. Processors P_1 and P_2 finish their jobs at $T = 5$, but since L is empty they stop. Processor P_3 completes J_3 at $T = 12$. This particular schedule is illustrated in Fig. 3.2.3 in a timing diagram known as a *Gantt chart*. The schedule is clearly not optimum. Processors P_1 and P_2 have a lot of unnecessary idle time. The schedule $L^* = (J_3, J_2, J_5, J_1, J_4, J_6)$ completes all the jobs by $T^* = 8$, and it must be optimum since no schedule can complete all the jobs in less time than it takes to do the longest job.

Let L_0 denote an optimum schedule, and let T_0 be the corresponding shortest possible finishing time. The construction of L_0 is a difficult problem requiring complicated techniques, such as branch and bound (see Sec. 3.4).

Consider the following extremely simple heuristic. Let L^* denote a schedule for the jobs in which the job with the longest run time is listed first, the job with the second longest run time is listed second, . . . , and the job with the shortest run time is listed last. This heuristic generates a schedule L^* which lists the jobs in descending order by run time (ties are broken arbitrarily).

Returning to our specific example, we have $L^* = (J_3, J_2, J_5, J_1, J_4, J_6)$. The

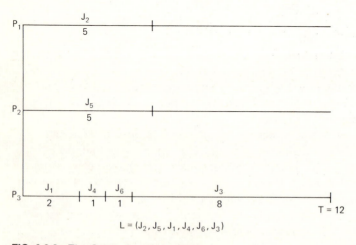

$$L = (J_2, J_5, J_1, J_4, J_6, J_3)$$

FIG. 3.2.3 The Gantt chart for schedule L.

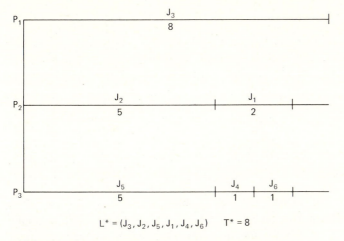

$$L^* = (J_3, J_2, J_5, J_1, J_4, J_6) \quad T^* = 8$$

FIG. 3.2.4 The Gantt chart for an optimum schedule L^*.

schedule L^* completes all the jobs by $T^* = 8$, as shown in Fig. 3.2.4. Thus, the heuristic does generate an optimum schedule in this example.

Of course, it is hoping for too much to think that such a simple heuristic is an exact algorithm. In fact, it is easy to construct a problem in which it does not yield an optimal solution. An example—for two processors and $t_1 = 3$, $t_2 = 3$, $t_3 = 2$, $t_4 = 2$, $t_5 = 2$—is shown in Fig. 3.2.5. Figure 3.2.5a shows the L^* schedule and Fig. 3.2.5b shows an optimum schedule.

Some very useful theory comes with this particular heuristic. As before, let T^* denote the time to complete all jobs on an n-processor problem using our descending-order heuristic schedule. Let T_0 denote the time to complete these jobs using an optimum schedule. One can then prove that

$$\frac{T^*}{T_0} \leq \frac{4}{3} - \frac{1}{3n}$$

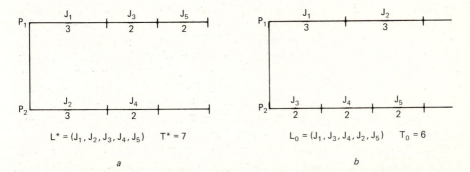

$$L^* = (J_1, J_2, J_3, J_4, J_5) \quad T^* = 7$$

$$L_0 = (J_1, J_3, J_4, J_2, J_5) \quad T_0 = 6$$

a

b

FIG. 3.2.5 A nonoptimum heuristic schedule L^* and an optimum schedule L_0.

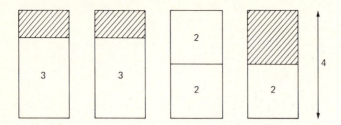

FIG. 3.2.6 The minimum number of boxes of size 4 required to hold objects of sizes 2, 2, 2, 3, and 3.

With this result it is possible to establish an upper bound on the error that we might incur if we use this heuristic rather than go to the effort of obtaining a guaranteed optimal schedule. For $n = 2$, $T^*/T_0 \leq \frac{7}{6}$, and this maximum error is possible, as Fig. 3.2.5 shows. For a large number of processors, the maximum error may be as high as 33 percent.

Tight upper bounds on the worst-case performance of heuristics are not easy to produce. In fact, such bounds are known for very few heuristics.

We shall now consider a different kind of multiprocessor scheduling problem. Instead of asking for the earliest completion time for a set of jobs on a fixed number of processors, we now ask for the minimum number of processors necessary to complete the set of jobs by a fixed time T_0. Of course, the time T_0 will be at least as long as the run time of the longest running job.

This scheduling problem is equivalent to the following packing problem. Let each processor P_j correspond to a box B_j of size T_0. Let each job J_i correspond to an object of size t_i, the run time of job J_i, for $i = 1, \ldots, n$. The scheduling problem then asks for an algorithm which enables us to put all the objects into the fewest number of boxes. Of course, no box can be filled beyond its capacity T_0, and no object can be broken up into smaller objects.

Consider the set of objects shown in Fig. 3.2.5. There are five objects: two of size 3 and three of size 2. What is the minimum number of boxes of size 4 which are needed to hold all the objects? The answer is shown in Fig. 3.2.6, where the shaded portions of the boxes denote empty space.

There are a number of straightforward heuristics available for this problem. They can all be described in a few lines. Let us look at four such algorithms:

H1 (*first fit of a given list*, FF) Let L be some given ordering of the objects. The first object in L is put into B_1. The second object in L is put into B_1 if it will fit. Otherwise, it is placed in the next box B_2. In general, the next object in L is placed in the box B_i of lowest index i in which it will fit. If it does not fit in any of the k partially filled boxes, it is placed in box B_{k+1}. This basic step is repeated until L is depleted.

H2 (*first fit decreasing*, FFD)   This algorithm is the same as FF, except that the list L is ordered from the largest to the smallest object.

H3 (*best fit of a given list*, BF)   Let L be some given ordering of the jobs.   The general step is the same as in FF, except that the next object is placed in that box which results in the smallest unused capacity.   Thus, if the next object has size 3, and we have four partially filled boxes of size 6, and if these boxes have 2, 3, 4, and 5 units of *un*filled capacity left, then we would place the object in the second box, leaving it completely full.

H4 (*best fit decreasing*, BFD)   This algorithm is the same as BF, except that L is ordered from the largest to the smallest object.

Some respectable upper bounds have been discovered for this particular packing problem.   One of the best is the following, which is due to Graham.   Let N_0 be the minimum number of boxes needed, as found by an exact algorithm.   If

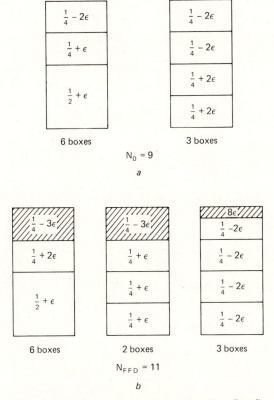

FIG. 3.2.7 An example in which the first-fit-decreasing heuristic does as badly as possible: $N_{FFD}/N_0 = \frac{11}{9}$.

N_{FFD} denotes the approximate solution as found by the FFD algorithm, then, for any $\epsilon > 0$ and N_0 sufficiently large,

$$\frac{N_{FFD}}{N_0} < \frac{11}{9} + \epsilon$$

That is, the FFD algorithm will produce a result that cannot be more than about 23 percent too high. This much is guaranteed; for any particular problem the error may be much less.

It is not easy to construct an example in which the FFD heuristic does as badly as possible. Try to experiment a little before reading further. We will present one such "bad case." Let $\epsilon > 0$ be an arbitrarily chosen, but small, positive real number. Assume that all of the boxes are of size 1 and that we have the task of packing the following list of items:

  6 items of size $\frac{1}{2} + \epsilon$

  6 items of size $\frac{1}{4} + \epsilon$

  12 items of size $\frac{1}{4} - 2\epsilon$

  6 items of size $\frac{1}{4} + 2\epsilon$

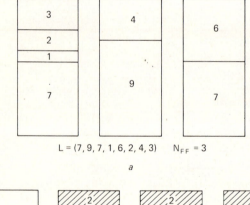

$$L = (7, 9, 7, 1, 6, 2, 4, 3) \qquad N_{FF} = 3$$

a

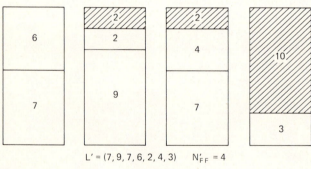

$$L' = (7, 9, 7, 6, 2, 4, 3) \qquad N'_{FF} = 4$$

b

FIG. 3.2.8 An anomaly using the first-fit heuristic; the packing is worse when an object is deleted.

An optimum packing using $N_0 = 9$ boxes is shown in Fig. 3.2.7a. This packing is clearly optimum since all 9 boxes are completely full. If the FFD heuristic H2 is used on this problem, we obtain the packing shown in Fig. 3.2.7b, using $N_{FFD} = 11$ boxes.

Packing problems can be surprisingly deceptive. For example, if items of sizes $L = (760, 395, 395, 379, 379, 241, 200, 105, 105, 40)$ are put into boxes of size 1000, then the H2 heuristic will do this in $N_{FFD} = 3$ boxes. This is, in fact, an optimum solution (check it). Let us *decrease* all the sizes by one unit, resulting in the list $L' = (759, 394, 394, 378, 378, 240, 199, 104, 104, 39)$. Now the FFD heuristic gives us $N'_{FFD} = 4$. This is clearly not optimal and is totally unexpected. Why does this example not violate the $\frac{11}{9}$ result?

Let us look at another anomaly. Using heuristic H1, let us pack $L = (7, 9, 7, 1, 6, 2, 4, 3)$ into boxes of size 13. We find that $N_{FF} = 3$, as shown in Fig. 3.2.8a; this result is clearly optimum. *Delete* the item of size 1, yielding the list $L' = (7, 9, 7, 6, 2, 4, 3)$. Now $N'_{FF} = 4$, as shown in Fig. 3.2.8b.

Other examples of anomalies for scheduling heuristics are given in Graham (1972).

Exercises 3.2

L3.2.1 *Algorithm* GTS2 (*implementation*). Write a program for Algorithm GTS2. Perform an experimental expected performance analysis.

3.2.2 *Algorithm* GTS2. Algorithm GTS2 uses a number of cities as the "initial" city. What if the salesman has a single initial city, say, where he lives. Does that mean that he might not be able to use the tour produced by the algorithm?

*****3.2.3** *Traveling salesman problem heuristic* (*design*). Assume that we have found a tour (which is not necessarily optimal) in a symmetric traveling salesman problem. Arbitrarily choose two nonadjacent edges in this tour, say, edges (i, j) and (k, l). Assuming that these four cities are encountered in the order i, j, k, l (with other cities between j and k), we can transform the current tour into a new one by deleting edges (i, j) and (k, l) and replacing them with edges (i, k) and (j, l). Note that some edges may have to be traversed in the opposite direction in the new tour.

Use this transformation to design a heuristic for the traveling salesman problem.

*****L3.2.4** *Comparison of heuristics* (*testing*). Comparatively test Algorithm GTS2 against your algorithm from Exercise 3.2.3. Run the same test problems on both algorithms. Compare the cost of the tours found and the means and variances of the run times.

*****3.2.5** *Knapsack problem heuristic* (*design, analysis*). We have a knapsack of volume V and an unlimited stockpile of each of N different items. For

$i = 1, \ldots, N$, one unit of item i has a known volume v_i and a known value m_i. Integer numbers of the various items may be put into the knapsack. The objective is to pack as much value as possible, subject to the constraint that the total volume of the packed items is not greater than V. Considerations of shape do not enter into the problem.

Design and analyze a greedy heuristic algorithm for the knapsack problem.

**3.2.6 *Set covering problem* (*design, analysis*). S is a set of elements. $\mathcal{F} = \{F_i\}$, for any $i = 1, \ldots, n$, is a set of n sets, each of which contains elements in S. Our problem is to find the smallest number of sets in $\mathcal{F}$ such that the union of these sets contains all the elements in S. This is known as the minimum-cardinality set covering problem.

Design a heuristic algorithm which produces a candidate solution to this problem. Analyze the effort required to execute this heuristic.

*3.2.7 *Knight's tour* (*model, design*). Reconsider the knight's tour heuristic of Sec. 2.1. Design another heuristic algorithm for finding a knight's tour.

3.3 BACKTRACK PROGRAMMING

The algorithm design technique known as *backtrack programming* can be described as an organized exhaustive search which often avoids searching all possibilities. This technique is generally suitable for solving problems where a potentially large, but finite, number of solutions have to be inspected.

The Bicycle Lock Problem

As an example, consider a combination lock for a bicycle that consists of a set of N switches, each of which can be "on" or "off." Exactly one setting of all the switches, with $\lfloor N/2 \rfloor$ or more in the on position, will open the lock. Suppose we have forgotten this combination and must get the lock open. Suppose also that we are willing to try (if necessary) all combinations. We need an algorithm for systematically generating these combinations.

If we ignore the $\lfloor N/2 \rfloor$ condition, there are 2^N possible combinations for the lock. (Show this.) There may be a reasonable chance of finding the right combination if $N \le 10$. However, the $\lfloor N/2 \rfloor$ condition will enable us to ignore (or better, never generate) many combinations.

We model each possible combination with an N-tuple of 0s and 1s. The ith digit is 1 if switch i is on and 0 if switch i is off. The set of all possible N-tuples is conveniently modeled using a binary tree (see Sec. 2.2). Each vertex on the kth level of this tree will correspond to a distinct setting of the first k digits of the N-tuple. The two branches downward from a vertex at this level correspond to the

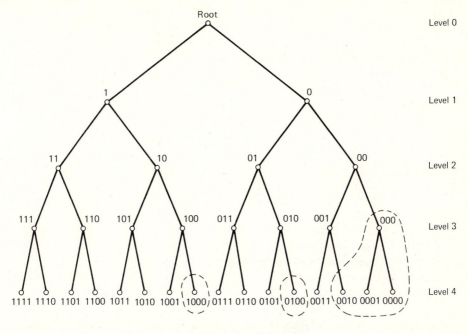

FIG. 3.3.1 A binary tree representing N-tuples of 0s and 1s.

two possible settings for the $(k + 1)$st digit in the N-tuple. The tree will have N levels. Figure 3.3.1, for $N = 4$, should make the general construction clear.

The condition that the number of on switches must be at least $\lfloor N/2 \rfloor$ enables us to avoid generating parts of the tree which cannot possibly provide a correct combination. For example, suppose we find ourselves at the vertex marked 00 in Fig. 3.3.1. Since the right branch (to 000) could not lead to an acceptable combination, there is no need to generate it. If any of the successors of a particular vertex do not satisfy a restriction on the problem, then these successors need not be considered. In this particular problem, none of the vertices within the dotted circles need to be investigated or even generated.

Using this binary tree as a model, we can now state a backtrack procedure for generating only those combinations with at least $\lfloor N/2 \rfloor$ switches on. This algorithm amounts to a traversal of the tree. Move down the tree as far as possible to the left until we can move no further. Upon reaching an end-vertex, try the corresponding combination. If it fails, backtrack up one level and see if we can move down again along an unused branch. If it is possible, take the leftmost unused branch. If not, backtrack up one more level and try to move down from this vertex. Before moving down, check to see if it is possible to satisfy the $\lfloor N/2 \rfloor$ restriction at any successor vertex. In Fig. 3.3.1, this algorithm will visit the following sequence of vertices:

1	
11	
111	
1111	Check this combination
111	Backtrack since 1111 is an end-vertex
1110	Take the only unused branch down; check this combination
111	Backtrack again
11	Backtrack further since 111 has no unused branches
110	Take the only unused branch
1101	Check combination
110	Backtrack from 1101
1100	Check combination
110	Backtrack from 1100
11	Backtrack since no unused branches
1	Backtrack since no unused branches
10	Take only unused branch
101	Take leftmost unused branch
1011	Check combination
101	Backtrack
1010	Check combination
101	Backtrack
10	Backtrack
100	Take only unused branch
1001	Check combination
100	Backtrack
10	Backtrack; note that we do not move down to 1000 since this left successor violates the constraints that we have at least two 1s
1	Backtrack
root	Backtrack
0	Take only unused branch

.
.
.

etc.

The algorithm stops when we return to the root and there are no unused branches remaining.

This simple example illustrates the basic features that are common to every backtrack algorithm. If a problem can be formulated so that all candidate solutions can be generated by building up the elements of N-tuples, then it can be solved by a backtrack procedure.

The 8-Puzzle Problem

Figure 3.3.2 illustrates what is known as an *8-puzzle*. There are eight movable squares and one empty space (denoted X) in the 3×3 box. Any numbered square

2	X	3
1	8	4
7	6	5

a

2	3	X
1	8	4
7	6	5

b

1	2	3
8	X	4
7	6	5

c

1	2	3
4	5	6
7	8	X

d

FIG. 3.3.2 The 8-puzzle.

adjacent to the empty space can be moved into it, which effectively moves the space into the position vacated by the numbered square. For example, in Fig. 3.3.2a square 3 can be moved into the position denoted by X, creating an empty space in the position vacated by 3, as shown in Fig. 3.3.2b. Let us try to find a sequence of moves which will transform the configuration shown in Fig. 3.3.2a into the one shown in Fig. 3.3.2c.

It is not obvious that backtrack programming is suitable for the 8-puzzle. A somewhat artificial, but nevertheless effective, N-tuple structure will have to be set up. Each vertex of the backtrack tree will correspond to a configuration of the 8-puzzle. The root (at level 0) will correspond to the initial configuration (Fig. 3.3.2a) and will have branches leading to vertices at level 1, each of which will correspond to a configuration which is attainable in one move from the root configuration. The vertices immediately below any vertex in the tree will be ordered from left to right by the direction in which the space moves. The leftmost configuration will correspond to a leftward movement of the empty space; the remaining configurations will correspond to the upward, downward, and rightward movements of the empty space, respectively. The first two levels of our tree are shown in Fig. 3.3.3. Note that no upward movement of the empty space from the root configuration is possible.

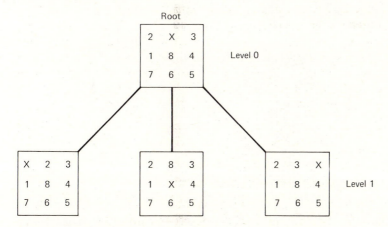

FIG. 3.3.3 Construction of the backtrack tree for the 8-puzzle.

The vertices on level k correspond to all the configurations that can be reached in k moves from the root configuration. Without losing any potential path to the desired configuration, we shall not permit any vertex to have a successor configuration which is the same as its predecessor. For example, consider the rightmost vertex at level 1 in Fig. 3.3.3. This vertex could have two successors, corresponding to the leftward and downward movements of the empty space. But the leftward movement would reproduce the root configuration and would not get us closer to the final configuration.

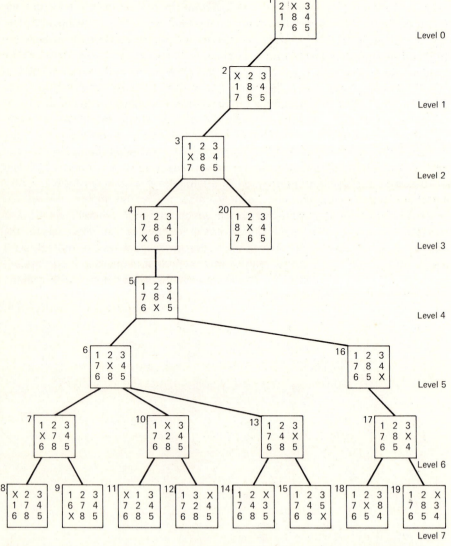

FIG. 3.3.4 The backtrack tree constructed in attempting to reach the configuration at vertex 20.

Thus the elements in these N-tuples, which correspond to configurations, must satisfy the conditions that the $(k + 1)$st element must be obtainable from the kth in exactly one move, and the $(k + 1)$st element cannot be the same as the $(k - 1)$st. What about the value of N? The tree depth N denotes the maximum number of moves that we are willing to consider along a path from the initial to the final configuration. Since we have no idea how many moves this might take, N will have to be chosen on the basis of how much patience or computer time we have available. For example, if $N = 7$, then the backtrack procedure will tell us whether the final configuration can be obtained in seven or fewer moves from the initial configuration.

We are now in a position to use a backtrack procedure for the 8-puzzle problem. As in the bicycle lock problem, we shall always try to move down and to the left in the search tree. Figure 3.3.4 illustrates the backtrack tree. The order in which vertices are generated as we backtrack is shown by the numbers next to the configurations. The final configuration at vertex 20 is reachable in three moves from the initial configuration. As an exercise, continue the backtrack procedure in an effort to obtain the configuration of Fig. 3.3.2d.

Backtrack algorithms are potentially exponential in worst-case behavior because they may amount to an exhaustive search through an exponentially large solution space. The bicycle lock problem earlier in this section may have 2^N vertices at level N since the search is binary. A backtrack procedure which eliminates 99 percent of the candidate solutions is still exponential since $2^N/100$ still grows exponentially as $N \to \infty$.

Backtrack programming has often been called a "method of last resort." Arguments can be made that it is only one level of efficiency above uninspired exhaustive search methods. One should certainly try to use a more efficient technique, but this is easier said than done. Backtrack programming is an important tool which every computer programmer should know how to use.

Exercises 3.3

3.3.1 *8-puzzle example.* Continue the backtrack procedure demonstrated in the 8-puzzle problem in an effort to obtain the configuration of Fig. 3.3.2d. Do not go deeper than seven levels in the search tree.

L3.3.2 *8-puzzle example* (*implementation*). Give a complete, formal specification of the backtrack algorithm in the 8-puzzle problem. Implement the algorithm as a computer program and use it for Exercise 3.3.1.

*3.3.3 *8-queens problem* (*design*). Show that a maximum of eight queens can be placed on a standard 8×8 chessboard in such a manner that no queen can be taken by any other. Design a backtrack algorithm that will explicitly construct such a configuration.

L3.3.4 *8-queens problem* (*implementation*). Implement the algorithm of Exercise 3.3.3.

**3.3.5 *Backtrack algorithms* (*general formulation*). Try to give a detailed, general, set-theoretic formulation of the basic structure common to all backtrack algorithms.

***3.3.6 *Backtrack algorithms* (*analysis*). It is usually close to impossible to give a very refined expected performance analysis of a backtrack algorithm. How might one go about making coarse average run-time estimates for backtrack algorithms? Assess the strengths and weaknesses of these estimation procedures. Try them out on an actual backtrack program (see Exercises 3.3.2 and 3.3.4).

3.4 BRANCH AND BOUND

The design technique known as *branch and bound* is similar to backtracking in that it searches a tree model of the solution space and is applicable to a wide variety of discrete combinatorial problems. Backtracking algorithms try to find one or all configurations, modeled as N-tuples, which satisfy certain properties. Branch-and-bound algorithms are oriented more toward optimization. The problem being solved specifies a real-valued cost function for each of the vertices that appear in the search tree. The goal is to find a configuration for which the cost function is maximized or minimized.

The traveling salesman problem discussed in Sec. 1.3 is a good candidate for a branch-and-bound algorithm. This section will be developed around the salesman example. It is only fair to warn you that branch-and-bound algorithms tend to be quite complicated, and the one to be presented here is no exception. A large and varied assortment of serious real-world problems have been solved by branch-and-bound algorithms (see Chap. 7); these algorithms are rarely simple.

Recall that the salesman's problem is to find a least-cost tour of the N cities in his sales region. The tour is to visit each city exactly once. In network terminology, we want a least-cost spanning cycle of the network of cities. To help find an optimum tour, the salesman has a cost matrix C, where element c_{ij} equals the cost (usually in terms of time, money, or distance) of direct travel between city i and city j. The problem is called *symmetric* if $c_{ij} = c_{ji}$ for all i and j—that is, if the cost of traveling between every pair of cities is the same regardless of direction. Assume $c_{ii} = \infty$ for all i.

Branch-and-bound algorithms for the traveling salesman problem can be formulated in a variety of ways. The algorithm which we develop is due to Little, Murty, Sweeny, and Karel. It is something of a classic.

Let us first consider *branching*. Figure 3.4.1*a* shows the cost matrix for the five-city, asymmetric (nonsymmetric) traveling salesman problem in Fig. 3.4.1*b*. Note that we use a directed network to model the costs since the cost of going from city i directly to city j is not necessarily the same as the cost of going

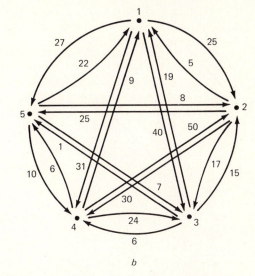

	1	2	3	4	5
1	∞	25	40	31	27
2	5	∞	17	30	25
3	19	15	∞	6	1
4	9	50	24	∞	6
5	22	8	7	10	∞

a

b

FIG. 3.4.1 A traveling salesman problem: (*a*) cost matrix; (*b*) five-city network.

from city *j* directly to city *i*. The root of our search tree will correspond to the set of "all possible tours"; that is, this vertex represents the set of all 4! possible tours in our five-city problem. In general, for any asymmetric N-city problem, the root will represent the entire set R of $(N-1)!$ possible tours. The branches from the root are determined by the selection of a single edge, say (i, j). The objective is to split the set of all tours into two sets: one which is very likely to contain an optimum tour and one which is not. To do this we choose an edge (i, j), which we hope will be in an optimum tour, and partition R into two sets $\{i, j\}$ and $\{\overline{i, j}\}$. The set $\{i, j\}$ denotes those tours in R which contain edge (i, j), and $\{\overline{i, j}\}$ denotes those that do not.

   In the example, suppose we branch on edge $(i, j) \doteq (3, 5)$, the least costly edge in the entire matrix. The root and first level of our solution space tree would then be as shown in Fig. 3.4.2. Note that every tour in R is contained in exactly one of the sets on level 1. If we could somehow conclude that set $\{\overline{3, 5}\}$ does *not* contain an optimum tour, we would only have to search the set $\{3, 5\}$. We then partition the set $\{3, 5\}$ in the same way that we partitioned R. The next cheapest edge in the matrix is $(2, 1)$ with cost $c_{21} = 5$. We might therefore partition set $\{3, 5\}$ into tours which include edge $(2, 1)$ and those which do not. This is shown on level 2 of Fig. 3.4.2. *The path to any tree vertex from the root specifies certain edges which must or must not be included in the sets represented by the tree vertex.* For example, the left vertex on level 2 of Fig. 3.4.2 represents the set of all tours that contain edge $(3, 5)$ and do not contain edge $(2, 1)$. In general, if X denotes a vertex in the tree and (i, j) is the branching edge, the immediate descendants of X will be denoted by Y and $\bar{Y}$. The set Y will denote the subset of tours in X *with* edge (i, j), and the set $\bar{Y}$ will denote the subset of X *without* (i, j).

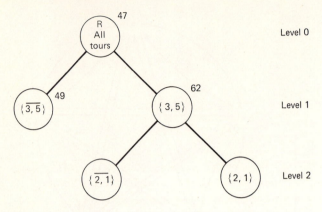

FIG. 3.4.2 The construction of a branch-and-bound search tree.

This discussion should give you some idea of what is meant by branching. Before going into an explicit description of our traveling salesman algorithm, we shall describe what is meant by *bounding*.

With each vertex in the tree we associate a lower bound on the cost of any tour in the set represented by the vertex. The computation of these lower bounds is the major labor-saving device in any branch-and-bound algorithm. Therefore, much thought should be given to obtaining tight bounds. The reason for this is as follows. Assume that we have constructed a specific complete tour with cost m. If the lower bound associated with the set of tours represented by vertex v_k equals $M \geq m$, we need never consider vertex v_k or any of its descendants in the remainder of our search for an optimum tour (why?).

The basic step in the computation of lower bounds is known as *reduction*. It is based on the following two observations:

1 In terms of the cost matrix C, every full tour contains exactly one element (an edge and its associated cost) from each row and each column. Note that the converse statement is not necessarily true. A set of elements chosen such that there is exactly one element in each column and row of C does not necessarily represent a tour. For example, in the problem of Fig. 3.4.1, the set $\{(1, 5), (5, 1), (2, 3), (3, 4), (4, 2)\}$ satisfies this condition but does not form a tour.

2 If a *constant h* is subtracted from every entry in any row or column of the cost matrix C, the cost of any tour under the new matrix C' is exactly h less than the cost of the same tour under C. Since any tour must contain an edge from this row or column, we have reduced the cost of all tours by h. This subtraction is called a *row (or column) reduction*.

Let t be an optimum tour under the cost matrix C. Then the cost of tour t is

$$z(t) = \sum_{(i,j) \in t} c_{ij}$$

If C′ is a row-reduced (or column-reduced) version of C, then t must still be an optimum tour under C′ and

$$z(t) = h + z'(t)$$

where $z'(t)$ is the cost of tour t under C′.

By a *reduction of the entire cost matrix* C we mean the following. Sequentially go down the rows of C and subtract the value of each row's smallest element h_i from every element in the row. Then do the same for each column. If $h_i = 0$ for any row or column, just go on to the next row or column since this one is already reduced. Let

$$h = \sum_{\substack{\text{all rows} \\ \text{and columns}}} h_i$$

The resulting cost matrix will be called the *reduction of* C. Figure 3.4.3 shows the reduction of the cost matrix in Fig. 3.4.1a. The values of h_i are at the end of each row and column (the rows and columns are numbered consecutively).

The total reduction is by $h = 47$ units. Therefore, a lower bound on the cost of any tour in R is also 47; that is,

$$z(t) = h + z'(t) \geq h = 47$$

since $z'(t) \geq 0$ for any tour t under the reduced matrix C′. This bound is shown next to the root of the tree in Fig. 3.4.2.

	1	2	3	4	5	
1	∞	0	15	3	2	$h_1 = 25$
2	0	∞	12	22	20	$h_2 = 5$
3	18	14	∞	2	0	$h_3 = 1$
4	3	44	18	∞	0	$h_4 = 6$
5	15	1	0	0	∞	$h_5 = 7$

$h_6 = 0 \quad h_7 = 0 \quad h_8 = 0 \quad h_9 = 3 \quad h_{10} = 0$

$h = 25 + 5 + 1 + 6 + 7 + 3 = 47$

FIG. 3.4.3 The reduction of the cost matrix in Fig. 3.4.1a.

Consider lower bounds for the vertices at level 1, that is, for the sets $\{3, 5\}$ and $\{\overline{3, 5}\}$. We shall work with the reduced matrix in Fig. 3.4.3 while keeping in mind that a cost of 47 must be added to the cost of any optimum tour t under C′ in order to obtain the true cost of t under C.

The edge $(3, 5)$ is, by definition, in every tour in set $\{3, 5\}$. This fact prohibits our choice of edge $(5, 3)$ since edges $(3, 5)$ and $(5, 3)$ form a cycle, and this is not permitted in any tour. Edge $(5, 3)$ is avoided by setting $c_{53} = \infty$. Row 3 and column 5 can also be deleted from further consideration with respect to set $\{3, 5\}$. This is because we already have an edge from 3 to 5. The part of the reduced cost matrix in Fig. 3.4.3 which will be of any use in further searching of the tour set $\{3, 5\}$ is shown in Fig. 3.4.4a. It can then be reduced to the cost matrix shown in Fig. 3.4.4b, with $h = 15$. A lower bound for any tour in the set $\{3, 5\}$ is now $47 + 15 = 62$, which is placed next to this vertex in Fig. 3.4.2.

A lower bound for the set $\{\overline{3, 5}\}$ is obtained in a somewhat different fashion. Edge $(3, 5)$ cannot be in this set, so set $c_{35} = \infty$ in the matrix of Fig. 3.4.3. Any tour in $\{\overline{3, 5}\}$ will use *some edge from city 3* and *some edge into city 5*. The cheapest edge from city 3, excluding the old value of $(3, 5)$, has cost 2; the cheapest edge to city 5 has value 0. Therefore, a lower bound on any tour in set $\{\overline{3, 5}\}$ is given by $47 + 2 + 0 = 49$, and this is shown next to the $\{\overline{3, 5}\}$ vertex in Fig. 3.4.2.

At this stage we have managed to *reduce the size* of the cost matrix to be considered at vertex $\{3, 5\}$. Also, if we can find an explicit tour in the set $\{\overline{3, 5}\}$ with cost less than or equal to 62, *then there is no reason for further branching and bounding on vertex $\{3, 5\}$*. In this case we say vertex $\{3, 5\}$ is *fathomed* in the tree. The next objective might then be a branching on vertex $\{\overline{3, 5}\}$ in the hope of finding an explicit tour with cost c in the range $49 \le c \le 62$.

A rough flowchart for this branch-and-bound algorithm is shown in Fig. 3.4.5. We shall fill in a number of important details shortly. Some of the notation used is as follows. The letter X will denote the current vertex in the search tree, and $w(X)$ will be the corresponding lower bound. The successors to X will be called Y and $\bar{Y}$, which are chosen by branching on some edge (k, l). The symbol

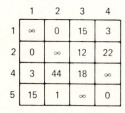

	1	2	3	4
1	∞	0	15	3
2	0	∞	12	22
4	3	44	18	∞
5	15	1	∞	0

a

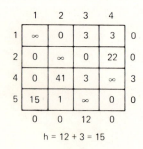

	1	2	3	4	
1	∞	0	3	3	0
2	0	∞	0	22	0
4	0	41	3	∞	3
5	15	1	∞	0	0
	0	0	12	0	

$h = 12 + 3 = 15$

b

FIG. 3.4.4 (*a*) The reduced cost matrix upon deleting row 3 and column 5 and setting $c_{53=\infty}$; (*b*) the reduction of the cost matrix in (*a*).

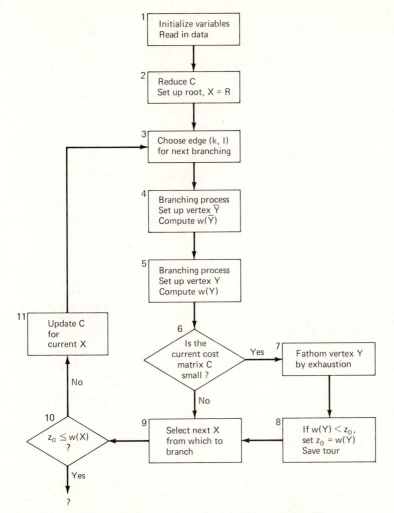

FIG. 3.4.5 A rough flowchart for a branch-and-bound algorithm.

z_0 is the value of the cheapest currently known tour. Initially $z_0 = \infty$. Spend some time studying this flowchart.

Now let us develop the content of some of the boxes in our flowchart in more detail.

Box 1 The initialization is straightforward, and the details are left as an exercise.

Box 2 The first reduction is a straightforward implementation of the procedure described earlier, and it is left as an exercise.

Box 3 The choice of the next branching edge (k, l) determines sets Y and $\bar{Y}$, the descendants of the current X. Edge (k, l) shall be chosen so as to try to get a large lower bound on the set $\bar{Y} = \overline{\{k, l\}}$. This makes it easier to fathom $\bar{Y}$. It is usually preferable to fathom $\bar{Y}$ since its cardinality and associated cost matrix are generally larger than those of Y (row k and column l are deleted from the matrix for Y). Hopefully, Y will also be more likely to contain an optimum tour.

How do we translate these ideas into a specific choice of branching edge (k, l)? In the reduced cost matrix C' associated with X, each row and column has at least one zero entry (if not, then C' is not fully reduced). One would think that the edges corresponding to these zero costs would be more likely to be in an optimum tour than edges with high costs. Therefore, we shall choose one of these. But which one? Let edge (i, j) have $c_{ij} = 0$ in C'. We want to give $\bar{Y} = \overline{\{i, j\}}$ as large a lower bound as possible. By recalling the method for computing the lower bound for $\overline{\{3, 5\}}$ in our example, we see that the lower bound for $\bar{Y}$ is given by

$$w(\bar{Y}) = w(X) + (\text{smallest cost in row } i, \text{ omitting } c_{ij}) + (\text{smallest cost in column } j, \text{ omitting } c_{ij})$$

Consequently, of all the edges (i, j) with $c_{ij} = 0$ in the current C' matrix, we choose the one which gives the largest value of $w(\bar{Y})$. Let this edge be (k, l).

Therefore, a more complete description of the decision represented by box 3 is as follows:

Step 1. Let S be the set of edges (i, j) such that $C_{ij} = 0$ in the current cost matrix C.

Step 2. Let D_{ij} equal the smallest cost in row i, omitting c_{ij}, plus the smallest cost in column j, omitting c_{ij}. Compute D_{ij} for every $(i, j) \in S$.

Step 3. Choose the next branching edge (k, l) from

$$D^*_{kl} = \max_{(i, j) \in S} D_{ij}$$

Consider again the five-city problem in Fig. 3.4.1. From the reduced matrix C, we see that the first value of X, the root R, has $w(X) = 47$. Using the subalgorithm above, we find our first branching edge as follows:

Step 1. $S = \{(1, 2), (2, 1), (3, 5), (4, 5), (5, 3), (5, 4)\}$

Step 2. $D_{12} = 2 + 1 = 3$

$\quad\quad D_{21} = 12 + 3 = 15$

$\quad\quad D_{35} = 2 + 0 = 2$

$\quad\quad D_{45} = 3 + 0 = 3$

$\quad\quad D_{53} = 0 + 12 = 12$

$\quad\quad D_{54} = 0 + 2 = 2$

Step 3. Choose edge $(k, l) = (2, 1)$ since D_{21} is the maximum of the set of $\{D_{ij}\}$.

Box 4 Set up the $\bar{Y}$ successor to X exactly as we did in our earlier discussion.

In our current development $X = R$ and $\bar{Y} = \{\overline{2, 1}\}$, that is, the set of all tours *not* containing edge (2, 1). Compute the lower bound $w(\bar{Y})$ as described in the discussion of box 3; that is,

$$w(\bar{Y}) = w(X) + D^*_{kl}$$

and

$$w(\{\overline{2, 1}\}) = 47 + 15 = 62$$

Box 5 The Y successor to X is the subset of tours of X that *contain* the edge (k, l), which was chosen in box 3. In our current example, $Y = \{2, 1\}$. The computation of $w(Y)$ requires some care. An explicit subalgorithm follows:

Step 1. Delete row k and column l from C.
Step 2. The tours in the set represented by the vertex Y all contain zero or more previously chosen edges in addition to edge (k, l). Edge (k, l) will either be isolated from these other edges or will be part of a path formed with some or all of these edges. Let p and q denote the starting and ending cities in this path. It is possible that $p = k$ and/or $q = l$. Set $c_{qp} = \infty$. This measure prevents us from choosing edge (q, p) as a successor to Y, thereby forming a closed cycle of required edges of length $<N$. This, of course, is not permitted in the construction of a tour. Is there any occasion when we do not set $c_{qp} = \infty$?
Step 3. Reduce the current C. Let h equal the sum of the reducing constants.
Step 4. Compute $w(Y)$ from $w(Y) = w(X) + h$.

Returning to the example, delete row 2 and column 1 from the C matrix in Fig. 3.4.3. Since edge (2, 1) is the only chosen edge, set $p = 2$, $q = 1$, and $c_{12} = \infty$. After these steps, which correspond to steps 1 and 2 in the preceding subalgorithm, the current matrix is given in Fig. 3.4.6a. After reduction, we obtain the

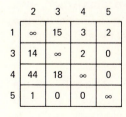

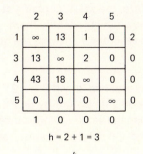

$h = 2 + 1 = 3$

a b

FIG. 3.4.6 (a) The reduced cost matrix upon deleting row 2 and column 1 and setting $c_{12=\infty}$; (b) the reduction of the cost matrix in (a).

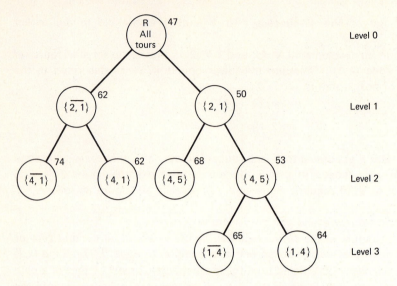

FIG. 3.4.7 The search tree constructed for the sample problem of Fig. 3.4.1.

matrix shown in Fig. 3.4.6b, with $h = 3$ and

$$w[(2, 1)] = w(X) + h$$
$$= 47 + 3 = 50$$

Our current status is shown on levels 0 and 1 in Fig. 3.4.7.

Box 6   We ultimately have to get down to sets that contain so few tours that we can inspect each of them and fathom this vertex without branching any further.   Box 6 checks for this.   Every edge which we insist be in every tour of Y reduces the size of C by one row and one column.   If we originally have an N-city problem and the current C matrix is 2×2, then $N - 2$ of the edges of every tour in Y have been chosen.   Therefore, the set Y contains at most two tours (why?).   We leave it as an exercise to show how to identify them.   Thus, box 6 checks if C is a 2×2 matrix.   Note that this essentially answers the question at the end of step 2 in the discussion of box 5.

Boxes 7 and 8   Box 7 is reached only if C is a 2×2 matrix.   This box finds the cheapest tour in Y and denotes its weight by $w(Y)$.   Box 8 checks to see if the value of this tour is better than the value z_0 of the currently known best tour.   If it is not, the new tour is discarded.   If it is, the new tour becomes our current best tour and we set $z_0 = w(Y)$.

Box 9   We now need to select the next X from which to branch.   This choice is fairly obvious.   Choose that vertex *which currently has no successor* and *which* *has the smallest lower bound.* Therefore, this box consists of the following subalgorithm:

Step 1. Find the set S of end-vertices of the current search tree.
Step 2. Let X be chosen such that

$$w(X) = \min_{v \in S} w(v)$$

In our current example:

Step 1. $S = \{\{\overline{2,1}\}, \{2,1\}\}$
Step 2. $w(\{\overline{2,1}\}) = 62$
$\quad\quad w(\{2,1\}) = 50$

Therefore $X = \{2,1\}$.

Box 10   Our discussion helps us decide what to do with that annoying question mark at box 10.   You should have noticed that the algorithm shown in the flowchart of Fig. 3.4.5 has no way of terminating.   Box 10 lets us know if we should stop.   If the current value of our best tour z_0 is less than or equal to $w(X)$—the value of the lowest unexplored lower bound—then there is no way that any successor of X can give rise to a better tour.   From the way X was chosen in box 9, none of the other unfathomed end-vertices can produce a better tour either.   The whole search tree is now fathomed and we stop.

   If $w(X) < z_0$, the search must continue.   Currently, our example has $z_0 = \infty$; therefore, we do not terminate.

Box 11   This portion of the algorithm obtains the correct cost matrix C for the current X.   The updating procedure is as follows:

Step 1. Is the current X equal to the Y set most recently generated by box 5?   If so, then our current C is what we need and we return to box 3.   This is usually the case on level 2 of the tree.
Step 2. Set C $\leftarrow$ original cost matrix.
Step 3. Set $S \leftarrow$ {set of all (i,j) pairs that must be edges in X}.
Step 4. Compute $g = \Sigma_{(i,j) \in S} c_{ij}$
Step 5. For each $(i,j) \in S$, delete row i and column j in C.   For each path among the (i,j), find the starting and ending cities p and q and set $c_{qp} = \infty$.   For each edge (k,l) prohibited from the tours of X, set $c_{kl} = \infty$.
Step 6. Reduce C.   Let h equal the sum of the reducing constants.
Step 7. Compute $w(X) = g + h$.

Step 5 is a nuisance because it amounts to a repetition of something we did earlier.   There is an obvious alternative that would require a great deal of storage—that is, retain the C's for each end-vertex in the tree.   This is usually impractical. In the current example, we simply exit from the subalgorithm at step 1.

Let us continue the example. We are now at box 3, $X = \{2, 1\}$, $w(X) = 50$, and the tree contains only levels 0 and 1 in Fig. 3.4.7. We need an edge (k, l) to determine the successors of X. The appropriate C is shown in Fig. 3.4.6b. Using the subalgorithm described with box 3:

> *Step 1.* $S = \{(1, 5), (3, 5), (4, 5), (5, 2), (5, 3), (5, 4)\}$
> *Step 2.* $D_{15} = 1 + 0 = 1$
> $\quad\quad D_{35} = 2 + 0 = 2$
> $\quad\quad D_{45} = 18 + 0 = 18$
> $\quad\quad D_{52} = 13 + 0 = 13$
> $\quad\quad D_{53} = 13 + 0 = 13$
> $\quad\quad D_{54} = 0 + 1 = 1$
> *Step 3.* $D_{kl}^* = D_{45} = 18$ (in case of a tie, break it arbitrarily). Thus $(k, l) = (4, 5)$.

Now set up $\bar{Y}$ using box 4:

$$\bar{Y} = \overline{\{4, 5\}}$$

and

$$w(\overline{\{4, 5\}}) = w(\{2, 1\}) + D_{45}^*$$

$$= 50 + 18 = 68$$

Next comes vertex $Y = \{4, 5\}$. First delete row 4 and column 5 from C. Since edge $(4, 5)$ does not meet edge $(2, 1)$, $p = 4$ and $q = 5$. Set $c_{54} = \infty$, and reduce C. We find $h = 3$ and $w(Y) = 50 + h = 53$. The reduced C is shown as Fig. 3.4.8a. Notice that the lower bounds are nondecreasing as we go deeper into the tree.

We are now at box 6 in the flowchart. Is the current C a 2×2 matrix? Since C is 3×3, continue to box 9. The subalgorithm for box 9 is executed as follows.

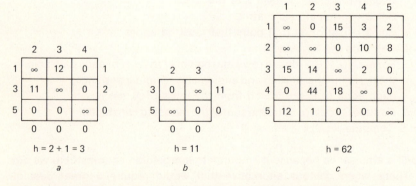

FIG. 3.4.8 Additional reduced cost matrices for the sample problem.

Step 1. $S = \{\{\overline{2, 1}\}, \{\overline{4, 5}\}, \{4, 5\}\}$

Step 2. $w(\{\overline{2, 1}\}) = 62$

$\quad\quad w(\{\overline{4, 5}\}) = 68$

$\quad\quad w(\{4, 5\}) = 53$

Therefore $X = \{4, 5\}$.

At box 10 $z_0 = \infty$, and therefore we continue. At box 11 we are fortunate and exit at step 1. We are at box 3 again with $X = \{4, 5\}$, $w(X) = 53$ and C is given in Fig. 3.4.8a.

One more time might do it! The subalgorithm of box 3 gives:

Step 1. $S = \{(1, 4), (3, 4), (5, 2), (5, 3)\}$

Step 2. $D_{14} = 12 + 0 = 12$

$\quad\quad D_{34} = 11 + 0 = 11$

$\quad\quad D_{52} = 11 + 0 = 11$

$\quad\quad D_{53} = 12 + 0 = 12$

Step 3. $D_{kl}^* = D_{14} = D_{53} = 12$. We arbitrarily choose $(k, l) = (1, 4)$.

Now $\bar{Y} = \{\overline{1, 4}\}$, and

$$w(\bar{Y}) = w(\{4, 5\}) + D_{14}^*$$

$$= 53 + 12 = 65$$

Since $Y = \{1, 4\}$, delete row 1 and column 4 from C. Edge (1, 4) forms a path with edges (2, 1) and (4, 5). Therefore, $p = 2$ and $q = 5$. Set $c_{52} = \infty$, and reduce the current C. We find $h = 11$ and $w(Y) = 53 + h = 64$. The reduced C is shown as Fig. 3.4.8b.

We are now at box 6 and have a 2×2 matrix C. Box 7 produces the tour with city order

$$3 \quad 2 \quad 1 \quad 4 \quad 5 \quad 3$$

and cost $z = 64$ (check this). At box 8, set $z_0 = 64$; this is now the current best tour.

Are we finished? There is no need to consider the successors to vertices $\{\overline{4, 5}\}$ and $\{\overline{1, 4}\}$ since their lower bounds are greater than 64. However, at box 10 we see that end-vertex $\{\overline{2, 1}\}$ has a lower bound of $62 < 64$. Consequently, it is possible that a tour in this subset may be a bit better than the one we have. There is more work to do.

We find that $X = \{\overline{2, 1}\}$, $w(X) = 62$, and the update of C, using the subalgorithm for box 11, is shown in Fig. 3.4.8c. Box 3 next picks edge (4, 1), with $D_{41}^* = 12$, as the next branching edge. Boxes 4 and 5 yield $w(\{\overline{4, 1}\}) = 62 + 12 = 74$ and $w(\{4, 1\}) = 62$. Another iteration is necessary. This will be left as an exercise. Is there a tour with cost 62 or 63?

Although the algorithm we just developed seemed to plod along on our little five-city example, it is really quite powerful. A carefully implemented version will usually solve traveling salesman problems with 20 to 30 cities in well under a minute on CDC 6000 or IBM 360/1xx series machines. Problems with 40 to 50 cities can often be solved in respectable times (less than 10 minutes of central processor time). Contrast this with the outrageous performance of the exhaustive search Algorithm ETS (see Sec. 1.3) on a supercomputer for a 20-city problem.

There are a variety of heuristics which will make this basic branch-and-bound algorithm faster (some of which were used to obtain the above times). Two of these were discussed in Sec. 3.2.

Algorithm GTS2 can be used as a "primer" for the branch-and-bound algorithm of this section. As we saw during the development of that algorithm, it might take some time before the first full tour is constructed and z_0 is set to a realistic estimate of the cost for an optimum tour. If a reasonably good tour is known at the start of the algorithm, say from Algorithm GTS2, then z_0 starts at a fairly low level. Any vertex in the search tree which shows up with a lower bound greater than or equal to z_0 can then be immediately considered fathomed. In this way, a lot of worthless searching can be avoided early in the execution of the exact algorithm.

This algorithm was one of the best for the traveling salesman problem until about 1970. Since that time a number of faster algorithms have appeared, but they use techniques that are beyond the scope of this text.

All branch-and-bound algorithms of any significance are known or suspected to be exponential in worst-case performance. The analysis of expected performance is very difficult and often beyond current analytical powers. Most branch-and-bound algorithms are reported in the literature with nothing more than some experimental statistics.

Exercises 3.4

3.4.1 Complete the solution of the five-city example in this section.

3.4.2 Solve the following six-city traveling salesman problem using the branch-and-bound algorithm of this section.

	1	2	3	4	5	6
1	∞	21	42	31	6	24
2	11	∞	17	7	35	18
3	25	5	∞	27	14	9
4	12	9	24	∞	30	12
5	14	7	21	15	∞	48
6	39	15	16	5	20	∞

3.4.3 *Initialization subalgorithm.* Design a detailed subalgorithm for the initialization step (box 1) of the flowchart in Fig. 3.4.5.

3.4.4 *Initial reduction subalgorithm.* Design a detailed subalgorithm for the initial reduction step (box 2) of the flowchart in Fig. 3.4.5.

3.4.5 *Branching process for set $\bar{Y}$.* Design a detailed subalgorithm for the $\bar{Y}$ generation step (box 4) of the flowchart in Fig. 3.4.5.

3.4.6 *Exhaustive search subalgorithm.* Design a detailed subalgorithm for the exhaustive fathoming steps (boxes 6, 7, and 8) in Fig. 3.4.5.

L**3.4.7** *Complete statement of the traveling salesman algorithm.* Assemble a complete detailed statement of the entire branch-and-bound algorithm developed in this section. Organize the algorithm so that it will be ready for direct implementation as a computer program. See Exercises 3.4.3 to 3.4.6.

*3.4.8** *Correctness.* Prove the correctness of the algorithm developed in this section.

*3.4.9** *Symmetric case.* What improvements might be made to the algorithm of this section if the cost matrix is symmetric?

Each of the next four problems should be done in teams of two to five students.

*L**3.4.10** *Implementation.* Implement the algorithm of this section (see Exercise 3.4.7) as a computer program. Care in the design and coding stages will save a lot of debugging grief. Special care should be taken to handle the various altered cost matrices correctly.

*L**3.4.11** *Testing.* Use the program of Exercise 3.4.10 to experimentally ascertain the quality of the traveling salesman algorithm studied in this section. Limit runs to $N \leq 20$ cities.

***L**3.4.12** *Knapsack problem (complete development).* We have a knapsack of volume V and an unlimited stockpile of each of N different items. For $i = 1, \ldots, N$, one unit of item i has known volume v_i and known value m_i. Integer numbers of the various items may be put into the knapsack. The objective is to pack as much value as possible into the knapsack, subject to the constraint that the total volume of the packed items is not greater than V. Considerations of shape do not enter into the problem. Completely develop a branch-and-bound algorithm for the knapsack problem.

***L**3.4.13** *Parallel processor scheduling (complete development).* Three identical central processors are available to run M jobs. Any job may be run on any processor, and once a job is put on a processor it runs there until it is completed (that is, no job is interrupted or shared among two or more processors). For $i = 1, \ldots, M$, job i requires time t_i to run. For any linear ordering of the jobs, the next job on the list is run on the first available processor. The jobs may be listed in any order.

   Completely develop a branch-and-bound algorithm for finding an optimum list—that is, one which permits all the jobs to be completed in the shortest possible total time. As an example, consider four jobs with $t_1 = 3$, $t_2 = 3$, $t_3 = 3$, and $t_4 = 6$. Taken in the order (1, 2, 3, 4) the total elapsed time from start to completion of all jobs is $T = 9$. For the order (4, 1, 2, 3), $T = 6$, and this is clearly a best possible schedule.

*L3.4.14 *Evaluation of Algorithm* GTS2 (*testing*). This exercise can only be done if you have programs for both Algorithm GTS2 and the branch-and-bound algorithm developed earlier. Experimentally test the quality of Algorithm GTS2 against the exact solutions produced by the branch-and-bound algorithm for randomly generated problems with no more than 20 cities. Use Algorithm GTS2 as a primer for the branch and bound as described in this section. How do the experimental means and variances for the run times compare?

3.5 RECURSION

In mathematics and computer programming *recursion* is the name given to the method of defining or expressing a function, procedure, language construct, or the solution of a problem in terms of itself. A few examples will give this idea concrete meaning.

Factorials and Fibonacci Numbers

The factorial function is defined recursively as

$$0! = 1$$
$$N! = N \times (N - 1)! \qquad \text{if } N > 0$$

or, in programming notation,

$$FAC(0) = 1 \qquad\qquad (1)$$

$$FAC(N) = N * FAC(N - 1) \qquad \text{if } N > 0 \qquad (2)$$

The domain of the FAC function is the set of nonnegative integers.

Equation (2) is an example of a *recurrence relation*. Recurrence relations express function values in terms of other values computed with smaller arguments. Equation (1) is a nonrecursively defined *initial value* of the function. Every recursive function needs at least one such initial value or it can never be explicitly evaluated.

Similarly, the Fibonacci numbers are defined by the following infinite sequence of integers: 1, 1, 2, 3, 5, 8, 13, 21, 34, 55, 89, ... Inspection shows that the

N*th* element of this sequence is simply the sum of the two immediately preceding elements. That is, if FIB(N) denotes the N*th* Fibonacci number, FIB(N) can be defined as a recurrence relation

$$FIB(N) = FIB(N-1) + FIB(N-2)$$

Since FIB(N) is defined in terms of *two* different values with smaller arguments, *two* initial values are necessary. These are taken as

$$FIB(1) = 1$$
$$FIB(2) = 1$$

As defined here, the Fibonacci numbers[1] form a recursive solution to the following problem:

Each month the female of a pair of rabbits gives birth to a pair of rabbits (a male and a female). Two months later the newborn female gives birth to a like pair of rabbits. Find the number of rabbits at the end of the year if there was one newborn pair of rabbits at the beginning of the year, and no rabbits die.

Consider the amount of work required to compute FAC(N), for an arbitrary natural number N. In order to compute FAC(N), we must make a *recursive call* and compute FAC(N − 1). This in turn requires yet another recursive call to compute FAC(N − 2), etc. Thus, in order to compute FAC(N), we must make N recursive calls, the last of which is for FAC(0) = 1. We say that the *depth of recursion* required to compute FAC(N) is N. Stated in terms of computer programs, depth of recursion refers to the longest sequence of procedure calls required to evaluate a function before a RETURN is encountered. Depth of recursion is therefore a measure of the computational complexity of a recursively defined function.

For the Fibonacci function, two function evaluations are required [FIB(N − 1) and FIB(N − 2)] in order to compute FIB(N). Each of these evaluations in turn requires two evaluations—two for FIB(N − 1) and two more for FIB(N − 2), etc. This suggests that the depth of recursion required to compute FIB(N) is roughly 2^{N-2}. However, a moment's reflection reveals considerable redundancy in this approach. Certainly if we know the N − 1 values, FIB(1), FIB(2), ..., FIB(N − 1), then we can compute FIB(N). Furthermore, since we are given FIB(1) and FIB(2), by definition, it will require only N − 3 evaluations to compute FIB(3), ..., FIB(N − 1). Thus, N − 2 function evaluations should suffice to compute FIB(N).

[1] These numbers are named after the Italian mathematician Fibonacci, who published the problem stated here in 1202.

Ackermann's Function

The two recursive functions considered so far have been fairly simple. So as not to give a false impression of the complexity of recursive functions, we present the following, rather innocent-looking, *doubly recursive function* known as *Ackermann's function*. A function is doubly recursive if the function *and* one of its arguments is defined in terms of itself.

$$A(M, N) = \begin{cases} N + 1 & \text{if } M = 0 \\ A(M - 1, 1) & \text{if } N = 0 \\ A[M - 1, A(M, N - 1)] & \text{otherwise} \end{cases}$$

A brief inspection of Fig. 3.5.1 should indicate how difficult it is to compute this function for even such small arguments as $M = 4$ and $N = 2$. Note, for example, that $A(4, 1) = A(3, 13)$.

Partitions of an Integer

A partition of a positive integer M is an expression of M as a sum of integers. A classical counting problem is to determine the number $P(M)$ of partitions of M.

For $M = 6$, the partitions are

$$6$$
$$5 + 1$$
$$4 + 2, 4 + 1 + 1$$
$$3 + 3, 3 + 2 + 1, 3 + 1 + 1 + 1$$
$$2 + 2 + 2, 2 + 2 + 1 + 1, 2 + 1 + 1 + 1 + 1$$
$$1 + 1 + 1 + 1 + 1 + 1$$

An interesting way to express the function $P(M)$ is in terms of a second function $Q(M, N)$, which is defined to equal the number of partitions of the integer M in which no summand is greater than N. A bit of recursive reflection reveals the following:

1 $Q(M, 1) = 1$. That is, there is only one partition of the integer M in which the largest summand is 1—namely, $M = 1 + 1 + \cdots + 1$.
2 $Q(1, N) = 1$. Obviously there is only one partition of the integer 1, regardless of the size N of the largest summand.
3 $Q(M, N) = Q(M, M)$ if $M < N$. Clearly no partition of M can contain a summand N larger than M.
4 $Q(M, M) = 1 + Q(M, M - 1)$. There is exactly one partition of M with a summand equal to M. All other partitions of M have a largest summand $N \leq M - 1$.

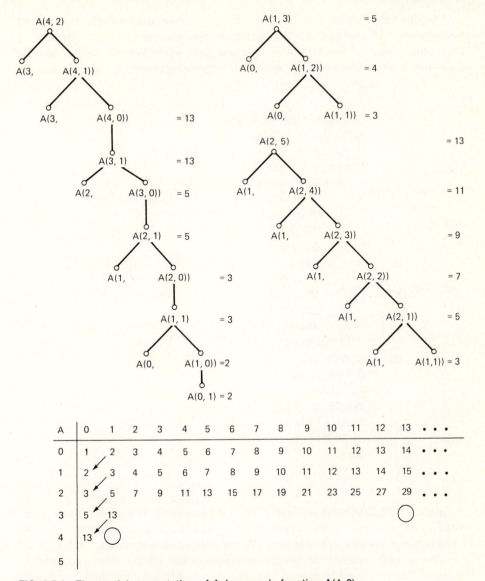

FIG. 3.5.1 The partial computation of Ackermann's function A(4, 2).

5 $Q(M, N) = Q(M, N - 1) + Q(M - N, N)$. This states that any partition of M with a largest summand less than or equal to N either does not contain N as a summand—in which case the partition is also in $Q(M, N - 1)$—or it does contain N and the remaining summands form a partition of $M - N$.

Equations 1 through 5 recursively define the function $Q(M, N)$. They define $P(M)$ since $P(M) = Q(M, M)$.

Anyone familiar with Fortran knows that one cannot execute recursive calls to subroutines in this language. This would seem to prevent us from implementing the computation of the recursive function Q(M, N) in Fortran. However, the following is an iterative routine which correctly computes Q(M, N) in Fortran.

```
        INTEGER FUNCTION Q(M, N)
        INTEGER M, N, VAL(M, N)
        IF (M .LT. 1 .OR. N .LT. 1) GO TO 70
        DO 60   K = 1, M
            DO 50   L = 1, N
                IF (K .EQ. 1 .OR. L .EQ. 1) GO TO 40
                IF (K − L) 10, 20, 30
10              VAL(K, L) = VAL(K, K)
                GO TO 50
20              VAL(K, L) = 1 + VAL(K, K − 1)
                GO TO 50
30              VAL(K, L) = VAL(K, L − 1) + VAL(K − L, L)
                GO TO 50
40              VAL(K, L) = 1
50          CONTINUE
60      CONTINUE
        Q = VAL(M, N)
        RETURN
70      WRITE (6, 1000) M, N
1000    FORMAT (1H0, 21H IMPROPER ARGUMENTS   , 2I6)
        RETURN
        END
```

Notice that Q(M, N) is evaluated by first computing and storing in an array VAL(I, J) *all* previous values of Q(M, N) for $I \le M$ and $J \le N$ so that what appear to be recursive calls (for example, line 10) are only array references.

The previous example shows that with some effort we can write a program to implement a recursive function in Fortran. Contrast this, on the other hand, with the naturalness of implementing the same function in Algol:

```
begin if M < 1 OR N < 1  then PRINT 'IMPROPER ARGUMENTS'
    else if M = 1 OR N = 1  then QP: = 1
    else if M < N           then QP: = QP(M, M)
    else if M = N           then QP: = 1 + QP(M, M − 1)
    else                         QP: = QP(M, N − 1) + QP(M − N, N)
end
```

Language Identifiers

Recursion occurs naturally throughout computer science. For example, a Fortran identifier (variable, function, or subroutine name) is usually defined as consisting of from one to six letters or digits, the first of which is a letter. In Algol, identifiers are defined in almost the same way, except for removing the restriction on the length. The specification of an identifier is usually given as follows:

$$\langle\text{digit}\rangle := 0/1/2/3/4/5/6/7/8/9$$
$$\langle\text{letter}\rangle := A/B/C/ \ldots /X/Y/Z$$
$$\langle\text{identifier}\rangle := \langle\text{letter}\rangle$$
$$\langle\text{identifier}\rangle := \langle\text{identifier}\rangle \langle\text{digit}\rangle$$
$$\langle\text{identifier}\rangle := \langle\text{identifier}\rangle \langle\text{letter}\rangle$$

Notice that the definition of an identifier is expressed in terms of itself in the last two specifications.

Statements like those above are used by Algol compilers to determine if all variables in a source program are properly formed. Suppose that we define a function VAR such that for any string of characters X, VAR(X) = "YES" if and only if X is a proper identifier; otherwise, VAR(X) = "NO". Function VAR is defined recursively as follows:

$$VAR(X) = \begin{cases} YES & \text{if } X = \langle\text{letter}\rangle \\ VAR(Y) & \text{if } X = Y\langle\text{digit}\rangle \\ VAR(Y) & \text{if } X = Y\langle\text{letter}\rangle \\ NO & \text{otherwise} \end{cases}$$

where $X = Y\langle\text{digit}\rangle$ signifies that X is a character string, the last character of which is a digit.

Depth-First and Breadth-First Search

In a variety of network theoretic problems, one must find an arbitrary spanning tree in a network G (for example, to determine if G is connected) or examine every edge of G at least once. Tarjan has given a simple recursive algorithm for doing both of these. The algorithm is called *depth-first search*, the basic idea of which can be used in a variety of situations where one seeks to find an optimum of some sort by searching through a large tree structure. We illustrate this algorithm (Algorithm DFS) with the network in Fig. 3.5.2, which is represented by adjacency lists.

Algorithm DFS, which is expressed recursively, requires as initial input the network G, an arbitrary starting vertex V, and initial values of I = 0 and T = ∅.

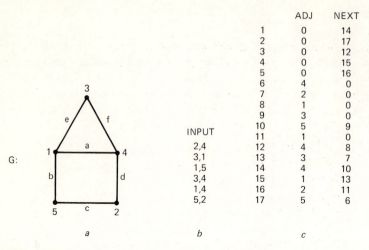

	ADJ	NEXT
1	0	14
2	0	17
3	0	12
4	0	15
5	0	16
6	4	0
7	2	0
8	1	0
9	3	0
10	5	9
11	1	0
12	4	8
13	3	7
14	4	10
15	1	13
16	2	11
17	5	6

G:

INPUT
2,4
3,1
1,5
3,4
1,4
5,2

a   b   c

FIG. 3.5.2 A linked lists representation of a network: (a) network, (b) edges, (c) linked lists.

Algorithm DFS (*Depth-First Search*) To find a spanning tree T in a connected network G, whose vertices are numbered 1, 2, ..., M. The algorithm is recursive and calls itself with the statement CALL DFS(V), where vertex V is the new vertex being visited; if VISIT(W) = I, then vertex W was the I*th* new vertex visited: VISIT(W) is undefined if it has not been visited.

Step 1. [Visit vertex] **Set** I ← I + 1; **and** VISIT(V) ← I.

Step 2. [Find an unvisited vertex adjacent to V]
    For all vertices W adjacent to V **do** step 3 **od**; **and** RETURN.
    Step 3. [Has vertex W been visited?]
        If VISIT(W) is undefined **then** set T ← T + (V, W);
        and CALL DFS(W) **fi**.

Let us offer an intuitive explanation of how this algorithm works. The variable V indicates the current vertex, that is, the vertex at which we are now located. Algorithm DFS proceeds by traversing an arbitrary edge from V, say, to vertex W. If vertex W has not yet been visited, the algorithm recursively calls itself with CALL DFS(W). If, on the other hand, vertex W has already been visited, the algorithm tries another edge from V, always looking for unvisited vertices to visit next. If no unvisited vertices adjacent to V are found, the algorithm backs up to the vertex from which V was visited and tries new edges from there. If the network is connected, Algorithm DFS will "examine" every edge twice and will find a spanning tree.

We next trace out the steps of Algorithm DFS, working on the network in Fig. 3.5.2, starting (arbitrarily) at vertex 4. The initial call is to DFS(4).

```
DFS(4)
  V = 4, T = ∅, I = 0
  I = 1
  VISIT(4) = 1
  W = 1                              We are now in step 3.
    T = T + (4, 1)
    DFS(1)
      V = 1
      I = 2
      VISIT(1) = 2
      W = 4
      W = 5
        T = T + (1, 5)
        DFS(5)
          V = 5
          I = 3
          VISIT(5) = 3
          W = 2
            T = T + (5, 2)
            DFS(2)
              V = 2
              I = 4
              VISIT(2) = 4
              W = 5
              W = 4
            RETURN to DFS(5)
          W = 1
        RETURN to DFS(1)
      W = 3
        T = T + (1, 3)
        DFS(3)
          V = 3
          I = 5
          VISIT(3) = 5
          W = 4
          W = 1
        RETURN to DFS(1)
    RETURN to DFS(4)
  W = 3
  W = 2
RETURN
```

The edges of the network G are traced out in the order abcdef, as indicated in Fig. 3.5.3a; the final spanning tree found by Algorithm DFS is shown in Fig. 3.5.3b.

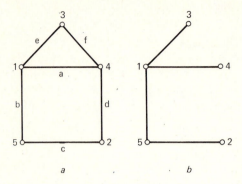

FIG. 3.5.3 The spanning tree found by Algorithm DFS.

In order to implement Algorithm DFS, it would be natural to write a computer program for it in a programming language, such as Algol or PL/1, in which it is possible to make recursive procedure calls. If you are familiar with such a language, we encourage you to do so.

We will present a Fortran implementation of Algorithm DFS because it serves to illustrate: (1) the creation and use of a linked list representation of a network; (2) the use of a pushdown store; and (3) a method by which a recursive algorithm can be implemented iteratively.

In order to understand how a pushdown store can be used to implement recursive calls, consider again the sequence of operations performed by Algorithm DFS in finding a spanning tree in the network G of Fig. 3.5.2, starting at vertex 4.

Every time we make a recursive CALL like DFS(5), we interrupt the process of examining all vertices adjacent to vertex $V = 1$ and reset the value of V (for example, $V = 5$). Upon RETURN from the CALL to DFS(5), we must somehow remember where we were—that is, we were at vertex $V = 1$ and we had just examined the next vertex $W = 5$ adjacent to V.

In order to remember where we were at the time we CALLed DFS(5), we store the current values of V and W in a pushdown store (that is, $V = 1$ and $W = 5$). Values V and W are called the *current environment* of Algorithm DFS. If, during the CALL to DFS(5), another CALL is made [for example, to DFS(2)], then the new current environment is placed on top of the pushdown store (that is, $V = 5$ and $W = 2$). On every RETURN from a procedure call, we take the most recent environment off the top of the pushdown store and use it to restore the previous values of V and W.

Figure 3.5.4 illustrates what the contents of the pushdown store would be in this example. Figure 3.5.5 is a Fortran implementation of the recursive Algorithm DFS. Note that SUBROUTINE DFS stores on a pushdown store the values of the variable V and a *pointer* K to the vertex W, instead of the vertex W itself.

Several additional observations should be made about Algorithm DFS. The first concerns its name: Why is it called depth-first search? This algorithm is effectively a backtracking algorithm (see Sec. 3.3) which has the property of searching through a tree structure in such a manner as to find a "bottom" vertex as quickly as possible. Figure 3.5.6 illustrates the tree structure searched by DFS in Fig. 3.5.2; the circled numbers indicate the order in which the vertices of this tree are visited (they correspond exactly to the sequence of values of W in DFS). An X under a vertex means that it has already been visited. Notice that by continually moving to the first unvisited vertex from a given vertex, DFS reaches the bottom of this tree (vertex 5) as quickly as possible. Observe that in Fig. 3.5.6 there are exactly twice as many edges in the tree T(G) as there are in G, and each edge of G appears exactly twice in T(G).

A proof of the correctness of Algorithm DFS could be based on the following observations:

1 An edge is added to T only if one of its two vertices has not yet been visited. This implies that T cannot contain a cycle.
2 If each of the M − 1 vertices other than the starting vertex *are* in fact visited, then M − 1 edges will be added to T.
3 A spanning tree T in a network G with M vertices consists of M − 1 edges which do not form a cycle.

Given these observations you might try to construct a correctness proof for Algorithm DFS.

We complete our discussion of Algorithm DFS by analyzing its complexity. The number of operations required to carry out the algorithm on a network G = (V, E) is O(|E|), that is, a linear function of the number of edges in the network. This follows from the fact that the algorithm examines each edge of G exactly twice and the processing of any edge takes no more than about 12 steps. Note also that exactly |V| calls are made to DFS.

The technique of searching through a tree in a depth-first manner should be contrasted with another technique known as *breadth-first search*. In a sequential

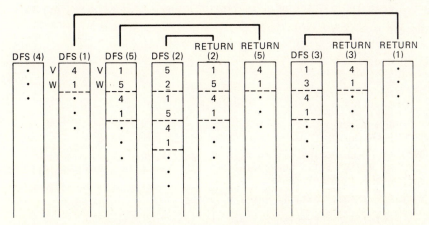

FIG. 3.5.4 Contents of the pushdown store when implementing Algorithm DFS.

```
       PROGRAM SPAN (INPUT,OUTPUT,TAPE5=INPUT,TAPE6=OUTPUT)
C
C      THIS IS A PROGRAM WHICH FINDS A SPANNING TREE OF AN UNWEIGHTED,
C      NETWORK G.  THIS PROGRAM ILLUSTRATES THE USE OF A LINKED LIST
C      REPRESENTATION OF A NETWORK, AND IT ILLUSTRATES, IN SUBROUTINE
C      DFS, THE USE OF A PUSHDOWN STORE AS A MEANS OF IMPLEMENTING A
C      RECURSIVE ALGORITHM IN FORTRAN.
C
C      VARIABLE       DESCRIPTION
C
C      ADJ(K)         ARRAYS USED TO STORE THE P LINKED LISTS OF VERTICES
C      NEXT(K)        ADJACENT TO A GIVEN VERTEX.  FOR 1 .LE. K .LE. P,
C                     ADJ(K) = 0, AND IF J=NEXT(K), THEN ADJ(J) IS THE
C                     FIRST VERTEX ADJACENT TO VERTEX K.  THE NEXT VERTEX
C                     ADJACENT TO K IS CONTAINED IN ADJ(NEXT(J)), ETC.
C
C      TREE(J,1)      THE J-TH EDGE CHOSEN FOR THE SPANNING TREE.
C      TREE(J,2)
C
C      P, Q           THE NUMBER OF VERTICES AND EDGES, RESPECTIVELY, IN G.
C                     THE VERTICES OF G ARE LABELED 1,2,...,P.
C
C      U, V           AN EDGE IN G BETWEEN VERTICES U AND V.
C
C      WORDS          WORDS = P + 2*Q, THE NUMBER OF WORDS OF MEMORY
C                     REQUIRED BY ARRAYS ADJ AND NEXT.
C
       INTEGER P, Q, T, U, V, WORDS
       INTEGER ADJ(1000), NEXT(1000), TREE(100,2)
C
C          READ IN THE NUMBER OF VERTICES AND EDGES IN G.
C
       READ (5,1000) P,Q
 1000  FORMAT (I4,I4)
       I = P + 1
       WORDS = P + 2 * Q
C
C          INITIALIZE THE ARRAYS ADJ AND NEXT.
C
       DO 100 M = 1, P
            ADJ(M) = 0
            NEXT(M) = 0
  100  CONTINUE
C
C
C          READ THE Q EDGES OF G AND SET UP LINKED LIST REPRESENTATION.
C
       DO 200 N = 1, Q
            READ (5,1000) U,V
            NEXT(I) = NEXT(U)
            ADJ(I) = V
            NEXT(U) = I
            I = I + 1
            NEXT(I) = NEXT(V)
            ADJ(I) = U
            NEXT(V) = I
            I = I + 1
  200  CONTINUE
C
C          CALL SUBROUTINE DFS TO FIND A SPANNING TREE OF G, STARTING
C          AT VERTEX V=1.  SUBROUTINE DFS WILL PLACE THE SPANNING TREE
C          EDGES IN ARRAY TREE.
C
       CALL DFS ( ADJ, NEXT, 1, TREE, P, WORDS, T )
C
C          PRINT OUT THE NETWORK G AND THE SPANNING TREE OF G.
```

FIG. 3.5.5 A Fortran implementation of Algorithm DFS.

```
C
      WRITE (6,2000) (I,ADJ(I),NEXT(I), I = 1,WORDS)
 2000 FORMAT ( 1H1,38H THE LIST REPRESENTATION OF NETWORK G ,///,
     +    23H        I      ADJ   NEXT ,/, ( 1H0,I8,I6,I6))
      WRITE (6,2100)
 2100 FORMAT ( 1H1,22H  SPANNING TREE EDGES )
      K = T - 1
      WRITE (6,2200) (( TREE(I,J), J=1,2), I=1,K )
 2200 FORMAT ( 1H0, I10, I6 )
C
      IF ( T .EQ. P ) STOP
C
      WRITE (6,2300)
 2300 FORMAT ( 1H1,41H NOTE THAT THE NETWORK IS NOT CONNECTED. )
C
      STOP
      END
      SUBROUTINE DFS ( ADJ, NEXT, V, TREE, P, WORDS, T )
C
C     THIS SUBROUTINE IS AN ADAPTATION OF TARJAN S RECURSIVE DEPTH-FIRST
C     SEARCH ALGORITHM. DFS WILL FIND A SPANNING TREE OF A CONNECTED,
C     UNWEIGHTED NETWORK G, HAVING P .LE. 100 VERTICES AND Q EDGES.
C     THE NETWORK G IS REPRESENTED BY LINKED LISTS, USING ARRAYS
C     ADJ(WORDS) AND NEXT(WORDS), WHERE WORDS = P + 2*Q.  DFS PLACES
C     THE EDGES CHOSEN FOR THE SPANNING TREE IN ARRAY TREE, AND BEGINS
C     ITS SEARCH FOR A SPANNING TREE AT VERTEX V.  IF G IS NOT CONNECTED
C     DFS WILL FIND A SPANNING TREE OF THE CONNECTED COMPONENT OF G
C     CONTAINING V.  DFS SIMULATES A PUSHDOWN STORE IN ORDER TO
C     IMPLEMENT THE RECURSIVE CALLS IN TARJAN S ALGORITHM.
C
C     VARIABLES       DESCRIPTION
C
C     V               AT ANY POINT IN TIME, WE ARE CONSIDERING VERTEX V.
C
C     W               THE NEXT VERTEX ADJACENT TO V.
C
C     VISIT(V)=I      MEANS THAT VERTEX V WAS THE I-TH VERTEX VISITED
C                     FOR THE FIRST TIME. VISIT(V)=0 MEANS THAT VERTEX V
C                     HAS NOT YET BEEN VISITED.
C
C     STORE           THE PUSHDOWN STORE USED TO REMEMBER THE PAST
C                     SEQUENCE OF VERTICES VISITED.  THE PUSHDOWN STORE
C                     IS NEEDED IN ORDER TO REMEMBER THE CURRENT VERTEX V,
C                     AND HOW FAR WE HAVE PROGRESSED POINTER K THROUGH
C                     V S ADJACENCY LIST.  IF P .LE. 100 THEN NO MORE
C                     THAN 200 ITEMS WILL EVER BE STORED IN STORE.
C
C     PTR             THE POINTER TO THE TOP OF THE PUSHDOWN STORE.
C
C     T               THE COUNT OF THE NUMBER OF EDGES CURRENTLY IN THE
C                     SPANNING TREE.
C
C     K               A POINTER USED IN TRAVERSING THE LINKED LISTS OF
C                     ADJACENCIES.
C
      INTEGER P, PTR, T, V, W, WORDS
      INTEGER ADJ(WORDS), NEXT(WORDS), STORE(200), TREE(100,2)
      INTEGER VISIT(100)
C
C         INITIALIZE VARIABLES.
C
      DO 100 I = 1,100
          VISIT(I) = 0
 100  CONTINUE
      PTR = 0
      T = 1
```

FIG. 3.5.5 *(Continued)*

```
C
C              VISIT ALL OF THE VERTICES.
C
       DO 400 I = 1,P
C
C                  V IS THE I-TH NEW VERTEX VISITED.
C
           VISIT(V) = I
           K = V
C
C                  GET THE NEXT VERTEX ADJACENT TO V.
C
  200      K = NEXT(K)
C
C                  ANY MORE VERTICES ADJACENT TO V.
C
           IF ( K .GT. 0 ) GOTO 300
C
C                      ANYTHING LEFT ON THE PUSHDOWN STORE.
C
           IF ( PTR .EQ. 0 ) RETURN
C
C                      REMOVE THE TOP THREE ITEMS
C                      FROM THE PUSHDOWN STORE.
C
               V = STORE(PTR)
               K = STORE(PTR-1)
               STORE(PTR) = 0
               STORE(PTR-1) = 0
               PTR = PTR - 2
               GOTO 200
C
C                      GET THE NEXT VERTEX ADJACENT TO V.
C
  300      W = ADJ(K)
C
C                  HAS VERTEX W ALREADY BEEN VISITED.
C
           IF ( VISIT(W) .GT. 0 ) GOTO 200
C
C                      ADD EDGE VX TO THE SPANNING TREE
C
               TREE(T,1) = V
               TREE(T,2) = W
               I = T + 1
C
C                      DO WE HAVE A SPANNING TREE YET.
C
           IF ( T .EQ. P ) RETURN
C
C                          STORE K, V, AND U ON THE PUSHDOWN STORE
C                          AND VISIT W.
C
               STORE(PTR+1) = K
               STORE(PTR+2) = V
               PTR = PTR + 2
               V = W
C
  400  CONTINUE
C
C          THIS STATEMENT SHOULD NEVER BE REACHED.
C
       WRITE(6,1000)
 1000  FORMAT(1H1,25H ERROR IN SUBROUTINE DFS.)
       RETURN
       END
```

FIG. 3.5.5 *(Continued)*

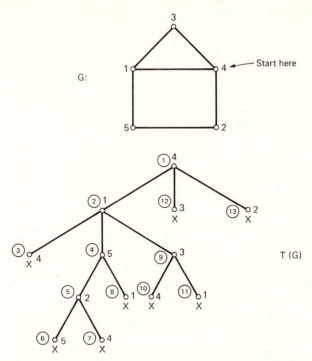

FIG. 3.5.6 The depth-first search tree produced by Algorithm DFS.

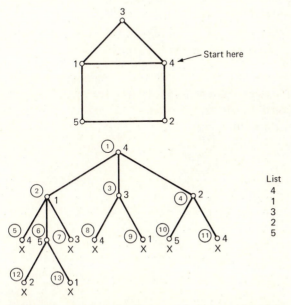

FIG. 3.5.7 The breadth-first search tree produced by Algorithm BFS.

fashion, a breadth-first search visits all vertices in a tree at level k, then all vertices at level $k+1$, etc. A breadth-first search for a spanning tree in the network G in Fig. 3.5.2 would produce a tree like the one shown in Fig. 3.5.7.

For the sake of completeness we next present a breadth-first search algorithm for finding a spanning tree in a network G.

Algorithm BFS starts at an arbitrary vertex V and adds to a list LIST all vertices adjacent to V which have not been visited, marking each of these vertices "visited" as they are added to the LIST. On each successive iteration of the algorithm, the next vertex W on the LIST is examined to see if there are any unvisited vertices adjacent to it which can be added to the LIST. Whenever a new vertex is added to the LIST, the edge from it to the current vertex being examined is added to the spanning tree.

> **Algorithm BFS** (*Breadth-First Search*) To find a spanning tree T in a connected network G, whose vertices are numbered 1, 2, ..., M. The algorithm starts at vertex U; VISIT(W) = 1 means that vertex W has already been visited; VISIT(W) = 0 if W has not been visited.
>
> *Step 0.* [Initialize] **Set** I ← 1; J ← 1; **for** K ← 1 to M **do set** LIST(K) ← 0; **and** VISIT(K) ← 0 **od**; **set** LIST(1) ← U; VISIT(U) ← 1; **and** T ← ∅.
>
> *Step 1.* [Examine all vertices] **While** LIST(J) ≠ 0 **do through** step 3 **od**; **and** STOP.
>
> > *Step 2.* [Get the next vertex] **Set** V ← LIST(J); **and** J ← J + 1.
> >
> > *Step 3.* [Find all unvisited vertices adjacent to V]
> > **For** all vertices W adjacent to V **do** step 4 **od**.
> >
> > > *Step 4.* [Add unvisited vertex of LIST and edge to T]
> > > **If** VISIT(W) = 0 **then set** I ← I + 1; LIST(I) ← W;
> > > VISIT(W) ← 1; **and** T ← T + (V, W) **fi**.

The following is a simple, nonrecursive implementation of Algorithm BFS. The output VECTOR produced by SUBROUTINE BFS is the recursive representation of a spanning tree T of G which was discussed at the end of Sec. 2.3. Figure 3.5.8 illustrates this representation of T. An explicit program for finding a spanning tree using breadth-first search is shown in Fig. 3.5.9.

	1	2	3	4	5
Vector	4	4	4	0	2

FIG. 3.5.8 A vector representation of a spanning tree.

```
        PROGRAM BFSPAN (INPUT,OUTPUT,TAPE6=OUTPUT,TAPE5=INPUT)
C
C       THIS IS A PROGRAM WHICH FINDS A SPANNING TREE OF AN UNWEIGHTED
C       NETWORK G USING A SUBROUTINE BFS WHICH EMPLOYS A BREADTH FIRST
C       SEARCH METHOD.
C
C       VARIABLE     DESCRIPTION
C
C       ADJ(I)       ARRAYS USED TO STORE THE P LINKED
C       NEXT(I)      LISTS OF VERTICES ADJACENT TO A GIVEN VERTEX.
C
C       P            THE VERTICES OF G ARE LABLED 1,2,...,P
C
C       M,N          AN EDGE IN G WHICH IS READ IN.  IF M .LT. 0
C                    THEN THERE ARE NO MORE EDGES.
C
C       V            THE INITIAL VERTEX FROM WHICH THE BREADTH FIRST SEARCH
C                    BEGINS.
C
        INTEGER ADJ(1000), NEXT(1000)
        INTEGER V, P
C
C       READ IN THE NUMBER OF VERTICES.
C
        READ (5,1000) P
 1000 FORMAT ( I4, I4 )
        I = P + 1
C
C       INITIALIZE THE ARRAYS ADJ AND NEXT.
C
        DO 50 II = 1,P
            ADJ(II) = 0
            NEXT(II) = 0
   50 CONTINUE
C
C       READ IN THE EDGES OF G.
C
  100 READ (5,1000) M,N
        IF ( M .LT. 0 ) GO TO 200
        NEXT(I) = NEXT(M)
        ADJ(I) = N
        NEXT(M) = I
        I = I + 1
        NEXT(I) = NEXT(N)
        ADJ(I) = M
        NEXT(N) = I
        I = I + 1
        GO TO 100
C
C       READ IN THE INITIAL VERTEX V AND CALL SUBROUTINE BFS.
C
  200 READ (5,1000) V
        CALL BFS (V, ADJ, NEXT, P )
        STOP
        END

        SUBROUTINE BFS (V, ADJ, NEXT, P )
C
C       THIS SUBROUTINE INPLEMENTS A BREADTH FIRST SEARCH ALGORITHM
C       FOR FINDING A SPANNING TREE OF AN UNWEIGHTED NETWORK G.
C
C       *** FORMAL PARAMETERS ***
C
C       V            INITIAL VERTEX FROM WHICH BREADTH FIRST SEARCH BEGINS.
C
```

FIG. 3.5.9 A Fortran implementation of Algorithm BFS.

```
C         ADJ,NEXT        ARRAYS USED TO STORE A LINKED LIST REPRESENTATION
C                         OF THE NETWORK G.
C
C         P               THE NUMBER OF VERTICES IN G.
C
C         *** LOCAL VARIABLES ***
C
C         LABLE(I)        AN ARRAY USED ONLY FOR FORMATTING PURPOSES, TO
C                         PRINT OUT THE SPANNING TREE.
C
C         VECTOR(I)       IF VECTOR(I)=J THEN EDGE(I,J) IS IN THE SPANNING TREE.
C
C         VISIT(J)=I      MEANS THAT THE VERTEX WAS THE I-TH VERTEX VISITED FOR
C                         THE FIRST TIME.  VISIT(V)=0 MEANS THAT VERTEX V
C                         HAS NOT YET BEEN VISITED.
C
C         LIST(I)         LIST IS AN ARRAY OF VERTICES TO BE VISITED FOR THE
C                         FIRST TIME.
C
C         N               THE INDEX WHICH RUNS THROUGH THE ARRAY LIST.
C
C         I               THE INDEX WHICH IS USED TO ADD VERTICES TO THE ARRAY
C                         LIST.
C
C         PTR             THE INDEX WHICH RUNS THROUGH THE LINKED LIST OF
C                         ADJACENCIES.
C
          INTEGER ADJ(1000), NEXT(1000)
          INTEGER VECTOR(100), VISIT(100)
          INTEGER LABEL(100)
          INTEGER LIST(100)
          INTEGER V, P, PTR
C
C         INITIALIZE ARRAYS.
C
          DO 10 I = 1,P
              LABEL(I) = I
              LIST(I) = 0
              VISIT(I) = 0
              VECTOR(I) = 0
       10 CONTINUE
          LIST(P+1) = 0
          I = 1
          N = 1
C
C         VERTEX V IS VISITED FIRST.
C
          LIST(1) = V
          VECTOR(V) = 0
          VISIT(V) = 1
C
C         GET NEXT UNVISITED VERTEX M.
C
       50 M = LIST(N)
          PTR = M
C
C         EXAMINE VERTICES ADJACENT TO M.
C
      100 PTR = NEXT(PTR)
          IF ( PTR .EQ. 0 ) GO TO 150
          J = ADJ(PTR)
C
C         CHECK IF VERTEX HAS BEEN VISITED.
C
          IF ( VISIT(J) .NE. 0 ) GO TO 100
```

FIG. 3.5.9 *(Continued)*

```
C
C      ADD VERTEX TO UNVISITED LIST AND TO SPANNING TREE.
C
          I = I + 1
          LIST(I) = J
          VISIT(J) = I
          VECTOR(J) = M
          GO TO 100
  150 N = N + 1
      IF ( LIST(N) .NE. 0 ) GO TO 50
      WRITE (6,2000) (LABEL(K), K=1,P)
 2000 FORMAT(1H1,30H  THE SPANNING TREE VECTOR IS .//,(1H0,40I3))
      WRITE (6,2100) (VECTOR(K),K=1,P)
 2100 FORMAT (1H0, 40I3)
      RETURN
      END
```

FIG. 3.5.9 (*Continued*)

A proof of correctness and an analysis of the complexity of Algorithm BFS can be given in exactly the same manner as for Algorithm DFS. We leave these to you. Also consider the following question: Which algorithm, DFS or BFS, is preferable? Or can this not be determined in all cases? You are encouraged to *test* both of these algorithms in order to answer these questions.

Recursion versus Iteration

A complete discussion of the advantages and disadvantages of recursive and iterative algorithms is beyond the scope of this book. So, too, is a discussion of the relationship between recursion and iteration, which is theoretically interesting and deep. Some have argued that any recursive algorithm should be transformed into an equivalent iterative algorithm. Others argue that it is senseless to do this in all cases.

Our view is simply that recursion is a natural technique for representing the algorithmic solution to a variety of problems in mathematics and computer science, and it is a design tool that should be kept in mind. Once an algorithm has been stated recursively, one has several options regarding implementation. The first and most obvious is to implement it in a recursive programming language. A second option is to implement it in a nonrecursive language simulating a pushdown store, as we did with Algorithm DFS. A third possibility is to consult the literature on a variety of "automatic" procedures for transforming a recursive algorithm into an iterative one. Finally, one could rethink the problem to see if recursion is really necessary—that is, one could design a new algorithm.

Exercises 3.5

3.5.1 *Factorials.* What would happen if one attempted to compute N! in Fortran using the recursive definition given at the beginning of this section?

3.5.2 *Binomial coefficients.* Write a recursive algorithm for computing the binomial coefficients:

$$\binom{n}{m} = \frac{n!}{m!(n-m)!} \qquad \text{for } n \geq m \geq 0$$

Implement your algorithm if a language which permits recursive calls is available.

*3.5.3 Let $G(n)$ denote the number of n-digit sequences of 0s and 1s that do not contain two or more consecutive 1s. Express $G(n)$ recursively. How does the $G(n)$ sequence compare with the Fibonacci numbers?

3.5.4 *Depth-first search.* Use depth-first search to find a spanning tree for the complete bipartite network $K_{3,3}$ (see Exercise 2.2.12).

3.5.5 *Breadth-first search.* Use breadth-first search to find a spanning tree for the complete bipartite network $K_{3,3}$. Compare this tree with the one found in Exercise 3.5.4.

3.5.6 *Partitions of integers.* Write a computer program to compute P(N) for $N = 1, 2, 3, \ldots, 50$.

3.5.7 *Partitions of integers.* Determine the number of computations which FUNCTION Q(M, N) performs in order to compute Q(M, N). Do we need to know *all* values of Q(A, B) for $A \leq M$ and $B \leq N$ to compute Q(M, N)?

3.5.8 *Partitions of integers.* Suppose we want to mail a package and the postage comes to 84 cents. Suppose further that all we have are large supplies of 4-, 6-, and 10-cent stamps. In how many different ways can we select stamps for the package? Let S(N) denote the number of partitions of the integer N using only the integers 4, 6, and 10. Express S(N) recursively by generalizing the recurrence relation for the Fibonacci numbers.

3.5.9 *Fortran identifiers.* Write a computer program that accepts as input an arbitrary character string X and outputs a YES if X is a proper identifier. Assume X is read in one character at a time.

***3.5.10 *Probabilistic recursion.* You have an opportunity to win some money playing the following game. In front of you is a large number of boxes containing money. The amount of money in any box is a random variable with a uniform distribution on [0, 1]. You pick a box, open it, and either accept or reject the money inside. If you accept, the game ends. Otherwise, you can pick another box. This procedure is repeated up to a maximum of five boxes (the fifth box must be accepted if it is opened). How would you try to maximize your expected winnings?

**3.5.11 We want to draw a set of n closed curves $C_1, \ldots, C_n$ in the plane according to the following rules: (a) no curve intersects itself; (b) C_1 is drawn arbitrarily; (c) for every $i \geq 2$, C_i intersects each of $C_1, C_2, \ldots, C_{i-1}$ in exactly two distinct points; (d) no three curves meet at a single point. Let R(n) denote the number of regions in the plane defined by constructing n closed curves by the rules above.   Check that R(1) = 2 and R(2) = 4.   (Note that there is always an unbounded region that includes the "point" at infinity.)

Derive a general recurrence relation for R(n) in terms of R(n − 1). Compute R(1), R(2), ... , R(25). If you do not have a recursive language available, do this by working your way up from R(1) to R(25).

3.6 SIMULATION

The majority of algorithms presented in this book solve relatively simple problems.   Most of these problems are easy to state and easy to model.   They do not involve many parameters, and they can usually be solved analytically. Furthermore, the resulting algorithms are reasonably short.

These problems contrast sharply with those involving large-scale systems, such as those for (1) military logistics, (2) NASA space flights, (3) administrative decision making, (4) factory production, (5) communication networks, or (6) files and inventories.

Problems relating to large systems are considerably more difficult to model, analyze, and solve.   For example, it is difficult to define all the variables that influence the system's behavior.   Interrelationships between variables are hard to determine.   Probability distributions of system random variables are typically unknown, and the inherent concurrency and continuous nature of system functions are not easy to model.

The advent of computers has made it feasible to approach the study of such complex systems by means of simulation.   *Computer simulation* is the process of conducting experiments on a computer model of a dynamic system.   The immediate purpose of these experiments is to observe the behavior of a system under a given set of assumptions, conditions, and parameter values.   The ultimate purpose might be to (1) formulate management policies, (2) determine optimal or feasible system configurations, (3) establish realistic production schedules, or (4) decide upon optimal economic strategies.

The advantages of computer simulations are numerous.   They enable one to study all parts of a fully integrated system in as much detail as desired, whereas analytically, only individual parts of a system can be studied.   All variables can be controlled and measured.   They enable one to obtain information about a real system when direct experimentation on the system is impractical.   Simulations make it possible to test a system before any time or money is invested in a corresponding real system.

Simulations can also be run with different time scales.   Time can be slowed down to examine features on a microscopic level that are difficult to analyze in a real system.   Time can be sped up to gain insight on a macroscopic level, for example, in order to study the long-term effects of various assumptions.   Time can also be stopped, backed up, and replayed to study unusual behavior patterns in greater detail. Often in real systems, once an experiment has been started, it cannot be stopped.

One might well ask the question: Why not simulate all the time? There are several partial answers to this question. First of all, simulation is an experimental technique. As such there is always the serious question of how to interpret the results. It is important to understand that the validity of the output depends on the degree to which the model and the underlying assumptions reflect the system's characteristics. Computer simulations can also be costly if the detail incorporated in the model becomes excessive.

The subject of simulation is too large to be treated comprehensively here. It will suit our purposes to present several of the important considerations that go into the design of a computer simulation; we shall also illustrate these with an example or two. This should help you to approach the design and analysis of a computer simulation algorithm in a reasonably intelligent fashion.

Perhaps the simplest and most common of all simulation algorithms are those which model waiting lines. These will be used as a point of departure for our discussion since they serve to illustrate the concepts that enter into many computer simulations. Waiting lines are also subject to a large number of different assumptions and extensions, which make them good examples for further study.

The basic objects of a simple waiting line are customers, who arrive at random intervals of time, and a server, who services each customer in a random service time. When customers arrive they are either served immediately, or they get in line, forming a queue, and are serviced on a first-come, first-served basis. Figure 3.6.1 illustrates a single-queue/single-server system.

The functioning of such a queue is determined by the following characteristics and assumptions:

1 There is a random variable X which determines the arrival time of the next customer. There are several possibilities for deciding when a customer arrives. We will assume that if customer K arrives at time t, then customer $K + 1$ arrives at time $t + T$, where T is a random variable, between 1 and some fixed integer MAXA, with a given probability distribution.

2 There is a random variable S which determines how long it will take to service customer K. The range of S is assumed to lie between 1 and some other fixed integer MAXC, with a given probability distribution. Once

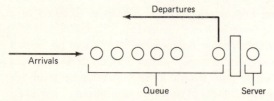

FIG. 3.6.1 A single-queue/single-server system.

initiated, this service continues until completed; that is, there is no interruption or preemption.

3 There is a queue of customers, serviced on a first-come, first-served basis. Once a customer gets into the queue, he or she remains there until serviced. Once serviced, the customer leaves the system.

4 All activities in the system are described by discrete "events," and hence the name "discrete-event simulation." An event, roughly speaking, can be described as anything which changes the "state" or configuration of the system. An event is said to be *primary* or *independent* if no other event can cause it to take place; otherwise it is called a *secondary* or *conditional* event. The independent events in the queuing system are

(*a*) The arrival of a customer
(*b*) The completion of service to a customer

5 There is an initially empty system. At time $t = 0$ the server is "idle" and there is no one in the queue awaiting service.

6 There is a discrete and fixed-increment time clock which governs the flow of activities. This clock moves in fixed units of time, which could be seconds, nanoseconds (when discussing simulations of computer operating systems), or months or years (when considering population simulations).

7 There is a random number generator used to determine the interarrival times for customers and the service times required by the server.

In order to design an algorithm for simulating a specific single-queue/single-server system, we must decide upon a number of matters:

1 What are the probability distributions for the interarrival and service times?
2 Which random number generator will be used to generate random times, and how will it be used to get these times?
3 What is the *queue discipline* (the properties of the queue)? For example, will those customers having the highest priorities go first? Will a customer ever become impatient and leave, either because the line is too long or is moving too slowly? Is there a limit on the number of customers that can be in the queue at the same time?
4 How long should the simulation be run? And should the clock move one unit at a time, or should it advance to the time of the next determined event?
5 How will events be "scheduled" which have been determined (randomly or nonrandomly) to occur at specific times? That is, how do we make sure that these events, and all other events which must follow because of them, actually take place, and take place on time? What is done in case of "ties"—that is, when two or more events occur simultaneously?
6 What data is to be gathered during the simulation? Typical data that one might be interested in obtaining are:

(*a*) Number of arrivals during the simulation

(*b*) Average queue length

(*c*) Average waiting time in the queue

(*d*) Maximum queue length

(*e*) Server utilization, that is, the percentage of time that the server was busy

(*f*) Average, maximum, and minimum service times

(*g*) Frequency distributions of queue length, that is, the percentage of time that the queue was of length *t*

(*h*) Number of no-wait customers during the simulation

Answers to the questions raised in 1 through 6 depend upon the specifics of the queuing system being modeled. But how does one begin to answer them?

One can start by observing the actual queuing system for a period of time and gathering data of the kind indicated in item 6 by recording the interarrival and service times. With most queuing systems, arrival times are subject to wide fluctuations depending on the time of day (peak-period phenomena). Given this data several additional questions arise. For example, what can be inferred from the data? Is the sample large enough? Can these times be approximated by certain standard distributions? Intelligent answers to these questions require an understanding of hypothesis testing, sampling theory, and the like. The interested reader can consult the references in Chap. 7.

Virtually all computing installations provide their users with a system random number generator for the uniform distribution on the interval [0, 1). This distribution can be made to simulate other random variable distributions using the techniques described in Sec. 6.3.

Most queuing systems have previously established queuing disciplines which are not subject to change. For these systems, therefore, the queuing discipline is not a design problem. But in other cases, such as computer operating systems, the determination of optimal queuing disciplines is an important objective of the simulation.

A basic assumption in discrete-event systems is that the state of a system changes only when events occur; otherwise the state remains constant. Thus, there is no need to continually advance a clock when nothing else is happening. The most common approach is to make all changes necessary because of the occurrence of an event, and then to advance the simulation time to that of the next event. This is called the *event-scheduling approach* to discrete-event simulation.

In order to illustrate this approach, we present in Fig. 3.6.2 a rough flowchart of an algorithm for simulating a single-queue/single-server system. Some reworking of this flowchart is necessary in order to produce a simulation program. In particular, there is no provision for stopping (or returning) in Fig. 3.6.2. For this purpose we set up three distinct integer variables ARR, COMP, and TERM, which denote the next ARRival time, service COMPletion time, and TERMination time for the simulation, respectively. We also create the variable CLOCK to record the current time. Since we are using the event-scheduling approach, set CLOCK equal to the time of the next scheduled event, which is either the next arrival or

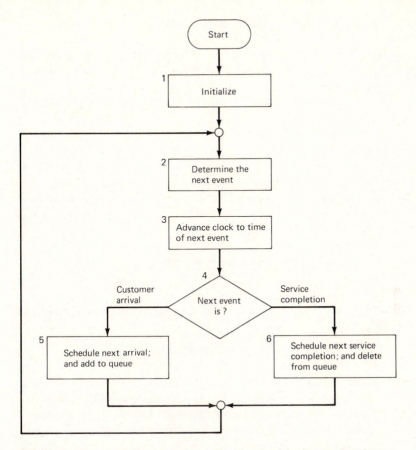

FIG. 3.6.2 Flowchart for simulating a single-queue/single-server system.

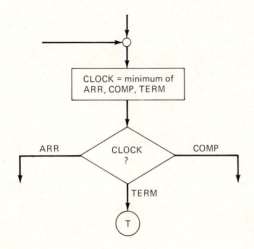

FIG. 3.6.3 Flowchart for determining the next event.

service completion time, or the termination time. Boxes 2, 3, and 4 then become as shown in Fig. 3.6.3.

Consider next what must be done in box 5 of Fig. 3.6.2 when a new arrival has taken place. First, we can determine the next arrival time according to a rule like

$$ARR = CLOCK + RANARR(1, MAXA)$$

where RANARR(1, MAXA) is a function which produces a random integer between 1 and some fixed constant MAXA with a specified probability distribution.

The second task to be performed when a new arrival occurs is either to add the customer to the queue or to move the customer directly to the front for servicing if the queue is empty. If the queue is empty (the length of the queue is defined by a variable QUEUE), we can determine the time this customer will depart (that is, the service completion time) by a statement of the form

$$COMP = CLOCK + RANCOM(1, MAXC)$$

Box 5 then looks like Fig. 3.6.4.

The completion of box 6 will also require the determination of the next service completion time:

$$COMP = CLOCK + RANCOM(1, MAXC)$$

However, we must take into account the special situation in which the queue becomes empty. Certainly, in this case the next completion time is meaningless. Therefore, we arbitrarily assign COMP = TERM + 1 to ensure that a completion is not the next scheduled event. Box 6 then looks like Fig. 3.6.5.

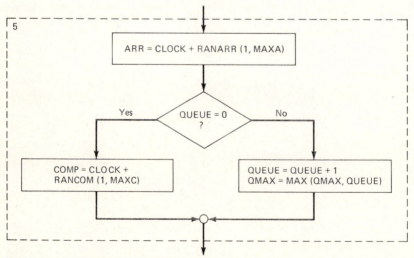

FIG. 3.6.4 Flowchart for a new arrival.

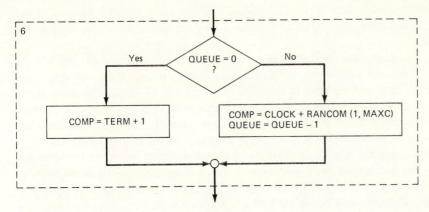

FIG. 3.6.5 Flowchart for a service completion.

What now remains to be done? First of all, we need to initialize all variables, such as ARR, TERM, QUEUE, QMAX, MAXA, MAXC, and COMP. We then need to define subprograms for computing RANARR and RANCOM. Lastly, we need to produce some output—at the circle labeled T in Fig. 3.6.3. Notice that this flowchart is still reasonably stripped down. For example, we have arranged for no data gathering to speak of; that is, we have only recorded QMAX.

We leave it to you to provide for the computation of any statistics you may desire. Notice also the implicit assumptions made in regard to queue discipline and size.

The queuing example above is not terribly complex. Therefore, we shall now present a more complicated, yet still manageable, problem which serves to illustrate the interdependence of several parameters on overall system behavior.

The Wheat-Mice-Cats Problem

The people of a certain village grow wheat as their major food source. They harvest 2 million pounds of wheat every July and store it in a barn. Although they consume only 100,000 pounds of wheat per month (their harvest is therefore a 20-month supply), they occasionally run out of wheat since mice in the barn eat away at their supplies.

The villagers, being primitive people, do not use poisons; instead, they try to control the mice by keeping a colony of cats in the barn. They discover that for some reason the cats do not solve their problem, for there are still occasional wheatless periods.

The only recourse of the villagers is to move the wheat from the barn whenever there is less than 1.5 million pounds remaining. The villagers then kill the mice by flushing them out. This mouse hunt is not terribly desirable, however, since it represents considerable work and manages to eliminate only 80 percent of the mice. In any case, the villagers decide that they are willing to do this once a year at most.

At this point, the villagers ask us to help solve the problem. We initially discover several additional variables that could significantly influence the situation. The first variable is the minimum number of cats to be kept in the barn. A second variable is the number of barns used to store the wheat. A third variable is the amount of wheat harvested per year (the villagers obviously are harvesting at peak efficiency, but maybe they should harvest *less* wheat!).

At this point it is clear that we need a mathematical model to simulate the wheat-mice-cat system on a computer. This will enable us, in a short time, to perform a large number of "experiments" in order to compare the effects of different strategies and hopefully find an optimum one.

In order to build a model, we need more facts and/or assumptions. For example:

1 Each mouse eats about 10 pounds of wheat per month.
2 Each mouse lives about 12 months—that is, approximately one-twelfth of all mice die of old age each month.
3 All mice will die within a month if there is no wheat in the barn. Unfortunately, 20 mice will then migrate in from the fields. Consequently, there are never less than 20 mice in the barn.
4 If there is more than 100 pounds of wheat per mouse, the number of mice will double each month. (If $W > 100 * M$, then births $= M$.) With less wheat, the number of births is the smaller of M (the current number of mice) and $W/100$.
5 The cats flourish with an abundant supply of mice. If there are more than 50 mice per cat (that is, $M > 50 * C$), then each cat eats 30 mice per month. When $M \leq 50 * C$ the number of mice eaten is 30 times the smaller of C and $M/50$.
6 Whenever $M < 25 * C$ (that is, there are fewer than 25 mice per cat), some cats die of starvation. When there are no mice, one-half of the cats die each month; otherwise, when $M < 25 * C$, $(25 * C - M)/50$ cats die per month.
7 When there are plenty of mice ($M > 50 * C$), each female cat (one-half of the total of cats) has a litter of six cats during both March and September. But when $M < 25 * C$, the cats are so undernourished that they do not breed at all. For intermediate mice/cat ratios, $25 * C \leq M \leq 50 * C$, the number of cats born (in March and September) varies from 0 when $M = 25 * C$ to $3 * C$ when $M = 50 * C$. The number is $3(M/25 - C)$ cat births.
8 Each cat lives about 10 years. Therefore, about 1 out of every 120 cats dies of old age each month. When $C < 120$, one cat dies each month with a probability of $C/120$. The number of cats is never allowed to fall below some minimum value MINCATS.

Now that we have all of this information, what is to be done with it? What solution are we seeking? What assumptions should be made?

Assume that we (1) want to study the effect that the minimum number of cats has on the number of mice, (2) will not undertake any mouse hunts, (3) will maintain only one barn, and (4) will continue to harvest 2 million pounds of wheat

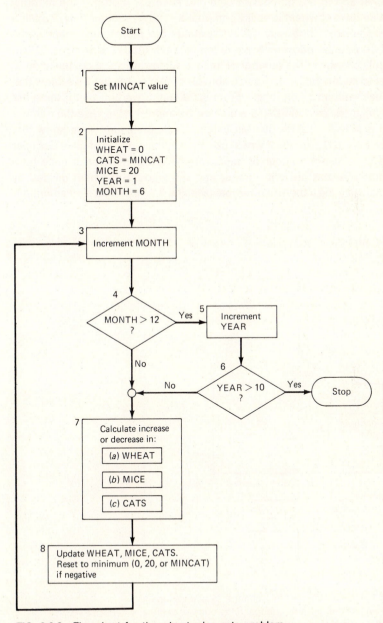

FIG. 3.6.6 Flowchart for the wheat-mice-cats problem.

each July. Let us now devise an algorithm for simulating the wheat-mice-cat system for a period of, say, 10 years, varying with each experiment the minimum number of cats. A rough flowchart of the algorithm for doing this is given in Fig. 3.6.6.

Let us examine box 7 in some detail. Here we compute the change in the amount of wheat and in the number of cats and mice per month. The monthly change in the amount of wheat is easily computed. If the month is July, 2 million pounds are produced. Otherwise 100,000 pounds per month are eaten by the villagers, and 10 pounds per month are eaten by each mouse (see Fig. 3.6.7a).

The monthly change in the number of mice is somewhat more complicated to compute (refer to statements 2, 3, 4, and 5 above). From statement 2 we know that MICE/12 die each month of old age. From statement 5 we find that if there are more than 50 mice per cat, 30 * CATS are eaten per month; otherwise the number of mice eaten is MIN(30 * CATS, 30 * MICE/50). From statement 4 we know that if there is more than 100 pounds of wheat per mouse, the number of mice born per month equals the present number of mice; otherwise the number of mice born equals the smaller of the present number and the amount of wheat divided by 100. Finally, all mice die if there is no wheat (see Fig. 3.6.7b). In a similar manner

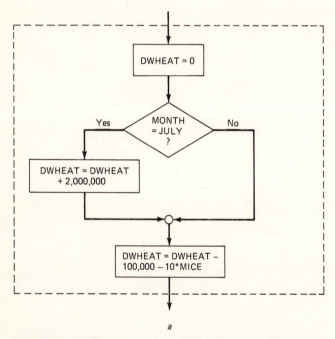

a

FIG. 3.6.7 (*a*) Flowchart for monthly change in wheat supply; (*b*, page 163) flowchart for monthly change in the number of mice; (*b*, *c*, page 164) flowchart for monthly change in the number of cats.

we can compute the monthly change in the cat population using statements 6, 7, and 8 (see Fig. 3.6.7c).

Figure 3.6.8 contains an explicit program and some sample output for this problem. The variables DWHEAT, DMICE, and DCATS represent the monthly changes (increase or decrease) in the WHEAT supply, MICE population, and CAT population, respectively.

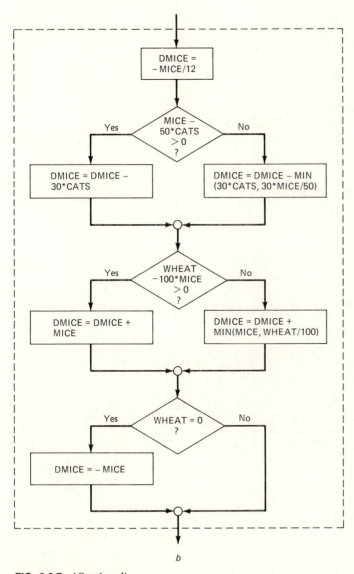

b

FIG. 3.6.7 (*Continued*)

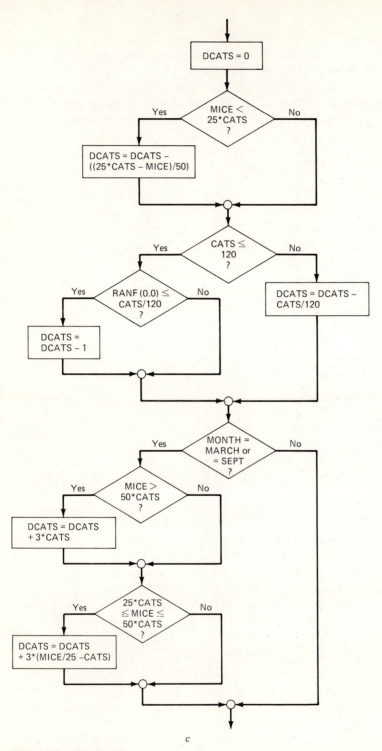

FIG. 3.6.7 (*Continued*)

```
      PROGRAM BARN(OUTPUT,TAPE6=OUTPUT)
C
C     THE ECOLOGY OF A BARN
C
C
C
C     WHEAT  -  NUMBER OF POUNDS OF WHEAT IN THE BARN
C     CATS   -  NUMBER OF CATS IN THE BARN
C     MINCATS-  MINIMUM NUMBER OF CATS
C     MICE   -  NUMBER OF MICE IN THE BARN
C     MINMICE-  MINIMUM NUMBER OF MICE
C     WHEAT  -  INCREASE OR DECREASE IN POUNDS OF WHEAT FOR A MONTH
C     ICATS  -  INCREASE OR DECREASE IN CAT POPULATION FOR A MONTH
C     MICE   -  INCREASE OR DECREASE IN MICE POPULATION FOR A MONTH
C     MONTH  -  1,2,3,....,12
C     YEAR   -  1,2,3,....,10
C
          INTEGER WHEAT,CATS,MINCATS,MICE,MINMICE,MONTH,YEAR
          INTEGER DWHEAT,DCATS,DMICE
C
C             VARY MINIMUM NUMBER OF CATS ,MINCATS,FROM 2 THRU 8
C
      DO 900 MINCATS = 2,8
C
C             INITIALIZE ALL VARIABLES
C
          WHEAT = 0
          MICE = 20
          MINMICE = 20
          YEAR = 0
          MONTH = 6
          CATS = MINCATS
C
C             PRINT INITIAL HEADING
C
      WRITE(6,1) MINCATS
    1 FORMAT(/////,15H NEW EXPERIMENT,//,9H MINCATS=,I2)
C
C             STEP EACH MONTH AND WRAP AROUND FROM DEC TO JAN IF NECESSARY
C             EACH YEAR IS 12 MONTHS STARTING WITH JUNE
C
C
   40 MONTH = MONTH + 1
      IF ( MONTH .GT. 12 ) MONTH = 1
      IF ( MONTH .NE. 7 ) GOTO 10
      YEAR = YEAR + 1
      IF ( YEAR .GT. 10 ) GOTO 900
      WRITE (6,2) YEAR
    2 FORMAT(//,5H YEAR,I3//,2X,5HMONTH,3X,5HWHEAT,5X,4HMICE,4X,4HCATS)
C
C             CALCULATE MONTHLY CHANGES IN WHEAT, CATS, AND MICE.
C
   10 IWHEAT = DWHEAT(MICE,MONTH)
      ICATS = DCATS(CATS,MICE,MONTH)
      IMICE = DMICE(WHEAT,CATS,MICE)
C
C             ADD MONTHLY CHANGES TO CURRENT LEVELS OF WHEAT, MICE, AND
C             CATS BEING CAREFUL TO MAINTAIN MINIMUM LEVELS OF EACH.
C
      WHEAT = MAX0(WHEAT+IWHEAT,0)
      MICE = MAX0(MICE+IMICE,MINMICE)
      CATS = MAX0(CATS+ICATS,MINCATS)
C
      WRITE (6,34) MONTH,WHEAT,MICE,CATS,IWHEAT,IMICE,ICATS
   34 FORMAT(4X,I2,3X,I7,3X,I6,3X,I4,4X,7HDWHEAT=,I9,2X,6HDMICE=,I6,2X,
     +   6HDCATS=,I5)
C
      GOTO 40
C
  900 CONTINUE
C
C             WHEN MINCATS VALUES HAVE BEEN USED, STOP.
C
      STOP
      END
```

FIG. 3.6.8 A Fortran implementation of the wheat-mice-cats problem.

```
         INTEGER FUNCTION DCATS(CATS,MICE,MONTH)
         INTEGER CATS,MICE,MONTH
C
C        CALCULATE INCREASE OR DECREASE, DCATS, IN NUMBER OF CATS.
C        CATS DIE OF STARVATION, DIE OF OLD AGE, AND HAVE LITTERS.
C        CATS HAVE A LIFE EXPECTANCY OF 10 YEARS.
C
         DCATS = 0
         IF ( MICE .LT. 25*CATS ) DCATS = DCATS - ((25*CATS-MICE)/50)
C
C        USE RANDOM NUMBERS TO DECIDE WHEN CATS DIE OF OLD AGE.
C
         IF ( RANF(0.) .LT. FLOAT(CATS)/120. ) DCATS=DCATS-MAX0(1,CATS/120)
         IF ( MONTH .NE. 3 .AND. MONTH .NE. 9 ) GOTO 20
         IF ( MICE .GT. 50*CATS ) DCATS = DCATS+3*CATS
         IF ( MICE .GE. 25*CATS .AND. MICE .LE. 50*CATS )
        +        DCATS = DCATS + 3*(MICE/25 - CATS)
   20    RETURN
         END



         INTEGER FUNCTION DMICE (WHEAT,CATS,MICE)
         INTEGER WHEAT,CATS,MICE
C
C        CALCULATE INCREASE OR DECREASE IN MICE POPULATION, DMICE.
C
C        MICE DIE OF OLD AGE, ARE KILLED BY CATS, AND INCREASE THEIR
C        NUMBER BY BIRTHS.  IF THERE IS NO WHEAT, ALL THE MICE DIE.
C
         DMICE = -MICE/12
         IF ( MICE .GT. 50*CATS ) DMICE = DMICE-30*CATS
         IF ( MICE .LE. 50*CATS ) DMICE = DMICE-MIN0(30*CATS,30*MICE/50)
         IF ( WHEAT .GT. 100*MICE ) DMICE = DMICE+MICE
         IF ( WHEAT .LE. 100*MICE ) DMICE = DMICE+MIN0(MICE,WHEAT/100)
         IF ( WHEAT .EQ. 0 ) DMICE = -MICE
         RETURN
         END



         INTEGER FUNCTION DWHEAT (MICE,MONTH)
         INTEGER MICE,MONTH
C
C        CALCULATE MONTHLY INCREASE OR DECREASE IN WHEAT, DWHEAT.
C        IF JULY THEN WHEAT HARVEST OF TWO MILLION POUNDS.
C        PEOPLE EAT 100,000 POUNDS OF WHEAT PER MONTH,
C        MICE EAT 10 POUNDS EACH.
C
         DWHEAT = 0
         IF ( MONTH .EQ. 7 ) DWHEAT = DWHEAT+2000000
         DWHEAT = DWHEAT-100000-10*MICE
         RETURN
         END
```

FIG. 3.6.8 (*Continued*)

NEW EXPERIMENT

MINCATS= 2

YEAR 1

MONTH	WHEAT	MICE	CATS			
7	1899800	20	2	DWHEAT= 1899800	DMICE= -20	DCATS= -0
8	1799600	27	2	DWHEAT= -100200	DMICE= 7	DCATS= -0
9	1699330	36	2	DWHEAT= -100270	DMICE= 9	DCATS= -0
10	1598970	48	2	DWHEAT= -100360	DMICE= 12	DCATS= -0
11	1498490	64	2	DWHEAT= -100480	DMICE= 16	DCATS= -0
12	1397850	85	2	DWHEAT= -100640	DMICE= 21	DCATS= -1
1	1297000	112	2	DWHEAT= -100850	DMICE= 27	DCATS= 0
2	1195880	155	2	DWHEAT= -101120	DMICE= 43	DCATS= 0
3	1094330	238	8	DWHEAT= -101550	DMICE= 83	DCATS= 6
4	991950	315	8	DWHEAT= -102380	DMICE= 77	DCATS= 0
5	888800	415	8	DWHEAT= -103150	DMICE= 100	DCATS= 0
6	784650	556	8	DWHEAT= -104150	DMICE= 141	DCATS= 0

YEAR 2

MONTH	WHEAT	MICE	CATS			
7	2679090	826	8	DWHEAT= 1894440	DMICE= 270	DCATS= 0
8	2570830	1344	8	DWHEAT= -108260	DMICE= 518	DCATS= 0
9	2457390	2336	32	DWHEAT= -113440	DMICE= 992	DCATS= 24
10	2334030	3518	32	DWHEAT= -123360	DMICE= 1182	DCATS= 0
11	2198850	5783	31	DWHEAT= -135180	DMICE= 2265	DCATS= -1
12	2041020	10155	31	DWHEAT= -157830	DMICE= 4372	DCATS= 0
1	1839470	18534	31	DWHEAT= -201550	DMICE= 8379	DCATS= 0
2	1554130	34454	31	DWHEAT= -285340	DMICE= 15920	DCATS= 0
3	1109590	46194	124	DWHEAT= -444540	DMICE= 11740	DCATS= 93
4	547650	49720	123	DWHEAT= -561940	DMICE= 3526	DCATS= -1
5	0	47363	122	DWHEAT= -597200	DMICE= -2357	DCATS= -1
6	0	20	121	DWHEAT= -573630	DMICE=-47363	DCATS= -1

YEAR 3

MONTH	WHEAT	MICE	CATS			
7	1899800	20	60	DWHEAT= 1899800	DMICE= -20	DCATS= -61
8	1799600	27	31	DWHEAT= -100200	DMICE= 7	DCATS= -29
9	1699330	36	16	DWHEAT= -100270	DMICE= 9	DCATS= -15
10	1598970	48	9	DWHEAT= -100360	DMICE= 12	DCATS= -7
11	1498490	64	6	DWHEAT= -100480	DMICE= 16	DCATS= -3
12	1397850	85	5	DWHEAT= -100640	DMICE= 21	DCATS= -1
1	1297000	112	5	DWHEAT= -100850	DMICE= 27	DCATS= -0
2	1195880	148	5	DWHEAT= -101120	DMICE= 36	DCATS= -0
3	1094400	196	5	DWHEAT= -101480	DMICE= 48	DCATS= 0
4	992440	259	5	DWHEAT= -101960	DMICE= 63	DCATS= 0
5	889850	347	5	DWHEAT= -102590	DMICE= 88	DCATS= 0
6	786380	516	5	DWHEAT= -103470	DMICE= 169	DCATS= 0

YEAR 4

MONTH	WHEAT	MICE	CATS			
7	2681220	839	5	DWHEAT= 1894840	DMICE= 323	DCATS= 0
8	2572830	1459	5	DWHEAT= -108390	DMICE= 620	DCATS= 0
9	2458240	2647	20	DWHEAT= -114590	DMICE= 1188	DCATS= 15
10	2331770	4474	20	DWHEAT= -126470	DMICE= 1827	DCATS= 0
11	2187030	7976	20	DWHEAT= -144740	DMICE= 3502	DCATS= 0
12	2007270	14688	20	DWHEAT= -179760	DMICE= 6712	DCATS= 0
1	1760390	27552	20	DWHEAT= -246880	DMICE= 12864	DCATS= 0
2	1384870	42259	20	DWHEAT= -375520	DMICE= 14707	DCATS= 0
3	862280	51986	80	DWHEAT= -522590	DMICE= 9727	DCATS= 60
4	242420	53876	79	DWHEAT= -619860	DMICE= 1890	DCATS= -1
5	0	49441	79	DWHEAT= -638760	DMICE= -4435	DCATS= 0
6	0	20	78	DWHEAT= -594410	DMICE=-49441	DCATS= -1

FIG. 3.6.8 *(Continued)*

YEAR 5

MONTH	WHEAT	MICE	CATS						
7	1899800	20	39	DWHEAT=	1899800	DMICE=	-20	DCATS=	-39
8	1799600	27	20	DWHEAT=	-100200	DMICE=	7	DCATS=	-19
9	1699330	36	11	DWHEAT=	-100270	DMICE=	9	DCATS=	-9
10	1598970	48	7	DWHEAT=	-100360	DMICE=	12	DCATS=	-4
11	1498490	64	5	DWHEAT=	-100480	DMICE=	16	DCATS=	-2
12	1397850	85	4	DWHEAT=	-100640	DMICE=	21	DCATS=	-1
1	1297000	112	4	DWHEAT=	-100850	DMICE=	27	DCATS=	-0
2	1195880	148	4	DWHEAT=	-101120	DMICE=	36	DCATS=	0
3	1094400	196	7	DWHEAT=	-101480	DMICE=	48	DCATS=	3
4	992440	259	7	DWHEAT=	-101960	DMICE=	63	DCATS=	0
5	889850	342	7	DWHEAT=	-102590	DMICE=	83	DCATS=	0
6	786430	451	7	DWHEAT=	-103420	DMICE=	109	DCATS=	0

YEAR 6

MONTH	WHEAT	MICE	CATS						
7	2681920	655	7	DWHEAT=	1895490	DMICE=	204	DCATS=	0
8	2575370	1046	7	DWHEAT=	-106550	DMICE=	391	DCATS=	0
9	2464910	1795	28	DWHEAT=	-110460	DMICE=	749	DCATS=	21
10	2346960	2601	28	DWHEAT=	-117950	DMICE=	806	DCATS=	0
11	2220950	4146	28	DWHEAT=	-126010	DMICE=	1545	DCATS=	0
12	2079490	7107	28	DWHEAT=	-141460	DMICE=	2961	DCATS=	0
1	1908420	12782	27	DWHEAT=	-171070	DMICE=	5675	DCATS=	-1
2	1680600	23689	27	DWHEAT=	-227820	DMICE=	10907	DCATS=	0
3	1343710	37711	107	DWHEAT=	-336890	DMICE=	14022	DCATS=	80
4	866600	44796	106	DWHEAT=	-477110	DMICE=	7085	DCATS=	-1
5	318640	46549	105	DWHEAT=	-547960	DMICE=	1753	DCATS=	-1
6	0	42706	104	DWHEAT=	-565490	DMICE=	-3843	DCATS=	-1

FIG. 3.6.8 (*Continued*)

Exercises 3.6

L3.6.1 *Barn problem.* Modify the algorithm developed in this section for the wheat-mice-cats problem to take into account one or more of the following: (*a*) an annual mouse hunt; (*b*) a second barn; (*c*) a smaller annual harvest; (*d*) the effects of random fluctuations in the size of the harvest; (*e*) owls and snakes.

L3.6.2 *Random walk.* An intoxicated beetle starts out in the exact center of a 10-inch × 10-inch square which is suspended above a vat of boiling oil. Once every second, the beetle moves 1 inch in an arbitrary direction. Using a simulation, compute P(N)—the probability that the beetle will have been boiled alive by time T = N. Also compute the average distance a *live* beetle will be from the center after N seconds.

L3.6.3 *Waiting line.* Simulate the following single-line/two-server system. Service times for server 1 have a uniform U(0, 3) distribution, while those for server 2 are uniform U(0, 4) distributed. The single line queues up before the two servers, and the customer at the front of the line goes to the first free server and to server 1 if both are available. The arrival times are normally $N(\frac{3}{2}, \frac{1}{4})$ distributed (be careful here). All times are in minutes. Simulate the system for 1 and 2 hours. Compute the average queue length and customer waiting time. What fraction of the customers do not wait at all?

L3.6.4 Modify the waiting line problem in Exercise 3.6.3 as follows. Customers become discouraged and do not bother to enter the line if five or more people are already waiting. What fraction of potential customers are lost? What is the average queue length and customer waiting time?

L3.6.5 *Computation of* π. Try the following procedure for computing an approximate value for $\pi = 3.14159\ldots$. The following equations describe a quarter circle with unit radius and area $\pi/4$ in the first quadrant of a 2-dimensional cartesian coordinate system.

$$x^2 + y^2 \le 1 \qquad \begin{array}{l} x \ge 0 \\ y \ge 0 \end{array}$$

Now consider the unit square $0 \le x, y \le 1$. Choose N uniformly distributed points at random in the square. If n of these points lie in the quarter circle, then n/N should approximate the area; that is, $n/N \simeq \pi/4$. An estimate of π is now possible. Estimate π for N = 100, 500, 1000, 5000. One member of the class might try N = 50,000 or more.

*L3.6.6 *More beetles.* At time $t = 0$ four beetles start at the four corners of a 10-inch × 12-inch rectangle. A fifth beetle starts at a random point inside the rectangle. Each beetle can move at the rate of 1 inch per second, and each continuously moves toward its closest neighbor. Simulate the activity of this system. Try various time-step sizes and plot the movements of the beetles.

4 A COMPLETE EXAMPLE

In Chap. 1 several basic steps that go into the complete development of an algorithm were discussed. Chapters 2 and 3 presented some basic design tools and methods which can be used in developing an algorithm. In this chapter many of these ideas are illustrated with a concrete example—a completely developed algorithm for finding a minimum-weight spanning tree in a network. This example is also used to illustrate many of the ideas that are involved in program testing and documentation.

The length of this chapter also makes it clear that we cannot develop other algorithms in this text as completely. Therefore, in subsequent chapters, we shall only highlight the more interesting aspects of the development of a given algorithm.

4.1 THE DEVELOPMENT OF A MINIMUM-WEIGHT SPANNING TREE ALGORITHM

Statement of the Problem

The director of a major computing facility is faced with the decision of whether or not to recommend the establishment of a computer network involving smaller computer facilities at N different sites. This decision is a rather complex one involving a large number of factors. The factors include computing resources available at each site, anticipated site usage levels, peak demands on the system, possible system degradation of the major facility, and, above all, the cost of the proposed network. This cost includes equipment purchases, establishment of communications links, systems maintenance, and the costs of running a job of a given type at a given site. The director asks us to determine the cost of such a communications network.

Thinking about the matter, we decide that what is needed is a minimum-cost network in which any site can communicate with any other. By calling a telephone company representative, we can determine the cost c_{ij} of establishing a direct communications link (leased line) between any two sites i and j in the proposed network. The telephone company representative informs us that the cost of a leased line is a function of the geographic distance between the sites, the desired transmission rate, and the desired communications capacity of the line.

After discussing this matter further with both the director and the representative, we succeed in determining the appropriate costs $c_{ij} > 0$; that is, we have a symmetric cost matrix similar to that used for the traveling salesman problem in Sec. 1.3.

Development of a Model

What constitutes a solution to the problem? We must decide which specific communications links should be established and which ones should not. That is, for every pair i and j, we must decide whether or not to establish a link at cost c_{ij}.

Therefore, a solution will consist of a modified matrix C′ of the original cost matrix in which the (i, j) and (j, i) entries equal ∞ if we do not establish the link; the entries equal c_{ij} if we do. Also, since every site is supposed to be able to communicate with every other site in the final network, each row (and each column) of C′ will have at least one finite entry. But will any modified matrix satisfying this condition on the rows and columns be a solution? While you are thinking about this question, let us consider a second model for the problem. Figure 4.1.1 demonstrates how any symmetric cost matrix can be represented by a weighted, complete network. Figure 4.1.1a presents a hypothetical cost matrix C for a communications network consisting of five sites, labeled 1, 2, 3, 4, and 5. For convenience the costs c_{ij}, for $i \neq j$, are assumed to be positive integers. Notice that $c_{ij} = c_{ji}$; that is, C is a symmetric matrix. Each element along the main diagonal is set to infinity to avoid establishing a communications link from a site to itself. The five vertices of the weighted, complete network in Fig. 4.1.1b, labeled 1, 2, 3, 4, and 5, correspond to the five sites of the communications network. For every distinct pair of vertices v_i and v_j, the edge between them is labeled by the cost c_{ij}.

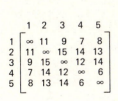

a

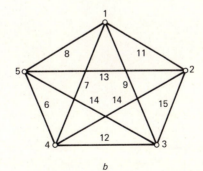

b

FIG. 4.1.1 (a) Cost matrix C; (b) corresponding weighted complete network G.

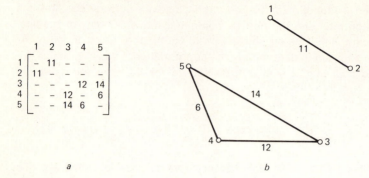

	1	2	3	4	5
1	–	11	–	–	–
2	11	–	–	–	–
3	–	–	–	12	14
4	–	–	12	–	6
5	–	–	14	6	–

a

b

FIG. 4.1.2 (a) C′; (b) G′.

Returning to the question of what constitutes a solution to the problem, consider the modified matrix C′ of C in Fig. 4.1.2, which satisfies the condition that every row (and column) has at least one finite entry. Could this possibly represent a solution? An examination of the corresponding subnetwork G′ of G reveals *visually* that this could not possibly be a solution since in G′ there is no way for sites 3, 4, or 5 to communicate with sites 1 or 2.

What we have discovered in Fig. 4.1.2 is that the subnetwork G′ is not connected. Therefore, let us form a connected network by adding a (cheapest) communications link between sites 1 or 2 and sites 3, 4, or 5—that is, the link between sites 1 and 4 with cost $c_{14} = 7$ (see network G″ in Fig. 4.1.3a). Could network G″ represent a solution? The cost of this network is the sum of the costs of all the communications links it contains. Notice what would happen if we were to delete the link between sites 3 and 5 (see network G‴ in Fig. 4.1.3b). The resulting network is cheaper and is still connected; that is, any site can communicate with any other site through the links.

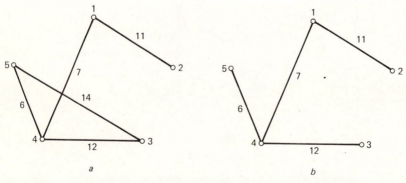

a

b

FIG. 4.1.3 (a) G″; (b) G‴.

What this illustrates is that a network corresponding to a solution to the problem will not contain a *cycle* of communication links. If a solution were to contain a cycle, then a cheaper solution could be found by removing the most costly link in the cycle. Therefore, a solution to the problem will consist of a cheapest subnetwork which is connected, contains no cycles, and contains every vertex. Thus, according to Theorem 2.2.4, this subnetwork will be a spanning tree.

Our original problem can now be stated mathematically as follows: Given a weighted, connected, and complete network G, find a minimum-cost (or weight) spanning tree of G.

Design of an Algorithm

Now that we have stated our problem mathematically, we must find a solution. Perhaps the most natural thing to do is to try a greedy algorithm—that is, select the cheapest edge first, then the next cheapest edge, and so forth. But in selecting edges we must keep in mind our three requirements: (1) the final subnetwork must contain all vertices and must be connected; (2) the final network must not contain any cycles; and (3) the final network must have the minimum possible weight. Looking ahead a bit, we must also be prepared to prove that our final network is indeed one of minimum weight.

Let us attempt to formulate this procedure as an algorithm.

Algorithm A To find a minimum-weight spanning tree T in a weighted, connected, and complete network G with M vertices and N edges.
Step 0. [Initialize] **Set** T ← a network consisting of M vertices and no edges; **set** H ← G.
Step 1. [Iterate] **While** T is not a connected network **do through** step 3 **od; and** STOP.
    Step 2. [Pick a lightest edge] Let (U, V) be a lightest (cheapest) edge in H; **if** T + (U, V) has no cycles **then** [add (U, V) to T] **set** T ← T + (U, V) **fi.**
    Step 3. [Delete (U, V) from H] **Set** H ← H − (U, V).

There are several questions we should ask about this algorithm:

1   Does it always STOP?
2   When it STOPs, is T always a spanning tree of G?
3   Is T guaranteed to be a minimum-weight spanning tree?
4   Is it self-contained (or does it contain hidden, or implicit, subalgorithms)?
5   Is it effective?

For the moment, you might think about questions 1, 2, and 3; the answer to all three is "yes." We shall concentrate instead on questions 4 and 5.

The answer to question 4 is "no," and the answer to question 5 is "maybe." Step 1 requires a subalgorithm to determine if a network is connected, and step 2 requires a subalgorithm to decide if a network has a cycle. These two steps can make the algorithm ineffective in that these subalgorithms might be time-consuming.

This suggests that we might improve Algorithm A if we could discover a method of constructing a spanning tree which guarantees, without having to check, that a connected network with no cycles is created.

The following algorithm, due to Prim, does just what we want. It is so simple that it is difficult to believe it always works. Its correctness will be proved in the next section.

Algorithm PRIM To find a minimum-weight spanning tree T in a weighted, connected network G with M vertices and N edges.

Step 0. [Initialize] Label all vertices "unchosen"; **set** T ← a network with M vertices and no edges; choose an arbitrary vertex and label it "chosen".

Step 1. [Iterate] **While** there is an unchosen vertex **do** step 2 **od**; **and** STOP.

Step 2. [Pick a lightest edge] Let (U, V) be a lightest edge between any chosen vertex U and any unchosen vertex V; label V as "chosen"; **and set** T ← T + (U, V).

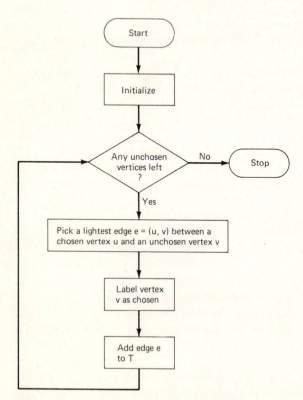

FIG. 4.1.4 Flowchart for Algorithm PRIM.

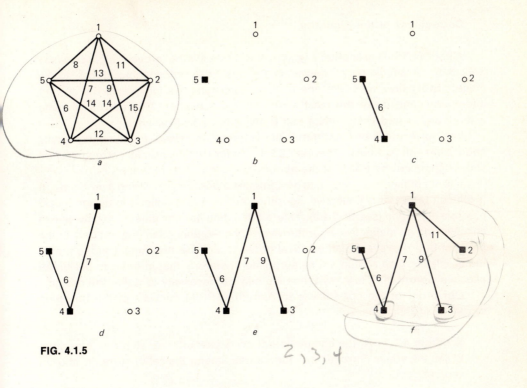

FIG. 4.1.5

2, 3, 4

A flowchart for Algorithm PRIM is given in Fig. 4.1.4.

Figure 4.1.5a shows the network of Fig. 4.1.1b; Fig. 4.1.5b through f illustrate the growth of the minimum-weight spanning tree T produced by Algorithm PRIM; a chosen vertex is indicated by a solid square, and an unchosen vertex by a circle. The initial vertex in Fig. 4.1.5b is 5.

Notice that both minimum-weight spanning tree algorithms could be used on an arbitrary connected network G; that is, input need not be restricted to complete networks. Edges which do not exist in G should be given infinite weight.

Working backward is often used to gain insight into the design of an algorithm. The key idea which led to the design of Algorithm PRIM could have been found by working backward. Assume that we have found by some method a minimum-weight spanning tree T in a network G. Somehow the edges of G that are not in T must have been eliminated from consideration. Let us put one of them back in T, say, edge e. By Theorem 2.2.4f, T + e has exactly one cycle, which we will call C. The weight of edge e must be greater than or equal to the weight of any other edge on C. This follows from the observation that if edge f on C had weight *greater* than e, then T + e − f would be a spanning tree of G with weight less than that of T. This would contradict the assumption that T is a minimum-weight spanning tree of G.

This suggests a forward procedure for finding a minimum-weight spanning tree that repeatedly finds a cycle in G and breaks it by removing that edge on the cycle with the greatest weight.

Correctness of the Algorithm

Algorithm PRIM is another example of what is called a "greedy" algorithm (see Sec. 3.2). A sequence of decisions (in this case, edge choices) has to be made. Every time we make one of these decisions, we look at all the current information and make the least costly choice possible. This choice is made without any regard to the effect that it might have on later choices.

The correctness of Algorithm PRIM is based on several fundamental results about trees—in particular, Theorem 2.2.4. Before we discuss its correctness, we should comment on a fact of life about the design of algorithms.

It is not difficult, in general, to design *some* algorithm for solving a problem. It is difficult to design an effective algorithm, and it is very difficult to design a best possible algorithm (see Sec. 1.3). More often than not, the difference between an effective and an ineffective algorithm is a very clear understanding not only of the problem but of relevant mathematical properties of the structures used to model the problem. One should not be surprised, therefore, that in order to design an effective algorithm, a few key theorems may be necessary to guide the design.

Our proof of the correctness of Algorithm PRIM consists of the following sequence of theorems.

Theorem 4.1.1 At the completion of every execution of step 2 of Algorithm PRIM, the edges currently in T form a tree among the set of currently chosen vertices.

Proof We proceed by induction on the number of times K that step 2 has been executed. Certainly, if K = 1, then there will be two chosen vertices and one edge in T between them.

Thus, let us assume that at the end of K executions of step 2, the edges currently in T form a tree, call it T_c, among the currently chosen vertices. Consider the (K + 1)st execution of step 2.

This essentially involves adding one new vertex and one new edge to T_c. Since this new edge is the only edge between the new vertex and T_c, the addition of this vertex and edge cannot create a cycle in T_c and leaves the new T_c connected. Thus, T_c is still a tree.

Theorem 4.1.2 At the end of Algorithm PRIM, T is a spanning tree of G.

Proof This now follows immediately from Theorem 4.1.1, which assures us that T is a tree, and the fact that T contains every vertex of G—that is, the algorithm stops only when all vertices are chosen.

Theorem 4.1.3 Let T be a subtree of a network G and let e be a lightest edge between a vertex in T and a vertex not in T. Then there is a spanning tree T′ in G which contains T and e such that if T″ is any spanning tree of G that properly contains T, then $W(T') \le W(T'')$.

Proof Let T″ be a spanning tree of G which contains T and has minimum weight among all spanning trees which contain T. Suppose further that T″ does not contain e. Consider the network $T'' \cup \{e\}$ and the unique cycle C of $T'' \cup \{e\}$ which contains e. Now C must contain an edge $f \neq e$ which joins a vertex of T to a vertex not in T. Why? By our assumptions, however, we know that $w(e) \leq w(f)$. Therefore, the tree obtained from T″ by deleting f and adding e,

$$T'' - \{f\} \cup \{e\} = T'$$

is a spanning tree of G which contains T and e and satisfies $W(T') \leq W(T'')$.

Theorem 4.1.3 essentially provides the justification for step 2 of Algorithm PRIM; it asserts that the basis for choosing a new edge in step 2 is sufficient to guarantee that there will exist a minimum-weight spanning tree of G which contains the chosen edge. Hereafter we will use MWST to denote a minimum-weight spanning tree.

Theorem 4.1.4 Let $G = (V, E)$ be a weighted, connected network, and let $e = (v, w)$ be a lightest edge incident to a vertex v. Then there exists a MWST T which contains e.

Proof Let T be a MWST of G which does not contain e. Consider the network $T \cup \{e\}$. According to Theorem 2.2.4f, $T \cup \{e\}$ contains exactly one cycle. This cycle contains two edges incident to vertex v, including $e = (v, w)$ and another edge, say, $f = (u, v)$. By the hypothesis, $w(e) \leq w(f)$, and thus $T - \{f\} \cup \{e\}$ is a MWST of G which contains e.

Theorem 4.1.5 Algorithm PRIM finds a MWST T in a weighted, connected network G with M vertices.

Proof By Theorem 4.1.2 we know that Algorithm PRIM finds a spanning tree.

By Theorem 4.1.4 we know that there exists a MWST T_1 which contains the first edge—call it e_1—chosen by Algorithm PRIM.

By Theorem 4.1.3 we know that there is a spanning tree T_2 which contains the first edge e_1 and second edge e_2 chosen by Algorithm PRIM. T_2 also has a minimum weight among all spanning trees which contain e_1; that is, $W(T_2) = W(T_1)$ since T_1 is our MWST.

By iterating this process, Theorem 4.1.3 guarantees the existence of a MWST which contains the first k edges chosen by Algorithm PRIM, for all $k = 1, 2, \ldots, M - 1$.

Finally, since the $M - 1$ edges chosen form a spanning tree T itself, it must follow that T is a minimum-weight spanning tree of G.

Implementation of the Algorithm

It is now time to write a computer program which finds a MWST using Algorithm PRIM. The algorithm will be implemented as a subroutine. This convention is used to avoid certain matters of input and output which depend on local computing requirements and questions of style. By this convention we do not mean to suggest that matters of input and output are always trivial matters. For example, input/output (I/O) time can be significantly greater than the time required to compute a MWST for very large networks.

The first question that might be asked is: What should be the input and output parameters for this subroutine? The opening statement of Algorithm PRIM partially answers this question: The input should be a weighted, connected network G with M vertices and N edges, and the output should be a minimum-weight spanning tree T of G.

We must decide therefore how to store a network in memory. In Secs. 2.2 and 2.3 we discussed several ways of representing a network in a computer. For now, we shall arbitrarily decide to use an $M \times M$ array C (that is, a cost matrix), where c_{ij} equals the weight of the edge in G between v_i and v_j. If there is no edge between v_i and v_j, then use $c_{ij} = 1{,}000{,}000$, that is, some value greater than the weight of any edge in G. We shall also assume, for convenience, that all weights are positive integers.

The output will consist of a sequence of $M - 1$ ordered triples, the elements of which are stored in three arrays—FROM(I), TO(I), and COST(I). The pair FROM(I), TO(I) represents the I*th* edge in the MWST T, whose weight is COST(I).

Having decided how to represent the input and output of the subroutine, we proceed to implement each step of Algorithm PRIM. Steps 0 and 1 suggest the need for an array CHOSEN, where CHOSEN(I) = 1 once vertex I has been "chosen," and CHOSEN(I) = 0 if vertex I is, so far, "unchosen."

However, step 2 suggests the need for two arrays, CHOSEN and UNCHOSEN, in order to find the minimum weight of an edge between a vertex in CHOSEN and a vertex in UNCHOSEN. With this in mind, we can imagine implementing step 2 by examining all edges between a vertex in CHOSEN and a vertex in UNCHOSEN. Once a minimum-weight edge has been found, the unchosen vertex on the edge can be deleted from the UNCHOSEN array and added to the CHOSEN array. Step 2 can then be repeated with the updated arrays.

A closer look at this approach to implementing step 2 reveals that a lot of redundant edge examination will occur, and that some difficulty will be involved in updating the CHOSEN and UNCHOSEN arrays. A more efficient implementation of step 2 is obtained by keeping only a list of unchosen vertices UNCHSN(I), which initially contains NUMUN = $M - 1$ vertices, and creating two additional arrays. The arrays are LIGHT(I), which equals the value of the lightest edge between the I*th* unchosen vertex and a chosen vertex, and VERTEX(I), which contains the chosen vertex on this edge.

With these arrays step 2 can be implemented as follows: (1) search through the array LIGHT for the lightest edge, say, LIGHT(K); (2) delete the K*th* element from the

UNCHSN list [by placing the last unchosen vertex UNCHSN(NUMUN) in UNCHSN(K)]; (3) decrease the value of NUMUN, which is the number of unchosen vertices, by 1; (4) record, or print out, the newly chosen LIGHT edge; and (5) using UNCHSN(K) as the newly chosen vertex, update the values of the remaining unchosen vertices by comparing LIGHT(I) with C(I, UNCHSN(K)).

Having decided how to implement the most difficult step of Algorithm PRIM, we can now settle upon an implementation of the remaining steps. Step 0 is handled by arbitrarily selecting vertex M as our initial vertex and placing vertices 1, 2, 3, . . . , M − 1 in array UNCHSN. Step 1 is implemented by checking to see if there are any remaining unchosen vertices, that is, if NUMUN = 0. These ideas are collected in the flowchart shown in Fig. 4.1.6.

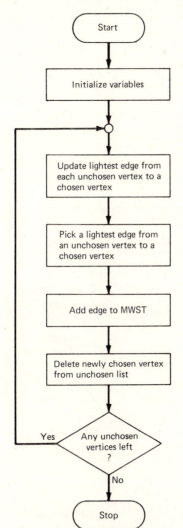

FIG. 4.1.6 Expanded flowchart for Algorithm PRIM.

```
      SUBROUTINE PRIM (C,M,FROM,TO,COST,WEIGHT)
C
C         THIS SUBROUTINE FINDS A MINIMUM WEIGHT SPANNING TREE (MWST)
C         IN A WEIGHTED, CONNECTED NETWORK G USING AN ALGORITHM DUE TO
C         PRIM (BELL SYSTEM TECH. J. 36 (NOV. 1957), 1389-1401).  THIS
C         IMPLEMENTATION IS A MODIFICATION OF A PROGRAM DUE TO V. KEVIN
C         M. WHITNEY (COMM. ACM (APRIL,1972), ALGORITHM 422).
C
C   ***FORMAL PARAMETERS***
C
C         C(I,J)    THE WEIGHT OF THE EDGE BETWEEN VERTICES I AND J,
C                   WHERE  1 .LE. C(I,J) .LE. 999999.
C                   IF THERE IS NO EDGE BETWEEN I AND J,
C                   THEN C(I,J) = 1000000, AN ARBITRARY LARGE NUMBER.
C
C         M         THE VERTICES OF G ARE NUMBERED 1,2,...,M,
C                   WHERE 2 .LE. M .LE. 100.
C
C         FROM(I)   THE I-TH EDGE IN THE MWST IS FROM VERTEX
C         TO(I)     -FROM(I)- TO VERTEX -TO(I)- OF COST -COST(I)-.
C         COST(I)
C
C         WEIGHT    TOTAL WEIGHT OF THE MWST.
C
C   ***SUBROUTINE VARIABLES***
C
C         EDGES     NUMBER OF EDGES IN MWST SO FAR.
C
C         LIGHT(I)  WEIGHT OF LIGHTEST EDGE, FROM VERTEX(I) TO UNCHSN(I).
C
C         NEXT      NEXT VERTEX TO BE ADDED TO MWST.
C
C         NUMUN     NUMBER OF UNCHOSEN VERTICES.
C
C         UNCHSN(I) ARRAY OF UNCHOSEN VERTICES.
C
C         VERTEX(I) VERTEX OF PARTIAL MWST CLOSEST TO VERTEX UNCHSN(I).
C
      INTEGER EDGES,LIGHT(100),NEXT,NUMUN,UNCHSN(100),VERTEX(100)
      INTEGER C(100,100),M,FROM(100),TO(100),COST(100),WEIGHT
C
C         CHECK FOR PROPER INPUT
C
      CALL CHECK(C,M)                                                1
C
C         INITIALIZE VARIABLES.
C
      EDGES = 0                                                      1
      NEXT = M                                                       1
      NUMUN = M - 1                                                  1
      WEIGHT = 0                                                     1
      DO 100 I = 1,NUMUN                                             1
          UNCHSN(I) = I                                              M-1
          LIGHT(I) = C(I,NEXT)                                       M-1
          VERTEX(I) = NEXT                                           M-1
  100 CONTINUE                                                       M-1
C
C         UPDATE LIGHTEST EDGE FROM EACH UNCHOSEN VERTEX
C         TO A CHOSEN VERTEX.
C
  200 DO 300 I = 1,NUMUN                                             M-1
          J = UNCHSN(I)                                              M(M-1)/2
          JK = C(J,NEXT)                                             M(M-1)/2
          IF ( LIGHT(I) .LE. JK ) GO TO 300                         M(M-1)/2,A
              VERTEX(I) = NEXT                                       B
              LIGHT(I) = JK                                          B
  300 CONTINUE                                                       M(M-1)/2
C
C         PICK A LIGHTEST EDGE FROM AN UNCHOSEN VERTEX
C         TO A CHOSEN VERTEX.
C
      K = 1                                                          M-1
      L = LIGHT(1)                                                   M-1
      DO 400 I = 1,NUMUN                                             M-1
          IF ( LIGHT(I) .GE. L ) GO TO 400                          M(M-1)/2,C
              L = LIGHT(I)                                           D
              K = I                                                  D
  400 CONTINUE                                                       M(M-1)/2
C
C         ADD EDGE TO MWST.
C
      EDGES = EDGES + 1                                              M-1
      FROM(EDGES) = UNCHSN(K)                                        M-1
      TO(EDGES) = VERTEX(K)                                          M-1
      COST(EDGES) = L                                                M-1
      WEIGHT = WEIGHT + L                                            M-1
      NEXT = UNCHSN(K)                                               M-1
C
C         DELETE NEWLY CHOSEN VERTEX FROM UNCHOSEN LIST.
C
      LIGHT(K) = LIGHT(NUMUN)                                        M-1
      UNCHSN(K) = UNCHSN(NUMUN)                                      M-1
      VERTEX(K) = VERTEX(NUMUN)                                      M-1
C
C         ANY UNCHOSEN VERTICES LEFT.
C
      NUMUN = NUMUN - 1                                              M-1
      IF ( NUMUN .NE. 0 ) GO TO 200                                 M-1,M-2
      RETURN                                                         1
      END
```

FIG. 4.1.7 SUBROUTINE PRIM.

In the Fortran program shown in Fig. 4.1.7, we arbitrarily decide to provide enough memory to handle a network having 100 vertices. The symbols on the far right of the code will be explained shortly; the numbers to the left will be discussed in the next section.

The CALL CHECK statement in Fig. 4.1.7 refers to a subroutine whose job it is to check that the value for M and the values of C are proper. If an improper value is found, SUBROUTINE CHECK will print an appropriate error message and stop execution. We leave the development of this simple subroutine to the reader.

Analysis of the Algorithm

We will now take up a complexity analysis of Algorithm PRIM. The objective is to try to determine the largest number of operations that this algorithm has to perform in order to find a MWST in an arbitrary, connected network with M vertices.

Before considering a detailed analysis of the implementation in Fig. 4.1.7, let us first give a rougher "order-of-magnitude" analysis.

Step 0 of Algorithm PRIM requires $O(M)$ operations in order to initialize the list of unchosen vertices. In our implementation, this involves $O(M)$ operations to initialize each of three $M - 1$ element arrays, plus a constant number (independent of M) of "bookkeeping" operations. Since the effort here is directly proportional to M, step 0 has $O(M)$ complexity.

Step 1, the iteration step, essentially requires $O(M)$ tests to determine if there are any more unchosen vertices.

Step 2 is executed exactly $M - 1$ times. Each execution of step 2 requires that we search through the current LIGHT list to find the edge of least weight from an unchosen to a chosen vertex. This effort requires $O(NUMUN)$ operations, where NUMUN is the current number of unchosen vertices (see Algorithm MAX of Sec. 1.2). Since $NUMUN \le M - 1$, this part of step 2 is bounded from above by $O(M)$ operations. After the newly chosen vertex I is identified, we need to update the unchosen list UNCHSN. For each unchosen vertex K, we must compare the current value of LIGHT(K) with C(K, I) in order to see if it is now cheaper to link any of the unchosen vertices to a chosen vertex using the newly chosen vertex I. One pass through the current LIGHT list is required; the updating process is bounded above by $O(M)$ operations. Since none of the other substeps of step 2 requires more than $O(M)$ operations, the complexity of step 2 is bounded from above by $O(M)$ [recall that $O(M) + O(M) = O(M)$].

We have shown that step 2 is $O(M)$ and that it is executed $M - 1$ times. Therefore, the entire effort expended on step 2 is $(M - 1)[O(M)] = O(M^2)$; that is, Algorithm PRIM has overall complexity of $O(M^2)$.

Algorithm PRIM is very efficient, particularly when we consider that we may have to examine $O(M^2)$ edges.[1] Thus, no MWST algorithm could do any better than $O(M^2)$, and Algorithm PRIM attains this lower bound.

[1]Observe that a complete network with M vertices has $M(M - 1)/2$ edges.

The most important objective in an analysis is to obtain the functional dependence of the number of operations performed by the algorithm on the problem size parameters. Of course, an algorithm that uses $2M^2 + 1$ operations on a network with M vertices is more efficient than one which uses $30M^2 + 500$ operations. However, both are $O(M^2)$ algorithms and their run times, which are roughly proportional to the number of operations, increase in essentially the same way as M gets larger. Contrast this with the case where there are two algorithms, one of which requires $1000M^2 + 2000M + 3000$ operations while the other needs $\frac{1}{2}M!$ operations to solve the same problem. For values like M = 2, the second algorithm is superior, but we are usually interested in larger values of M. How do the algorithms compare for M = 10, M = 20, or M = 100?

We now take up a more detailed analysis of Algorithm PRIM. This kind of analysis looks carefully at the coded implementation and counts the number of times each statement is executed, or at least tries to obtain a tight upper bound on this number. The sum of all these numbers gives a fairly precise estimate of the number of operations required by the algorithm for a problem of size M. This type of analysis is usually more tedious than an order-of-magnitude analysis, but it provides a more refined estimate of the complexity of the algorithm and the particular implementation under consideration.

In Fig. 4.1.7, on the far right of each statement is an upper bound for the number of times it is executed. Many of these numbers are readily verified and the reader should do so. However, some segments of code deserve special comment.

We are ignoring a detailed analysis of the complexity of the CALL CHECK statement, which is executed only once. It is not difficult to see that any implementation of this subroutine will have complexity $O(M^2)$ since all of the M^2 entries in the cost matrix must be examined.

The DO 300-loop is executed $M - 1$ times. Each execution of this loop involves NUMUN iterations, where the value of NUMUN changes from $M - 1$, to $M - 2, \ldots$, to 1. Thus the statement J = UNCHSN(I), which is placed after the DO 300 statement, is executed $M - 1$ times the first time that this DO-loop is executed, $M - 2$ times the second time the DO-loop is executed, and so forth. Therefore, it is executed

$$(M - 1) + (M - 2) + \cdots + 1 = \sum_{i=1}^{M-1} i = \frac{M(M - 1)}{2}$$

times.

The number of times each of the remaining statements in SUBROUTINE PRIM is executed is now easily determined. The only execution numbers remaining to be explained are those labeled A, B, C, and D. These can be seen to satisfy the equations

$$A + B = \frac{M(M - 1)}{2} \quad \text{and} \quad C + D = \frac{M(M - 1)}{2}$$

If we sum all execution numbers we can see that the number of statements executed by SUBROUTINE PRIM is bounded above by

$$4M^2 + 16M - 14 + B + D$$

Since B and D are both bounded above by $M(M-1)/2$, the total number of statements executed is bounded above by

$$5M^2 + 15M - 14$$

Thus the overall complexity is $O(M^2)$. Note that there is relatively little "play" in SUBROUTINE PRIM. That is, the number of statements executed for two different networks with M vertices varies only in the numbers B and D.

Although we count each statement as one operation, these statements do not take the same amount of time to be executed. Comparisons take longer than additions, for example. Such refinements in the analysis require a detailed knowledge of compilers and operating systems.

Exercises 4.1

4.1.1 MWST *algorithms* (*extension*).   Although our communications network problem was formulated in terms of a complete network, the algorithms of this section can easily be used to find minimum-weight spanning trees on arbitrary connected networks.   Show this explicitly.

4.1.2 Are there situations where Algorithm A might be better than Algorithm PRIM?

4.1.3 *Binary-decimal conversion* (*complete development*).   Completely develop an algorithm which converts binary numbers to decimal numbers, and vice versa.   You might restrict your attention to integer conversion.

4.1.4 *Pascal's triangle* (*complete development*).   Completely develop an algorithm which constructs the first n rows of Pascal's triangle.   If you need it, a definition (and short history) of the triangle can be found in Knuth (1969a), p. 52.

**4.1.5 *Algorithm* A (*design*).   Explicitly fill in all the missing subalgorithms in Algorithm A.

***L4.1.6 The Ace Security Agency is a private security patrol company.   They have n patrol cars and m customers.   Ace knows how long it takes to check out each customer's establishment, and how long it takes to travel between any two customers.   For obvious security reasons, Ace likes to vary its patrol schedules.   The patrolmen are paid on an hourly basis.

Completely develop an algorithm for this problem.   Make up whatever additional information you think is necessary.

*4.1.7 *Integer multiplication* (*complete development*).   Develop an algorithm which computes the product of two integers using only the three operations of addition, doubling, and halving.

4.1.8 Show explicitly that the average run time $T(M)$ of SUBROUTINE PRIM is $O(M^2)$.

*4.1.9   *Cycle algorithm* (*design, correctness*). Design an algorithm to determine if an arbitrary network has a cycle.   Prove that the algorithm is correct.

**4.1.10   *Tree algorithm* (*design, correctness*).   Design an algorithm to determine
if an arbitrary network is a tree.   Prove that the algorithm is correct.

**4.1.11   *Spanning-tree algorithm* (*hill climbing*).   Does the following procedure
always find a minimum-weight spanning tree T in a network G?

Algorithm **EXCHANGE**   To find a minimum-weight spanning tree T in a
weighted, connected network G with M vertices and N edges.

Step 0. [Initialize] **Set** T ← an arbitrary spanning tree of G; **and** let
the edges of G not in T be $e_1, e_2, \ldots, e_K$.

Step 1. [Examine each edge not in T] **For** I ← 1 **to** K **do** step 2 **od**; **and**
STOP.

Step 2. [Exchange heaviest edge] Let f be a heaviest edge in the
unique cycle in $T + e_I$; **set** $T = T + e_I - f$.

4.2   PROGRAM TESTING

There are three ways to test a program: (1) for correctness, (2) for implementation
efficiency, and (3) for computational complexity.   Taken together, these tests try to
provide experimental answers to the questions: Does the algorithm work?   How
well does it work?

Tests for correctness are supposed to verify that a program does exactly what it
was designed to do.   This is much more difficult than it may at first appear, especially for large programs.   It is important to realize that the fact that an algorithm
is mathematically rigorous does not guarantee that its translation into code is
correct.   Similarly, neither a lack of compiler diagnostics nor output that "looks
reasonable" is sufficient to guarantee that a program is correct.   This is amply
demonstrated by many examples of computer programs that ran for months or years
before errors were detected in them.

Tests for implementation efficiency attempt to find ways to make a correct
program faster or use less storage.   It is a code-refining process which reexamines
the implementation phase of algorithm development.

Tests of computational complexity amount to an experimental analysis of the
complexity of an algorithm or an experimental comparison of two or more
algorithms which solve the same problem.   Tests of this type are also used to check
a theoretical analysis of an algorithm.   If a theoretical analysis is too difficult to
obtain, there is still an obligation to gather some computational experience for the
algorithm.   This can be used, for example, to predict how long a program will run on
a given set of inputs.   Experimental analyses are rarely comprehensive, however,
and care must be taken not to overinterpret them.

Testing Correctness

Assume that we have a program that compiles and produces correct results for a few simple inputs.[1] The problem now is to test it so that it can be used confidently. We next present several ideas that should be part of any testing plan.

Preventive measures It is easier to test the correctness of a program if the earlier steps in its development have been carefully organized and carried out. To a considerable extent, the development of top-down structured programming was motivated by such considerations.

Plan for testing a program as it is being designed. Think about how each module can be tested and what data should be used as it is being written.

Also, plan ahead for anticipated modifications in a program at a later date. Ask the question: What changes are most likely to be made? A healthy concern for program generality can avoid costly revisions of entire segments of code.

Spot checks A number of simple tests or checks can be performed by hand:

1 Test the correspondence between an algorithm statement or flowchart and the program implementation. Make a slow pass over every statement, or block of statements in the program, and try to understand the purpose of each and its relationship to the algorithm or flowchart.
2 Make spot checks for such things as declaring all variables, changing *all* occurrences of a variable whose name has been changed, watching dimensions of arrays, and inserting debug or print statements. Make any changes as soon as they are perceived, or at least make a note of them; otherwise they are easily forgotten.
3 Test for improper values. In any statement, see if it is possible for a variable to have an improper value, and if it is possible determine how it could happen. Make sure that all variables are properly initialized, for example, on *every* call to a subroutine or procedure. Make sure that subscripts can never have values which are either too small or too large. Also check that improper values can never be passed to a subroutine or procedure.
4 Test for infinite loops. Attempt to determine whether or not there is any apparent way that a program could get into an infinite loop.

Testing all parts of the program Use a minimum testing standard: Test until every statement in the program has been used to produce a correct result. In particular, try each branch and each error condition at least once. Attempt to check as many different paths through the program as possible. Note that treelike programs have far fewer paths than those with complicated cycle structures.

[1]Many programmers would say that such a program is "debugged" but not "tested." Some use the two words interchangeably. Others use "testing" for the process of finding errors and "debugging" for the process of pinpointing and removing them. We distinguish three types of testing and use debugging for testing correctness.

Test data   A serious effort should be made to obtain good data for early testing.   The initial collection of test data must cover a broad range of cases, and correct answers should be known.   Data should be included which test all error conditions.   Some "nonsense" data might also be run to see if such data are handled correctly.

Avoid running data that essentially require the program to do the same thing over and over.   Also try to avoid test data whose answers cannot be verified.   Random data usually suffers from both of these defects.

Test the program on data at the extremes of the input range.   If the input range is defined by problem size, make a special effort to check very large and very small problems.   Pay particular attention to all null cases, for example, empty strings, networks with no vertices or edges, zero matrices, and so forth.   If a program will be used often, you can be sure that every possible extreme case will show up sooner or later.   Test them now.

Test the program for data that are outside the acceptable input range.   Watch out for the dangerous situation where the program produces appealing (but incorrect) results.

If another program is available which solves the same problem, use it as a check against the one being tested.   Although it is unlikely, keep in mind that it is possible for both programs to be wrong.

Some effort should also be made to test the program with real-world data if it is going to be used by others.   The cooperation of some potential users may be necessary.

Looking for trouble   Try everything you can think of to force a program into an error.   If possible, get someone else to do this for you.   An unbiased and fresh point of view might be just what is needed to locate errors that you have missed.

Time for testing   Testing usually requires a considerable amount of time and should not be rushed.   Budget time for it.

Retesting   If errors are found during testing, changes must be made to correct them.   Care should be taken not to pile one error correction upon another and to locate all places in a program affected by a given error.   Be sure that one error correction does not introduce others.   For this purpose, old test data might be saved and used to retest the program.

When to stop testing   There is no general answer to this question.   For any particular program, the answer depends on its potential use and the level of confidence desired by the programmer.   Large programs intended for important commercial use may have to be tested for months.   In fact, they have to be monitored for some time after release for production runs.   Often the question is answered by considerations of time and money.

Testing Implementation Efficiency

This kind of testing is concerned with finding ways to make programs run faster or use less storage. It is a waste of time for simple programs or programs that will rarely be used, but it is highly recommended for programs that are likely to be run frequently.

We should draw a distinction between implementation or coding efficiency and computational complexity. Suppose that we have designed an algorithm, and a theoretical analysis shows that it has $O(n^3)$ complexity, where n is some measure of problem size. Suppose further that a detailed analysis of an implementation of the algorithm reveals a tight upper bound of $2n^3 + 5n + 17$ on the number of statements executed. What do we expect to accomplish by testing implementation efficiency? It is important to realize that streamlining the code will usually not change the basic $O(n^3)$ behavior; this is essentially a property of the algorithm and its associated data structures. However, a more efficient code can change the work function associated with the implementation. For example, some reordering of the code might produce a tighter upper bound of $\frac{1}{2}n^3 + 5n + 20$. The new implementation will tend to run in one-quarter of the time required by the original implementation; the basic complexity is still $O(n^3)$.

A word of warning is in order. Extremely efficient code can destroy the clarity of a program and make it much more difficult to test for correctness. In general, changes which compromise clarity should be avoided unless they can be justified by substantial saving in time and/or storage.

There are many techniques which can be used to make a program more efficient. Many of them depend on a detailed knowledge of the local compiler or operating system. We shall ignore these and simply mention several of the more commonly used machine-independent techniques. We shall then discuss a useful and general testing procedure known as *profiling*.

Arithmetic operations The arithmetic operations of addition and subtraction are faster to perform than multiplication and division. Exponentiation is the slowest. Furthermore, integer arithmetic is generally faster than real arithmetic. Thus, the quantity X^2 is more rapidly computed as $X * X$ than $X ** 2.0$, and $X + X$ may be faster than $2.0 * X$.

Redundant calculations If a complicated expression is used in more than one place, compute it once and assign it to a variable. A good example of this involves the formula for finding the roots of a quadratic equation. Instead of writing

$$ROOT1 = (-B + SQRT(B ** 2 - 4.0 * A * C))/(2.0 * A)$$
$$ROOT2 = (-B - SQRT(B ** 2 - 4.0 * A * C))/(2.0 * A)$$

it is more efficient to use

$$\text{DENOM} = A + A$$
$$\text{DISCRIM} = \text{SQRT}(B * B - 4.0 * A * C)$$
$$\text{ROOT1} = (-B + \text{DISCRIM})/\text{DENOM}$$
$$\text{ROOT2} = (-B - \text{DISCRIM})/\text{DENOM}$$

(We suppress the test for an imaginary square root.) The amount of time saved depends on the local compiler.

Order in logical expressions Many compilers will stop evaluating certain logical expressions as soon as the result is known. For example, in

A .OR. B .OR. C

the evaluation will stop as soon as a TRUE value is found. Some time can be saved by ordering A, B, and C so that A is the most likely to be true, B the next most likely, and C the least likely.

Loop elimination The greatest potential for improving execution efficiency is with code segments that are repeated often. Such segments are almost invariably in the form of loops.

One way to cut down time spent in loops is to decrease the number of loops. This eliminates costly index incrementation and testing. For example, consider the following initialization code.

```
        DO  10  I = 1, 1000
            A(I) = 0.0
10      CONTINUE

        DO  20  J = 1, 1000
            B(J) = 0.0
20      CONTINUE
```

These statements involve 2000 incrementations and tests. All of this can be saved by initializing with a DATA statement at compile time. If this cannot be done, then the two loops should be combined.

Loop unrolling Further saving in loop overhead is possible using a technique known as *loop unrolling*. The overhead in the last example can be reduced with

```
        DO  10  I = 1, 1000, 2
            A(I) = 0.0
            B(I) = 0.0
            A(I + 1) = 0.0
            B(I + 1) = 0.0
10      CONTINUE
```

Excessive unrolling compromises clarity and makes the program unnecessarily long.

Inner loop streamlining Unquestionably, the single most valuable speedup technique involves streamlining inner loops. If nothing else is done to test efficiency, at least see if the computation performed in inner loops can be reduced.

For example, consider the following nested loop structure.

```
DO  30  I = 1, 50
   DO  20  J = 1, 100
      DO  10  K = 1, 200
                .
                .
                .

         STATEMENT X
                .
                .
                .

10             CONTINUE
20          CONTINUE
30       CONTINUE
```

What if STATEMENT X does not depend on I, J, or K in any way? As it stands, this statement is executed 1 million times. If it is removed from the entire loop structure and placed before the DO 30 statement, it is executed only once.

Execution profiles We should mention at this point that many compilers have built-in optimization routines which can automatically improve the efficiency of a program. However, we do not want to recommend that these compilers are the only means of improving the efficiency of a program, especially when improvements in efficiency can be obtained by redesigning the logic of an algorithm.

Time is valuable, and we do not want to waste it by going over every line of code in order to save a few microseconds of CP time. Is there an experiment that will enable us to find out what parts of the code take up most of the execution time? If we can isolate these segments, then we can concentrate our efficiency testing effort on them.

One good way to do this is by constructing an *execution profile* for the program. The program is monitored with an assortment of timers and counters, and an output listing is given which shows how many times each statement was executed and the total number of time units spent on each statement. Library programs which generate such profiles are becoming increasingly common at computer installations.

If a ready-made profiling package is not available, it is not too difficult to put together rough profiles. Counters can be placed throughout the program to keep track of the number of times statements or groups of statements are executed. Obtaining accurate timing costs is somewhat more difficult. Many internal clocks are not suitable for finding execution times for single instructions. One way to obtain a rough estimate of times is as follows. Find out how long it takes to execute the simplest possible assignment statement, such as A = 2.0. Define this as one unit of time. Then find the relative times needed to execute more complicated statements; for example, it may take two units to execute a simple assignment statement involving a subscripted variable, such as A(I) = 2.0. With a little effort and computational experience, a fairly complete table of relative times can be constructed.

Statistical studies using execution profiles reveal the remarkable fact that less than 5 percent of the code in most programs accounts for approximately 50 percent of the execution time. As we might expect, inner loops are responsible for much of this concentration.

Execution profiles are not only useful for testing implementation efficiency, but they are valuable for the two other types of testing. In testing correctness, profiles can be used to see what segments of code are, or are not, executed. Thus, profiles can help to check whether all parts of the program are tested. Profiles are also useful for verifying or experimentally constructing detailed complexity analyses on a statement-by-statement basis.

Testing Computational Complexity

It is difficult to test the computational complexity of most algorithms seriously and convincingly. There are two major problems: (1) the choice of input data and (2) the translation of experimental results into empirical complexity curves.

How do we choose data to test the complexity of an algorithm? The standard technique is to run the algorithm on a quantity of random data and to plot the run times against one or more problem size parameters. But how much random data should we generate, and how random are the random data? The quantity of data generated is usually determined by the programmer's patience and computer budget. Randomness is most often defined by the uniform or normal distribution because these distributions are the most convenient.

How about the translation of output data into empirical complexity curves? This problem is essentially hopeless if the input data depend on three or more parameters. Calculations become very complicated, and often an unbelievably large volume of output is needed to reach even the crudest conclusions. Fortunately, for many programs problem size is reasonably measured by a single parameter N—for example, some network problems and sorting.

What is done with these programs? Random data are run for some range of N, and average run times are computed for each value of N. These are plotted against N, and some method is used to fit a curve of a specified form to the data. This technique can be informative, particularly if it is used to support a theoretical complexity analysis.

How seriously should we take the fitted curve? We cannot give a definitive answer to this question, but there are some useful guidelines. (Warning: it is not hard to find a counterexample for every one of the following rules.)

1 Confidence in a fitted curve should increase with sample size. The rate of increase should be slower for more complex algorithms. Thus, roughly speaking, one should have more confidence in a good linear fit than in a good exponential fit.

2 Confidence in a fitted curve should decrease as N increases. The rate of decrease should be faster for more complex algorithms.

3 Never trust a polynomial fit to an algorithm that is suspected to be exponential. One may have a reasonable interpolating curve for the experimental range of N, but any stronger claim is probably unjustified.

4 Try to do a theoretical complexity analysis before an experimental analysis. The reverse order tends to produce the larger psychological bias.

5 Keep alert for experimental error and misinterpretation. In particular, do not confuse expected performance with worst case performance. Be alert for biases induced by random number generators.

6 It is remarkably easy to miss fractional powers or logarithmic factors in an experimental analysis. An $O(N^{5/2})$ algorithm is likely to be seen as an $O(N^2)$ or $O(N^3)$ algorithm.

7 Do not be overly trustful of "goodness-of-fit" parameters computed in conjunction with curve-fitting algorithms (such as least-squares library packages).

8 Do not forget the possibility of an error in the program. All of your results could be spurious.

Our discussion has been rather negative, but it is difficult to be otherwise. Nevertheless, complexity testing should be considered an important part of the development of any algorithm. Crude information, carefully obtained and cautiously evaluated, is a major improvement over no information at all. Experimental confirmation of a theoretical complexity analysis is a valuable addition to any program. Disagreement between theory and experiment should be taken seriously. The importance of computational experience is fairly self-evident.

Is it easier to compare two algorithms that solve the same problem? Can relative computational complexity be measured more confidently than absolute complexity? The answer to these questions is a qualified "yes" (in contrast to a "yes!"). Of course, there are serious problems:

1 It is important to remove "nuisance parameters" that artificially complicate matters. These include differences in machines, languages, and programmers. A clever programmer can implement an exponential algorithm so efficiently that it may appear to be superior to a polynomial algorithm implemented by a novice. Direct run-time comparisons will be meaningless if such differences are not eliminated or otherwise scaled out of the experiment.

2 How do we choose a set of problems on which to base the comparison? This is the same question that shows up whenever any kind of testing is discussed. The simplest answer is to use the union of all the

nontrivial problems which were used to develop and test the two algorithms separately. This is likely to produce some cases where each algorithm does very well (people who develop algorithms usually manage to find a few such cases) and a respectable mixture of random problems. Unfortunately, poor documentation often makes it difficult to follow this plan.

3 Care must be taken not to jump to conclusions. One algorithm beating a second on two out of three tests does not necessarily demonstrate the superiority of the first algorithm. As always, extensive testing is required before any sort of conclusion can be drawn. Keep alert for special classes of problems where the overall "loser" outperforms the "winner."

4 Absolute run time (corrected for differences in machines, etc.) is not the only way to measure relative quality. Storage requirements, special features, program length, and simplicity are others. A user may find it more attractive to use an algorithm that will solve a problem in 5 seconds of central processor time than to use one which requires 1 second. Why? Possibly because it would take several hours to learn to use the second algorithm and only a few minutes to learn to use the first.

Let us conclude this section with a discussion of how we might test SUB-ROUTINE PRIM (Sec. 4.1) for correctness, implementational efficiency, and computational complexity.

Unfortunately, it is difficult to approach the question of the correctness of SUBROUTINE PRIM in an unbiased manner since we are told in the program prologue that a modification of it has appeared in a journal and presumably is correct. However, we can still consider checking or testing a number of aspects of the subroutine.

First, is the subroutine (reasonably) structured? A check of the flowchart (Fig. 4.1.6) shows that it is. Secondly, does the flowchart correspond directly with the code? The comments (and blocks of code between them) can be seen to correspond to those in the flowchart. At this point we might make a mental check to verify that the logic of each block of code agrees with the intended purpose in the flowchart. Let us next make a list of *all* variables in the subroutine in order to (1) see if they are properly declared, (2) see if they are properly initialized, (3) determine the range of values of each variable, (4) count the number of statements which contain each variable, and (5) determine which variables are used as subscripts. See, for example, the accompanying table.

We should point out that most compilers automatically generate a listing of all variables in a program, together with the statements in which each appears.

For variables which are not declared, we can check to see if they need to be declared and if they are of the correct type. For variables which are not initialized (FROM, TO, COST), we can decide whether they need to be; in this case they do not. A check of the range of each variable can be used to aid in verifying that their use agrees with their intended purpose.

A count of the number of statements in which a variable appears can be helpful not only in determining the range of values it might assume but in determining

Variable name	Declared	Subscript	Initialized	Range	Number of statements
EDGES	Yes	*	Yes	$1 \rightarrow (M-1)$	5
NEXT	Yes	*	Yes	$1 \rightarrow (M-1)$	6
NUMUN	Yes	*	Yes	$(M-1) \rightarrow 0$	6
M	Yes		Input	$2 \rightarrow 100$	2
WEIGHT	Yes		Yes	$0 \rightarrow (M-1) * 1,000,000$	2
I	No	*	DO-loop	$1 \rightarrow$ NUMUN	13
J	No	*	Yes	$1 \rightarrow$ NUMUN	2
JK	No		Yes	$1 \rightarrow 1,000,000$	3
K	No	*	Yes	$1 \rightarrow$ NUMUN	3
L	No		Yes	Same as LIGHT	5
LIGHT(100)	Yes		Yes	$1 \rightarrow 1,000,000$	7
UNCHSN(100)	Yes		Yes	$1 \rightarrow$ NUMUN	5
VERTEX(100)	Yes		Yes	$1 \rightarrow (M-1)$	4
FROM(100)	Yes		No	Same as UNCHSN	1
TO(100)	Yes		No	Same as VERTEX	1
COST(100)	Yes		No	Same as L	1
C(100, 100)	Yes		Input	$1 \rightarrow 1,000,000$	1

which statements must be changed if the name of the variable is changed. For example, the names of the variables I, J, JK, K, and L in SUBROUTINE PRIM give little or no indication of their use in the subroutine. Furthermore, the variable I serves several different purposes. Let us therefore make the changes listed in the accompanying table.

Replace	By		Number of statements
I	I1	in DO 100 loop	4
I	I3	in DO 300 loop	5
I	I4	in DO 400 loop	4
J	VTX		2
JK	NEWCST		3
K	NEWVTX		3
L	LEAST		5

The listing of variables used as subscripts, together with the range of values they can assume, is useful in deciding if a subscript can get out of bounds. In this case all subscripts range in value from 1 to $M-1$ or 1 to NUMUN, and M and NUMUN are bounded above by 100 and below by 0. The possibility that a subscript can have the value 0 is prevented by the last two statements:

```
IF (NUMUN .NE. 0) GO TO 200
RETURN
```

With regard to the question—Could the subroutine get into an infinite loop?—it appears that this can happen if for some reason NUMUN never equals 0. It can be seen from the above list that while NUMUN appears in six statements, its value changes in only two:

$$NUMUN = M - 1 \qquad \text{(at the beginning of the program)}$$
$$NUMUN = NUMUN - 1 \qquad \text{(near the end of the program)}$$

Insofar as M is declared to be an integer and SUBROUTINE CHECK determines that M is an integer between 2 and 100, we can be reasonably confident that no infinite loop occurs because NUMUN never equals 0.

In regard to the question of looking for anything which could make SUBROUTINE PRIM fail, we might ask: Could the subroutine ever select an edge with weight 1,000,000? And if it did, what would it mean?

In regard to testing SUBROUTINE PRIM with data, let us suggest the following sample: (1) a network in which the values $C(I, J)$ or M are improper; (2) networks with $M = 2$ and $M = 100$ vertices; (3) several small networks with MWSTs which can be hand-verified; (4) a network in which all values $C(I, J)$ are the same; (5) a network in which $C(I, J) < C(I, J + 1)$ for $J = 1, \ldots, M - 1$, and $I < J$. In order to test that all instructions are executed, and in order to test the efficiency of the implementation, let us now examine an execution profile for SUBROUTINE PRIM.

The numbers to the left of each statement in Fig. 4.1.7 indicate the number of times it was executed when SUBROUTINE PRIM was used to find a MWST in a randomly generated network with 50 vertices. The profiler which we used did not indicate the number of times that statements GO TO 300 and GO TO 400 were executed. However, since we know that $A + B = 1225$ and $C + D = 1225$, we can conclude that they were executed $1225 - 151 = 1074$ and $1225 - 122 = 1103$ times, respectively.

This profile not only shows that each statement is executed at least once, but it confirms our complexity analysis of the previous section. For example, if $M = 50$, then $M(M - 1)/2 = 25(49) = 1225$. The profile also indicates that SUBROUTINE PRIM spends the vast majority of its time executing the six statements with execution numbers of 1225. Therefore, it is on these statements that we should focus attention in an effort to improve the implementation.

A close examination of the logic of the DO 300 and DO 400 loops reveals two places where execution time can be saved. First, it is not necessary to execute the DO 300 loop immediately after the DO 100 loop. We could insert the statement GO TO 350 immediately after 100 CONTINUE, where 350 becomes the label for the statement immediately after 300 CONTINUE—that is

```
300     CONTINUE
350     K = 1
```

Since this change in SUBROUTINE PRIM would eliminate the first execution of the DO 300 loop—involving $(M - 1)$ statements (at a cost of one new statement)—and since it does not unduly increase the complexity of the logic, it is worth making.   Secondly, the DO 400 loop could (with care) be made to read DO 400 I = 2, NUMUN.   This would save setting I = 1, as well as M − 1 comparisons of LIGHT(1) with itself, M − 1 GO TO 400 executions, and M − 1 CONTINUE executions; that is, 3(M − 1) + 1 statements would not be executed.   However, when NUMUN = 1, this DO-loop should not be executed.   This can be prevented by changing

```
          IF (NUMUN .NE. 0) GO TO 200
          RETURN
          END
```

to read

```
          IF (NUMUN .GE. 2) GO TO 200
              J = UNCHSN(1)
              JK = C(J, NEXT)
          IF (LIGHT(1) .LE. JK) GO TO 500
              VERTEX(1) = NEXT
              LIGHT(1) = JK
  500       EDGES = EDGES + 1
            FROM(EDGES) = J
            TO(EDGES) = VERTEX(1)
            COST(EDGES) = LIGHT(1)
            WEIGHT = WEIGHT + LIGHT(1)
          RETURN
          END
```

These new statements in turn can be seen to save the execution of 16 statements, with the added risk that the complexity of the logic has increased to the point where there might be an error.

Thus, the total saving attained by these changes is $5(M − 1) − 1 + 3(M − 1) + 1 + 16 = 8M + 8$ statements.   When compared with the upper bound of $5M^2 + 15M − 14$ total statements executed by SUBROUTINE PRIM, a saving of $8M + 8$ statements would amount to an improvement of roughly 14 percent for M = 10, 6 percent for M = 25, 3 percent for M = 50, and 1 percent for M = 100.

In Fig. 4.2.1, SUBROUTINE PRIM has been revised according to the preceding observations.   The execution numbers, for the same random network as in Fig. 4.1.7, indicate a saving of 3 percent over the unrevised subroutine.   However, this improvement should not be taken too seriously since it does not necessarily imply the same percentage improvement in execution time.   The amount of time actually saved in execution depends on the compiler used and the degree of optimization employed.

In an effort to determine how much computer time was really saved by these revisions, you might run a number of time trials of the original and revised subroutines for varying sizes of randomly generated networks.

Before concluding the discussion of profiling, we must point out that one should not expect one profile (as in this case) to give an accurate indication of where a program spends most of its time.   A large number of profiles may be necessary in order to build an accurate average profile.   We were lucky in this case since most of the upper bounds on the statement execution numbers were exact (only numbers B and D could not be predicted in advance).   If these upper bounds had been loose, the value of execution profiles would have been greater.

Finally, let us consider the problem of testing the computational complexity of SUBROUTINE PRIM by timing its execution.   This effort will not be terribly sophisticated, but it should give us an idea of what we might try to do.

We could record the central processor time used by the program on a given run.   We could also query a clock immediately before and after the execution of the main part of the code and print out the difference in times.

This method suffers an inherent inaccuracy, namely, the inaccuracy in measuring these times.   Most computers are capable of executing thousands of instructions in the time it takes to update a clock.   On the CDC 6400, for example, the clock is measured to three decimal places (.001 seconds), yet the basic instruction time for a statement might be roughly 10^{-6} seconds.   There is also an

```
      SUBROUTINE PRIM (C,M,FROM,TO,COST,WEIGHT)
C
C
C         THIS SUBROUTINE FINDS A MINIMUM WEIGHT SPANNING TREE (MWST)
C         IN A WEIGHTED, CONNECTED NETWORK G USING AN ALGORITHM DUE TO
C         PRIM (BELL SYSTEM TECH. J. 36 (NOV. 1957), 1389-1401).  THIS
C         IMPLEMENTATION IS A MODIFICATION OF A PROGRAM DUE TO V. KEVIN
C         AND M. WHITNEY (COMM. ACM (APRIL, 1972), ALGORITHM 422).
C
C    ***FORMAL PARAMETERS***
C
C         C(I,J)      THE WEIGHT OF THE EDGE BETWEEN VERTICES I AND J,
C                     WHERE  1 .LE. C(I,J) .LE. 999999,
C                     IF THERE IS NO EDGE BETWEEN I AND J,
C                     THEN C(I,J) = 1000000, AN ARBITRARY LARGE NUMBER.
C
C         M           THE VERTICES OF G ARE NUMBERED 1,2,...,M,
C                     WHERE 2 .LE. M .LE. 100.
C
C         FROM(I)     THE I-TH EDGE IN THE MWST IS FROM VERTEX
C         TO(I)       -FROM(I)- TO VERTEX -TO(I)- OF COST -COST(I)-.
C         COST(I)
C
C         WEIGHT      TOTAL WEIGHT OF THE MWST.
C
C    ***SUBROUTINE VARIABLES***
C
C         EDGES       NUMBER OF EDGES IN MWST SO FAR.
C
C         LIGHT(I)    WEIGHT OF LIGHTEST EDGE, FROM VERTEX(I) TO UNCHSN(I).
C
C         NEXT        NEXT VERTEX TO BE ADDED TO MWST.
C
C         NUMUN       NUMBER OF UNCHOSEN VERTICES.
C
C         UNCHSN(I) ARRAY OF UNCHOSEN VERTICES.
C
C         VERTEX(I) VERTEX OF PARTIAL MWST CLOSEST TO VERTEX UNCHSN(I).
C
```

FIG. 4.2.1 Revised SUBROUTINE PRIM.

```
   *        INTEGER EDGES,LIGHT(100),NEXT,NUMUN,UNCHSN(100),VERTEX(100)
   *        INTEGER C(100,100),M,FROM(100),TO(100),COST(100),WEIGHT
   *        INTEGER LEAST,NEWCST,NEWVTX,VTX
  * C
  * C          CHECK FOR PROPER INPUT AND INITIALIZE VARIABLES
  * C
  1*        CALL CHECK(C,M)
  1*        EDGES = 0
  1*        NEXT = M
  1*        NUMUN = M - 1
  1*        WEIGHT = 0
  1*        DO 100 I1 = 1,NUMUN
 49*            UNCHSN(I1) = I1
 49*            LIGHT(I1) = C(I1,NEXT)
 49*            VERTEX(I1) = NEXT
 49*    100 CONTINUE
  1*        GO TO 350
  * C
  * C          UPDATE LIGHTEST EDGE FROM EACH UNCHOSEN VERTEX
  * C          TO A CHOSEN VERTEX.
  * C
 47*    200 DO 300 I3 = 1,NUMUN
1175*            VTX = UNCHSN(I3)
1175*            NEWCST = C(VTX,NEXT)
1175*            IF ( LIGHT(I3) .LE. NEWCST ) GO TO 300
 151*                VERTEX(I3) = NEXT
 151*                LIGHT(I3) = NEWCST
1175*    300 CONTINUE
  * C
  * C          PICK A LIGHTEST EDGE FROM AN UNCHOSEN VERTEX
  * C          TO A CHOSEN VERTEX.
  * C
 48*    350 NEWVTX = 1
 48*        LEAST = LIGHT(1)
 48*        DO 400 I4 = 2,NUMUN
1176*            IF ( LIGHT(I4) .GE. LEAST ) GO TO 400
 122*                LEAST = LIGHT(I4)
 122*                NEWVTX = I4
1176*    400 CONTINUE
  * C
  * C          ADD EDGE TO MWST.
  * C
 48*        EDGES = EDGES + 1
 48*        NEXT = UNCHSN(NEWVTX)
 48*        FROM(EDGES) = NEXT
 48*        TO(EDGES) = VERTEX(NEWVTX)
 48*        COST(EDGES) = LEAST
 48*        WEIGHT = WEIGHT + LEAST
  * C
  * C          DELETE NEWLY CHOSEN VERTEX FROM UNCHOSEN LIST.
  * C
 48*        LIGHT(NEWVTX) = LIGHT(NUMUN)
 48*        UNCHSN(NEWVTX) = UNCHSN(NUMUN)
 48*        VERTEX(NEWVTX) = VERTEX(NUMUN)
  * C
  * C          ANY UNCHOSEN VERTICES LEFT.
  * C
 48*        NUMUN = NUMUN - 1
 48*        IF ( NUMUN .GE. 2 ) GO TO 200
  1*            VTX = UNCHSN(1)
  1*            NEWCST = C(VTX,NEXT)
  1*            IF ( LIGHT(1) .LE. NEWCST ) GO TO 500
  0*                VERTEX(1) = NEXT
  0*                LIGHT(1) = NEWCST
  1*    500 EDGES = EDGES + 1
  1*        FROM(EDGES) = VTX
  1*        TO(EDGES) = VERTEX(1)
  1*        COST(EDGES) = LIGHT(1)
  1*        WEIGHT = WEIGHT + LIGHT(1)
  1*        RETURN
   *        END
```

FIG. 4.2.1 (*Continued*)

inherent variability in the manner in which those clocks are updated, and this introduces an error that is difficult to measure.

In any event, this mechanism is the one we will use to test SUBROUTINE PRIM. By making many test runs on large networks, some of this variability can be partially averaged out.

Just before the variables are initialized in SUBROUTINE PRIM, insert a statement like

$$\text{TIMIN} = \text{SECOND(T)}$$

where SECOND(T) is a locally defined, real-valued system function using a dummy argument T, which gives the time accurate to a few milliseconds.

Since the program finishes the job of finding a MWST at the RETURN, we precede that statement with the statements

$$\text{TIMOUT} = \text{SECOND(T)}$$
$$\text{TIME(I)} = \text{TIMOUT} - \text{TIMIN}$$

which query the clock a second time and record the difference in times in a new array TIME(I).

As input data for test runs, we use a locally defined random number generator RANF(0.0) to generate random complete networks on M vertices. This can be done with the following code:

```
       MM = M − 1
       DO 10 I = 1, MM
         K = I + 1
         DO 10 J = K, M
           C(I, J) = C(J, I) = 1 + INT(RANF(0.0) ∗ 1000000.0)
   10    CONTINUE
```

The function RANF(0.0) generates a random REAL number between 0.0 and 1.0; the function INT produces the integer part of the REAL number RANF(0.0) ∗ 1000000.0; we add 1 to ensure that no weight has a value of 0 and arbitrarily decide that the weights of all edges will lie between 1 and 1,000,000. One might ask if the range of the edge weights can significantly influence run times? Apparently this is not the case. This conclusion can be supported by arguments from Sec. 4.1 and elementary probability theory, but the most convincing evidence is experimental. Networks were run with edge weights ranging between 1 and 100 and between 1 and 10^6, and variations in the average run times only occurred in the third decimal place (which is already subject to system error).

Let us now test the complexity analysis of Sec. 4.1. The primary objective is to determine the average run time for a network with M vertices.

How many random networks with M vertices should be run to obtain an average that can be used with reasonable confidence? An adequate sample size will be determined experimentally (with an implicit appeal to the law of large numbers[1]). Start with M = 50 since smaller values of M run so fast that inaccuracies in the third decimal place can be a nontrivial fraction of total run time. Now make runs on varying numbers of random complete networks with 50 vertices. We ran between 25 and 200 random networks and noticed an average of approximately .034 seconds per network for all sample sizes. This indicates that the average "settles down" quickly. Just to be safe, and in anticipation of the possibility that larger values of M might require larger sample sizes, we use a sample size of 100 randomly generated complete networks in the testing to follow. If the cost per run were much more expensive, we might not be so cavalier.

Consider M = 75. Before performing a run of 100 networks with 75 vertices, let us first test the predictions of Sec. 4.1. If SUBROUTINE PRIM requires run times proportional to M^2, and if networks with 50 vertices have average run times of .034 seconds, then networks with M = 75 vertices have average run times of about $(75/50)^2(.034) = .076$ seconds. A test of 100 networks with 75 vertices produced an experimental average of .075 seconds.

With M = 100, the average run time should be roughly four times that for M = 50 (why?). We would therefore expect an average of approximately .136 seconds. An experimental run of 100 networks produced an average of .129 seconds.

It does indeed appear that SUBROUTINE PRIM runs in time proportional to M^2. Let us now construct a function that predicts run time. Let T(M) denote the average run time using SUBROUTINE PRIM for a network with M vertices. Since $T(M) = O(M^2)$, we might be more explicit and write $T(M) = AM^2 + BM + C$, where A, B, and C are constants to be determined experimentally.

The T(M) curve is required to pass through our three experimental points:

$$M = 50 \qquad T(M) = .034$$
$$M = 75 \qquad T(M) = .075$$
$$M = 100 \qquad T(M) = .129$$

Since each of these points is on the T(M) curve, the following three equations must hold:

$$(50)^2A + (50)B + C = .034$$
$$(75)^2A + (75)B + C = .075$$
$$(100)^2A + (100)B + C = .129$$

This set of linear equations is easily solved for the coefficients A, B, and C. We find

$$A = 1.04(10^{-5})$$
$$B = 3.4(10^{-4})$$
$$C = 9.0(10^{-3})$$

so that

$$T(M) = [1.04(10^{-5})]M^2 + [3.4(10^{-4})]M - 9.0(10^{-3})$$

---

[1]In the present example, the law of large numbers essentially states that the experimental average is close to the true average as the sample size becomes very large.

Now consider M = 150. Using this equation, we would predict an average run time of T(150) = .276 seconds for networks with 150 vertices. We found an experimental value of .284, which indicates an "error" of $\frac{8}{284}$ = .028, or approximately 3 percent.

Some comments are in order concerning this error. The activity of trying to fit a curve of a certain kind to data in a certain range, and then using this curve to make predictions beyond that range, is known as *extrapolation*. Extrapolation with polynomials is dangerous. Small errors in the fitted data will change the values of the polynomial coefficients slightly. These small errors in the coefficients produce much larger errors as the argument of the polynomial increases beyond the fitted range. The experimental T(M) values are subject to errors in the third decimal places for reasons which we discussed earlier. The 2.8 percent "too low" error could easily be affected by changes in the observed last decimal places. A good, elementary discussion of extrapolation and the errors that plague it can be found in Hamming (1971).

Exercises 4.2

4.2.1 *Statement counts (testing).* Modify SUBROUTINE PRIM so that it will print out the total number of statements executed in finding a MWST. For random inputs, compute the averages for the statements with execution numbers A, B, C, and D in Fig. 4.1.7.

4.2.2 *Bowling score (development of an algorithm).* Develop an algorithm for keeping score of a bowling game. Use the standard rules covering strikes, spares, frames, etc. Implement and test your algorithm.

*L4.2.3 *Prime numbers (complete development, comparative testing).* Completely develop an algorithm which outputs all the prime numbers from 2 to some input value N. You might use the literature to find two such algorithms and comparatively test them.

*4.2.4 *Relative execution times (analysis).* Find approximate relative execution times for a variety of statement types on your local computing system. Express these times in terms of a unit which equals the time it takes to execute an assignment statement of the form A = 1.0. Then, for example, you might find that it takes two such time units to execute a simple assignment for a subscripted variable like A(I) = 1.0. Be careful. This problem is not as straightforward as it sounds.

*L4.2.5 *8-puzzle (implementation and testing).* Implement and test the backtrack algorithm for the 8-puzzle given in Sec. 3.3.

*4.2.6 *Interpolation and extrapolation (program testing).* Define and contrast "interpolation" and "extrapolation." Which is likely to be more reliable? You might consult a text on numerical analysis for help [for example, Hamming (1971)].

*__4.2.7__ *Least-squares data fit* (*program testing*). Look at a text on numerical analysis and learn about fitting curves to data using the *method of least squares.* Compare this procedure with the use of interpolating and extrapolating polynomials (see Exercise 4.2.6).

*L__4.2.8__ *Polynomial data fitting* (*program testing*). Code up and continue testing SUBROUTINE PRIM. Is the polynomial T(M) of this section a good interpolating polynomial (see Exercise 4.2.6)? Recomputation of A, B, and C will be necessary to fit your local machine. Why? How widely do individual run times differ from the average run times? Try using the least-squares method (see Exercise 4.2.7) to obtain a quadratic polynomial fit. How does the least-squares polynomial compare with T(M)?

L__4.2.9__ *Algorithm* PRIM (*design and implementation*). Implement Algorithm PRIM using linked lists. Compare the performance of the altered version of the program with the program in Fig. 4.2.1.

L__4.2.10__ Many people have observed that most programs appear to spend a large fraction of the total run time executing a small fraction of the statements in the code. Collect some old programs and use profiles to test this observation.

L__4.2.11__ Test the complexity of either PROGRAM KNIGHT (Sec. 2.1) or the heuristic outlined in Exercise 2.1.2.

__4.2.12__ What modifications or additions might be made to the discussion in this section if storage were a prime testing consideration?

4.3 DOCUMENTATION AND MAINTENANCE

General Discussion

One measure of the quality of a programmer is the degree to which he or she understands the overall programming process. An important and often neglected aspect of this is the process of communicating to others the details of a given program.

Many programmers learn to appreciate documentation the hard way. Situations like the following are common. A programmer's first assignment on the new job is to update an important program whose author is no longer present. The program consists of several thousand cards that are stored in a box in the corner of the office. The program contains very few comment cards, no flowcharts, and no other forms of documentation or instructions!

The primary purpose of documentation is to help a reader, or even the author, understand a computer program. It is essential to the usability and longevity of a program, and it can often save considerable time and frustration. Ideally, code should be written so that it is virtually self-documenting, but this is rarely possible in medium and large programs. For all but the simplest programs, code must be supplemented by both (1) external documentation and (2) program documentation.

External Documentation

In essence, external documentation is anything about the program that is not in the program itself. This is often collected in the form of a user's manual or technical report. It can be argued that some of the textual material in this book is really external documentation for the programs we present.

Depending on the size and complexity of the program, external documentation can take a variety of forms. Some of these include (1) flowcharts, (2) user instructions, (3) sample input and output, (4) complete record of the top-down development, (5) verbal statement of the algorithm, (6) references to sources of information, (7) directories of variable and routine names and their roles in the program, and (8) discussion of various special features (for example, results of testing, limitations, history, and mathematical background).

Program Documentation

We do not propose to offer any hard and fast rules for program documentation. There really are no such rules. However, we shall present a number of guidelines which are used by many good programmers.

Comments should be correct and informative Although this guideline is obvious, it is often violated. Consider the following code segment:

```
C
C      CHECK IF K IS LARGER THAN L;
C      THEN GO TO 150
C

       IF (K .GE. L) GO TO 150
          .
          .
          .
```

The comment preceding the IF statement is neither correct nor informative. It merely echoes the statement and provides no information about the purpose of the IF statement or what takes place at statement 150. The comment also gives the impression that statement 150 will be executed even if K is not larger than L. Furthermore, statement 150 is executed when K = L. Such a comment is worse than useless.

Comments which simply restate the code do nothing but clutter the program. Incorrect comments are dangerous; people will be inclined to believe them without checking the code itself.

Write comments as you write the code This practice helps to integrate documentation into the design and implementation stages. Useful comments can often be taken directly from flowcharts or verbal statements of algorithms. By writing comments as the code is being written, they are more likely to accurately reflect the logical steps in the program than if they are written later. Of course, it is a good idea to review all documentation after the program is finished.

Mnemonic names should be used for variables and subroutines   Variable and subroutine names should suggest their function in the algorithm. This practice helps the code document itself.

Start every program with a prologue   Give the reader useful information at the beginning of every program. The prologue might contain:

1   A good descriptive title, author identification, date of last revision, etc.
2   A brief description of what the program does, and possibly how it does it (or at least give references)
3   A list of all subroutines used, with a brief description of the purpose of each
4   A list and description of all variables whose function is not immediately obvious
5   Information on error returns and defaults
6   Information on input required and output produced

For some programs, all of the above may be unnecessary. One need not preface a 10-statement program with 100 comment cards.

Mini-prologues should be provided for most subroutines. Particular attention should be given to the documentation of communications between routines.

Do not overdocument   Do not use so much documentation that it is hard to find the program. This hardly helps the reader.

Avoid bad or overly clever code   The best documentation is clear code. Bad code and overly clever code breed errors and require extra documentation. Do not try to compensate for such code with many comments; rewrite the code.

Aim for neatness   It is easier to read clear, well-spaced code than it is to try to work through a congested program. Let us mention several specific visual aids.

1   Order variable and array declarations, either in some logical sequence or alphabetically. This makes it easier to check whether all variables have been declared, and whether their sizes and types are correct.
2   Order statement numbers. Statement numbers for executable statements should increase down the program listing. Also use higher statement numbers for formats than for executable statements.
3   Indent segments of code to reflect levels of logic in a program; indent, in particular, after DO and IF statements. See Sec. 2.1 and Appendix A for some guidelines.

4 Indent comments and separate them from code by means of blank comment cards.

5 Use good visual spacing. For example,

IF (ALPHA .LE. 0.5 + EPS) GO TO 100

is easier to read than

IF(ALPHA.LE..5+EPS)GOTO 100

6 Break up long expressions. Avoid logical or arithmetic expressions that take up most of a card or require continuation cards.

Generally, follow the golden rule on matters of neatness: Write the sort of program you would want to read.

Avoid nonstandard features If you expect a program to be used by others, and particularly if you expect it to be used at other installations, it is a good idea to identify all nonstandard Fortran features contained in the program [see ANSI Standard Fortran (1966)]. One might do this, without cluttering the body of the program with additional comment cards. The appropriate statements could be labeled by symbols in columns 73 through 80.

Properly define all input and output Documentation should provide the program user with all the information necessary to successfully input the data. This information may be included in the program if there is not too much program documentation already. Extensive input specifications should be put into a user's manual, and the prologue should make explicit reference to it.

One can argue that the output is the most important documentation of any program since it may be the only documentation that many users see. The program designer should strive to make all output self-contained.

The programmer has a responsibility to protect the user. It is usually a good idea to output the input in some easy-to-read fashion. This gives the user a good opportunity to recheck the input, and it provides a more complete record of the run. The program designer should also protect the user by providing meaningful error messages. One should try to anticipate what could go wrong and make provisions for the occurrence of errors since they will occur sooner or later. Particular attention should be given to potential input errors and degenerate cases—for example, DO-loops that do nothing for the given input, input arrays and variables that are too large or too small, etc.

One of the most tedious and unexciting parts of the implementation/documentation stages is the job of formatting visually attractive output. However, this should be treated carefully since unsightly or undecipherable output casts aspersions on the whole program.

Maintenance

Many programmers believe that no large program is ever fully tested or free of error.   Since the number of possible paths through a program is an exponential function of the number of IF statements in the code, it is rarely possible or practical to test them all.   Therefore, it is common to hear of errors in reasonably large programs that were not detected until months or years after the program was thought to be correct.   Repairing such programs can be difficult if they are not properly documented.

There are a variety of other reasons why programs need to be .updated, upgraded, or otherwise altered in time.   For example, it may be necessary to change the values of program variables, to increase the size of the input that a program can accept, to calculate and output some additional statistical information, to substitute a more efficient algorithm for an existing one, or to recode a program entirely, either for a new machine or system configuration, or in a different programming language.

This activity falls under the heading of *program maintenance*.   It is an important activity which extends the useful life of a program.   It has become such an increasingly important and time-consuming function that program maintainability can be more important than program efficiency.   Programs that are extremely clever, tight, efficient, and fast are generally harder to maintain.   If is often better to sacrifice a measure of speed in a program in order to improve one's ability to understand and maintain it.

Never update or otherwise alter the one and only deck or tape of any program (there should always be more than one copy, in any case).   All maintenance should be done on a copy of the program.   A copy of the old version should be kept for a respectable period just to be safe.   All maintenance changes should be carefully recorded.   Old documentation should be updated; this includes removing outdated or incorrect documentation in addition to the description of the changes.   An appendix should be added to any external documentation.   This appendix should thoroughly describe the maintenance operation, including such information as date of changes, reasons for making them, etc.

SUBROUTINE PRIM

Figure 4.2.1 provides a reasonably well-documented implementation of Algorithm PRIM, which is the result of improvements suggested during the analysis of the first implementation in Fig. 4.1.7.

The program prologue could contain more information, but what is given adequately explains the purpose, the nature of the input and output, and the definition of all variables.   Comments within the code have been held to a minimum, set apart with blank comment cards, and directly reflect the flowchart in Fig. 4.1.6.   The code has been partitioned into manageable pieces, and it has been split between pages at natural junctures in the logical flow.   Some statement indentation has been used to reflect the logic within the program.

5 COMPUTER SCIENCE ALGORITHMS

In the first four chapters of this text we discussed the majority of the fundamentals that are involved in the complete development of an algorithm. In this chapter these fundamentals will be applied to several problem areas in computer science.

Sections 5.1 and 5.2 develop a variety of algorithms in the practical and important area of computing that considers sorting and searching for information. In Sec. 5.1 we discuss and analyze two of the more sophisticated sorting algorithms, QUICKSORT and HEAPSORT, and prove that no comparison sorting algorithm can have better than an $O(N \log N)$ expected performance behavior. Section 5.2 discusses two efficient algorithms for finding a given record in a set of records which has been sorted by some key value. We also consider an algorithm for optimally storing records in a tree structure, according to a given set of probabilities that these records will occur. With this tree structure, the average number of comparisons required to find an arbitrary record is shown to be a minimum.

In this chapter we provide examples of algorithms in three other areas of computer science: arithmetic expressions, paging in virtual-memory computer systems, and parallelism.

Section 5.3 presents an inductive definition of both arithmetic and logical expressions. The infix, prefix, and postfix forms for describing an arithmetic expression as a linear sequence of symbols are given, along with a means of representing these expressions using binary trees. Two algorithms are given—one for evaluating an arithmetic expression in postfix form, and another for converting an arithmetic expression from infix to postfix form.

Section 5.4 provides an elementary discussion of memory allocation in a virtual-storage computer. After presenting five algorithms for handling page faults in such a computer, a simple model of program behavior is presented. This is used to test the relative effectiveness of these algorithms.

Section 5.5 concludes this chapter with an introduction to parallel algorithms, a subject currently in its infancy but one which may play an important role in future computing.

5.1 SORTING

Sorting has become an important subject in computer science primarily because considerable time is spent doing it. The realization that as much as 25 percent of all computer time is spent sorting data has placed a premium on efficient sorting algorithms.

Unfortunately, no sorting algorithm is best for every situation. It is even difficult to decide which algorithm is best for a given situation since a variety of factors can influence the effectiveness of a sorting algorithm. For example, the factors could include: (1) the number of elements to be sorted; (2) whether or not all elements will fit into the available main memory; (3) the degree to which the elements are already sorted; (4) the range and distribution of values of the elements to be sorted; (5) whether the elements are on disk, tape, or cards; (6) the length, complexity, and storage requirements of the sorting algorithm; (7) whether elements are likely to be deleted or added periodically; or (8) whether elements can be compared in parallel.

Sorted data are obviously easier to work with than random data. Elements are easier to find (as in a telephone book), update, delete, insert, and merge when they are sorted. With sorted data, it is easier to determine if any elements are missing (as in a deck of playing cards), and it is easier to make certain that all elements have been examined. It is also simpler to find all elements in common between two sets if they are both sorted. Sorting is used in compiling computer programs when symbol tables are constructed, and it is also an important means for speeding up almost any algorithm in which specific elements must be located frequently.

Usually the elements to be sorted are data records of some kind. Each record has a *key* field and an *information* field. The key field contains a positive number, usually an integer, and the records are ordered by key value.

In this section we present and analyze two of the most efficient sorting algorithms known—QUICKSORT and HEAPSORT—and establish theoretical best bounds for all comparison sorting algorithms. Two additional sorting algorithms are discussed in other sections: Straight Insertion Sort (SIS) in Sec. 2.4 and Parallel Sort (PARSORT) in Sec. 5.5.

QUICKSORT: An Expected Performance O(N log N) Sorting Algorithm

The main reason for the slowness of Algorithm SIS is that all comparisons and exchanges between keys in a sequence $a_1, a_2, \ldots, a_N$ take place between adjacent pairs. In this way it takes a relatively long time for a key that is badly out of place to work its way into its proper position in the sorted sequence. A natural way to try to speed up this process is to compare two items that are far apart in the sequence.

C. A. R. Hoare has devised a very efficient way of implementing this idea (Algorithm QUICKSORT) that improves the $O(N^2)$ behavior of Algorithm SIS with an expected performance that is O(N log N). This algorithm is explained in the following example.

	I↓														J↓	
	1	2	3	4	5	6	7	8	9	10	11	12	13	14	15	16	
Line	38	08	16	06	79	76	57	24	56	02	58	48	04	70	45	47	Action
1	38															47	decrease j
2	38														45		
3	38													70			
4	38												04				>
5	04												38				swap
6		08											38				increase i
7			16										38				
8				06									38				
9					79								38				>
10					38								79				swap
11					38							48					
12					38						58						
13					38					02							>
14					02					38							swap
15						76				38							increase i, >
16						38				76							swap
17						38		56									decrease j
18						38	24										>
19						24	38										swap
20							57	38									increase i, >
21							38	57									swap, decrease j
22	04	08	16	06	02	24	38	57	56	76	58	48	79	70	45	47	
	(1	2	3	4	5	6)	7	(8	9	10	11	12	13	14	15	16)	

FIG. 5.1.1 The initial steps of Algorithm QUICKSORT in sorting a sequence of integers.

Suppose that we want to sort the sequence in the first line of Fig. 5.1.1. Let us start by assuming that the *first* key in this sequence (38) is a good approximation to the key which will ultimately appear in the middle of the sorted sequence. Use this value as a pivot around which keys may be interchanged and proceed as follows. Maintain two pointers I and J, where I initially starts at the left (I = 1) and J at the right (J = N) of the sequence. Compare $a_I : a_J$. If $a_I \le a_J$, set $J \leftarrow J - 1$ and make another comparison. Continue *decreasing* J until a point is reached where $a_I > a_J$. Then interchange $a_I \leftrightarrow a_J$ (in Fig. 5.1.1, line 5, interchange 38 and 04), set $I \leftarrow I + 1$, and continue *increasing* I until $a_I > a_J$. After another interchange (at line 10, 79 ↔ 38), resume decreasing J. By alternating in this way—between decreasing

	1	2	3	4	5	6	7	8	9	10	11	12	13	14	15	16	Pushdown store
1	(04	08	16	06	02	24)	38	(57	56	76	58	48	79	70	45	47)	(8, 16)
2	02				04												(8, 16)
3		04			08												(8, 16)
4	(02	04	16	06	08	24)											(8, 16)
5			08		16												(8, 16)
6			(08	06)	16	(24)											(8, 16)
7	02	04	06	08	16	24	38	(57	56	76	58	48	79	70	45	47)	(8, 16)
8								47								57	
9										57						76	
10										45					57		
11											57				58		
12											48	57					
13								(47	56	45	48)	57	(79	70	58	76)	(13, 16)
14								45		47							(13, 16)
15									47	56							(13, 16)
16								(45)	47	(56	48)						(10, 11)(13, 16)
17								45	47	48	56	57	(79	70	58	76)	(13, 16)
18													76			79	
19													(76	70	58)	79	(13, 15)
20								45	47	48	56	57	58	70	76	79	

FIG. 5.1.2 The completion of Algorithm QUICKSORT in sorting the sequence in Fig. 5.1.1.

J and increasing I—work toward the "middle" of the sequence from both ends until I = J.

At this point two things will have happened. First, the original first key (38) will have worked its way to its proper position in the sorted sequence. Secondly, all keys to the left of this element will be less in value, and all keys to the right of it will be greater in value.

The same procedure can then be reapplied to the left and right subsequences in order to finish sorting the entire sequence. The last row (line 22) of Fig. 5.1.1 indicates that when I = J occurs, I = 7. The procedure is then reapplied to the subsequences (1, 6) and (8, 16).

The recursive nature of this algorithm suggests that one should put the subscript bounds of the larger of the two unsorted subsequences (8, 16) on a pushdown store and then proceed to sort the smaller subsequence (1, 6).

At line 4 of Fig. 5.1.2, 04 has worked its way to position 2, and the subsequences (1, 1) and (3, 6) must be sorted. Since (1, 1) is already sorted (that is, 02), we sort (3, 6), which in turn leads to line 6 where (3, 4) and (6, 6) must be sorted. At line 7 the subsequence (1, 6) is sorted. Now pop (8, 16) off the pushdown store and commence sorting this subsequence. At line 13 the subsequences (8, 11) and (13, 16) must be sorted. Place (13, 16) on the pushdown and sort (8, 11), etc. At line 20 the entire sequence has been sorted.

Before stating Algorithm QUICKSORT formally, we should indicate more precisely how it works. We use a pushdown [LEFT(K),RIGHT(K)] to store the left and right subscripts of subsequences yet to be sorted. Since it is faster to sort small subsequences using a more conventional sorting algorithm, Algorithm QUICKSORT has an input parameter M which specifies how small a subsequence must be before it is sorted in a more conventional way. We use Straight Insertion Sort for this purpose.

Algorithm QUICKSORT To sort a sequence of N keys A(1), A(2), . . . , A(N), N $\geq$ 2, in place, into ascending order. Subsequences of size less than M are sorted by Straight Insertion Sort. This algorithm makes use of a pushdown store (LEFT(K),RIGHT(K)) which contains the left and right subscripts of subsequences yet to be sorted. The variable K records the number of entries on the pushdown store.

Step 0. [Initialize pushdown] **Set** K $\leftarrow$ 1; LEFT(K) $\leftarrow$ 1; **and** RIGHT(K) $\leftarrow$ N.

Step 1. [Iterate] **While** K $>$ 0 **do through** step 12 **od; and** STOP.

> *Step 2.* [Pop off pushdown] **Set** L $\leftarrow$ LEFT(K); R $\leftarrow$ RIGHT(K); **and** K $\leftarrow$ K $-$ 1.

> *Step 3.* [Sort large set] **While** R $-$ L $\geq$ M **do through** step 11 **od.**

>> *Step 4.* [Initialize] **Set** I $\leftarrow$ L; J $\leftarrow$ R; **and** MID $\leftarrow$ A(I).

>> *Step 5.* [Compare MID :A(J)] **While** MID $<$ A(J) **do set** J $\leftarrow$ J $-$ 1 **od.**

Step 6. [Pass complete?] **If** J ≤ I **then set** A(I) ← MID; **and goto** step 11 **fi**.

Step 7. [Interchange] **Set** A(I) ← A(J); A(J) ← MID; **and** I ← I + 1.

Step 8. [Compare A(I) : MID] **While** A(I) < MID **do set** I ← I + 1 **od**.

Step 9. [Pass complete?] **If** J ≤ 1 **then set** I ← J; **and goto** step 11 **fi**.

Step 10. [Interchange] **Set** A(J) ← A(I); J ← J − 1; **and goto** step 5.

Step 11. [Pushdown] **Set** K ← K + 1; **if** R − I ≤ I − L
then set LEFT(K) ← I + 1; RIGHT(K) ← R; **and** R ← I − 1
else set LEFT(K) ← L; RIGHT(K) ← I − 1; **and** L ← I + 1 **fi**.

Step 12. [Start INSERTION] **For** J ← L + 1 **to** R **do through** step 15 **od**.

  Step 13. [Take next key] **Set** B ← A(J); **and** I ← J − 1.

  Step 14. [Compare B : A(I)] **While** B < A(I) AND I ≥ L **do set** A(I + 1) ← A(I); **and** I ← I − 1 **od**.

  Step 15. [Insert] **Set** A(I + 1) ← B.

Before discussing the complexity of Algorithm QUICKSORT, let us consider its proof of correctness. This algorithm presents another example where a proof by induction can be given. The induction hypothesis is that QUICKSORT correctly sorts all N − 1 element sequences. Let A(1), A(2), . . . , A(N) be an arbitrary N-element sequence. If the following three conditions are met after one pass through the sequence (step 11), it is immediate by the induction hypothesis that QUICKSORT will correctly sort the subsequences (1, I − 1) and (I + 1, N).

1 QUICKSORT correctly locates the proper final position of A(1), say, I.
2 All elements to the left of the I*th* position are less than A(1).
3 All elements to the right of the I*th* position are greater than A(1).

But the three conditions all follow from the fact that QUICKSORT compares every element of the sequence A(2), . . . , A(N) against A(1) on the first pass, making every interchange necessary to bring elements smaller than A(1) to the left and every element larger than A(1) to the right.

In order to analyze the performance of QUICKSORT, let Q(N) be the expected number of steps required to sort N elements. Let us also assume that M = 1—that is, that no improvement in speed is obtained by using Straight Insertion Sort on small subsequences.

On the first pass, QUICKSORT examines every element in the sequence and executes no more than cN steps, where c is some constant. At this point, two subsequences, whose lengths are I − 1 and N − 1, remain to be sorted. The expected number of steps required to sort N elements therefore depends on the expected number of steps required to sort I − 1 and N − 1 elements, where I varies from 1 to N.

If we assume that every value of I between 1 and N is equally likely for the final position of I in the sorted sequence, then

$$Q(N) \le cN + \frac{1}{N}\sum_{I=1}^{N} [Q(I-1) + Q(N-I)]$$

Since this sum can be seen to equal

$$Q(0) + Q(N-1) + Q(1) + Q(N-2) + \cdots + Q(N-2) + Q(1) + Q(N-1) + Q(0)$$

we have
$$Q(N) \le cN + \frac{2}{N}\sum_{I=0}^{N-1} Q(I) \qquad (1)$$

Let us show by induction on N that for $N \ge 2$, $Q(N) \le KN \log_e N$, where $K = 2c + 2b$ and $b = Q(0) = Q(1)$. That is, QUICKSORT requires a constant b number of steps to sort 0 or 1 elements.

For $N = 2$, $Q(2) \le 2c + \frac{2}{2}(Q(0) + Q(1)) = 2c + 2b = K$. Assume therefore that $Q(I) \le KI \log_e I$ for $I = 2, 3, \ldots, N-1$, and rewrite (1) as

$$Q(N) \le cN + \frac{2}{N}(Q(0) + Q(1)) + \frac{2}{N}\sum_{I=2}^{N-1} KI \log_e I$$

or
$$Q(N) \le cN + \frac{4b}{N} + \frac{2}{N}\sum_{I=2}^{N-1} KI \log_e I \qquad (2)$$

Now since $I \log_e I$ is concave upwards (see Fig. 5.1.3),

$$\sum_{I=2}^{N-1} I \log_e I \le \int_2^N x \log_e x \, dx \le \frac{N^2 \log_e N}{2} - \frac{N^2}{4}$$

Substituting this inequality into (2) leads to

$$Q(N) \le cN + \frac{4b}{N} + \frac{2K}{N}\left(\frac{N^2 \log_e N}{2} - \frac{N^2}{4}\right)$$

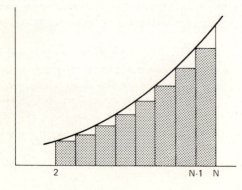

FIG. 5.1.3 A function which is concave upward.

or
$$Q(N) \leq cN + \frac{4b}{N} + KN \log_e N - \frac{KN}{2}$$

Finally, since $N \geq 2$,

$$cN + \frac{4b}{N} \leq \frac{KN}{2} = \frac{(2c + 2b)N}{2} = cN + bN$$

Thus,
$$Q(N) \leq KN \log_e N + \left(\frac{4b}{N} - bN\right) \leq KN \log_e N$$

The expected performance of QUICKSORT is therefore $O(N \log_e N)$. One final comment about QUICKSORT concerns the value of M to use in sorting small subsequences; a more detailed analysis of the complexity of QUICKSORT (see Knuth, vol. 3, p. 122) reveals that $M = 9$ is a good value to choose.

HEAPSORT: A Worst Case O(N log N) Sorting Algorithm

There are relatively few sorting algorithms which can guarantee no more than $O(N \log N)$ comparisons in the worst case. One of these is an ingenious algorithm due to Williams, which makes use of a special tree structure called a *heap*. A heap consists of a labeled, rooted binary tree of a given height h which has the following three properties:

1 Every end-vertex has height h or $h - 1$.
2 Every end-vertex of height h appears to the left of every end-vertex of height $h - 1$.
3 The label of every vertex is greater than the label of every one of its descendants.

An immediate consequence of property 3 is that the label of the root of a heap is the largest label in the tree. Figure 5.1.4 illustrates three labeled, rooted, binary trees which are not heaps and one (T_4) which is a heap. Notice that tree T_i violates property 1 for $i = 1, 2, 3$.

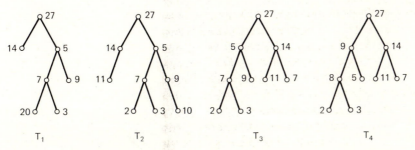

$$T_1 \qquad\qquad T_2 \qquad\qquad T_3 \qquad\qquad T_4$$

FIG. 5.1.4 Only tree T_4 is a heap.

The special structure of heaps allows them to be stored compactly in memory. In particular, we can store a heap with n vertices in an array A, where we store the two immediate descendants of the vertex in $A(i)$ in positions $A(2i)$ and $A(2i + 1)$. For example, the heap T_4 in Fig. 5.1.4 can be stored in a nine-element array A as follows:

	1	2	3	4	5	6	7	8	9
A	27	9	14	8	5	11	7	2	3

Notice, for example, that elements 11 and 7 in $A(6)$ and $A(7)$ are the two descendants of element 14 in $A(3)$. If $2i > n$, then $A(i)$ has no descendants and is an end-vertex of the heap. This order for storing the elements of a heap is the same as that produced by a breadth-first search of the tree (see Sec. 3.5).

Using this array representation, it is easy to sort the vertices in a heap. We illustrate this with heap T_4.

1 Interchange $A(1)$ with $A(n)$. That is,

27	9	14	8	5	11	7	2	3

becomes

3	9	14	8	5	11	7	2	27

which is equivalent to changing T_4 into the tree T_5 in Fig. 5.1.5.

2 Set $n \leftarrow n - 1$. This is equivalent to deleting vertex 27 from T_5 in Fig. 5.1.5.

3 Reconvert the modified tree into another heap. This is accomplished by repeatedly interchanging the new root with the larger of its two new descendants until a point is reached where it is larger than both of its

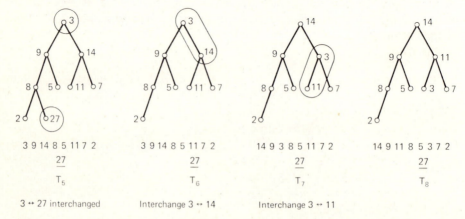

FIG. 5.1.5 The first four steps in sorting the vertices of the heap T_4 in Fig. 5.1.4.

descendants. In T_7, vertices 3 and 14 have been interchanged, and in T_8, vertices 3 and 11 have been interchanged according to this procedure. The tree T_8 is therefore the reconverted heap.

4 Repeat steps 1, 2, and 3 until $n = 1$.

Figure 5.1.6 illustrates the completion of this sorting process for the heap T_4 in Fig. 5.1.5.

Since this sorting procedure requires a heap as input, we need an algorithm to convert an arbitrary array of integers into a heap. The algorithm for doing this uses step 3 of the previous process. It is illustrated with the array of integers in Fig. 5.1.7a. Start by imagining that the integers in this array are stored in a rooted binary tree as if it were a heap (see Fig. 5.1.7b). Then proceed from right to left through the array, checking to see if $A(i)$ is greater than $A(2i)$ and $A(2i + 1)$, for $i = \lfloor n/2 \rfloor, \dots, 1$ (see Fig. 5.1.8). If for some value of i, $A(i)$ is not greater than $A(2i)$ and $A(2i + 1)$, then apply the procedure indicated in step 3 and interchange $A(i)$ with the larger of $A(2i)$ and $A(2i + 1)$.

Figure 5.1.8 shows that the array in Fig. 5.1.7a has been converted after 15 steps into the heap T_4 in Fig. 5.1.4.

It is now time to state Algorithm HEAPSORT formally. First we state Algorithm HEAP, the "subroutine" used by HEAPSORT to convert a linear array into a heap.

Algorithm HEAP   To place an element A(J) into its proper place in a heap having elements A(1), A(2), . . . , A(M), $M \geq 3$, and $1 \leq J \leq M$.

Step 1. [Place A(J) in heap] **While** $2J + 1 \leq M$ AND $(A(J) < A(2J)$ OR $A(J) < A(2J + 1))$
   do [Interchange with A(J)] **If** $A(2J) > A(2J + 1)$
      then set TEMP $\leftarrow$ A(J); A(J) $\leftarrow$ A(2J); A(2J) $\leftarrow$ TEMP; **and** J $\leftarrow$ 2J
      else set TEMP $\leftarrow$ A(J); A(J) $\leftarrow$ A(2J + 1); A(2J + 1) $\leftarrow$ TEMP; **and** J $\leftarrow$ 2J + 1 **fi od**.

Step 2. [Is 2J = M?] **If** $2J = M$ AND $A(J) < A(2J)$
   then set TEMP $\leftarrow$ A(J); A(J) $\leftarrow$ A(2J); **and** A(2J) $\leftarrow$ TEMP **fi**; **and** RETURN.

Algorithm HEAPSORT   To sort (in place) an array of integers A(1), A(2), . . . , A(N), $N \geq 2$, into ascending order.

Step 0. [Initialize] **Set** I $\leftarrow \lfloor N/2 \rfloor$; **and** M $\leftarrow$ N.

Step 1. [Create heap] **Do through** step 3 **while** I $\geq$ 1 **od**.
   Step 2. [Place A(I) in heap] CALL HEAP(I, A, M).
   Step 3. [New value of I] **Set** I $\leftarrow$ I − 1.

Step 4. [Sort] **Do through** step 6 **while** M $\geq$ 1 **od**; **and** STOP.
   Step 5. [Interchange   A(1) $\leftrightarrow$ A(M)]   **Set**   TEMP $\leftarrow$ A(1);   A(1) $\leftarrow$ A(M); A(M) $\leftarrow$ TEMP; **and** M $\leftarrow$ M − 1.
   Step 6. [Place A(1) in heap] CALL HEAP (1, A, M).

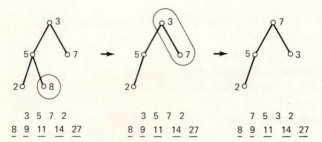

FIG. 5.1.6 The complete sequence of steps in sorting the vertices of the heap T_8 in Fig. 5.1.5.

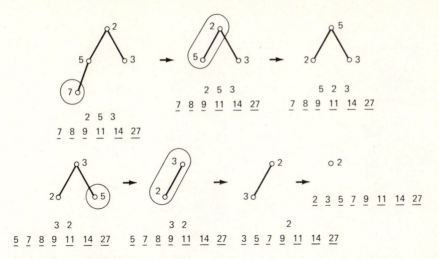

FIG. 5.1.6 (*Continued*)

Implementations of Algorithms HEAP and HEAPSORT follow (see Figs. 5.1.9 and 5.1.10). The proof of correctness of Algorithm HEAPSORT is rather long and tedious. The interested reader should consult Knuth (1973).

The complexity analysis of SUBROUTINE HEAPSORT is relatively simple. The maximum number of times that a statement can be executed is indicated to the right of each statement in Fig. 5.1.10. The only execution numbers that require more than a cursory examination are the two labeled H1 $*$ N/2 and (N − 1) $*$ H2, where H1 and H2 denote the number of statements executed in SUBROUTINE HEAP.

The quantities A, B, C, and D (Fig. 5.1.9) are related as follows:

$$A + B \le \log_2 N \le \lceil \log_2 N \rceil$$
$$C + D = 1$$

One has only to explain why the number of times that statement 100 is executed is bounded above by $\lceil \log_2 N \rceil$. In the worst case, the initial value of J = 1 and the values of K are 2, 4, 8, 16, . . . (that is, powers of 2). The maximum number of times

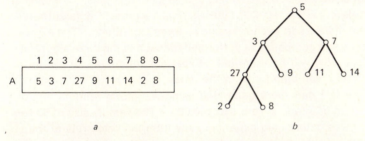

a

b

FIG. 5.1.7 Creating a tree from a random-input sequence of integers.

Step	1	2	3	4	5	6	7	8	9	Array A
1	5	3	7	27↑	9	11	14	2	8	A(4) > A(8), A(9)
2	5	3	7↑	27	9	11	14	2	8	A(3) ⊁ A(6) or A(7) Interchange A(3) ↔ A(7)
3	5	3	14↑	27	9	11	7↑	2	8	A(7) is an end-vertex
4	5	3↑	14	27	9	11	7	2	8	A(2) ⊁ A(4) or A(5) Interchange A(2) ↔ A(4)
5	5	27↑	14	3↑	9	11	7	2	8	A(4) ⊁ A(9) Interchange A(4) ↔ A(9)
6	5	27↑	14	8	9	11	7	2↑	3↑	A(9) is an end-vertex
7	5↑	27	14	8	9	11	7	2	3	A(1) ⊁ A(2) or A(3) Interchange A(1) ↔ A(2)
8	27↑	5↑	14	8	9	11	7	2	3	A(2) ⊁ A(4) or A(5) Interchange A(2) ↔ A(5)
9	27↑	9	14	8	5↑	11	7	2	3	A(5) is an end-vertex
10	27↑	9	14	8	5	11	7	2	3	STOP

FIG. 5.1.8 Creating a heap from the sequence in Fig. 5.1.7.

that statement 100 can be executed is bounded by the smallest integer k such that $2^k + 1 > N$; that is, $k = \lceil \log_2 (N-1) \rceil$.

SUBROUTINE HEAP therefore can be seen to execute no more than $2N(11\lceil \log_2 N \rceil + 6) + 11N + 3$, or $22N\lceil \log_2 N \rceil + 23N + 3$, statements in the worst case.

Having discussed the expected performance of Algorithms SIS, QUICKSORT, and HEAPSORT, let us do some simple testing to check our analyses. For each of three different sample sizes ($N = 100, 200, 500$), we shall generate 50 different sets of N random integers and then sort each set using all three algorithms. The average number of exchanges and comparisons performed for each of the three algorithms and the three values of N will be recorded. Experimental curves, of the forms predicted by the theory, will then be fit to the data.

The keys for the test data were generated using a uniform random number generator over a range of integers from 1 to 100,000. The sample size of 50 sets for each value of N was determined experimentally from the same rule of thumb used to test Algorithm PRIM in Chap. 4.

We are interested in both the number of comparisons and the number of exchanges made by each algorithm. A comparison consists of a statement like **if** $A(I) < A(J)$ or **if** $B < A(J)$. An exchange consists of a set of three assignment statements, such as

$$T \leftarrow A(I) \qquad A(I) \leftarrow A(J) \qquad A(J) \leftarrow T$$

However, for Algorithm SIS an exchange takes on a slightly different form; one first picks up a comparison value $B \leftarrow A(I)$, which counts as one-third of an exchange. One then performs an assignment $A(I+1) \leftarrow A(I)$, representing one-third of an exchange. Finally, the initial value is replaced with a statement like $A(I) \leftarrow B$, counting another one-third of an exchange.

The table at the top of page 220 shows the average values observed in these tests for each value of N and each algorithm. We shall analyze only the observed number of comparisons for Algorithm QUICKSORT; the other cases are handled similarly and are left to the interested reader.

```
      SUBROUTINE HEAP (I,A,N)
C
C     THIS SUBROUTINE PLACES THE ELEMENT A(J) INTO ITS PROPER PLACE
C     IN A HEAP OF INTEGERS A(1), A(2), ..., A(N).

      INTEGER A(N),TEMP
C
C     (PLACE A(J) IN THE HEAP)
C
      J = I                                                          1
  100 K = 2*J                                                        LOG N
      L = K+1                                                        LOG N
      IF (L .LE. N .AND. (A(J) .LT. A(K) .OR. A(J) .LT. A(L))) GOTO 200   LOG N , LOG N -1
          GOTO 500                                                  1
C
C         THEN (INTERCHANGE WITH A(J))
C
  200     IF (A(K) .GT. A(L)) GOTO 300                              LOG N , A
              GOTO 400                                              B
C
C             THEN
C
  300             TEMP = A(J)                                       A
                  A(J) = A(K)                                       A
                  J = K                                             A
                  A(K) = TEMP                                       A
                  GOTO 100                                          A
C
C             ELSE
C
  400             TEMP = A(J)                                       B
                  A(J) = A(L)                                       B
                  A(L) = TEMP                                       B
                  J = L                                             B
                  GOTO 100                                          B
C
C         ELSE (IS I*J .EQ. N)
C
  500 IF (K .EQ. N .AND. A(J) .LT. A(K)) GOTO 600                   1, C
          GOTO 700                                                  D
C
C         THEN
C
  600             TEMP = A(J)                                       C
                  A(J) = A(N)                                       C
                  A(N) = TEMP                                       C
  700 RETURN                                                        1
      END
```

FIG. 5.1.9 A Fortran implementation of Algorithm HEAP.

RESULTS OF TESTING COMPLEXITY OF ALGORITHMS SIS, QUICKSORT, AND HEAPSORT

N	Algorithm QUICK	Algorithm HEAP	Algorithm INSERT
Average number of comparisons in 50 trials			
100	712	2842	2595
200	1682	9736	10,307
500	5102	53,113	62,746
Average number of exchanges in 50 trials			
100	148	581	899
200	328	1366	3503
500	919	4042	21,083

Since our complexity analysis indicated that QUICKSORT has an expected performance of $O(N \log_2 N)$, it would be reasonable to try to fit a curve of the form

$$f_0(N) = C_1 N \log_2 N + C_2 N + C_3$$

to the data. However, for the time being, let us consider only the leading term $C_1 N \log_2 N$. We shall (somewhat arbitrarily) fit the leading term to the data at

```
      SUBROUTINE HPSORT (A,N)
C
C     THIS SUBROUTINE (HEAPSORT) SORTS AN ARRAY OF INTEGERS A(1),
C     A(2), A(3), ...., A(N) USING AN ALGORITHM DUE TO J. WILLIAMS
C     (CACM 7(1964),347-348).
C
      INTEGER A(N),TEMP
C
C     (INITIALIZE I,M)
C
      I = N/2                                                1
      L = I                                                  1
      M = N                                                  1
C
C     (CREATE HEAP)
C
      DO 100 K = 1,L                                         1
            CALL HEAP (I,A,M)                                H1*N/2
            I = I-1                                          N/2
  100 CONTINUE                                               N/2
C
C     (SORT)
C
      DO 200 K = 2,N                                         1
            TEMP = A(1)                                      N-1
            A(1) = A(M)                                      N-1
            A(M) = TEMP                                      N-1
            M = M-1                                          N-1
            CALL HEAP (1,A,M)                                (N-1)*H2
  200 CONTINUE                                               N-1
      RETURN                                                 1
      END
```

FIG. 5.1.10 A Fortran implementation of Algorithm HEAPSORT.

$N = 100$ and 500, use the average of these two values of C_1 to predict the average number of comparisons for $N = 200$, and then compare the prediction with the observation (see Exercise 4.2.6 on interpolation and extrapolation).

For $N = 100$, we find $C_1 \, 100 \log_2 100 = 712$, or $C_1 \approx 1.07$. For $N = 500$, we have $C_1 \, 500 \log_2 500 = 5102$, or $C_1 \approx 1.14$. This yields the average value

$$\bar{C} = \frac{1.07 + 1.14}{2} = \frac{2.21}{2} = 1.105$$

from which, for $N = 200$, we predict $1.105(200)(\log_2 200) \approx 1690$ comparisons; we had found an experimental value of 1682. Although the virtual lack of error is somewhat fortuitous, this simple analysis does lend considerable support to the theory.

Lower Bounds on Sorting by Comparisons

In regard to the sorting algorithms we have seen so far, Algorithm SIS is worst case $O(N^2)$ and expected performance $O(N^2)$, Algorithm QUICKSORT has expected performance $O(N \log N)$, and Algorithm HEAPSORT is worst case $O(N \log N)$. It is natural to wonder if it is possible to design a sorting algorithm whose worst case or expected performance is better than $O(N \log N)$. Unfortunately, such an algorithm is not possible. That is, one can prove that any algorithm which works by making a series of comparisons of two elements has both worst case and expected performance of at least $O(N \log N)$.

We first observe that any comparison algorithm for sorting N elements can be represented by an N-element *decision tree*, as illustrated in Fig. 5.1.11. Each interior vertex of a decision tree represents a comparison (or decision) made by the algorithm at some point in its execution. The edges emanating downward from a

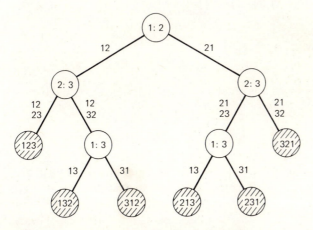

FIG. 5.1.11 A decision tree for $N = 3$ elements.

vertex represent the two possible results of a comparison. The end-vertices of a decision tree represent the sorted sequences produced by the algorithm. Since any of N! permutations of N arbitrary elements $a_1, a_2, \ldots, a_N$ is a possible outcome of a sorting algorithm, the N-element decision tree of every comparison sorting algorithm must have at least N! end-vertices.

The length of a path from the root to an end-vertex of a decision tree represents the number of comparisons that are made in producing the sorted sequence represented by the end-vertex of the path. The length of a longest such path, which is the same as the height of the tree, is therefore the number of comparisons made by the algorithm in the worst case.

In the three-element decision tree in Fig. 5.1.11, $1:2$ denotes the comparison of a_1 with a_2; the edge labeled 12 indicates that $a_1 < a_2$; the end-vertices indicate the final sorted order of keys a_1, a_2, and a_3. Since the height of this tree is three, no more than three comparisons are required to sort three elements.

We would now like to consider the worst case performance of any comparison sorting algorithm. The N-element decision tree for every such algorithm must have at least N! end-vertices and will have some height h. What is the minimum value h such that an N-element decision tree of height h can have N! end-vertices?

We first prove by induction on h that any tree of height h has at most 2^h end-vertices. Certainly if $h = 1$, this is true. Assume then that every decision tree of height $h - 1$ has at most 2^{h-1} end-vertices. Let T be a decision tree of height h. If we remove the root vertex of T, two subtrees T_1, T_2 remain, each having at most a height of $h - 1$. It follows by the induction hypothesis that T_1 and T_2 have at most 2^{h-1} end-vertices each. Thus, since the number of end-vertices of T equals the number of end-vertices of T_1 and T_2, T has at most $2^{h-1} + 2^{h-1} = 2^h$ end-vertices.

A lower bound on the smallest value of h such that $2^h \geq N!$ or that $h \geq \log N!$ is constructed as follows:

$$N! \geq N(N-1)(N-2) \cdots \left(\left\lceil \frac{N}{2} \right\rceil\right) \geq \left(\frac{N}{2}\right)^{N/2}$$

Hence
$$h \geq \log N! \geq \frac{N}{2} \log \frac{N}{2}$$

A more refined lower bound on h is obtained by using Stirling's approximation to N! That is, for sufficiently large N, $N! = O(N/e)^N$. Hence

$$h \geq \log N! \approx N \log N - N \log e = N \log N - 1.44N$$

Thus, the decision tree of every comparison sorting algorithm has a height of at least $h \geq N \log N - 1.44N$; in other words, every such algorithm is at least $O(N \log N)$ in the worst case.

A lower bound of $O(N \log N)$ also exists for the expected performance of every comparison sorting algorithm. Again we use the N-element decision tree model.

Any expected performance result for a sorting algorithm depends on the probability distribution of inputs to the algorithm. The analysis which we shall give assumes the equally likely distribution function—that is, every permutation of N elements is equally likely to appear as an input to the comparison sorting algorithm. In practice, this assumption may not be valid since the input to a sorting algorithm might be a "partially" sorted set.

If each of the N! permutations is equally likely to occur for a given comparison sorting algorithm, then each of the corresponding N! end-vertices of the N-element decision tree is equally likely to be reached. All other end-vertices will therefore never be reached. The expected number of comparisons is then equal to the average height of these N! end-vertices.

Theorem 5.1.1 Under the assumption of an equally likely probability distribution, any N-element decision tree has an average height of at least $\log (N!) \geq N \log N$.

Proof Let $H(T, k)$ denote the sum of the heights of all end-vertices of a decision tree T with k end-vertices, and let $H(k) = \min \{H(T, k)\}$ be the minimum of the height sums of all decision trees with k end-vertices. If we can show that $H(k) \geq k \log k$, then the average height of any decision tree with k end-vertices will be at least $H(k)/k \geq \log k$.

We proceed by induction on the number k of end-vertices. Certainly if $k = 1$, the result is true. Assume therefore that $H(k) \geq k \log k$ for all decision trees with less than k end-vertices.

Consider all decision trees with k end-vertices. Each such tree T has two subtrees T_1 and T_2 immediately below the root, having k_1 and k_2 end-vertices, where $k_1, k_2 < k$ and $k_1 + k_2 = k$. Thus, $H(T, k) = k_1 + H(T_1, k_1) + k_2 + H(T_2, k_2)$, and the minimum of all $H(T, k)$'s is

$$H(k) = \min_{k_1 + k_2 = k} \{k + H(k_1) + H(k_2)\}$$

By the induction hypothesis, $H(k_1) \geq k_1 \log k_1$ and $H(k_2) \geq k_2 \log k_2$. That is,

$$H(k) \geq k + \min_{k_1 + k_2 = k} \{k_1 \log k_1 + k_2 \log k_2\}$$

It is easy to show that this minimum occurs when $k_1 = k_2 = k/2$. Thus,

$$H(k) \geq k + k \log \frac{k}{2} = k \log k$$

We can now conclude that since every N-element decision tree T has at least N! end-vertices,

$$H(N!) \geq N! \log N!$$

and the average height of every N-element decision tree is at least

$$\frac{H(N!)}{N!} \geq \log N! \sim N \log N$$

A corollary of Theorem 5.1.1 follows from the observations that the average height of every N-element decision tree is at least $\log N!$, and $\log N! \approx N \log N - 1.44N$; that is, every comparison sorting algorithm has an expected performance of at least $O(N \log N)$.

Exercises 5.1

5.1.1 Sort the following list using both QUICKSORT and HEAPSORT.

17   23   114   28   35   72   16   84   90   65

L5.1.2 BUBBLESORT (*complete development*). The basic idea behind the technique known as *bubblesort* is as follows. On each pass through the list, the first key is compared with the second, and the smaller is placed in the first position. The second key is compared with the third, and the smaller is placed in the second position. This procedure is continued until the entire list has been processed. Then a second, third, and so forth, pass is made through the list until we finally make a pass in which no exchanges are made—that is, until no key is moved. The list is then sorted.
Completely develop an algorithm based on this idea.

L5.1.3 QUICKSORT (*implementation*). Put together a flowchart and program for Algorithm QUICKSORT.

5.1.4 Explicitly show that the minimum value of

$$\min_{k_1+k_2=k} \{k_1 \log k_1 + k_2 \log k_2\}$$

occurs at $k_1 = k_2 = k/2$.

5.1.5 QUICKSORT (*analysis*). Show that the worst case performance of Algorithm QUICKSORT is $O(N^2)$.

5.1.6 Put together a decision tree similar to Fig. 5.1.11 which shows how Algorithm QUICKSORT sorts the keys in Exercise 5.1.1.

L5.1.7 *Sorting by finding the smallest key* (*complete development*). Completely develop an algorithm which sorts a list by searching it, finding the smallest key, the second smallest key, and so forth, until the list is depleted and all the numbers are arranged in ascending order.

*L5.1.8 *Merging* (*complete development*). Let $A = (a_1, a_2, \ldots, a_n)$, $B = (b_1, b_2, \ldots, b_m)$, and $C = (c_1, c_2, \ldots, c_p)$ be three finite sequences of real numbers. Assume each separate sequence is arranged in ascending order. *Merge* the three sequences into a single sequence $D = \{d_1, d_2, \ldots, d_{n+m+p}\}$ which is a list of all the numbers in A, B, and C (including repetitions) such that $d_1 \leq d_2 \leq \cdots \leq d_{n+m+p}$. Design and analyze an algorithm for doing this. You might first try the case where $n = m = p$.

*5.1.9 *Sorting by merging* (*design, analysis*). Design and analyze a sorting algorithm that operates using a merging technique (see Exercise 5.1.8). What opportunities can you find for parallelism?

*5.1.10 *Set intersection* (*design, analysis*). Let A and B be two sets of nonnegative integers with k members each. There is a fairly obvious way of constructing the set $A \cap B$ using $O(k^2)$ operations. By using a sorting technique, design and analyze an algorithm that will find $A \cap B$ in $O(k \log k)$ operations.

**L5.1.11 *Comparison of sorting methods* (*testing*). Consider all the sorting techniques that you know, including any that we have not covered in this section. On the basis of analysis and experimentation, determine which of these methods is most efficient (define!) over various ranges of N. The problem is essentially to determine which sorting method is best for "small" N, best for "medium" N, and best for "large" N. Give special attention to such problems as deciding where the small range ends and the medium range begins. You may find it necessary to have more than three ranges. Use randomly generated data.

5.2 SEARCHING

We now turn to the investigation of some basic search problems that are concerned with the retrieval of information from data structures. As in Sec. 5.1 on sorting, we assume that all information is stored in records which can be identified by key values; that is, record R_i has a key value denoted by K_i.

Assume that we have N randomly ordered records in a file in the form of a linear array. An obvious way to search for a given record is to sequentially inspect the keys, as was done in Algorithm MAX in Chap. 1. If the right key is found, we stop with a successful search; otherwise, all the keys will be inspected and the search is unsuccessful. If all possible orders of the keys are equally likely, then such an algorithm requires O(N) basic operations in both the worst and average cases (see Exercise 5.2.4). The search time can be substantially reduced if the file is first sorted by keys. This initial effort is well worth it if the file is large and accessed often.

Assume next that we have N records which have been ordered by keys so that $K_1 < K_2 < \cdots < K_N$. We are given a key K and asked to find the corresponding record in the file (successful search) or ascertain that it is not there (unsuccessful search).

Suppose we jump into the middle of the file, where we find key K_i, and compare

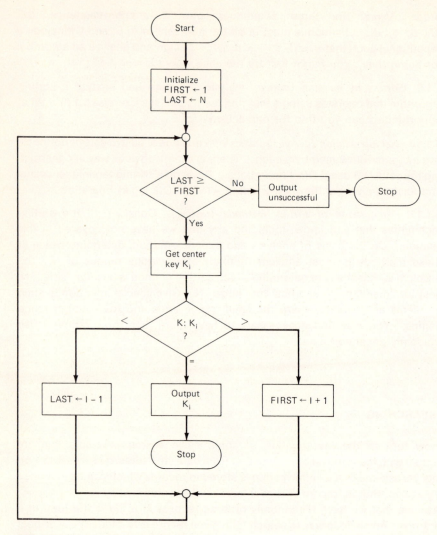

FIG. 5.2.1 Flowchart for binary search.

K with K_i.   If $K = K_i$, then the desired record has been found.   If $K < K_i$, then K must be in that portion of the file that precedes K_i, if it is there at all.   Similarly, if $K_i < K$, then further search is only necessary in that part of the file which follows K_i.   If we iterate this procedure of finding the middle key K_i of the unsearched portion of a file, then every unsuccessful comparison of K with K_i will eliminate roughly half the unsearched portion from consideration.

A flowchart for this procedure, known as *binary search*, is given in Fig. 5.2.1.

Algorithm BSEARCH (*Binary SEARCH*)   To search for a record with key K in a file with $N \geq 2$ records, whose keys are sorted in ascending order $K_1 < K_2 < \cdots < K_N$.

Step 0. [Initialize] **Set** FIRST $\leftarrow$ 1; LAST $\leftarrow$ N.   (FIRST and LAST are pointers which mark the first and last keys in the currently unsearched portion of the file.)

Step 1. [Basic iteration] **While** LAST $\geq$ FIRST **do through** step 4 **od**.

> *Step 2.* [Get middle key] **Set** I $\leftarrow$ $\lfloor$(FIRST + LAST)/2$\rfloor$.   (K_I is the middle, or left of middle, key in the current unsearched portion of the file.)
>
> *Step 3.* [Check for success] **If** $K = K_I$ **then** PRINT "SUCCESSFUL, KEY IS K_I"; **and** STOP **fi**.
>
> *Step 4.* [Compare] **If** $K < K_I$ **then set** LAST $\leftarrow$ I $-$ 1
> $\qquad\qquad\qquad\qquad$ **else set** FIRST $\leftarrow$ I $+$ 1 **fi**.

Step 5. [Unsuccessful search] PRINT "UNSUCCESSFUL"; **and** STOP.

Algorithm BSEARCH is used to find $K = 42$ in Fig. 5.2.2.

The binary search technique can also be used to represent an ordered file as a binary tree.   The value of the key found at the first execution of step 2 [K(8) = 53] is the root of the tree.   The key intervals to the right (9, 16) and left (1, 7) of this value are placed on a pushdown store.   The top interval on the store is popped off and the middle or left-of-middle element is found using step 2.   This key [K(4) = 33] becomes the left successor of the root if its value is less than that of the root; otherwise it becomes the right successor.   The subintervals of this interval to the right and left of the newly added key [(1, 3), (5, 7)] are now placed on the store.   This procedure is repeated until the store is empty.   Figure 5.2.3 illustrates the binary tree that would be constructed for the 16 ordered keys in Fig. 5.2.2.

1	2	3	4	5	6	7	8	9	10	11	12	13	14	15	16
7	14	27	33	42	49	51	53	67	70	77	81	89	94	95	99

$\uparrow$ FIRST = 1 $\qquad\qquad\qquad\qquad$ $\uparrow$ I = 8 $\qquad\qquad\qquad\qquad$ LAST = 16 $\uparrow$

7	14	27	33	42	49	51

$\uparrow$ FIRST = 1 $\quad$ $\uparrow$ I = 4 $\qquad$ $\uparrow$ LAST = 7

42	49	51

FIRST = 5 $\uparrow$ $\quad$ $\uparrow$ $\quad$ $\uparrow$ LAST = 7
$\qquad\qquad$ I = 6

42

$\uparrow$ FIRST = LAST = I = 5, K = K_5, RETURN

FIG. 5.2.2 Using Algorithm BSEARCH to find the record with KEY = 42.

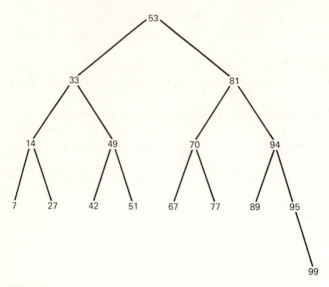

FIG. 5.2.3 A binary tree representation of the file in Fig. 5.2.2 which is constructed from Algorithm BSEARCH.

Binary search may now be interpreted as the traversal of this tree from the root to the record being sought. If an end-vertex is reached without finding the given key, the record is not in the file. Note that the number of vertices on the unique path from the root to the given key K equals the number of comparisons made by Algorithm BSEARCH in its effort to find K.

The binary tree representation of an ordered file provides a useful aid in the analysis of Algorithm BSEARCH. For convenience, we assume that the number N of records in the file is such that $N = 2^k - 1$ for some positive integer k. In this case the binary tree is *full*; that is, every interior vertex has both a left and a right successor, the tree has height $k - 1$, and the number of vertices at height l is 2^l for $l = 0, 1, \ldots, k - 1$.

First consider the worst case performance of Algorithm BSEARCH. Clearly the number of comparisons is the primary factor which determines its complexity. The number of comparisons needed to find a given key is equal to one more than the height of the key in the tree. In the worst case we have to traverse the tree to an end-vertex—that is, we make $k = \log_2(N + 1)$ comparisons. Thus, Algorithm BSEARCH is worst case $O(\log_2 N)$.

The calculation of the average number of comparisons in a successful search is somewhat more complicated. Assume that each record is equally likely to occur. Let NCOMP(i) be the height plus 1 of key K_i in the binary tree. Then NCOMP(i) equals the number of comparisons needed to find K_i. The average number of comparisons is

$$\bar{C} = \frac{1}{N} \sum_{i=1}^{N} \text{NCOMP}(i)$$

Since we have assumed that the binary tree is full and $N = 2^k - 1$, there are 2^{k-1} vertices with height $k - 1$. If σ is used to denote the summation $\sum_{i=1}^{N} \text{NCOMP}(i)$, then σ is the sum of the first N terms of the series

$$\sigma = 1 + 2 + 2 + 3 + 3 + 3 + 3 + \cdots$$
$$= 1 + 2(2) + 2^2(3) + 2^3(4) + \cdots + 2^{j-1}(j) + \cdots + 2^{k-1}(k)$$

A closed-form expression for the value of σ can be obtained using a standard technique from calculus. If S_k denotes the kth partial sum of the geometric series, then

$$S_k(y) = 1 + y + y^2 + \cdots + y^{k-1} = \frac{y^k - 1}{y - 1} \qquad y \neq 1$$

Let $y = 2z$, and then

$$S_k(2z) = 1 + 2z + (2z)^2 + \cdots + (2z)^{k-1} = \frac{2^k z^k - 1}{2z - 1}$$

Now

$$\frac{d}{dz}[\{S_k(2z) - 1\}z] = 2(2z) + 2^2(3z^2) + \cdots + 2^{k-1}(kz^{k-1})$$

where we have differentiated the series $\{S_k(2z) - 1\}z$ term by term. If we evaluate this derivative at $z = 1$ and add 1, we have σ, that is,

$$\sigma = 1 + \frac{d}{dz}[\{S_k(2z) - 1\}z] \qquad \text{at } z = 1 \text{ (check this)}$$

Using the closed-form expression for the partial sum of the geometric series, we obtain

$$\sigma = 1 + 2^k(k - 1)$$

and

$$\bar{C} = \frac{\sigma}{N} = \frac{1 + 2^k(k - 1)}{N}$$

$$= \frac{1 + (N + 1)[\log_2(N + 1) - 1]}{N}$$

$$= \frac{N + 1}{N} \log_2(N + 1) - 1$$

Thus the average complexity of binary search is $O(\log_2 N)$. Contrast this with the average of $N/2$ comparisons using a sequential search algorithm (see Exercise 5.2.4).

So far, we have discussed only files with a fixed number of records. Now consider the case where the file size changes, that is, where records are continually inserted and deleted.

Let us first develop an algorithm for maintaining a growing file of key-ordered records. This entails the choice of a convenient data structure and an associated algorithm which will quickly find a given record in the structure if it is there or insert the record in its proper place if it is not.

What data structure shall we use? Linked lists are a possibility. In Sec. 2.3, we saw that this type of data structure permits efficient insertion and deletion of elements. But unfortunately it is not easy to search a linked list in a binary search manner.

Is there another data structure which would permit us to retain the efficiency of binary search, but which permits efficient insertion and deletion of records? We next show that a binary tree is a good choice.

The table below contains 10 cities, listed by decreasing population (1970 census). The numbers on the right indicate alphabetical order. Let us read these cities in alphabetical order and store them in a binary tree in order of increasing population.

City	Population	Order
New York, N.Y.	7,868,000	7
Chicago, Ill.	3,367,000	3
Washington, D.C.	757,000	10
Pasadena, Calif.	114,000	8
Ann Arbor, Mich.	100,000	1
Charlottesville, Va.	39,000	2
Coatzocoalcos, Mexico	37,000	4
Goochland, Va.	400	6
Sleetmute, Alaska	109	9
Dry Lake, Nev.	10	5

Ann Arbor is read in first, and it becomes the root vertex. Charlottesville is read in next and is compared with the root vertex. Since the population of Charlottesville is less than that of Ann Arbor, Charlottesville becomes the left successor of Ann Arbor. Each succeeding city is read in and compared with the root. If its population is less than that of the root, it is next compared with the left successor of the root; otherwise it is compared with the right successor. Sooner or later each city is compared with a vertex having no right or left successor, and it becomes a new end-vertex of the tree. Numbered dummy vertices will be used to denote successors for cities that do not have two city successors. After the first nine cities have been read in, the binary tree appears as shown in Fig. 5.2.4.

Consider what happens next when Washington, D.C., is read in. Since Washington has a larger population than Ann Arbor, we move to its right successor. We then move to the left of Chicago since it has more people than Washington. Finally, we move to the right of Pasadena since it is smaller than Washington. Washington is then placed in the position marked $\boxed{7}$ and is given left and right dummy successors.

In what follows we assume that two distinct records do not have the same key values; for example, two distinct cities do not have identical populations.

The search procedure for this structure works just like the insertion procedure, with the exception that the search ends successfully when we reach a vertex whose key value equals that of the search key. If a dummy vertex is reached, then the record is not in the tree and the search is unsuccessful. If it is desired to add a record with the search key value, it can be added to the tree at the dummy vertex which is reached.

Algorithm BTSI (*Binary Tree Search and Insertion*)   To search for a given key K in a file with N $\geq$ 1 records, organized as a binary tree T. If K is not present, a new vertex will be created for it. K(P) denotes the key at vertex P; LEFT(P) and RIGHT(P) denote the left and right successors of vertex P. The root vertex of T is labeled ROOT; all dummy vertices are labeled Λ.

Step 0. [Initialize] **Set** P $\leftarrow$ ROOT.

Step 1. [Loop] **While** K $\neq$ K(P) **do** step 2 **od**.

> *Step 2.* [Compare and move] **If** K $<$ K(P)
> > **then if** LEFT(P) $\neq \Lambda$
> > > **then set** P $\leftarrow$ LEFT(P)
> > > **else** let Q denote a new vertex; **set** K(Q) $\leftarrow$ K;
> > > > LEFT(Q) $\leftarrow \Lambda$; RIGHT(Q) $\leftarrow \Lambda$;
> > > > LEFT(P) $\leftarrow$ Q; **and** STOP **fi**
> > **else if** RIGHT(P) $\neq \Lambda$
> > > **then set** P $\leftarrow$ RIGHT(P)
> > > **else** let Q denote a new vertex; **set** K(Q) $\leftarrow$ K;
> > > > LEFT(Q) $\leftarrow \Lambda$; RIGHT(Q) $\leftarrow \Lambda$
> > > > RIGHT(P) $\leftarrow$ Q; **and** STOP **fi fi**.

Step 3. [Successful search] Output "SUCCESSFUL SEARCH"; **and** STOP.

One would suspect that the worst Algorithm BTSI can do is to effectively behave like a sequential search. Unfortunately, this is possible. It happens if the records are read into the tree in sorted order. In this case, the binary tree degenerates into a simple path that is effectively a linear list. It is not difficult to show that this is a worst case.

What about the expected performance of Algorithm BTSI? This is not an easy question to answer. If the tree is full or nearly full, the algorithm is similar to binary search and is $O(\log_2 N)$. It appears that if the keys are inserted in random order, the average number of comparisons is still $O(\log_2 N)$. If every N-vertex binary tree is considered equally probable, the average number of comparisons is $O(\sqrt{N})$. The proofs of these statements are not simple and may be found in Knuth (1969a, 1973).

The problem of deleting a vertex from the binary tree representing an ordered file is somewhat involved. There is no problem if both of the successors of a vertex are dummy (empty) vertices. For example, to delete Sleetmute from the tree in Fig. 5.2.4, simply replace this key by Λ. In order to remove a vertex with one

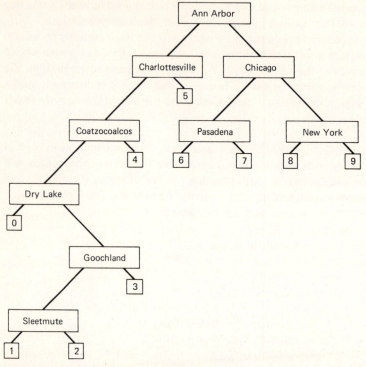

FIG. 5.2.4 The binary tree, ordered by population, which is created by reading in the first nine cities in alphabetical order.

dummy successor—for example, Coatzocoalcos in Fig. 5.2.4—merely move its left (or right) subtree up to take its place.

The linkage problem is more complicated if the vertex to be deleted has two nonempty successors. The general procedure is as follows: (1) replace the vertex to be removed by its right subtree RT; (2) make the left subtree of the deleted vertex the left subtree of the leftmost vertex of RT.

Figure 5.2.5 shows the tree of Fig. 5.2.4 after the removal of Ann Arbor. Exercise 5.2.10 asks for a more explicit statement of the deletion algorithm.

Consider the following general search problem. We are given a finite set of objects. One of these objects has been previously "selected" in some sense. We do not know which object has been selected, but we do know the probability distribution which governs this choice. Thus, object i has a known probability p_i of selection, and $\Sigma p_i = 1$, where the sum is taken over all objects. We are to find the selected object through a series of "yes and no" questions. We are allowed to select a subset of objects and ask: "Is the object a member of this subset?" Some referee will give us an honest "yes" or "no" answer. Our primary goal is to construct an algorithm which solves any search problem of this form with the minimum expected number of questions. Note that every question we ask divides the current set of unsearched objects into two sets, one of which is effectively searched and the other is unsearched.

For example, let D be a deck of 55 cards containing 1 ace, 2 deuces, 3 threes, ..., 9 nines, and 10 tens. A card is chosen at random and we have to guess its face value. In terms of the general problem statement, our set consists of 10 objects (ace, deuce, three, ..., ten) with probabilities $P(\text{ace}) = \frac{1}{55}$, $P(\text{deuce}) = \frac{2}{55}$, $P(\text{three}) = \frac{3}{55}, \ldots, P(k) = k/55, \ldots, P(\text{ten}) = \frac{10}{55}$.

Let us begin the algorithm design process by attempting to generalize the binary search. Assume that the objects are ordered by increasing values of p_i. Try to split the current set of unsearched objects in the middle. If the set is odd, put the middle object in the subset of objects with smaller p_i values. In this example, the first question is: "Is the object a six or greater?" This question and

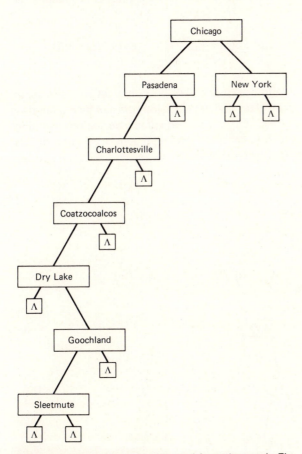

FIG. 5.2.5 The binary tree obtained from the tree in Fig. 5.2.4 by deleting Ann Arbor, moving its right subtree to the root, and adding its left subtree below Pasadena.

its answer divides the set of possible answers into two sets of equal cardinality. Suppose the answer to this question is "no." Then the next question is: "Is the object a four or five?" The decision tree for this example is shown in Fig. 5.2.6.

How do we compute the expected number of questions asked in finding the right card? The numbers on the far right of Fig. 5.2.6 indicate the number of questions that need to be asked to get to a vertex at this level for this algorithm. For example, if the chosen card was a five, it would take three questions to ascertain this. The expected number of questions that will be asked using binary search is computed from

$$EQBS = \sum_{\text{all objects}} P(\text{object } i \text{ chosen})[NQ(i)] = \sum_i p_i NQ(i)$$

where $NQ(i)$ is the number of questions that will be asked if object i is chosen. In the example,

$$EQBS = 4(\tfrac{1}{55}) + 4(\tfrac{2}{55}) + 3(\tfrac{3}{55}) + 3(\tfrac{4}{55}) + 3(\tfrac{5}{55}) + 4(\tfrac{6}{55}) + 4(\tfrac{7}{55}) + 3(\tfrac{8}{55}) + 3(\tfrac{9}{55}) + 3(\tfrac{10}{55})$$
$$= \tfrac{181}{55} = 3.291$$

Before we see if it is possible to design a better algorithm, let us make some general observations. It should be clear that any decision rule can be modeled as a binary decision tree (see Sec. 5.1). Every question splits a vertex representing an unsearched set into exactly two successors that represent a partition of this set. The terminal vertices of this tree—that is, those vertices without succes-

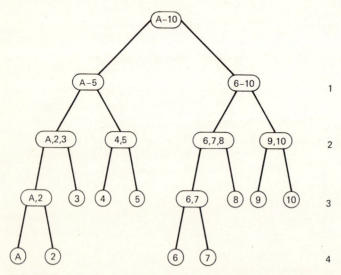

FIG. 5.2.6 A decision tree for finding a card selected at random from a deck containing aces, twos, ..., and tens.

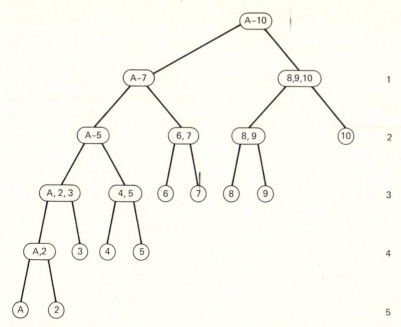

FIG. 5.2.7 The decision tree for finding a card selected at random from a deck containing aces, twos, ..., and tens, where sets are partitioned into two subsets with roughly equal probabilities.

sors—represent single objects in the original set. The interior vertices—that is, those with two successors—represent sets of two or more objects. The expected number of questions that will be asked for any rule is given by

$$EQ = \sum_i p_i I_i$$

where the sum is over the terminal vertices, and I_i is the length of the path from the root to the ith terminal vertex.

There is a fairly obvious way to improve the current binary search algorithm for the class of problems being considered. Let us try to split the set into two subsets, each with roughly the same probability of containing the chosen object. In the example, if we used this modification, our first question would be: "Is the object an eight or greater?" This question would generate two sets with P(eight or greater) equal to $\frac{27}{55}$ and P(seven or smaller) equal to $\frac{28}{55}$. The binary tree for this algorithm is shown in Fig. 5.2.7; for this tree $EQ = \frac{173}{55} = 3.145$ (check this).

One apparent handicap of this modification of binary search is that we are forced to group objects together in a manner that permits us to select only intervals of adjacent objects in the linear order. Is it possible to obtain a better "probabilistic balance" by asking such questions as:

Is it an odd-numbered object?

Is it one of objects 3, 17, 28, or 49?

We can take advantage of this extra flexibility using a remarkably simple algorithm which is guaranteed to produce a best possible solution to this search problem.

The following procedure was independently discovered by D. Huffman and S. Zimmerman. It is a recursive algorithm that constructs a binary search tree backward, that is, from the end-vertices to the root. The end-vertices represent the individual objects and their probabilities, the root represents the set of all objects, and the interior vertices represent assorted subsets and their probabilities. Let P_m be a search problem with $m \geq 2$ objects, where object i has

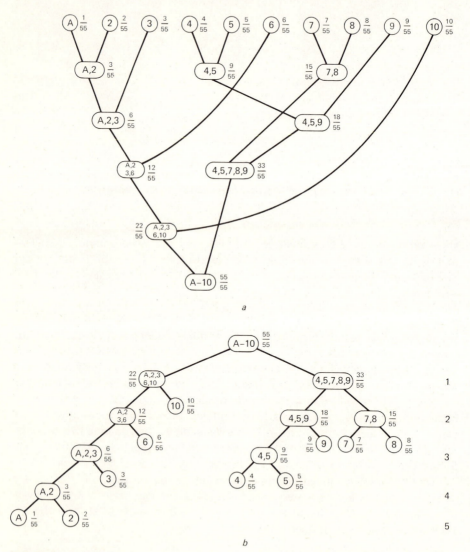

FIG. 5.2.8 An optimum decision tree obtained by iteratively combining the two sets with the smallest probabilities.

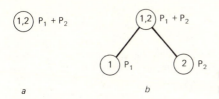

a   *b*

FIG. 5.2.9 Combining the two smallest probabilities P_1 and P_2.

probability p_i of being chosen and $p_1 \leq p_2 \leq \cdots \leq p_m$. The essential idea of the algorithm is to combine the two objects with the smallest probabilities into a single set, and then to solve the problem P_{m-1} with $m-1$ objects and probabilities $p'_1 = p_1 + p_2$, $p'_2 = p_3, \ldots, p'_{m-1} = p_m$. In practice, the explicit search tree is constructed backward, as illustrated in Fig. 5.2.8a for our example. After the tree in Fig. 5.2.8a is inverted and arranged by height, we obtain the search tree shown in Fig. 5.2.8b. A simple calculation yields EQOST $= \frac{173}{55} = 3.145$. Although this value is the same as that found using the modified binary search (which is a good heuristic), the associated trees are different. An explicit step-form statement of this algorithm is left as an exercise (see Exercise 5.2.14).

We conclude this section by proving that this algorithm produces a binary search tree which minimizes EQ $= \Sigma\, p_i l_i$. Assume that the p_i are ordered, that is, $p_1 \leq p_2 \leq \cdots \leq p_m$. The algorithm combines p_1 and p_2 into one vertex and then solves the reduced problem with $m-1$ objects. When the reduced problem is solved, the vertex of Fig. 5.2.9a in the tree corresponding to the reduced solution is replaced by the subtree shown in Fig. 5.2.9b. Let T_m be a tree which minimizes EQ, and let v be an internal vertex that is at maximum distance from the root. If p_1 and p_2 are not the probabilities assigned to the two successors of v, then it is possible to exchange these values with those of the actual successors of v without increasing the value of EQ. This new tree T'_m minimizes EQ and contains the subtree in Fig. 5.2.9b.

Let T'_{m-1} be the tree T'_m with the subtree in Fig. 5.2.9b replaced by the vertex in Fig. 5.2.9a. If we can show that T'_{m-1} is optimum for problem P_{m-1} if and only if T'_m is optimum for problem P_m, then a simple inductive argument will establish the correctness of the algorithm. We explicitly show that if T'_m is optimum for P_m, then T'_{m-1} will be optimum for P_{m-1}. Assume T'_{m-1} is not optimum for P_{m-1}, but T''_{m-1} is. Thus, $EQ(T''_{m-1}) < EQ(T'_{m-1})$. From the definition of problem P_{m-1}, T''_{m-1} must have a terminal vertex that looks like Fig. 5.2.9a. Break up this vertex in T''_{m-1} into the subtree of Fig. 5.2.9b and call this new tree T''_m. Then

$$EQ(T''_m) = EQ(T''_{m-1}) + p_1 + p_2 < EQ(T'_{m-1}) + p_1 + p_2 = EQ(T'_m)$$

which contradicts the statement that T'_m is optimum for P_m.

Exercises 5.2

5.2.1 Construct flowcharts for Algorithms BSEARCH and BTSI.

5.2.2 Construct a binary search tree for the following list of keys.

$$6 \quad 17 \quad 21 \quad 35 \quad 46 \quad 51 \quad 59 \quad 66 \quad 78 \quad 83$$

5.2.3 *Sequential search (design).* Design a simple sequential search algorithm (see the second paragraph of this section).

5.2.4 *Sequential search (analysis).* Analyze the sequential search algorithm from Exercise 5.2.3. Assume every possible arrangement of N keys is equally likely. Show that both the worst case and expected performance of the algorithm is O(N).

5.2.5 Use Algorithm BTSI to insert Scaggsville, Maryland (pop. 350), into the tree of Fig. 5.2.5.

5.2.6 Verify that $\sigma = 1 + d/dz[\{S_k(2z) - 1\}z]$ at $z = 1$.

L5.2.7 *Algorithm* BTSI *(implementation, testing).* Implement and test Algorithm BTSI.

L5.2.8 *Algorithm* BSEARCH *(implementation, testing).* Implement and test Algorithm BSEARCH. Experimentally verify its logarithmic complexity.

**5.2.9 *Algorithm* BSEARCH *(analysis).* Generalize the expected performance analysis given in this section to the case where the search tree is not full.

*5.2.10 Give an explicit step-form statement of the deletion algorithm described on pages 231 and 232.

5.2.11 Use the Huffman-Zimmerman procedure to construct an optimum search tree for a problem with seven objects and selection probabilities: $p_1 = .05$, $p_2 = .10$, $p_3 = .10$, $p_4 = .15$, $p_5 = .16$, $p_6 = .20$, and $p_7 = .24$.

*L5.2.12 *Probabilistic search (complete development).* Develop the following modification to the binary search: Instead of halving the remaining search interval at each stage, enter it at random with entry at any position equally likely. Compare the performance of this algorithm with that of binary search.

5.2.13 *Random requests with multiple responses (design).* We are searching a data base for *all* records of a certain type. Discuss some general ways of doing this. Formulate a reasonable real-world problem of this type and develop an algorithm for its solution.

**5.2.14 Give an explicit statement of the Huffman-Zimmerman algorithm.

*L5.2.15 *Selection problem (complete development).* Develop an algorithm for the selection problem: For an arbitrary set of n numerical inputs, find the kth largest input. The inputs are not presorted. Assume k is a fixed integer and $1 \le k \le n$.

5.2.16 *Path lengths in rooted binary trees (analysis).* Define the *external path length* EPL of a rooted binary tree as the sum, over all terminal vertices, of the lengths of the unique paths from the root to each terminal vertex. The *internal path length* IPL is defined similarly, with the sum taken over all internal vertices. If the tree has N internal vertices, show that EPL = IPL + 2N.

**L5.2.17 *A maze search* (*design, implementation*). Let M be a 15×15 matrix whose elements consist of O's (for "open") and B's (for "blocked"). Each element is chosen at random using the probabilities $P(O) = \frac{2}{3}$ and $P(B) = \frac{1}{3}$. Our objective is to find a path composed of horizontal or vertical movements to adjacent positions from position $(1, 1)$ to position $(15, 15)$. We can never move into a B position. Positions $(1, 1)$ and $(15, 15)$ are always O.

5.3 ARITHMETIC AND LOGICAL EXPRESSIONS

The subject of arithmetic and logical expressions pervades much of computer science since it involves the subjects of programming language syntax and semantics, compiling, formal languages, data structures, logic, recursion, and computational complexity. Insofar as these expressions form an integral part of virtually all computer programs, it is important to have algorithms which recognize and evaluate them as rapidly and efficiently as possible.

The problem of reading an arbitrary sequence $S = S(1), S(2), \ldots, S(N)$ of symbols and deciding or recognizing that it is a valid arithmetic or logical expression is a nontrivial one. Its solution involves the theory of formal languages and is an integral part of the theory of compiling. We do not have the space in this text to develop the theory necessary to explain these expression recognition algorithms. We shall therefore assume that all expressions presented to us are valid and shall concentrate on the easier problem of evaluating these expressions.

There are at least three distinct ways of defining arithmetic expressions. Textbooks for a first course in computer programming typically define them by example. The rationale for such an approach is that one can learn how to write correct expressions by seeing many examples, much like learning to speak a language. Since it has been observed that most programmers use rather simple expressions in their programs, this approach seems adequate for most people.

A more formal approach is to define the syntax and semantics of arithmetic and logical expressions by *context-free rewriting rules*, as is done in defining Algol. An intermediate approach which retains some of the mathematical precision of the Algol definitions and contains a fair degree of intuitive appeal is to define these expressions *inductively* or *recursively*.

An arithmetic expression, abbreviated ⟨a.e.⟩, is defined inductively as follows:

1 Any variable is an ⟨a.e.⟩.
2 Any constant is an ⟨a.e.⟩.
3 Any arithmetic function reference is an ⟨a.e.⟩.
4 If X is an ⟨a.e.⟩, so is (X).

5 If X and Y are both ⟨a.e.⟩, so are (X + Y), (X − Y), (X * Y), (X/Y), and (X ** Y).

6 Nothing is an arithmetic expression unless its being so follows from a finite number of applications of rules 1 through 5.

This definition effectively provides a set of rules which can be used to construct any arithmetic expression in terms of variables, constants, function references, and the operators +, −, *, /, and **. Notice that definitions of "variable," "constant," and "function reference" are missing from this definition. We assume that the reader is familiar with these terms.

Consider the expression

$$(((A - B) * C) + (D/(E ** F)))$$

If this is a valid arithmetic expression, then it must be possible to construct it from rules 1 through 5. One such construction is shown in Fig. 5.3.1.

An alternate way of describing this arithmetic expression is by means of the rooted binary tree in Fig. 5.3.2. Notice that all end-vertices in this tree correspond to variables, or operands, and that all interior vertices correspond to arithmetic operators. Given such a rooted binary tree, it is easy to evaluate an expression if the values of the variables are known. For example, suppose the variables have the following values: A = 4.0, B = 1.0, C = 5.0, D = 64.0, E = 2.0, and F = 5.0. The

Line	is an < a.e. >	according to rule,	using lines
1	A	1	
2	B	1	
3	(A – B)	5b	1, 2
4	C	1	
5	((A – B)*C)	5c	3, 4
6	E	1	
7	F	1	
8	(E**F)	5e	6, 7
9	D	1	
10	(D/(E**F))	5d	9, 8
11	(((A – B)*C) + (D/(E**F)))	5a	5, 10

FIG. 5.3.1 The construction of an arithmetic expression.

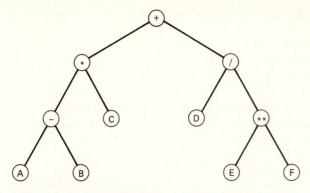

FIG. 5.3.2 A binary tree for describing the arithmetic expression $(((A-B)*C)+(D/(E**F)))$.

value of the arithmetic expression can be computed by working upward from the end-vertices to the root as indicated in Fig. 5.3.3.

It is interesting to observe how Fig. 5.3.3a and b make it obvious that several of the computations which must be carried out in evaluating an arithmetic expression can be done in parallel. For example, the subtraction $A-B$ can be done in parallel with the exponentiation $E**F$. One can find in the literature a variety of papers dealing with the parallel evaluation of arithmetic expressions; the interested reader is referred to Chap. 7 for references on this subject.

Logical expressions can be defined in the same way as arithmetic expressions. In order to do so, we first need to define a relational expression. A *relational expression* is an expression of the form ⟨a.e.⟩⟨rel. op.⟩⟨a.e.⟩, where ⟨rel. op.⟩ is one of the following six relational operators:

$$< \quad \leq \quad = \quad \neq \quad > \quad \geq$$

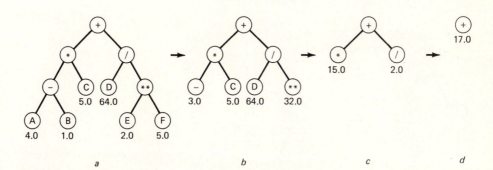

FIG. 5.3.3 Computing the value of an arithmetic expression.

A *logical expression*, abbreviated ⟨l.e.⟩, is defined inductively as follows:

1 Any logical constant is a ⟨l.e.⟩.
2 Any logical variable is a ⟨l.e.⟩.
3 Any relational expression is a ⟨l.e.⟩.
4 If X is a ⟨l.e.⟩, so is (X).
5 If X and Y are both ⟨l.e.⟩, so are (X AND Y), (X OR Y), and NOT (X).
6 Nothing is a ⟨l.e.⟩ unless its being so follows from a finite number of applications of rules 1 through 5.

An example of a valid logical expression is

$$((\text{NOT A}) \text{ AND B}) \quad \text{OR} \quad (\text{C AND (D OR E)})$$

the tree of which is given in Fig. 5.3.4.

You might have noticed by now that the definitions of an ⟨a.e.⟩ and a ⟨l.e.⟩ involve what seem to be an excessive number of parentheses. Definitions can be given which do not require as many parentheses, but such definitions invariably lead to ambiguities. For example, the expressions

$$A + B/C \quad \text{or} \quad \text{NOT A AND B}$$

must be evaluated using a priority scheme which requires that the slash (/) has a higher priority than the plus sign (+) and NOT has higher priority than AND. With these priorities the expression $A + B/C$ is equivalent to $A + (B/C)$, and NOT A AND B is equivalent to (NOT A) AND B. We include parentheses in this section to avoid these complications.

It is interesting to observe that three different ways of traversing the trees of Figs. 5.3.2 and 5.3.4 produce three different ways of writing the corresponding expressions as a linear sequence of symbols. Consider the tree in Fig. 5.3.5 for

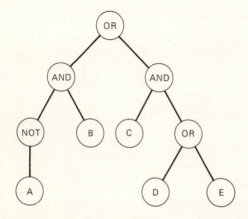

FIG. 5.3.4 The tree of a logical expression.

	TLR	Preorder	+ A B	Prefix
	LTR	Inorder	A + B	Infix
	LRT	Postorder	A B +	Postfix

FIG. 5.3.5 Three different traversals of a binary tree and the corresponding linear expressions.

the simple arithmetic expression (A + B). If we start at the root or top (T) of this tree and print +, then traverse to the left (L) descendant and print A, and then traverse back up to the root and down to the right (R) descendant and print B, we shall have performed what is called a *preorder* traversal of the tree. The sequence of symbols printed, + A B, is called the *prefix* form of the arithmetic expression; the operator (+) comes *before* the operands A and B.

The more familiar form of the arithmetic expression (A + B) is called the *infix* form; it is obtained by an *inorder* traversal of the tree, as indicated by LTR. The *postfix* form of an arithmetic expression—in which the operators appear *after* the operands, as in A B + — is obtained by a *postorder* traversal (LRT) of the tree.

It is instructive at this point to reconsider the tree of Fig. 5.3.2. In order to preorder traverse this tree, we start by visiting the TOP vertex (marked +). We next preorder traverse the left subtree (with root marked *), and we then preorder traverse the right subtree (with root marked /). The preorder traversal of this left subtree starts at the root (marked *), preorder traverses its left subtree (producing the sequence − A B), and then traverses its right subtree (producing the sequence C). Therefore, the total sequence produced by a preorder traversal of the left subtree of the TOP vertex is * − A B C. In the same way, the preorder traversal of the right subtree, with root marked /, produces the sequence /D **E F. Thus the preorder traversal of the entire tree of Fig. 5.3.2 produces the sequence

$$\underset{T}{+}\ \underset{L}{*\ -A\,B\,C}\ \underset{R}{/\,D\,**\,E\,F}$$

The inorder and postorder traversals of this tree produce the sequences

$$\underset{L}{A-B*C}\ \underset{T}{+}\ \underset{R}{D/E**F}\quad \text{(infix)}$$

and

$$\underset{L}{A\,B-C*}\ \underset{R}{D\,E\,F**/}\ \underset{T}{+}\quad \text{(postfix)}$$

respectively.

Notice that in all three expressions, the order of appearance of the variables is the same; only the order of the operators changes. Notice also that these sequences have no parentheses, and thus the value of the expression in infix form above is ambiguous if no priority scheme is given. For reasons which will become apparent, there is no ambiguity involved in determining the value of either the prefix or postfix forms of this expression. That is, for each form a simple algorithm can be constructed which will uniquely evaluate an expression in that form. We next present an algorithm for computing the value of an arithmetic expression in postfix form.

Algorithm POSTFIX To evaluate an arithmetic expression in postfix form; the expression consists of a sequence S(1) S(2) ... S(N), N ≥ 1, where S(I) is either a letter (that is, an operand or a variable) or one of +, −, *, /, or ** (that is, a binary arithmetic operator); the algorithm also uses a pushdown STORE.

Step 0. [Initialize] **Set** J ← 0.

Step 1. [Iterate] **For** I ← 1 **to** N **do** step 2 **od; and** STOP. (The value of the expression will be on the top of the pushdown STORE.)

> *Step 2.* [What is S(I)?] **If** S(I) is an operand
> > **then** [put S(I) on the pushdown] **set** J ← J + 1; **and** STORE(J) ← S(I)
> > **else** [evaluate subexpression] **set** T1 ← STORE(J); T2 ← STORE(J − 1); [perform operation S(I) on T1 and T2] **set** T3 ← T1 · S(I) · T2; **set** J ← J − 1; **and** STORE(J) ← T3
> > **fi**.

Figure 5.3.6 illustrates the execution of Algorithm POSTFIX on the arithmetic expression in postfix form: A B − C * D E F ** / + .

In line I = 5, for example, the input symbol S(5) = * causes the values of the top two elements on the pushdown, C and 3.0 (line 4), to be multiplied; these two elements are then removed from the pushdown and the product 15.0 is placed on top of the pushdown.

An outline of a proof of the correctness of Algorithm POSTFIX can be given by induction on the length N of the postfix expression S(1) S(2) ... S(N). Such a proof depends on the inductive definition of an arithmetic expression and the process of translating an arithmetic expression from infix to postfix form (discussed earlier).

Clearly, Algorithm POSTFIX works correctly on postfix expressions of length N = 1 or N = 3. (From the definition, there are no postfix expressions of length N = 2.) This can be verified by hand calculation. Assume therefore that Algorithm POSTFIX correctly evaluates all postfix expressions of length ≤ N.

Consider an arbitrary postfix expression S(1) S(2) ... S(N + 1) of length N + 1. Let k be the smallest integer such that S(k) is an operator. Then it is easy to see that this operator must be applied to S(k − 1) and S(k − 2), and furthermore, S(k − 1) and S(k − 2) are both operands. In general, S(I − 1) and S(I − 2) are not necessarily operands if S(I) is an operator. However, since S(k) is the first operator in the sequence, S(k − 1) and S(k − 2) must be operands. In step 2, Algorithm POSTFIX therefore removes S(k − 1) and S(k − 2) from the pushdown, evaluates T = S(k − 1)S(k)S(k − 2), and places T back on the pushdown, as though T were another operand.

I	Symbol read	Contents of store				Values of variables in store or operation performed
	A B − C * D E F ** / +	1	2	3	4	
1	A	A				A = 4.0
2	B	A	B			B = 1.0
3	−	3.0				A − B = 3.0
4	C	3.0				C = 5.0
5	*	15.0				3.0*C = 15.0
6	D	15.0	D			D = 64.0
7	E	15.0	D	E		E = 2.0
8	F	15.0	D	E	F	F = 5.0
9	**	15.0	D	32.0		E ** F = 32.0
10	/	15.0	2.0			D/32.0 = 2.0
11	+	17.0				15.0 + 2.0 = 17.0

FIG. 5.3.6 The evaluation of an arithmetic expression in postfix form using Algorithm POSTFIX.

At this point in the algorithm, the configuration of the pushdown is exactly the same as if the original postfix expression were the shorter expression $S(1) \ldots S(k-3) \, T \, S(k+1) \ldots S(N)$. But since the value of this modified expression (which can be shown to be a valid postfix expression) is the same as the original expression, and since by induction Algorithm POSTFIX works correctly on all postfix expressions of length $\leq N$, we conclude that Algorithm POSTFIX correctly evaluates the original expression.

A complete proof of the correctness of Algorithm POSTFIX would involve proofs of several of the above statements. We omit these proofs in the interest of brevity.

We can see that a postfix expression can be evaluated in O(N) time with the use of a pushdown store since no more than a constant number of operations must be performed in examining each of the N symbols $S(1), S(2), \ldots, S(N)$. We should point out several things about Algorithm POSTFIX:

1 It assumes that the input sequence is a valid postfix expression; no tests have been inserted to ensure that the input is in proper form.
2 It is not designed to handle expressions in which the operands can consist of several letters or digits.
3 No constants or function references can appear in an expression.
4 No unary operators — for example, $-A$ or $+A-B$ — can appear in an expression.

5 It neither initializes the values of the pushdown store to zero nor resets them to zero once they have been used; it may be aesthetically pleasing to do this but it is not necessary.

It is possible, however, to modify Algorithm POSTFIX so that each of these five conditions can be handled; we leave these as exercises, together with the problem of implementing Algorithm POSTFIX.

We have seen how easy it is to evaluate an arithmetic expression once it has been put into postfix form. In most programming languages, however, one is required to write arithmetic expressions in infix form. The next algorithm is designed to convert an expression from infix to postfix form. It is based on the following priority scheme:

Symbol	Priority
(,)	0
+, −	1
*, /	2
**	3

The algorithm proceeds by reading the symbols of the infix expression from left to right. All operands (variables) are output as soon as they are read; all other symbols are placed on a pushdown store and either removed or output later, depending on the above priority scheme.

Algorithm ITP (*Infix To Postfix*) To convert an infix expression $S(1) S(2) \ldots S(N)$, $N \geq 1$, into postfix form, where $S(I)$ is either a letter (that is, an operand or a variable), a left or right parenthesis, or an operator (that is, one of $+, -, *, /,$ or $**$). The algorithm uses a pushdown store STORE, and a priority function P, where "ϵ", "(", and ")" have priority 0, $P(+) = P(-) = 1$; $P(*) = P(/) = 2$; and $P(**) = 3$.

Step 0. [Initialize] **Set** STORE(1) $\leftarrow \epsilon$; **and** J $\leftarrow$ 1.

Step 1. [Iterate] **For** I $\leftarrow$ 1 **to** N **do through** step 6 **od**.

    Step 2. [Letter] **If** S(I) is a letter **then** PRINT S(I) **fi**.

    Step 3. [Left parenthesis] **If** S(I) = "(" **then** [put on pushdown] **set** J $\leftarrow$ J + 1; STORE(J) $\leftarrow$ S(I) **fi**.

    Step 4. [Right parenthesis] **If** S(I) = ")" **then** [remove from pushdown] **while** STORE(J) $\neq$ "(" **do** step 5 **od**; **and set** J $\leftarrow$ J − 1 **fi**.

        Step 5. [Print top of pushdown] PRINT STORE (J); **and set** J $\leftarrow$ J − 1.

    Step 6. [Operator] **While** $P(S(I)) \leq P(STORE(J))$ **do** PRINT STORE(J); **and set** J $\leftarrow$ J − 1 **od**; [put on pushdown] **set** J $\leftarrow$ J + 1; **and** STORE(J) $\leftarrow$ S(I).

Step 7. [Print rest of pushdown] **While** STORE(J) $\neq \epsilon$ **do** PRINT STORE(J); **and set** J $\leftarrow$ J − 1 **od**; **and** STOP.

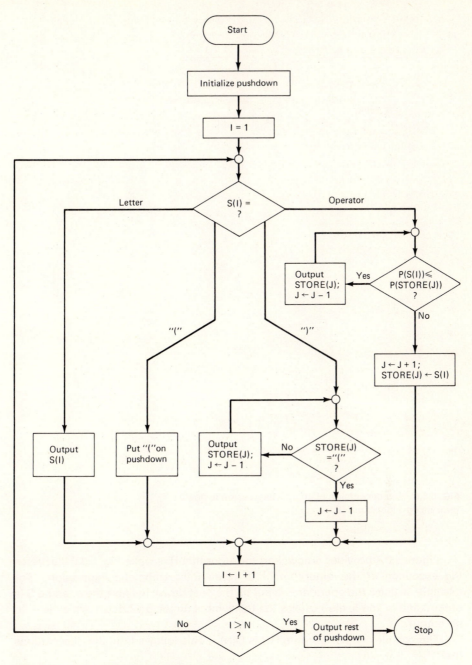

FIG. 5.3.7 A flowchart for Algorithm ITP.

Step	Input (A – B) * C + D / (E ** F)	Output	Contents of pushdown 1 2 3 4 5
			ϵ
1	(		ϵ (
2	A	A	ϵ (
3	–		ϵ (–
4	B	B	ϵ (–
5	)	–	ϵ
6	*		ϵ *
7	C	C	ϵ *
8	+	*	ϵ +
9	D	D	ϵ +
10	/		ϵ + /
11	(		ϵ + / (
12	E	E	ϵ + / (
13	**		ϵ + / (**
14	F	F	ϵ + / (**
15	)	**	ϵ + /
16		/+	

Output: AB – C*DEF**/+

FIG. 5.3.8 The conversion of an infix expression to postfix form using Algorithm ITP.

Figure 5.3.7 provides a flowchart for Algorithm ITP, while Fig. 5.3.8 illustrates the execution of this algorithm on a given infix arithmetic expression. For example, in line 3 the operator – is put on the pushdown; in line 4 the operand B is output; and in line 5, the) causes the top symbol on the pushdown, which is –, to be output.

The complexity of Algorithm ITP is O(N). This follows from the observations that:

1 One pass is made over the N symbols in the sequence.
2 At most N/2 symbols (that is, operators) can be placed on the pushdown.

3 All symbols remaining on the pushdown are output when all symbols have been read, requiring at most O(N) operations.

4 At most a constant number of operations are required to process an arbitrary symbol in the sequence.

Exercises 5.3

5.3.1 Consider the following arithmetic expression:

$$(((X_1 * Y_1) + (X_2 * Y_2)) ** \tfrac{1}{2}) - ((A + B) + C)$$

(*a*) Construct this expression using rules 1 through 5 for arithmetic expressions, and exhibit this construction in a table similar to Fig. 5.3.1.

(*b*) Construct a rooted binary tree representation similar to Fig. 5.3.2.

5.3.2 Evaluate the expression in Exercise 5.3.1 for the values $X_1 = 3$, $Y_1 = 4$, $X_2 = 4$, $Y_2 = 6$, $A = 5$, $B = 7$, and $C = 1$. Use a figure similar to Fig. 5.3.3.

5.3.3 Consider the following logical expression:

$$(X .OR. Y) .AND. ((.NOT. (A)) .OR. B) .OR. (.NOT. (X))$$

(*a*) Construct this expression using rules 1 through 6 for logical expressions, and exhibit this construction in a table similar to Fig. 5.3.1.

(*b*) Construct a rooted binary tree representation similar to Fig. 5.3.4.

5.3.4 Preorder, inorder, and postorder traverse the rooted binary trees constructed in Exercise 5.3.1 and/or Exercise 5.3.3.

**5.3.5 Prove the correctness of Algorithm ITP.

5.3.6 Use Algorithm POSTFIX to evaluate the expression in Exercise 5.3.1 for the values given in Exercise 5.3.2.

5.3.7 *Algorithm* POSTFIX(*implementation*). Implement Algorithm POSTFIX.

5.3.8 Use Algorithm ITP to process the expression in Exercise 5.3.1.

5.3.9 Give the prefix and postfix expressions corresponding to the logical expression in Fig. 5.3.4.

5.3.10 What property of an arithmetic expression determines the height of the corresponding rooted binary tree?

5.3.11 Construct a POSTFIX-type algorithm for logical expressions.

5.3.12 Construct a PREFIX-type algorithm for logical expressions.

*5.3.13 *Algorithm* POSTFIX (*analysis*). Provide a good upper bound for the maximum number of symbols that must be stored on a pushdown store in Algorithm POSTFIX.   Give an example of a worst case expression.

*5.3.14   *Algorithm* ITP (*analysis*).   Repeat Exercise 5.3.13 for Algorithm ITP.   What is the worst case behavior of this algorithm?

5.4   PAGING

One of the most valuable resources of a digital computer to a user is the amount of available core storage.   It is important therefore that it be used as efficiently as possible.   In many cases it is difficult to achieve maximum utilization of memory either because programs will not fit into core storage or because large parts of core are occupied by segments of programs that are seldom used.

It is not feasible or economical to structure a computer so that any program can use all of core.   Therefore, programs must be structured in such a way that different segments can be assigned to the same part of core at different times. Traditionally, overlay techniques have been used to do this by means of trading segments of a program between core storage and auxiliary storage (disks, drums, tapes, etc.).   However, for a variety of reasons, it is preferable to relieve a programmer of the task of using overlays.

Another approach is presented by a *virtual-storage computer* (VSC).   The central idea behind a VSC is to permit a programmer to write a program as though an unlimited, but imaginary (or *virtual*), storage is available.   When the VSC executes a virtual program, it automatically brings into core several segments of the program at a time, mapping the program's virtual address space into the physical addresses in core storage.   If, in executing the program, a reference is made to a segment of the program which is not in core, the VSC will *fetch* that segment from auxiliary storage and place it in core if there is a sufficient amount of unused core available.   If no core is available, it places a segment of the program which is in core in auxiliary storage to make room for the required segment.

In principle the VSC could fetch and replace one word of a program at a time, but in practice this would be uneconomical.   Since auxiliary storage devices require relatively long periods of time to access information, but relatively little time to transmit it, one can just as economically fetch an entire segment of a program at one time.   This is also justified by the observation that once a given word in a program has been referenced, the probability is high that an adjacent word or words will soon be referenced.

The problem thus arises of deciding how large, or small, a segment should be fetched in one VSC operation.   Experience with various fetching schemes indicates that it is convenient to fetch only fixed-size segments, which are called *pages*.   This avoids the complications of fetching variable-size segments and having to decide how to fit them in core.   It also prevents large segments from being fetched and using core inefficiently.

The number of words in a page is usually chosen to be a power of 2, say 2^m.   If the number of words in the program is 2^n, with $n > m$, then the program is automatically partitioned into 2^k pages, where $k = n - m$.   Core storage is also divided into segments of the same length, which are called *page frames.*

The sequence of VSC operations involved in swapping program pages in and out of core can now be described.

1   The virtual program is partitioned into pages, some of which are placed in core.   It is important to point out that some of these pages may contain only code, while others may contain only data.

2   During execution, access to a page which is not in core may be required.   This is detected by a reference to a *page table*, which indicates whether or not any given page is in core.

3   A *missing page fault* is said to occur.

4   A VSC program, called a *paging algorithm*, places the required page in core by replacing, if necessary, a page already in core; this is called *demand paging.*

5   The execution of the virtual program is interrupted while this page swap takes place, and another virtual program resumes its execution.

6   The interrupt of the given virtual program is completed when the required page has been placed in core.

7   When the virtual program resumes execution, reference is again made to the same page; at this time, no page fault occurs.

In this section we discuss, in somewhat idealistic terms, several of the algorithmic aspects of paging.   We shall present several simple paging algorithms of either theoretical or practical interest, and we shall test them in order to see what effect they have on the efficiency of memory utilization by a virtual-storage computer.

The main objective of a paging algorithm is to minimize the number of page faults which occur in executing an arbitrary program.   A secondary objective is to make the decisions regarding which pages to swap with a minimum amount of overhead.   Ideally, a paging algorithm replaces those pages that will not be used again for the longest time, and it retains those pages that will be used most often.   Unfortunately, there is usually no information available about subsequent references to a given page when a page fault occurs.

In such cases the decision about which page to replace must be based either on randomness or on some accumulation of information about previous references to the pages of the virtual program.

We shall discuss the following five paging algorithms:

RANDOM   This algorithm assumes that all pages are equally likely to be referenced at any time.   The page to be replaced is chosen at random.

FIFO (*first-in first-out*)   This algorithm always replaces the page that has been in core the longest.   Its justification is based on the notion of *program locality,* which states that the number of references in a program between two successive page replacements is relatively high. That is, programs tend to spend time executing instructions within a given set of pages, after which they move on to a different set of pages. Therefore, it is anticipated that the oldest page in memory is the least likely to be used in the future.

LRU (*least recently used*) This algorithm replaces the page in memory to which reference has not been made for the longest time. The hope is that since this page has not been referenced in the recent past, it will not be referenced in the near future.

LFU (*least frequently used*) This algorithm maintains a *frequency-of-reference* table for all pages in the program, both in and out of core, and replaces the page in core whose frequency of use is the lowest. The justification for this algorithm is that pages in a program tend to be divided into two categories: those which are used frequently (for example, those containing DO-loops) and those which are used infrequently (for example, those containing program initialization statements, input/output statements, or infrequently referenced data).

BEST This algorithm is primarily of theoretical interest since it assumes complete knowledge of all future page references and always makes the best possible choice of which page to replace; that is, it replaces the page whose next reference occurs later than any other page reference.

As we shall see, Algorithms RANDOM and BEST are very useful since they provide benchmarks against which to compare the performance of any paging algorithm.

For reasons of simplicity we assume that the input to each of these paging algorithms consists of an array REF(1), ..., REF(N) of integers, an integer FRAMES which indicates the number of page frames available in core, and an integer PAGES which indicates the number of pages in a given program. The array REF(1), ..., REF(N), which is called the *reference string*, represents the complete sequence of page references generated in executing a given virtual program, where we assume that these pages are numbered $1, 2, \ldots,$ PAGES. While it may be true in practice that a reference string will contain many subsequences of repeated page references, in studying paging algorithms such repeated page numbers are of no consequence. We assume therefore that REF(I) $\neq$ REF(I + 1) for $I = 1, \ldots, N - 1$.

Before presenting implementations of these paging algorithms, let us present an example which illustrates how Algorithm BEST works. Assume that we are given three page frames in core in which to run a program consisting of five pages. The reference string produced in executing this program is: 1 2 3 4 1 2 5 3 4 5 2 5.

Figure 5.4.1 shows the sequence of page replacements produced by Algorithm BEST. Even though one might say that page faults occur at lines 1, 2, and 3, we shall consider them to be "free" replacements. Note that for the page fault at line 4, we replace page 3 since its next reference is at time 8, while pages 1 and 2 are

	Page reference	Contents of page frames				Next contents of frames			
		1	2	3		1	2	3	
1	1				→	1			FREE
2	2	1			→	1	2		FREE
3	3	1	2		→	1	2	3	FREE
4	4	1	2	3	→	1	2	4	FAULT: 3 OCCURS LATEST
5	1	1	2	4	→	1	2	4	
6	2	1	2	4	→	1	2	4	
7	5	1	2	4	→	5	2	4	FAULT: 1 OCCURS LATEST
8	3	5	2	4	→	5	3	4	FAULT: 2 OCCURS LATEST
9	4	5	3	4	→	5	3	4	
10	5	5	3	4	→	5	3	4	
11	2	5	3	4	→	5	2	4	FAULT: 3 OCCURS LATEST
12	5	5	2	4	→	5	2	4	

FIG. 5.4.1 A sequence of page replacements using Algorithm BEST; that is, replace that page in core whose next page reference occurs the latest.

referenced at times 5 and 6, respectively. Note also that in case of ties (for example, at line 11), we replace the page with the smallest subscript. The reader is encouraged to construct a similar page replacement figure for at least one of the other paging algorithms before continuing.

We leave the implementation of Algorithms RANDOM and BEST as exercises, and concentrate on implementing Algorithms FIFO, LRU, and LFU.

In order to implement Algorithm FIFO, we set up a circular queue, FRAME(1), FRAME(2), . . . , FRAME(M), where M = FRAMES is the number of page FRAMES in core. As new page references occur, they are placed in the first available frame until all frames are used, at which point we resume loading new pages again from FRAME(1), FRAME(2), etc. This implementation is shown in Fig. 5.4.2.

In order to implement Algorithm LRU, we construct a page table TABLE, where TABLE(I) = J if page I is currently in page frame J. A doubly linked list with forward and backward links—BEFORE(I) and AFTER(I)—is used to order the set of pages currently in core according to the most recent reference. The variable FRONT points to the page in core which was least recently referenced. When a page fault occurs, the page at the FRONT of this list is deleted from the list (and from core) and the newly referenced page is inserted at the END of the list. When a page reference occurs to a page currently in some page frame, this page is deleted from this list and inserted at the END. Figure 5.4.3 gives this implementation of Algorithm LRU.

The implementation of Algorithm LFU is similar to that of the previous two algorithms. The major difference is that we use an array FREQ, where the current

```
      SUBROUTINE FIFO ( REF,N,FRAMES,PAGES )
C
C         THIS SUBROUTINE ACCEPTS AS INPUT A SEQUENCE REF(1), REF(2),...
C         REF(N) OF PAGE REFERENCES, AN INTEGER *FRAMES* WHICH SPECIFIES
C         THE NUMBER OF PAGE FRAMES GIVEN, AND AN INTEGER *PAGES* WHICH
C         SPECIFIES THE NUMBER OF DIFFERENT PAGES.  IT COMPUTES THE
C         NUMBER OF PAGE FAULTS PRODUCED BY THE SEQUENCE USING A FIFO
C         (FIRST-IN FIRST-OUT) REPLACEMENT ALGORITHM.  IT OUTPUTS THE
C         REFERENCE STRING REF(1)...REF(N), A SEQUENCE FAULT(1)...
C         FAULT(N), WHERE FAULT(I)=1 IF REF(I) PRODUCES A FAULT,
C         FAULT(I)=0 OTHERWISE.  IT ALSO OUTPUTS THE TOTAL NUMBER OF
C         PAGE FAULTS PRODUCED, AND THE FAULT RATE FOR THIS NUMBER OF
C         FRAMES.
C
C *** FORMAL PARAMETERS
C
C   REF(1)...REF(N)            REFERENCE STRING
C
C   FRAMES                     NUMBER OF FRAMES GIVEN
C
C   PAGES                      NUMBER OF DIFFERENT PAGES
C
C   *** LOCAL VARIABLES
C
C   FAULT(1)...FAULT(N)        =1 IF REF(I) PRODUCES A FAULT,=0 OTHERWISE
C
C   FRAME(I)                   CONTAINS THE PAGE NUMBER IN FRAME I
C
C   TABLE(I)                   =J IF PAGE I IS IN FRAME J, =0 OTHERWISE
C
C   TOTAL                      TOTAL NUMBER OF PAGE FAULTS PRODUCED
C
      INTEGER REF(N), FRAMES, PAGES
      INTEGER FAULT(1000),FRAME(50),P,TABLE(100),TOTAL
C
C     INITIALIZE VARIABLES
C
      DO 10 I = 1,N
         FAULT(I) = 0
   10 CONTINUE
      P = PAGES + 1
      DO 20 I = 1,P
         TABLE(I) = 0
   20 CONTINUE
      DO 30 I = 1,FRAMES
         FRAME(I) = P
   30 CONTINUE
      J = 1
      TOTAL = 0
```

FIG. 5.4.2 An implementation of Algorithm FIFO.

value of FREQ(K) equals the number of times page K has occurred in the reference string.   When a page fault occurs, we remove the page J in core which has the smallest value of FREQ(J).   If two or more pages in core have the same smallest frequency, we remove the page which has been in core the longest.   This is determined by examining an array ENTER, where ENTER(J) equals the time at which page J last entered core; that is, if REF(I) = K produces a page fault, we set ENTER(K) = I.   This implementation is shown in Fig. 5.4.4.

   Let us test each of these paging algorithms.   For each algorithm we shall construct a page reference string of length N and shall record the number of page

```
C
C         ITERATE ON REFERENCE STRING REF(1)...REF(N)
C
          DO 100 I = 1,N
C
C             IS PAGE K IN CORE
C
              K = REF(I)
              IF ( TABLE(K) .NE. 0 ) GO TO 100
C
C                 REMOVE PAGE FROM FRAME(J) AND INSERT PAGE K
C
                  L = FRAME(J)
                  TABLE(L) = 0
                  TABLE(K) = I
                  FRAME(J) = K
                  J = J - J/FRAMES*FRAMES + 1
                  FAULT(I) = 1
                  TOTAL = TOTAL + 1
  100 CONTINUE
C
C     OUTPUT RESULTS
C
      WRITE (6,900) FRAMES, PAGES
  900 FORMAT (1H0,31H THE FIFO PAGING ALGORITHM FOR ,I3,12H FRAMES AND
     1            I3,6H PAGES)
      WRITE (6,950)
  950 FORMAT (1H0,40H THE REFERENCE STRING AND FAULT SEQUENCE)
      WRITE (6,1000) (REF(I),I=1,N)
      WRITE (6,1000) (FAULT(I),I=1,N)
 1000 FORMAT (1H0,40I3)
C
C     THE FIRST *FRAMES* FAULTS ARE FREE
C
      TOTAL = TOTAL - FRAMES
      RATE = FLOAT(TOTAL) / (N-FRAMES)
      WRITE (6,1010) TOTAL, RATE
 1010 FORMAT (1H0,21H NUMBER OF FAULTS IS ,I3,17H AND THE RATE IS ,F6.3)
      RETURN
      END
```

FIG. 5.4.2 (*Continued*)

faults (TOTAL) produced by this string. The *fault rate* for each algorithm is the ratio (TOTAL − FRAMES)/(N − FRAMES), where FRAMES is the number of page frames available in core. The reason for subtracting FRAMES from both TOTAL and N is that we treat the first FRAMES faults to be "free" since all algorithms invariably fill up all page frames with pages.

In order to carry out this testing plan we must make a few simplifying assumptions:

1 The programs generating the reference strings will have 20 pages. The first 6 will be code pages, and the remaining 14 will be data pages (see Fig. 5.4.5).

2 Since the fault rate for any algorithm strongly depends on the ratio of PAGES to FRAMES, we shall vary the number of FRAMES from 2 to 18 in steps of 2. For each value of FRAMES, we shall use the same reference string to compute the fault rate.

```
       SUBROUTINE LRU ( REF,N,FRAMES,PAGES )
C
C          THIS SUBROUTINE IS AN IMPLEMENTATION OF THE LEAST RECENTLY
C          USED PAGING ALGORITHM, WHICH USES A DOUBLY LINKED LIST TO
C          ORDER THE PAGES IN CORE, ACCORDING TO THEIR MOST RECENT
C          REFERENCE.  IT ACCEPTS AS INPUT A PAGE REFERENCE STRING,
C          THE NUMBER OF DIFFERENT PAGES, AND THE NUMBER OF AVAILABLE PAGE
C          FRAMES.  IT OUTPUTS REFERENCE STRING REF(1)...REF(N),
C          A SEQUENCE FAULT(1)...FAULT(N), WHERE FAULT(I)=1 IF REF(I)
C          PRODUCES A PAGE FAULT, FAULT(I)=0 OTHERWISE.  IT ALSO OUTPUTS
C          THE TOTAL NUMBER OF PAGE FAULTS PRODUCED, AND THE FAULT RATE
C          FOR THIS NUMBER OF FRAMES.
C
C ***FORMAL PARAMETERS
C
C  REF(1)...REF(N)              THE PAGE REFERENCE STRING
C
C  FRAMES                       NUMBER OF PAGE FRAMES
C
C  PAGES                        NUMBER OF PAGES IN THE PROGRAM,
C
C ***LOCAL VARIABLES
C
C  BEFORE(I)                    LINKS IN THE DOUBLY LINKED LIST, BEFORE(I)
C  AFTER(I)                     (AFTER(I)) IS THE PAGE WHOSE MOST RECENT
C                               REFERENCE IMMEDIATELY PRECEDED (FOLLOWED)
C                               THE MOST RECENT REFERENCE TO PAGE I
C
C  FAULT(I)                     =1 IF REF(I) PRODUCES A PAGE FAULT
C                               =0 OTHERWISE
C
C  FRONT,END                    OF THE DOUBLY LINKED LIST, FRONT(END)
C                               POINTS TO THE LEAST (MOST) RECENTLY
C                               REFERENCED PAGE
C
C  J                            INDEX OF A FRAME
C
C  K                            CURRENT PAGE REFERENCE
C
C  TABLE(I)                     =J IF PAGE I IS IN FRAME J
C                               =0 IF PAGE I IS NOT IN CORE
C
C  TOTAL                        NUMBER OF PAGE FAULTS PRODUCED BY
C                               REF(1)...REF(N)
C
       INTEGER REF(N), FRAMES, PAGES
       INTEGER AFTER(100),BEFORE(100),END,FAULT(1000),FRAME(50),FRONT
       INTEGER J,K,TABLE(100),TOTAL,T1,T2
C
C      INITIALIZE VARIABLES
C
       J = 1
       DO 30 I = 1,PAGES
            TABLE(I) = 0
            BEFORE(I) = 0
            AFTER(I) = 0
   30 CONTINUE
C
C      FILL UP ALL PAGE FRAMES
C
       I = 1
       K = REF(1)
       TABLE(K) = 1
       FRONT = K
       END = K
       FAULT(1) = 1
       TOTAL = 1
       FRAME(1) = REF(1)
       DO 100 J = 2,FRAMES
   40       I = I + 1
```

FIG. 5.4.3 An implementation of Algorithm LRU.

256

```
C
C                    ARE WE FINISHED WITH THE REFERENCE STRING
C
                IF ( I .GT. N ) GO TO 170
C
C                        GET THE I-TH REFERENCE
C
                    K = REF(I)
C
C                        IS PAGE K IN CORE
C
                    IF ( TABLE(K) .NE. 0 ) GO TO 50
                        GO TO 90
C                        THEN ADD TO END OF FRAME LIST
      50                FAULT(I) = 0
C
C                            IS PAGE K AT END OF LIST
C
                        IF (AFTER(K) .EQ. 0 ) GO TO 40
C
C                                IS PAGE K AT THE FRONT OF THE LIST
C
                            IF ( FRONT .EQ. K ) GO TO 60
                                GO TO 70
C                                THEN DELETE FROM THE FRONT OF THE LIST
      60                            FRONT = AFTER(K)
                                    BEFORE(FRONT) = 0
                                    GO TO 80
C                                ELSE DELETE FROM THE MIDDLE OF THE LIST
      70                            T1 = BEFORE(K)
                                    T2 = AFTER(K)
                                    AFTER(T1) = T2
                                    BEFORE(T2) = T1
C
C                            ADD PAGE K TO THE END OF THE LIST
C
      80                    BEFORE(K) = END
                            AFTER(K) = 0
                            AFTER(END) = K
                            END = K
                            GO TO 40
C                        ELSE PLACE PAGE K IN FRAME J AND ADD IT AT END OF LIST
      90                    TABLE(K) = J
                            FRAME(J) = K
                            AFTER(END) = K
                            BEFORE(K) = END
                            END = K
                            FAULT(I) = 1
                            TOTAL = TOTAL + 1
     100 CONTINUE
C
C      ALL PAGE FRAMES ARE USED FROM HERE ON
C
      IN = I + 1
      DO 160 I = IN,N
          K = REF(I)
C
C          IS PAGE K IN CORE
C
          IF ( TABLE(K) .NE. 0 ) GO TO 110
                GO TO 150
C            THEN RECORD NO FAULT
     110      FAULT(I) = 0
C
C              IS PAGE K AT END OF LIST
C
              IF ( AFTER(K) .EQ. 0 ) GO TO 160
C
C                  IS PAGE K AT THE FRONT OF THE LIST
```

FIG. 5.4.3 (*Continued*)

```
C
                         IF ( FRONT .EQ. K ) GO TO 120
                             GO TO 130
C                          THEN DELETE PAGE K FROM THE FRONT OF THE LIST
   120                         FRONT = AFTER(K)
                               BEFORE(FRONT) = 0
                               GO TO 140
C                          ELSE DELETE PAGE K FROM THE MIDDLE OF THE LIST
   130                         T1 = BEFORE(K)
                               T2 = AFTER(K)
                               BEFORE(T2) = T1
                               AFTER(T1) = T2
C
C                         ADD PAGE K TO THE END OF THE LIST
C
   140                        BEFORE(K) = END
                              AFTER(K) = 0
                              AFTER(END) = K
                              END = K
                              GO TO 160
C
C                ELSE DELETE LEAST RECENTLY USED PAGE J FROM CORE
C                AND PUT PAGE K IN FRAME J
C
   150               J = TABLE(FRONT)
                     TABLE(K) = J
                     TABLE(FRONT) = 0
C
C                ADD PAGE K TO THE END OF THE LIST AND DELETE
C                THE LEAST RECENTLY USED PAGE FROM THE FRONT OF THE LIST
C
                     FRAME(J) = K
                     AFTER(END) = K
                     BEFORE(K) = END
                     END = K
                     T1 = AFTER(FRONT)
                     BEFORE(T1) = 0
                     AFTER(FRONT) = 0
                     FRONT = T1
                     FAULT(I) = 1
                     TOTAL = TOTAL + 1
   160 CONTINUE
   170 CONTINUE
C
C     OUTPUT RESULTS
C
      WRITE (6,900) FRAMES, PAGES
  900 FORMAT (1H0,30H THE LRU PAGING ALGORITHM FOR ,I3,12H FRAMES AND ,
     1         I3,6H PAGES)
      WRITE (6,950)
  950 FORMAT (1H0,40H THE REFERENCE STRING AND FAULT SEQUENCE)
      WRITE (6,1000) (REF(I),I=1,N)
      WRITE (6,1000) (FAULT(I),I=1,N)
 1000 FORMAT (1H0,40I3)
C
C     THE FIRST *FRAMES* FAULTS ARE FREE
C
      TOTAL = TOTAL - FRAMES
      RATE = FLOAT(TOTAL) / (N-FRAMES)
      WRITE (6,1010) TOTAL,RATE
 1010 FORMAT (1H0,21H NUMBER OF FAULTS IS ,I3,17H AND THE RATE IS ,F6.3)
      RETURN
      END
```

FIG. 5.4.3 *(Continued)*

3 The most important assumptions concern the mechanism for generating a reference string. Ideally, this string should be "representative" of the page references generated by a "typical" 20-page program with 14 data pages. Unfortunately, it is very difficult to define what is meant by a typical program. We shall therefore make several assumptions based on Fig. 5.4.5.

```
      SUBROUTINE LFU ( REF, N, FRAMES, PAGES )
C
C         THIS SUBROUTINE ACCEPTS AS INPUT A SEQUENCE REF(1)...REF(N) OF
C         PAGE REFERENCES, AN INTEGER *FRAMES* WHICH SPECIFIES THE NUMBER
C         OF AVAILABLE PAGE FRAMES, AND AN INTEGER *PAGES* WHICH
C         SPECIFIES THE NUMBER OF DIFFERENT PAGES.  IT COMPUTES THE
C         NUMBER OF PAGE FAULTS PRODUCED BY THE SEQUENCE USING A
C         LEAST FREQUENTLY USED REPLACEMENT ALGORITHM.  IT OUTPUTS THE
C         REFERENCE STRING REF(1)...REF(N), A SEQUENCE FAULT(1)...
C         FAULT(N), WHERE FAULT(I)=1 IF REF(I) PRODUCES A PAGE FAULT,
C         FAULT(I)=0 OTHERWISE.  IT ALSO OUTPUTS THE TOTAL NUMBER OF
C         PAGE FAULTS PRODUCED BY THE SEQUENCE AND THE FAULT RATE FOR
C         THIS NUMBER OF FRAMES.
C
C ***FORMAL PARAMETERS
C
C   REF(1)...REF(N)           PAGE REFERENCE STRING
C
C   FRAMES                    NUMBER OF PAGE FRAMES GIVEN
C
C   PAGES                     NUMBER OF PAGES IN THE PROGRAM
C
C ***LOCAL VARIABLES
C
C   ENTER(I)                  RECORDS THE MOST RECENT OCCURRENCE OF A
C                             REFERENCE TO PAGE I
C   FAULT(I)                  =1 IF REF(I) PRODUCES A PAGE FAULT
C                             =0 OTHERWISE
C   FRAME(I)                  =J IF PAGE J IS IN FRAME I
C
C   FREQ(I)                   THE NUMBER OF TIMES PAGE I HAS APPEARED
C                             IN THE REFERENCE STRING
C   TABLE(I)                  =J IF PAGE I IS IN FRAME J
C                             =0 IF PAGE I IS NOT IN CORE
C   TOTAL                     TOTAL NUMBER OF PAGE FAULTS PRODUCED BY
C                             REF(1)...REF(N)
      INTEGER   REF(N), FRAMES, PAGES
      INTEGER ENTER(100),FAULT(1000),FRAME(50),FREQ(100),TABLE(100)
      INTEGER TOTAL
C
C     INITIALIZE VARIABLES
C
      J = 1
      TOTAL = 0
      DO 10 I = 1, PAGES
         TABLE(I) = 0
         FREQ(I) = 0
         ENTER(I) = 0
   10 CONTINUE
```

FIG. 5.4.4 An implementation of Algorithm LFU.

```
C
C          ITERATE ON REFERENCE STRING
C
           DO 100 I = 1, N
C
C              GET THE I-TH REFERENCE AND INCREASE ITS FREQUENCY
C
               K = REF(I)
               FREQ(K) = FREQ(K) + 1
C
C              IS PAGE K IN CORE
C
               IF ( TABLE(K) .NE. 0 ) GO TO 20
                   GO TO 30
C                THEN NO PAGE FAULT
     20              FAULT(I) = 0
                   GO TO 100
C                ELSE A PAGE FAULT
     30              FAULT(I) = 1
                   TOTAL = TOTAL + 1
C
C                  ARE ALL PAGE FRAMES FULL
C
                   IF ( J .GT. FRAMES ) GO TO 40
                       GO TO 90
C                    THEN FIND THE LEAST FREQUENT PAGE TO DELETE
     40                  M = 1
                       M1 = FRAME(1)
                       MIN = FREQ(M1)
                       DO 80 L = 2,FRAMES
                           L1 = FRAME(L)
                           IF ( MIN - FREQ(L1) ) 80,70,50
     50                        MIN = FREQ(L1)
     60                        M = L
                               M1 = L1
                               GO TO 80
     70                    IF ( ENTER(M1) - ENTER(L1) ) 80,80,60
     80                CONTINUE
C
C                      DELETE LEAST FREQUENTLY USED PAGE AND ADD PAGE K
C                      TO CORE
C
                       J1 = FRAME(M)
                       FRAME(M) = K
                       ENTER(K) = I
                       TABLE(K) = M
                       TABLE(J1) = 0
                       GO TO 100
C                    ELSE ADD PAGE K TO FRAME J
     90                  TABLE(K) = J
                       FRAME(J) = K
                       ENTER(K) = I
                       J = J + 1
   100 CONTINUE
C
C      OUTPUT RESULTS
C
       WRITE (6,900) FRAMES,PAGES
   900 FORMAT (1H0,30H THE LFU PAGING ALGORITHM FOR ,I3,12H FRAMES AND ,
      1        I3,6H PAGES)
       WRITE (6,950)
   950 FORMAT (1H0,40H THE REFERENCE STRING AND FAULT SEQUENCE)
       WRITE (6,1000) (REF(I),I=1,N)
       WRITE (6,1000) (FAULT(I),I=1,N)
  1000 FORMAT (1H0,40I3)
C
C      THE FIRST *FRAMES* FAULTS ARE FREE
C
       TOTAL = TOTAL - FRAMES
       RATE = FLOAT(TOTAL) / (N-FRAMES)
       WRITE( 6, 1010 ) TOTAL, RATE
  1010 FORMAT (1H0,21H NUMBER OF FAULTS IS ,I3,17H AND THE RATE IS ,F6.3)
       RETURN
       END
```

FIG. 5.4.4 (Continued)

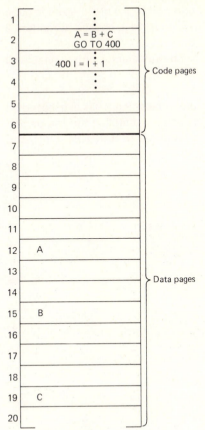

FIG. 5.4.5 Each program is assumed to have 6 code pages and 14 data pages.

Consider the statements $A = B + C$ and GO TO 400 on page 2 of this figure, where variables A, B, and C are stored in data pages 12, 15, and 19, respectively. When translated into assembly code, this statement is likely to produce the page reference string 2–19–2–15–2–12–2–3. This suggests that reference strings are likely to alternate between code pages and data pages, with an occasional pair of consecutive code pages. In addition, the idea of locality suggests that code page references will not vary considerably but will congregate around a small set of code pages for a period of time and then move on to another set of pages. We therefore assume that:

1 A code page reference will be followed by a data page 98 percent of the time; 2 percent of the time it is followed by a new code page chosen at random.

2 This data page is chosen on a most recently used basis. That is, a pushdown store is used to store data pages in order of most recent reference. New data pages are chosen from the top of the pushdown downwards with probabilities .50, .25, .125, .0625, .03125, etc.

3 Once a data page has been chosen, it is followed by the previous code page 98 percent of the time. It is followed by a code page chosen at random 2 percent of the time.

4 A reference string of length N = 10,000 will be sufficiently long to enable all pages to be referenced.

Figure 5.4.6 illustrates what a typical page reference string looks like, based on these assumptions. Figure 5.4.7 represents the results of testing the five paging algorithms. These results suggest that LRU is preferred to RANDOM, FIFO, and LFU—a fact which is confirmed in practice.

```
PAGE REFERENCE STRING FOR A PROGRAM WITH  20 PAGES.
PAGES  1... 6 ARE CODE PAGES.
PAGES  7...20 ARE DATA PAGES.
```

```
 1 11    1 11    1 11    1 11    1 11    1 11    6  9    6  7    6  7    6 10
 6 11    6 11    6 10    6 10    6 10    6 11    6  9    6  9    6  7    6  7
 6  7    6  9    6  9    6  7    6  7    6  7    6  7    6  9    6  7    6  7
 6  7    6  9    6  7    6  7    6  7    6 11    6 11    6  9    6  7    6  9
 6  7    6  7    6  7    6 10    6  7    6 11    6 10    6 10    6 11    6 11
 6 11    6 10    6 10    6 10    6 11    6 10    6 10    6 10    6 10    6 11
 6 11    6 11    6  7    6  7    6  7    6 11    6 11    6 10    6 10    6 11
 6 10    6 10    6 11    6  7    6  7    6  7    6  7    6 10    6 10    6 10
 6 10    6 10    6 10    6  9    6  9    6  9    6  9    6 10    6  8    6 10
 6 10    6 10    6 10    6 10    6  8    6  8    6  8    4  8    4 10    4  8
 4  9    4  9    4  9    4  9    4  9    4  7    4  7    4  7    4 15    4 15
 4  9    4  9    4  9    4  9    4 10    4 16    4 16    4 10    4 10    4 16
 4 10    4 10    4 10    4 16    4  9    4 15    4  7    4  7    4  7    4 15
 4  7    4  7    4  7    4  7    4 15    4  7    4  7    4  7    4  9    4  9
 4  9    4 10    4 10    4 15    4 15    4 15    4  9    4  9    4  9    4  9
 4 15    4  7    4  7    4 15    4 15    4 15    4 15    4 15    4 15    4  8
 4 10    4 10    4 10    4  8    4  8    4 10    4 10    4 10    4 10    4 10
 4 10    4 10    4 10    4 10    4 16    4 10    4  8    4 15    4 15    4  7
```

FIG. 5.4.6 A page reference string for a program with 20 pages; pages 1 through 6 are code pages, and pages 7 through 20 are data pages.

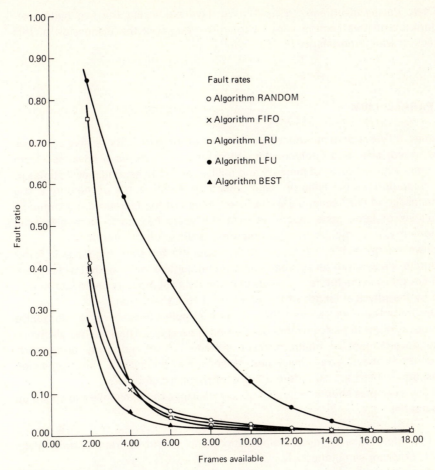

FIG. 5.4.7 Results of testing five paging algorithms.

Exercises 5.4

5.4.1 Construct page replacement figures, similar to Fig. 5.4.1, for at least one of the other paging algorithms of this section.

5.4.2 Implement Algorithm RANDOM.

5.4.3 Implement Algorithm BEST.

5.4.4 *Paging algorithms* (*testing*).   In order to keep the discussion of testing short and simple, we made a number of simplifying assumptions.   Critically assess these assumptions and the testing procedures followed in this section.

L5.4.5 *Paging algorithms* (*testing*).   Look into the paging procedures (if any) used by your computer(s).

L5.4.6 *Paging algorithms* (*testing*). We have not tested the five paging algorithms in this section very thoroughly. Augment the discussion of this section with experiments of your own.

5.5 PARALLELISM

In the past 30 years of computing, there have been some truly impressive advances in the speed, size, and sophistication of computers. We have advanced from computers with 8K words of memory and millisecond (10^{-3} seconds) cycle times to such computers as the Illiac IV, which has 512K 64-bit words of memory and a 240-nanosecond (10^{-9} seconds) cycle time. Much of the increased performance capabilities of large-scale machines over the years has come from advanced componentry, in particular through microminiaturization of circuits.

However, given the world's insatiable appetite for even bigger and faster computers, we seem to be approaching a technological impasse that will prevent major advances in the future. Speeds of present-day computers are in fact slowed down by the physical length of the wires used to transmit data.

One promising way around the apparent circuitry impasse is to reorganize computer systems to perform more operations in parallel. This idea has given rise to the development of multiprocessor systems, structured array processors, unstructured linear array machines, associative processors, and pipelined processors. These are all different kinds of parallel computers.

A few examples should indicate how parallelism can be exploited to speed up computations:

1 Performance of input, computation, and output operations on a given program simultaneously
2 Setting all values of an array to 0
3 Performance of vector, or array, arithmetic—for example, $A \leftarrow B + C$, where B and C are either vectors or matrices (this feature is already found in such languages as APL)
4 Simultaneous branching and bounding at various nodes of a tree structure
5 Performance of the same sequence of operations on different sets of data
6 Performance of different and independent operations on the same set of data
7 Pipelining, or looking ahead—that is, simultaneous processing of several instructions in a sequential list of instructions, where these instructions are in various stages of execution
8 Performance of simultaneous searching
9 Parallel sorting
10 Performance of simultaneous function evaluations, for example, in the search for a maximum or a zero of a function.

We do not mean to suggest that all computations can be "made" parallel.   In this regard, a general rule of thumb, called the *Amdahl effect*, seems to have developed in the brief history of parallel computing.   Roughly speaking, this states that in order for a computation to be reasonably effective on a parallel machine with m processors, it should be possible to divide the computation into m data streams, where substantially fewer than $1/m$ of its instruction segments have to be executed sequentially.   The Amdahl effect is based on observations of the inherent lack of parallelism in most of today's source programs.   Even though the real world is inherently parallel, our algorithmic view of it is basically sequential.   This is due in part to more than 300 years of sequential mathematics and more than 20 years of sequential Fortran programming.

A Parallel Spanning Tree Algorithm

Let us begin to develop some intuition about the design and analysis of parallel algorithms by returning to the minimum-weight spanning tree algorithm of Chap. 4.   We can attempt to construct a parallel version of this algorithm by considering what would happen if we simultaneously selected a lightest edge incident to every vertex in a weighted network G.

The example in Fig. 5.5.1 shows that if we did this, we could select an unwanted cycle of edges—for example, for v_1 select e_{12}, for v_2 select e_{24}, and for v_4 select e_{41}. We would also select e_{54} for v_5, e_{62} for v_6, and e_{32} for v_3. The simultaneously selected edges are indicated with bold lines.

If, however, we select for each vertex v_i that lightest edge which is incident to the vertex v_j ($j \neq i$) with a smallest subscript, then we cannot select a cycle of edges.   To see this, suppose that v_i, v_j, v_k, v_i is a cycle selected in this way—that is, e_{ij} is selected for v_i, e_{jk} is selected for v_j, and e_{ki} is selected for v_k.   Assume that i is the smallest subscript of i, j, k.   It then follows that weight $w_{ij} \geq w_{jk}$, since if $w_{ij} < w_{jk}$, then e_{ij} would have been selected for v_j.   By the same argument, $w_{jk} \geq w_{ki}$ and $w_{ki} \geq w_{ij}$.   Thus all weights must be the same.   If this is the case, then e_{ij} must have been selected for v_j since i is the smallest subscript.   This contradicts our

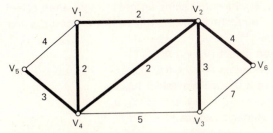

FIG. 5.5.1 A cycle of edges obtained by simultaneously selecting any lightest edge adjacent to each vertex.

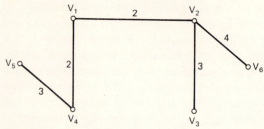

FIG. 5.5.2 A spanning tree found by simultaneously selecting lightest edges with the smallest vertex subscripts.

assumption that e_{jk} is selected for v_j. A similar argument can be given for a cycle of any number of edges.

Figure 5.5.2 shows the edges which would be selected with this modification. Notice that not only did this rule enable us to find a spanning tree of G in one parallel step, but this tree has minimum weight! The network G in Fig. 5.5.3, however, shows that this parallel algorithm is not always this fast.

Let us now state an algorithm, due to Sollin, which is a straightforward modification of this procedure.

Algorithm SOLLIN To find a minimum-weight spanning tree T in a weighted, connected network G with M vertices, $V_1, V_2, \ldots, V_M$, and N edges.

Step 1. [Select lightest edges] Simultaneously select, for each vertex V in G, a lightest edge incident to V; **if** two or more edges incident to V have the same lightest weight **then** select the edge which connects V to the vertex with the smallest subscript **fi**; **set** K ← the number of edges thus selected.

Step 2. [Have M − 1 edges been selected?] **While** K < M − 1 **do** step 3 **od**; **and** STOP.

Step 3. [Select edges between subtrees] Let $T_1, T_2, \ldots, T_L$ denote the subtrees of G formed by the edges selected so far; simultaneously select, for each subtree T_I, a lightest edge between a vertex in T_I and any other subtree T_J; **if** two or more edges, say (V_P, V_Q) and (V_R, V_S), have the same lightest weight, **then** select the edge according to the following rule, where we assume that P < Q and R < S:

    if P < R **then** select (V_P, V_Q) **fi**;

    if R < P **then** select (V_R, V_S) **fi**;

    if P = R **then if** Q < S **then** select (V_P, V_Q)

                         else select (V_R, V_S) **fi fi**;

    set K ← total number of edges selected so far.

Before commenting on the correctness and complexity of Sollin's parallel algorithm, let us illustrate it with an example.

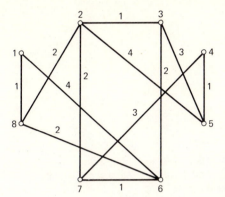

FIG. 5.5.3 A network requiring more than one parallel step to find a minimum-weight spanning tree.

After applying step 1 of Algorithm SOLLIN to the network G in Fig. 5.5.3, we shall have found the four subtrees T_1, T_2, T_4, and T_6 of Fig. 5.5.4. Three edges (e_{27}, e_{28}, and e_{36}) connecting T_2 with another tree have the same weight (2); of these edges we would choose e_{27} over e_{28} and e_{27} over e_{36} since 2 is the smallest subscript. For T_4 the choice is between e_{47} and e_{53}; we choose e_{53} since 3 is the smallest subscript. For T_6 the choice is between e_{72}, e_{68}, and e_{63}; we choose e_{72}. Finally, for T_1 the choice is between e_{82} and e_{86}; we choose e_{82}. Thus, after one application of step 3, we have the minimum-weight spanning tree in Fig. 5.5.5.

In order to establish the correctness of Algorithm SOLLIN, it suffices to show each of the following:

One application of step 1 produces a forest.

If the set of edges selected prior to step 3 forms a forest, then so does the set of edges selected after step 3.

Step 3 (and step 1) selects at least one edge; this guarantees that Algorithm SOLLIN stops in a finite number of steps.

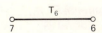

FIG. 5.5.4 The subtrees of the network in Fig. 5.5.3 formed by Algorithm SOLLIN in one step.

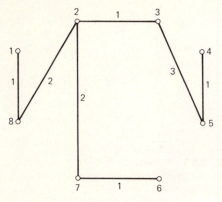

FIG. 5.5.5 The minimum-weight spanning tree found by Algorithm SOLLIN after two steps.

Given the above, one could assert that Algorithm SOLLIN finds a spanning tree T. It would only remain to show that:

The spanning tree T found by Algorithm SOLLIN has minimum weight.

Proofs of the above four suppositions can be constructed by generalizing those given for Algorithm PRIM in Chap. 4; they are left as exercises.

The example in Fig. 5.5.4 illustrates that the fewest possible number of edges selected in step 1 is $\lceil M/2 \rceil$ and that $\lfloor M/2 \rfloor$ subtrees would be formed in this case. It is easy to see, for the same reason, that if there are r subtrees formed on entry to step 3, then at least $\lceil r/2 \rceil$ additional edges will be selected in one application of step 3. One can see furthermore that each of these selected edges will reduce the number of subtrees remaining by one.

Therefore, if we let $n(k)$ denote the number of trees remaining after $k-1$ applications of step 3 and one application of step 1, then

$$n(1) \le \left\lfloor \frac{M}{2} \right\rfloor, n(2) \le \left\lfloor \frac{n(1)}{2} \right\rfloor, n(3) \le \left\lfloor \frac{n(2)}{2} \right\rfloor, \ldots$$

or, in general,

$$n(k) \le \left\lfloor \frac{M}{2^k} \right\rfloor$$

If K denotes the first integer for which $n(K) \le 1$, then in the worst case K satisfies $2^{K-1} < M \le 2^K$ — that is, $K \le \log_2 M$. Thus, Algorithm SOLLIN executes $O(\log_2 M)$ steps in the worst case.

This much of the complexity analysis of Algorithm SOLLIN is easy. How many operations and how much time is required to perform each step of the algorithm? The answer to this question depends on the type of computer being used and certain other assumptions.

Let us imagine that we have M processors (computers) $P_1, P_2, \ldots, P_M$, each of which is assigned to one of the M vertices $v_1, v_2, \ldots, v_M$ of G. In each step of

	1	2	3	4	5	6	7	8	Tree	Tree	Tree
$P_1 \to 1$	0	∞	∞	∞	∞	4	∞	1	1	1	1
$P_2 \to 2$	∞	0	1	∞	4	∞	2	2	2	2	1
$P_3 \to 3$	∞	1	0	∞	3	2	∞	∞	3	2	1
$P_4 \to 4$	∞	∞	∞	0	1	∞	3	∞	4	4	1
$P_5 \to 5$	∞	4	3	1	0	∞	∞	∞	5	4	1
$P_6 \to 6$	4	∞	2	∞	∞	0	1	2	6	6	1
$P_7 \to 7$	∞	2	∞	3	∞	1	0	∞	7	6	1
$P_8 \to 8$	1	2	∞	∞	∞	2	∞	0	8	1	1

FIG. 5.5.6 The use of parallel processors $P_1, P_2, \ldots, P_8$ to implement Algorithm SOLLIN.

Algorithm SOLLIN, each processor P_i will essentially walk down the ith row of the adjacency matrix of G, looking for the lightest edge with the smallest subscript, from v_i to a vertex in a tree other than the one containing v_i. Imagine that associated with each vertex is the label TREE(i) of the subtree to which v_i currently belongs. See Fig. 5.5.6, which shows the adjacency matrix for the network of Fig. 5.5.3 and the TREE labels as they might appear after step 1, after steps 2 and 3, and after the second execution of steps 2 and 3.

It follows that step 1 can be executed in parallel in O(M) time, but it will require O(M) steps from each of the M processors—that is, O(M^2) steps will be performed.

In step 3, processor P_i will again examine all edges incident to v_i to find the smallest subscript on a lightest edge to a vertex in another tree incident to v_i. For all processors, this will again require O(M) time and O(M^2) steps. After this, a second pass [O(M)] over all vertices will be required to select the lightest edge for each tree T_j. A final pass [O(M)] over all vertices will be required to update the vector TREE and merge subtrees.

Thus, Algorithm SOLLIN will require O(M) time for step 1 and O(M) time for each of the O($\lfloor \log_2 M \rfloor$) executions of steps 2 and 3; that is, it requires O($M \log_2 M$) time. However, it can be seen to perform O($M^2 \log_2 M$) operations. Contrast this with Algorithm PRIM which requires O(M^2) time and O(M^2) operations.

Parallel Programming Language Considerations

In order to implement a parallel algorithm like Algorithm SOLLIN, we would need a computing system with a sufficient number of processors capable of executing instructions independently and in parallel with each other. We would also need a programming language which would enable us to express the parallelism in the algorithm, that is, which will enable us to write instructions that implement the word "simultaneously."

Consider the flowchart form of Fig. 5.5.7a. If the blocks of instructions in Q_1, Q_2, and Q_3 can be executed simultaneously, but the instructions in Q_4 can only be executed after all instructions in Q_1, Q_2, and Q_3 have been finished, then we might

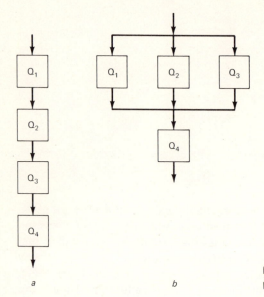

FIG. 5.5.7 The conversion of a sequential process to a parallel process.

reexpress the sequential flow of Fig. 5.5.7a using the parallel flow of Fig. 5.5.7b. In a programming language this might be expressed as

$$\{Q_1//Q_2//Q_3\}; Q_4$$

This indicates that the blocks Q_1, Q_2, and Q_3 are independent and can be executed in parallel. In order to ensure that we achieve the desired results with a statement of this type, we could insist that no variable subject to change in any of the Q_i is referred to in any Q_j $(i \neq j)$.

The effect of this statement is to initiate execution of each block of statements Q_i in parallel. The statement is completed—and Q_4 can be executed—only when all statements in all blocks Q_i are completed.

Within each block of statements, most of the usual kinds of statements, such as assignments, conditional statements, DO-loops, and subroutine calls, are allowed. Perhaps, an exception may be made for conditional jumps out of (or into) a given Q_j, which would be difficult to implement.

A similar type of statement is being implemented in a FORTRAN-like programming language, called IVTRAN, which is being designed for the highly parallel Illiac IV computer at the University of Illinois. It reads

$$\text{DO } k \text{ CONC FOR ALL } (i_1, i_2, \ldots, i_n) \in S$$

where k is a statement label of an executable statement which serves to define the range of the DO-loop.

$(i_1, i_2, \ldots, i_n)$ is a sequence of integer-valued index variables.

S is a finite set of n-tuples of integers which serves to define the range of values which the index variables may assume.

The intent of this statement is to assign one processor to each n-tuple, say, $(v_1, v_2, \ldots, v_n) \in S$. This processor will then execute all statements within the range of the DO-loop under the assumption that $i_1 = v_1, i_2 = v_2, \ldots, i_n = v_n$. Simultaneously, other processors, corresponding to different n-tuples, will execute the same statements within the DO-loop.

For example, consider the following code segment which computes in parallel the square root (SQRT) of each element of a 3×5 array B and places the result in an array A.

```
        DO 10 CONC FOR ALL (I, J) ∈ {1 ≤ I ≤ 3, 1 ≤ J ≤ 5)
          A(I, J) = SQRT(B(I, J))
10      CONTINUE
```

This concurrent DO-loop will require 15 different processors, each of which will execute the body of the DO-loop in what is called an *asynchronous* fashion—that is, no two processors need be executing the same instructions at precisely the same moment.

There are occasions in parallel processing when it is efficient to have all processors operating in complete synchrony. For the Illiac IV, this kind of parallelism can be expressed using the following type of statement.

$$\text{DO } k \text{ SIM FOR ALL } (i_1, i_2, \ldots, i_n) \in S$$

where S is a finite set of n-tuples of integers. This statement is similar to the DO k CONC statement with the exception that the instructions within the DO-loop are executed *synchronously* by all processors.

Occasionally, certain computations in a program must be done sequentially. In DO-loop form this could be expressed as

$$\text{DO } k \text{ SEQ FOR } K \in \{1 \leq K \leq 10\}$$

We can now combine these statements into a routine for multiplying two 10×10 matrices A and B; this will require $10 \times 10 = 100$ processors.

```
        DO 200 CONC FOR ALL (I, J) ∈ {1 ≤ I ≤ 10, 1 ≤ J ≤ 10}
          C(I, J) = 0
          DO 100 SEQ FOR K ∈ {1 ≤ K ≤ 10}
            C(I, J) = C(I, J) + A(I, K) * B(K, J)
100       CONTINUE
200     CONTINUE
```

A Parallel Sorting Algorithm

Consider the problem of sorting n integers or *keys*. Assume that we are given n processors $P_1, P_2, \ldots, P_n$. Into each of these is placed one of the keys. It is no loss of generality to assume that the integers $i_1, i_2, \ldots, i_n$ are the first n positive integers. Figure 5.5.8 illustrates one possible arrangement for $n = 8$.

Each processor P_i is only allowed to communicate and exchange keys with the two processors, P_{i-1} and P_{i+1}, to its immediate left and right. For example, in Fig. 5.5.8, P_6 can only communicate with P_5 and P_7.

Algorithm PARSORT (*PARallel Sort*)   To sort N keys $l_1, l_2, \ldots, l_N$ into ascending order.

Step 0. [Initialize] **Set** M $\leftarrow$ 0; **and** TIME $\leftarrow$ 0.

Step 1. [Alternate until no exchanges twice in a row]
   Do through step 3 **while** M $\neq$ 2 **od**; **and** STOP.

Step 2. [Odd or even] **If** TIME is even
   then simultaneously compare the keys l_{2K} in processors P_{2K} with the keys l_{2K-1} in processors P_{2K-1}, for all K = 1, 2, ..., N/2; if $l_{2K} < l_{2K-1}$ **then** exchange the keys in these two processors **fi**
   else simultaneously compare the keys l_{2K} in processors P_{2K} with the keys l_{2K+1} in processors P_{2K+1}, for all K = 1, 2, ..., N/2; **if** $l_{2K+1} < l_{2K}$ **then** exchange the keys in these two processors **fi fi**.

Step 3. [Did any exchanges take place?] **If** at least one exchange took place in step 2 **then** set M $\leftarrow$ 0 **else** set M $\leftarrow$ M + 1 **fi**; **set** TIME $\leftarrow$ TIME + 1.

Algorithm PARSORT alternates back and forth between steps 1 and 2 until two consecutive steps produce no exchanges.

Figure 5.5.9 illustrates how Algorithm PARSORT would sort the keys in Fig. 5.5.8. A figure of this kind is called a *sort diagram*. Notice that whereas the algorithm stops after executing $n + 1 = 9$ steps, it actually completes the sort in seven steps. We next prove that sorting is always completed in no more than n steps.

P_1	P_2	P_3	P_4	P_5	P_6	P_7	P_8
6	3	7	2	8	4	1	5
i_1	i_2	i_3	i_4	i_5	i_6	i_7	i_8

FIG. 5.5.8 Eight parallel processors for sorting the integers 1, 2, ..., 8 given an initial permutation.

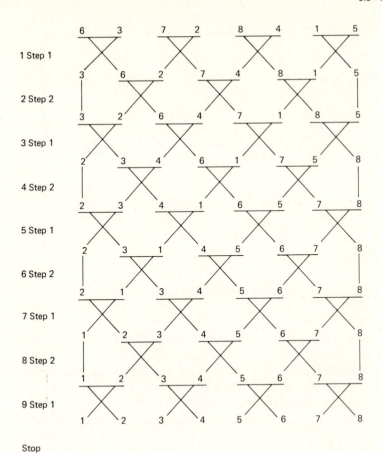

FIG. 5.5.9 The sort diagram produced by Algorithm PARSORT.

Theorem 5.5.1 Algorithm PARSORT sorts any set of n keys $i_1, i_2, \ldots, i_n$ into ascending order in at most n steps.

Proof The proof is by induction on the number of keys n. It is easy to see by exhaustion that for $n = 1, 2,$ or 3, Algorithm PARSORT works as indicated.

Assume then that Algorithm PARSORT can sort every set of m keys in at most m steps. We must show that it can sort every set $i_1, i_2, \ldots, i_{m+1}$ of $m + 1$ keys in at most $m + 1$ steps.

Consider the sort diagram produced by Algorithm PARSORT on keys $i_1, i_2, \ldots, i_{m+1}$. Also consider the path through this diagram created by the largest key — that is, consider the path of integers labeled $M = m + 1$. The general form of this path is indicated in Fig. 5.5.10a or b.

This path of M's serves to separate the sort diagram into two parts A and B. Consider the diagram that would result if we deleted this path of M's and

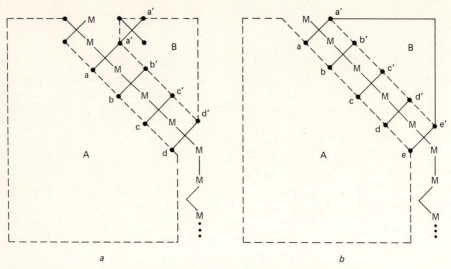

FIG. 5.5.10 The path through the sort diagram produced by the largest key M.

merged the two parts together again at points a and a', b and b', c and c', and so forth (see Fig. 5.5.11).

It can be seen that, excluding the partially completed top row of Fig. 5.5.11b, the remainder of Fig. 5.5.11b is a sort diagram for m keys. By our inductive hypothesis we know that the m elements on the second row of this diagram are sorted in at most m steps. Counting the top row as one more

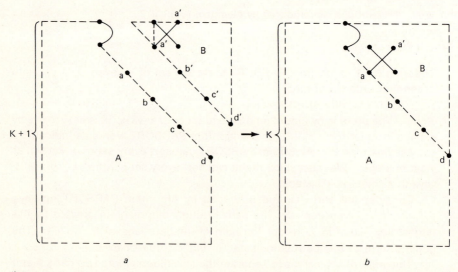

FIG. 5.5.11 Merging parts A and B of the sort diagram.

step, we conclude that the original $m + 1$ keys are sorted in at most $m + 1$ steps.

Notice that Algorithm PARSORT requires only a constant number c of operations to perform *in parallel* steps 1 and 2. Thus, Algorithm PARSORT sorts in real time — that is, $O(n)$ time steps — and it performs an average of $n/2$ comparisons at each step. Therefore, it requires $O(n^2)$ comparisons altogether.

Parallel Complexity Tradeoffs

In Algorithm SOLLIN, we have seen a case where parallelism enabled us to improve the speed of an algorithm from $O(M^2)$ to $O(M \log_2 M)$. We have seen that the best sequential sort algorithms are $O(M \log_2 M)$ but that Algorithm PARSORT is $O(M)$. There is sufficient evidence in the literature to indicate that, roughly speaking, an order-of-magnitude saving can be obtained if one can implement an algorithm in parallel. This statement is contained in what has been called *Minsky's conjecture*: Parallel machines executing a sequential program on n sets of data improve performance by at least a factor of $O(\log n)$.

While several counterexamples to Minsky's conjecture have been found, in sufficiently many cases it seems to be a reasonably good estimate of the observed improvement in computation.

Such improvements in speed are obviously not free. The cost is the addition of n processors, an order-of-magnitude increase in the total number of operations performed, and perhaps a reasonably low processor utilization rate. Generally, it seems difficult to keep every processor busy at all times.

Exercises 5.5

5.5.1 Use Algorithm SOLLIN (by hand) to find a minimum-weight spanning tree in the network of Fig. 5.5.12.

5.5.2 Use Algorithm PARSORT (by hand) to sort the sequence

$$12 \quad 4 \quad 8 \quad 11 \quad 7 \quad 5 \quad 6 \quad 2 \quad 9 \quad 3 \quad 1 \quad 10$$

*5.5.3 *Set and arithmetic operations.* What set and arithmetic operations do you think would be particularly amenable to parallel algorithms? Which do you think would be especially hard to implement in a parallel fashion?

5.5.4 Write a simple program using one or more of the special parallel language constructs described in this section.

*5.5.5 Show that it is always possible to number the vertices of any network in such a way that Algorithm SOLLIN finds a minimum-weight spanning tree in one parallel step. Is this fact of any practical use?

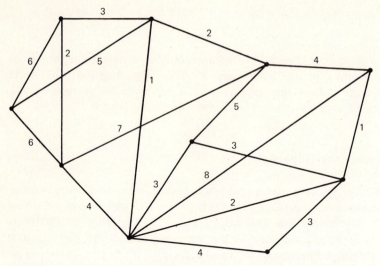

FIG. 5.5.12 Find a minimum-weight spanning tree using Algorithm SOLLIN.

**5.5.6 *Algorithm* SOLLIN (*proof*). Fill in the details for the proof of Algorithm SOLLIN.

5.5.7 *Algorithm* PARSORT (*analysis*). What arrangements force Algorithm PARSORT to perform the greatest number of exchanges?

**5.5.8 *Algorithm* PARSORT (*analysis*). Assuming every arrangement to be equally likely, what is the average number of exchanges performed by Algorithm PARSORT?

***5.5.9 *Shortest paths* (*complete development*). Completely develop a parallel algorithm for finding the shortest path between any two given vertices in a network whose edge weights denote edge length. Sequential algorithms for finding shortest paths are presented in Sec. 6.2.

6 MATHEMATICAL ALGORITHMS

Throughout this book we have illustrated many concepts and techniques by developing algorithmic solutions for mathematical problems. The three sections of this chapter contain several additional examples.

In Sec. 6.1 we consider two competitive games and a combinatorial puzzle. Extremely effective strategies and solutions will be developed for all three problems. These examples are representative of a large number of games and puzzles which have simple and clever solutions.

Section 6.2 takes up the problem of finding a shortest path between two specified vertices in a network. This problem has many important applications in operations research and computer science. As will be seen, the algorithm developed in this section turns out to be virtually identical to Algorithm PRIM in Chap. 4.

Section 6.3 considers algorithms requiring the use of random numbers. The first of these algorithms provides an efficient means for selecting a random set of M objects chosen from a set of N ($M \leq N$) objects. The remainder of this section is concerned with algorithms for generating random numbers.

6.1 GAMES AND COMBINATORIAL PUZZLES

In this section we shall study a classic combinatorial puzzle and two competitive games which illustrate a variety of interesting procedures.

Other games have been studied elsewhere in this book—for example, the 8-puzzle and the knight's tour in Secs. 2.1 and 3.3, respectively. Algorithms for these two problems used search and heuristic techniques that take advantage of the speed and computational power of the computer. Much of computer-oriented game playing has this flavor. The examples in this section will be different. Each contains a very efficient exact algorithm which is so simple that it is more trouble to implement the algorithm on a computer than it is to carry out with pencil and paper.

Magic Squares

A *magic square of order* N is an arrangement of integers in an N × N matrix such that the sums of all the elements in every row and column and along the two main diagonals are equal. Customarily, the integers are taken to be $1, 2, \ldots, N^2$. Figure 6.1.1a shows the only magic square of order 3. We shall investigate algorithms for constructing odd and double even (N = 4m, m = 1, 2, 3, ...) magic squares. The singly even case (N = 4m + 2, m = 1, 2, 3, ...) is left as an exercise.

Odd magic squares (N = 2m + 1, m = 0, 1, 2, ...) The following procedure will produce a magic square for odd N. Place the integer 1 into the top-center position. Then go up one square and over one square to find the location of the next integer. This move may take us outside the array, but a simple scheme, illustrated in Fig. 6.1.1b, shows where such a move "really" takes us in constructing an order 3 magic square. This "up one and over one" move is the basic operation in the construction of magic squares of odd order. However, at every Nth move we drop down one position to place the next integer (see Fig. 6.1.1c). The final moves in the construction of the order 3 square are shown in Fig. 6.1.1d.

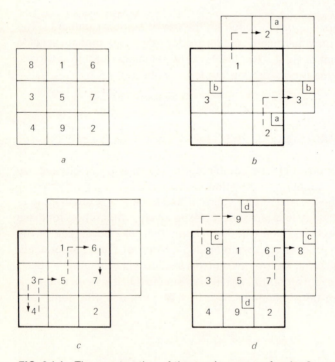

FIG. 6.1.1 The construction of the magic square of order 3.

Algorithm ODDMS (*ODD order Magic Square*) To construct a magic square of odd order N.

Step 0. [Initialize] **Set** I ← 1; **and** J ← (N + 1)/2.

Step 1. [Loop] **For** COUNT ← 1 **to** N^2 **do through** step 3 **od; and** STOP.

    Step 2. [Assign] **Set** SQUARE(I, J) ← COUNT.

    Step 3. [Find next position] **If** (COUNT)MOD(N) = 0

        then set I ← I + 1

        else if I = 1 **then set** I ← N **else set** I ← I − 1 **fi; and**

           if J = N **then set** J ← 1 **else set** J ← J + 1 **fi fi.**

To demonstrate the correctness of Algorithm ODDMS, it is convenient to consider every integer mod(N).[1] For every integer k from 1 to N^2, define the X and Y parts as Y = $(k − 1)$ mod (N) + 1 and X = $k − $Y (note that $k = $X + Y). Figure 6.1.2 shows the X and Y parts for the integers 1 through 9 in the 3×3 magic square.

In the discussion that follows, it is conceptually easier to visualize the N × N square as being drawn on a torus (a doughnut-shaped surface). Columns 1 and N are adjacent, as are rows 1 and N.

Since a detailed proof of Algorithm ODDMS is rather tedious, we shall only outline an argument that the algorithm places the integers from 1 to N^2 such that the row and column sums are equal. The diagonal sums are left as an exercise.

The integers from 1 to N^2 can be thought of as being placed into N groups of N consecutive integers. Each group has constant X parts with Y parts that run from 1 to N. The integers in any group are placed in an N × N array such that each row and column contains exactly one member of the group. This essentially follows from the facts that the algorithm places all the integers in any group consecutively and that the coordinates of any integer differ by one from that of the preceding integer; that is, if k is placed at position (I, J), then $k + 1$ is placed at (I − 1, J + 1). Thus, the algorithm places the integers in such a way that the X parts alone form a magic square.

Within each group the Y parts are the integers from 1 to N, and they are placed on the squares consecutively. Consider the position of all integers with a Y part of 1 (see Fig. 6.1.2). Given the position of a 1 at (I_1, J_1), the next Y = 1 is at $(I_1 + 2, J_1 − 1)$. This follows since the last member (Y = N) of the first group is placed at $(I_1 + 1, J_1 − 1)$, and the algorithm then "drops down" to place the first integer of the next group. You should be able to convince yourself that the algorithm places a Y = 1 in each row and column. A similar argument can be given to show that a

---

[1] By definition, if a(mod m) ≡ x for integers a and m, then x is the (integer) remainder after dividing a by m. For example, 5(mod 3) ≡ 2.

6, 2	0, 1	3, 3
0, 3	3, 2	6, 1
3, 1	6, 3	0, 2

FIG. 6.1.2 The (X, Y) parts of the integers $k = 1, 2, \ldots, 9$, where X = $k − $Y and Y = $(k − 1)$ mod (N) + 1.

$Y = j$, for $j = 1, \ldots, N$, is placed in each row and column. Therefore, the Y parts alone form a magic square.

Doubly even magic squares ($N = 4m$, $m = 0, 1, 2, \ldots$) This algorithm is somewhat more complicated than Algorithm ODDMS. We start with one quadrant of side $2m$, where $N = 4m$ for some positive integer m. For convenience, we choose the upper-left quadrant. Now mark the $4m^2$ squares in this quadrant in an arbitrary fashion subject to the restriction that there be exactly m marks in each row and column. For $m = 2$, this is illustrated in Fig. 6.1.3a.

Now reflect these marks about the vertical center line into the upper-right quadrant, and about the horizontal center line into the lower-left quadrant. Finally, reflect these marks into the lower-right quadrant about the lower-left to upper-right diagonal. This produces the set of marks shown in Fig. 6.1.3b.

Visit each of the squares in the upper half of the array in order, from left to right and downward. If the square does *not* contain a mark, put the first unused integer

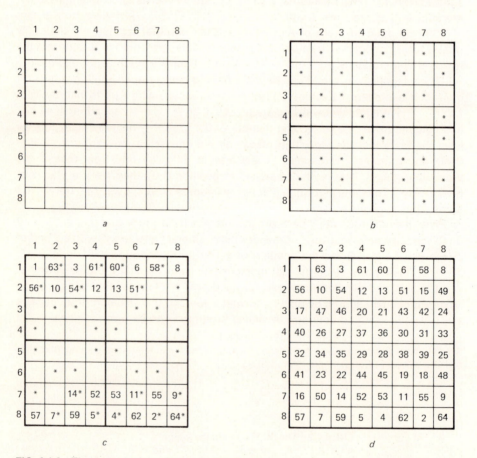

FIG. 6.1.3 The construction of an order 8 magic square.

K in the sequence $1, 2, \ldots, N^2$ into this square, *and* put the integer $(N^2 + 1) - K$ into the reflection of this square about the center point. If the square does contain a mark, put the integer $(N^2 + 1) - K$ into this square and K into its reflection. Continue until the entire array is filled. Figure 6.1.3*c* shows the example after 14 moves; Fig. 6.1.3*d* shows the completed magic square.

Algorithm DEMS (*Doubly Even Magic Square*)   To construct an $N \times N$ magic square, where $N = 4m$, for some positive integer m. The elements of the magic square are stored in a linear array MATRIX having N^2 entries.

Step 0. [Initialize] **Set** HALFN $\leftarrow$ N/2; MARK $\leftarrow$ 1; MIDDLE $\leftarrow$ N/2;
UPPER $\leftarrow N^2 + 1$; **and** HALF $\leftarrow N^2/2$.

Step 1. [Outer marking loop] **For** K $\leftarrow$ 1 **to** HALFN **do through** step 4 **od**.   (This loop and the following one give an initial marking to the first half of the array.)

Step 2. [Inner marking loop] **For** J $\leftarrow$ 1 **to** HALFN **do** step 3 **od**.

Step 3. [Put in marks] **Set** MATRIX(MIDDLE $-$ J $+$ 1) $\leftarrow$ MARK;
MATRIX(MIDDLE $+$ J) $\leftarrow$ MARK; **and** MARK $\leftarrow$ $-$MARK.

Step 4. [Move to next row] **Set** MIDDLE $\leftarrow$ MIDDLE $+$ N;
and MARK $\leftarrow$ $-$MARK.

Step 5. [Loop for placing integers] **For** I $\leftarrow$ 1 **to** HALF **do** step 6 **od**; **and** STOP

Step 6. [Insert integers] **Set** L $\leftarrow$ I;
if MATRIX(I) $<$ 0 **then** set L $\leftarrow$ UPPER $-$ I **fi** (L is the possibly interchanged coordinate of I);
set MATRIX(L) $\leftarrow$ I; **and** MATRIX(UPPER $-$ L) $\leftarrow$ UPPER $-$ I.
(Both I and its reflection are put into the array.)

Algorithm DEMS uses a checkerboard pattern of marks for the upper-left quadrant and MIDDLE to position itself in the middle of each row. Marks are put into both upper quadrants simultaneously. The complexity is readily seen to be $O(N^2)$.

To establish the correctness of this algorithm, we again use the (X, Y) coordinates defined earlier. Consider any two rows equidistant from the center—for example, rows $i - 1$ and $N - i$. These two rows are illustrated in Fig. 6.1.4. Each square has been numbered consecutively, starting in the upper-left corner and moving from left to right and downward. That is, each square has been numbered as if there were no marks in any of the squares. Note that each number k is represented in the form $k = X + Y$.

Observe that all elements originally in these two rows are still there after any interchanges caused by marked squares in the algorithm. In row $i - 1$, $2m$ X parts with value $X = (i - 1)N$ were traded for $2m$ X parts with value $X = (N - i)N$ from row $N - i$. By symmetry each exchange is paired with another, involving four numbers. The algorithm exchanges the Y parts of these four numbers in such a way that each row has a full set of Y parts—from $Y = 1$ to $Y = N$—after the exchanges are made. Therefore, after all the exchanges between the two rows are made, the Y parts of each row are a permutation of the integers from 1 to

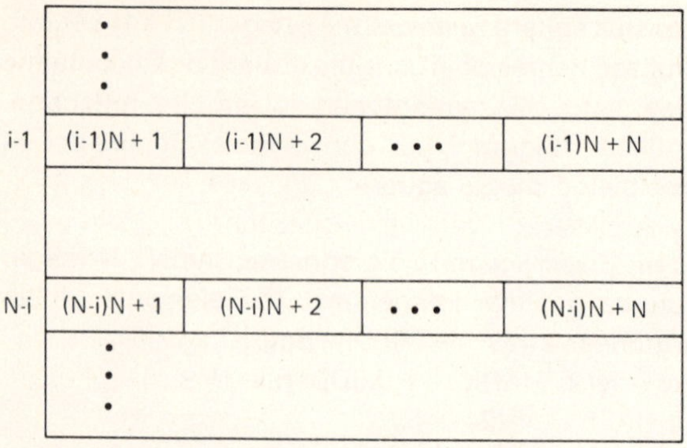

FIG. 6.1.4 The placement of integers in two rows equidistant from the center, using Algorithm DEMS.

N. Thus, the sum of the numbers of each row at the conclusion of the algorithm is

$$\text{ROWSUM} = 1 + 2 + 3 + \cdots + N + [(i-1)N + (N-i)N]\frac{N}{2}$$

$$= \frac{N(N+1)}{2} + \frac{N(N^2 - N)}{2}$$

$$= \frac{N(N^2 + 1)}{2}$$

This is the sum expected in a magic square (see Exercise 6.1.3).

Similar arguments can be given to show that the column and main diagonal sums are also $[N(N^2 + 1)]/2$ at the termination of the algorithm.

Extended Nimbi

Extended nimbi is a two-person game for which there exists a surprisingly simple winning strategy for one of the players.

The game board is a rectangular region divided into squares. Each player has a preferred direction, either vertical or horizontal, and the players alternate turns. On a given turn, the player who moves horizontally picks an unfilled square. The player then fills it and all other squares in that row which can be reached along that row without going off the board or meeting a square filled by an opponent. If the horizontal player moves first, as in Fig. 6.1.5, this first move will fill an entire row. The second player fills squares in columns in a similar manner. Play continues until one player cannot fill in a square, at which time the player loses. A complete sample game in which player B loses is shown in Fig. 6.1.5. This game is said to have full information, which means that each player is completely aware of the past moves and options available to the opponent.

Before developing a procedure for playing extended nimbi, let us try to gain some insight by considering a similar, but simpler, game. The rules of this game are the same, except that the board is a square $N \times N$ and the first player who cannot move is now the *winner*.

On all square $N \times N$ boards, the second player B wins. Player A initially has N possible moves. Every move by A fills a rectangular region (part of a row). If player B never divides a region into two parts with any move, then B will not interfere with A's monotonically decreasing number of moves. Since A went first, A will get the last move and lose; that is, after B's $(N-1)$st move, A is forced to fill the board. On nonsquare boards, the player moving parallel to the shorter dimension will win with B's strategy.

Let us now return to extended nimbi, where the first player who cannot move *loses*. All regions will be labeled by the parity of their dimensions, with the dimension facing A given first. Thus, in Fig. 6.1.5, the region that remains after A's first move is even-odd. It will be shown that A can guarantee a win on even-even, odd-odd, and odd-even boards; B can guarantee a win on an even-odd board. Thus, the player who moves parallel to the even dimension can win on boards with mixed parity, and A can win on all boards with matching parity.

Let us consider the three cases where A can guarantee a win. The even-odd case, where B wins, is left as an exercise.

Player A's objective will be to control the game in such a manner as to force B to leave an odd number of odd-odd regions after each move. Since 1 is the smallest natural odd number, A will always have at least one unfilled square available at each turn—that is, A will always be able to move.

For a first move on the even-even board, A should take out the top row. This will leave B with an odd-even board. Player B's first move must then leave A with one odd-odd region. In the odd-even case, A takes out the second row, leaving two odd-even regions. Player B's first move must be into one of these two regions, and B must create an odd-odd region. What should be A's first move in the odd-odd case?

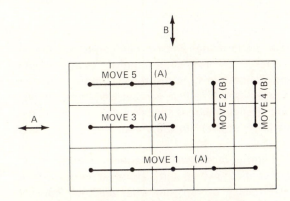

FIG. 6.1.5 A sample game of extended nimbi.

At later moves, A should find an odd-odd region. If the dimension of the first "odd" in the pair is 1, A covers the region. Otherwise, A should cover the second row of the region.

In order to demonstrate that this procedure will guarantee a win for A, we shall first show that all regions will be odd-odd or odd-even after the initial move. At each move, using the given strategy, A will either destroy an odd-odd region or create two new ones. If B moves in an odd-odd region, B must create one or two odd-even regions or two odd-odd regions. If B moves in an odd-even region, B must create one odd-odd region or one odd-odd and one odd-even region. Therefore, there can be no even-even or even-odd regions since such regions would be destroyed by the opening move and no new ones created later.

To prove that A wins, we must show that B always leaves an odd number of odd-odd regions. We have already shown that all of A's opening moves leave an even number (possibly 0) of odd-odd regions. By exhaustively considering B's possibilities, it is possible to see that B must change the parity of the number of odd-odd regions and that A may again change the parity. At a given move, B will be faced with an even number of odd-odd regions and an arbitrary number of odd-even regions. If B makes the next move into an odd-odd region, B must eliminate the region entirely (if the odd dimension is 1), turn it into an odd-even region (if B's move is at the ends), or create two odd-odd regions (if B's move is in the interior). If B moves into an odd-even region, B must create an odd-odd region (if B's move is at the ends) or one odd-odd and one odd-even region (if B's move is in the interior). In any case B must change the parity of the number of odd-odd regions. By reviewing A's strategy, it is possible to see that A can always leave B with an even number of odd-odd regions.

A formal statement of this algorithm (hereafter called EXNIM) and its computer implementation are left as exercises. The complexity of the algorithm is strongly dependent on the techniques used to implement it. The major problem, of course, is to come up with a procedure that quickly identifies odd-odd regions and updates the board.

Three-way Duel

This next example is an expected performance analysis of an unusually simple and effective strategy for playing a rather different kind of game. Sam, Bill, and John (hereafter denoted S, B, and J) agree to fight a three-way duel under the following rules: (1) they draw lots to see who fires first, second, and third; (2) they stand at the corners of an equilateral triangle; (3) they successively fire shots in the drawn order until two are dead; and (4) at each turn, the man who is firing can shoot at either of the others.

It is a fact that S is a dead shot and never misses at this range. At the given range, B hits his target about 80 percent of the time and J about 50 percent of the time. What is the best strategy for each player, and what are their survival probabilities if they play these strategies?

If S shoots first, he can do no better than to kill B. For if he kills J, then B (with probability .8) will have the next shot and must aim at S (since J is dead). Clearly, S would rather have J do the shooting.

Similarly, if B shoots first he will try to kill S. If he does not, S will shoot him at first opportunity, and S is a dead shot.

J has something of a dilemma. He does not really want to kill anyone if he goes first. For if he does, the survivor (who is a good shot) is guaranteed to try to kill him on the very next turn, regardless of the draw order. So J decides to miss on purpose until one of the other duelists is dead. It will then be J's turn, and he can make the most of his relatively poor shooting ability. This strategy dominates the duel in the sense that, if J adopts it, it will maximize J's survival probability. If either S or B choose to deviate from their previously given strategy (without calling off the whole duel), his corresponding survival probability will decrease.

We model the progress of the duel using a tree that initially has only two branches since J does not effectively enter the picture until either S or B is dead. In this way the tree is kept binary and fairly small.

Each vertex in the tree denotes an event (for example, J kills B), and the edges are weighted with the probability that the event at the end of the edge (the vertex farthest from root START) will occur given the event at the beginning of the edge (the vertex closest to the root). The tree for the duel is given in Fig. 6.1.6.

The dotted branch on the upper-right side in Fig. 6.1.6 denotes an infinite

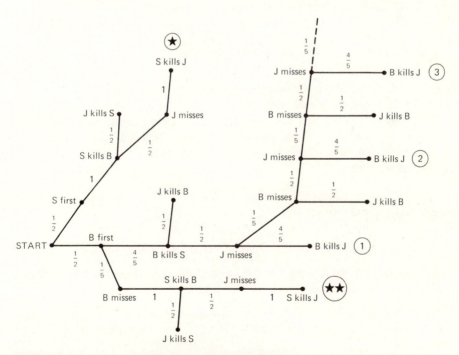

FIG. 6.1.6 The tree of probabilities for the three-way duel.

repetition of the basic pattern in which B and J keep shooting at each other (and possibly missing ad infinitum).

We now compute the various survival probabilities. Consider S first. There are two paths in the tree that denote a win by S, and they are labeled ★ and ★★. Since the two paths represent mutually exclusive events, their probabilities are additive. Consider the event ★. We have (from the definition of conditional probability in Sec. 2.4):

$$P(\bigstar) = P(\text{S first}) \times P(\text{S kills B} \mid \text{S first}) \times P(\text{J misses S} \mid \text{S first, S kills B})$$
$$\times P(\text{S kills J} \mid \text{S first, S kills B, J misses S})$$
$$= (\tfrac{1}{2})(1)(\tfrac{1}{2})(1) = \tfrac{1}{4}$$

Similarly,

$$P(\bigstar\bigstar) = (\tfrac{1}{2})(\tfrac{1}{5})(1)(\tfrac{1}{2})(1) = \tfrac{1}{20}$$

Note how the tree structure guarantees a one-to-one relationship between winning events and the unique paths from the root to the terminal vertices. The tree has been designed so that computation of the various complicated conditional probabilities amounts to nothing more than multiplying together all the numbers on the edges of the path. We are effectively computing compound probabilities as we "grow" the tree. Then $P_S = P(\text{S survives}) = \tfrac{1}{4} + \tfrac{1}{20} = \tfrac{3}{10}$. We next go to B.

$$P_B = P(\text{B survives}) = P(\text{B kills S}) \times P(\text{B kills J} \mid \text{B kills S})$$
$$= P(\text{B first}) \times P(\text{B kills S} \mid \text{B first}) \times P(\text{B kills J} \mid \text{B kills S})$$
$$= \left(\frac{1}{2}\right)\left(\frac{4}{5}\right) \sum_{n=1}^{\infty} \frac{4}{10^n} = \left(\frac{2}{5}\right)\left(\frac{4}{9}\right) = \frac{8}{45}$$

using the fact that all of B's winning events occur on the upper-right branch of the tree in Fig. 6.1.6 (all such events are denoted by circled numbers).

J's survival probability P_J can be obtained from the normalization $P_S + P_B + P_J = 1$. We find that $P_J = \tfrac{47}{90}$. So, with a little thought, J can guarantee himself the best chance of survival in what might, at first, appear to be a situation that is badly stacked against him.

Exercises 6.1

6.1.1 Use Algorithm ODDMS to construct a 7×7 magic square.

6.1.2 Explicitly exhibit the X and Y parts of the integers in the magic square constructed in Exercise 6.1.1 (see Fig. 6.1.2).

*6.1.3 *Magic squares.* Prove that the common sum associated with each row, column, and main diagonal of an $N \times N$ magic square is $[N(N^2 + 1)]/2$.

6.1.4 Use Algorithm DEMS to construct an 8×8 magic square. Is it the same square that was constructed in Fig. 6.1.3?

6.1.5 Explicitly illustrate the pattern of marks used in Algorithm DEMS.

**6.1.6 *Algorithm* ODDMS (*correctness*). Show that Algorithm ODDMS places integers along the two main diagonals so that the sum of the elements along each equals $[N(N^2 + 1)]/2$.

6.1.7 *Algorithms* ODDMS *and* DEMS (*complexity*). Explicitly show that Algorithms ODDMS and DEMS have $O(N^2)$ complexity.

*L6.1.8 *Latin squares* (*complete development*). A latin square is an $N \times N$ matrix whose elements are chosen from the integers 1 to N in such a way that exactly one copy of each integer is placed in each row and column. Note that each of the N integers is used N times. Completely develop an algorithm for constructing a latin square.

**L6.1.9 *A competitive matrix game.* Develop a winning strategy for one of the players in the following game. Two players, called "odd' and "even," alternate in placing 1s and 0s in unoccupied positions on an $N \times N$ board. Either player may place a 1 or a 0 in any empty position, thereby filling it. Note that odd is not limited to using 1s, and even is not limited to 0s. Play continues until all the positions are filled. Now the numbers along each row, column, and main diagonals are summed. The number ODD of sums that are odd is then compared to the number EVEN of even sums. If ODD > EVEN, player odd wins; if EVEN > ODD, player even wins; if ODD = EVEN the game is a draw.

**L6.1.10 *Algorithm* SEMS (*complete development*). Completely develop an algorithm—Algorithm SEMS (singly even magic squares)—for constructing an $N \times N$ magic square with $N = 4m + 2$, $m = 1, 2, 3, \ldots$.

6.1.11 Explicitly play A's winning extended nimbi strategy on 10×10, 9×9, and 9×10 boards.

6.1.12 What extended nimbi strategy should B play on an even-odd board?

**L6.1.13 *Algorithm* EXNIM (*statement, implementation*). State and program Algorithm EXNIM.

*6.1.14 *Algorithm* EXNIM (*complexity*). Analyze the complexity of the program in Exercise 6.1.13.

*L6.1.15 *Ordinary* NIM (*complete development*). This is a well-known two-person game in which the players alternately remove objects from sets. There are n sets of objects. Each set contains m_i objects for $i = 1, 2, \ldots, n$. The player whose turn it is removes one or more objects from any single set. Play alternates until all of the objects have been removed; the last player to remove an object is the winner.

Completely develop an algorithm for playing this game. *Hint*: Use binary numbers to represent the number of objects in each set.

*6.1.16 *Regular nimbi* (*heuristics*). Regular nimbi is played similarly to extended nimbi, except that there is now no need to fill all the squares that can be reached without bumping into the border or an opponent's square. There are also no preferred directions. For example, on the first move, A does not have to fill an entire row but can fill a string of adjacent squares of any size less than or equal to the row length. There is no known general winning strategy for this game. Design some useful heuristics for regular nimbi.

*6.1.17 *Counterfeit coins.* There are 12 identical-looking coins. One coin is a counterfeit and weighs more or less than the others. Only a simple balance scale is available. Decide which is the counterfeit. Try to devise an algorithm which uses only three weighings to identify the counterfeit and label it "heavy" or "light."

**6.1.18 *8-puzzle.* Reconsider the 8-puzzle example in Sec. 3.3. Design an efficient algorithm for checking if it is *possible* (without necessarily doing it) for one given configuration to be moved into another. Try to generalize your algorithm to an N-puzzle. *Hint*: Use parity considerations.

L6.1.19 *Tic-tac-toe.* Develop an algorithm for playing tic-tac-toe that never loses.

L6.1.20 *Three-dimensional tic-tac-toe.* This game is similar to ordinary tic-tac-toe but is played in a cube that has either three or four boxes on a side. A player wins by filling a row, column, or diagonal with marks. Design an algorithm for playing this game, and use it to test an assortment of playing strategies. Is there a winning strategy for the $3 \times 3 \times 3$ game?

6.1.21 Rework the analysis of the three-way duel for the general case of shooting probabilities p_1, p_2, and p_3, where $p_1 > p_2 > p_3 > 0$.

6.1.22 The spades and hearts are removed from an ordinary deck of cards. The 13 spades are laid out in order from ace to king. The hearts are shuffled, laid face down, and turned up one at a time. As each heart is turned up, the corresponding spade is removed from the line of spades. The player wins if the hearts turn up in such a way that a "gap" never appears between any two remaining spades. What is the probability of winning this game?

L6.1.23 *Probabilistic tic-tac-toe.* Number the boxes of the standard 3×3 tic-tac-toe game from 1 to 9. A player who attempts to place an X or an O in box i has a probability p_i $(0 < p_i < 1)$ of having the move nullified by God, thereby losing a turn. The center box always has a larger nullification probability than any of the others. Program and test this game using a variety of $\{p_i\}$ sets and playing strategies.

*6.1.24 *Modified roulette.* This game is played with a fair wheel with slots marked from 1 to N. A player who places \$D on slot k will win \$$(k + 2)D$ if this slot turns up on the play for that bet. Is it possible to play this game without *ever* losing?

*L6.1.25 *One is Zero (simulation).* Simulate the following game, sometimes called the One is Zero game, and experimentally decide on a good decision rule.

Two players each take a fixed number N of turns. At each turn a player rolls an ordinary die over and over until she either decides to stop and end her turn or rolls a 1, whichever comes first. If a player rolls a 1, her score for this turn is zero; otherwise her score for this turn is equal to the sum of all her rolls on the turn. A player's cumulative score is the sum of the scores on all her turns. The player with the highest cumulative score after N turns is the winner.

6.2 SHORTEST PATHS

Suppose that we are given a portion of a road map shown in Fig. 6.2.1 (where 32 @ 70 means 32 miles with a 70 miles per hour speed limit), and are asked to find the best route from Lexington to Danville. Such a request sounds simple enough, but a little reflection reveals that a variety of factors can determine a "best" route. For example, the factors include: (1) distance in miles; (2) time to travel the route, taking into consideration speed limits; (3) expected time, taking into consideration traffic and road conditions; (4) delays caused in passing through or bypassing cities; or (5) the number of cities which must be passed through, for example, in making deliveries along the route.

Let us solve the problem of finding a best route in terms of shortest distance. This problem is naturally modeled using networks. We are given a connected network G in which every edge is weighted with a positive integer denoting the length of the edge. The length of any path in such a network is the sum of the lengths of the edges in the path. Stated in terms of networks, the problem is to find a path of minimum length between two specified vertices.

Shortest-path problems are among the most fundamental of all combinatorial optimization problems since a large number of such problems can be reduced to finding a shortest path in a network. Furthermore, there are several types of shortest-path problems: (1) between two specified vertices; (2) between one specified vertex and all other vertices in a network; (3) between every pair of vertices in a network; (4) between two specified vertices which must pass through one or more specified vertices; and (5) the first, second, third, etc., shortest paths in a network.

It is somewhat surprising that among the dozens of shortest-path algorithms that have been designed, one of the best (due to Dijkstra) is virtually identical to the (greedy) minimum-weight spanning tree algorithm of Prim (see Chap. 4). Dijkstra's algorithm, which determines the shortest distance from a specified vertex to a final vertex, is best explained by an example. Consider the portion of the map of Fig. 6.2.1 which is shown in Fig. 6.2.2 as a network, where we desire a shortest path from LEX to BED. We represent the network by an adjacency matrix A, where:

FIG. 6.2.1 Find a "best" route from Lexington to Danville.

$A(I, J)$ = the length of the edge between vertices I and J

$A(I, J)$ = $+\infty$ if no edge exists between I and J

$A(I, I)$ = 0 for all I = 1, 2, ..., M

Dijkstra's algorithm repeatedly performs the following steps:

1 It starts by determining the direct distances (that is, one edge) from the specified vertex (LEX) to all other vertices (see Fig. 6.2.2a).

2 It then picks the smallest of these (distance 7 to BVA) as a "permanent" shortest distance (by selecting the heavy edge between LEX and BVA in Fig. 6.2.2b).

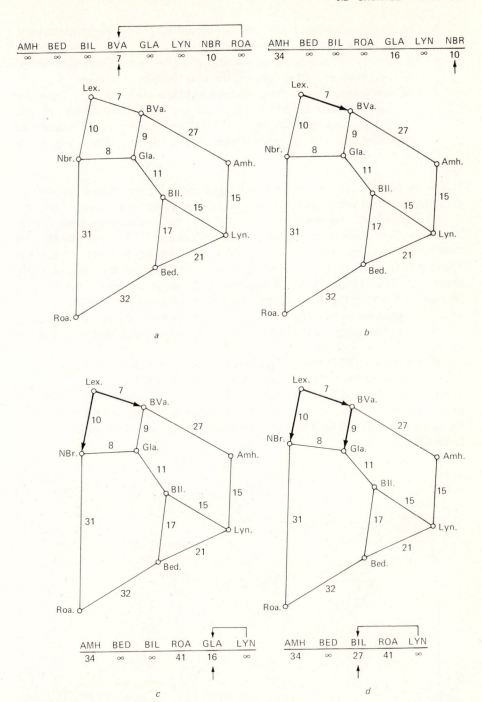

AMH	BED	BIL	BVA	GLA	LYN	NBR	ROA
∞	∞	∞	7	∞	∞	10	∞

a

AMH	BED	BIL	ROA	GLA	LYN	NBR
34	∞	∞	∞	16	∞	10

b

AMH	BED	BIL	ROA	GLA	LYN
34	∞	∞	41	16	∞

c

AMH	BED	BIL	ROA	LYN
34	∞	27	41	∞

d

FIG. 6.2.2 The first several steps of Dijkstra's algorithm for finding a shortest path from LEX to BED.

3 The algorithm then adds this smallest distance (7) to the length of the edge from the new vertex BVA to each other vertex.

4 It compares this sum with the previous distance from LEX to each vertex, and it updates the old distance if the new distance is smaller.

5 The new vertex BVA is then removed from the list of those vertices, the shortest distances to which have not yet been determined. In this example, the last vertex on this list (ROA) replaces the newly determined vertex BVA and the list is shortened by one (see the lists in Fig. 6.2.2*a* and *b*).

This entire process is then repeated, picking the new shortest distance on the list, etc., until the final vertex BED is joined to LEX by a path of permanent edges.

On the second iteration (see Fig. 6.2.2*b*), the distance to NBR (10) is minimum. This value is used to update the distance to ROA (from ∞ to 41), and then NBR is removed from the list. On the third iteration (see Fig. 6.2.2*c*), the distance to GLA (16) is minimum, which enables us to update the distance to BIL (from ∞ to 27). The final set of shortest distances is shown by the (rooted) *shortest-path tree* in Fig. 6.2.3, where the circled numbers indicate the order in which the edges are selected by the algorithm. An explicit shortest path to a given vertex is found by following the path in this tree from the root (LEX) to the vertex in question.

In this example, BED was the last vertex reached from LEX. Consequently, in order to compute the shortest distance from LEX to BED, we had to compute shortest paths from LEX to all other vertices. Therefore, in the worst case, the problem of finding the shortest distance from an initial vertex to a final vertex has the same complexity as the problem of finding shortest paths from the initial vertex to all other vertices.

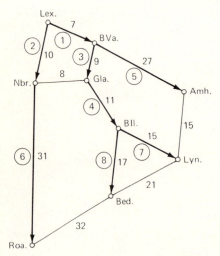

FIG. 6.2.3 A shortest-path tree rooted at LEX.

We are now ready to state Dijkstra's shortest-path algorithm.

Algorithm DIJKSTRA To determine the shortest distance DIST(W) from a specified initial vertex V0 to a final vertex W in a positively weighted, connected network G, with M vertices and N edges, which is represented by an adjacency matrix A.

Step 0. [Label all vertices] Label V0 "determined"; **and** label all other vertices "undetermined".

Step 1. [Initialize variables] **Set** DIST(U) ← A(V0, U) for all vertices U in G; **set** DIST(V0) ← 0; **and set** NEXT ← V0.

Step 2. [Iterate] **While** NEXT ≠ W **do through** step 4 **od; and** STOP.

    Step 3. [Update shortest distance to each undetermined vertex] For each undetermined vertex U, **set** DIST(U) ← the smaller of DIST(U) and DIST(NEXT) + A(NEXT, U).

    Step 4. [Pick a shortest distance to an undetermined vertex] Let U be an undetermined vertex having the smallest distance DIST(U) of all undetermined vertices; label U "determined"; **and set** NEXT ← U.

A proof of the correctness of Algorithm DIJKSTRA can be given by induction.

Theorem 6.2.1 Algorithm DIJKSTRA determines the shortest distance from V0 to W.

Proof We prove by induction that after n iterations of steps 3 and 4, for every vertex V which is labeled "determined" by Algorithm DIJKSTRA, DIST(V) equals the length of a shortest path from V0 to V. We also show that for every undetermined vertex U, DIST(U) is the length of a shortest path from V0 to U in which every vertex is determined except U.

For $n = 0$, after executing steps 0 and 1, there exists only one determined vertex—that is, V0—and DIST(V0) = 0 is clearly the length of a shortest path from V0 to itself. Also, for any undetermined vertex U, DIST(U) is clearly determined by the edge between V0 and U—that is, a path with two vertices, only one of which (U) is undetermined.

Assume the theorem is true for n iterations, and suppose that the $(n + 1)$st execution of step 3 has taken place. We must show that for all undetermined vertices U, DIST(U) is the length of a shortest path from V0 to U in which every vertex is determined except U.

Suppose that this is not the case—that is, there exists an undetermined vertex U and a path P from V0 to U in which U is the only undetermined vertex, and the length of P, say, m, satisfies $m < \text{DIST(U)}$. Let V be the determined vertex adjacent to U on P. If V ≠ NEXT, then, by our induction hypothesis, DIST(U) was determined after the nth iteration and $m = \text{DIST(U)}$. This contradicts our assumption that $m < \text{DIST(U)}$. If, on the other hand, V = NEXT, then $DIST(U) = DIST(NEXT) + A(NEXT, V) = m$. This again contradicts our assumption that $m < DIST(U)$.

Next assume that vertex V is chosen on the $(n + 1)$st execution of step 4—that is, V becomes the $(n + 1)$st determined vertex. We must show that DIST(V) is the length of a shortest path from V0 to V.

Suppose it is not. There must then exist a path P from V0 to V whose length is less than DIST(V). From the above, we know that DIST(V) is the length of a shortest path from V0 to V in which V is the only undetermined vertex. Therefore, P must contain at least one other undetermined vertex. Let U be the first undetermined vertex encountered on P proceeding from V0 to V. It must then follow that the distance from V0 to U is shorter than that from V0 to V; moreover, the subpath of P from V0 to U contains only one undetermined vertex, namely U. Therefore, by our inductive hypothesis, $DIST(U) < DIST(V)$, which contradicts the fact that V was chosen in step 4. Thus the path P does not exist, and DIST(V) is the length of a shortest path from V0 to V.

The fact that Algorithm DIJKSTRA determines the shortest distance from V0 to W now follows from the observations that the algorithm stops when $NEXT = W$—that is, W becomes determined. This must take place since G is finite and connected—that is, at most $M - 1$ iterations of steps 3 and 4 can take place.

It should be pointed out that the following implementation of Algorithm DIJKSTRA (Fig. 6.2.4) is virtually identical, statement for statement, to the implementation of Algorithm PRIM (see Chap. 4). In SUBROUTINE DIJKST, we input the adjacency matrix A, the number of vertices M, and the initial and final vertices V0 and W. The output of the subroutine consists of a set of triples—FROM(I), TO(I), and LENGTH(I)—which are the edges (FROM(I), TO(I)) of the shortest-path tree selected by the algorithm in finding the shortest distance to the vertex W; LENGTH(I) records the shortest distance from V0 to the vertex TO(I).

```
      SUBROUTINE DJIKST (A,M,VO,W,FROM,TO,LENGTH,EDGES)
C
C         THIS SUBROUTINE DETERMINES THE SHORTEST DISTANCE FROM AN
C         INITIAL VERTEX VO TO A FINAL VERTEX W IN A NON-NEGATIVELY
C         WEIGHTED, CONNECTED NETWORK G, USING AN ALGORITHM DUE TO
C         DIJKSTRA (NUMERISCHE MATHEMATIK, VOL. 1, PP. 269-271.)
C         THIS IMPLEMENTATION IS A MODIFICATION OF A PROGRAM DUE TO
C         V. KEVIN M. WHITNEY ( COMM. ACM (APRIL, 1972),
C         ALGORITHM 422).  THE OUTPUT OF THIS SUBROUTINE IS A
C         SHORTEST PATH TREE ROOTED AT VO.
C
C   ***FORMAL PARAMETERS***
C
C         A(I,J)    THE LENGTH OF THE EDGE BETWEEN VERTICES I AND J.
C                   IF THERE IS NO EDGE BETWEEN I AND J,
C                   THEN A(I,J) = 1000000, AN ARBITRARY LARGE NUMBER.
C
C         VO        THE INITIAL VERTEX.
C
C         W         THE FINAL VERTEX.
C
C         M         THE VERTICES OF G ARE NUMBERED 1,2,....,M,
C                   WHERE 2 .LE. M .LE. 100.
```

FIG. 6.2.4 An implementation of Algorithm DIJKSTRA.

```
C         FROM(I)    CONTAIN THE I-TH EDGE IN THE SHORTEST PATH TREE,
C         TO(I)      FROM VERTEX -FROM(I)- TO VERTEX -TO(I)-
C         LENGTH(I)  OF LENGTH -LENGTH(I)-.
C
C         EDGES      NUMBER OF EDGES IN SHORTEST PATH TREE SO FAR.
C
C   ***SUBROUTINE VARIABLES***
C
C         DIST(I)    THE SHORTEST DISTANCE FROM UNDET(I) TO THE PARTIAL
C                    SHORTEST PATH TREE.
C
C         NEXT       NEXT VERTEX TO BE ADDED TO THE SHORTEST PATH TREE.
C
C         NUMUN      NUMBER OF UNDETERMINED VERTICES.
C
C         UNDET(I)   LIST OF UNDETERMINED VERTICES.
C
C         VERTEX(I)  VERTEX OF PARTIAL SHORTEST PATH TREE ON SHORTEST
C                    PATH FROM UNDET(I) TO VO.
C
         INTEGER A(100,100),M,VO,W,FROM(100),TO(100),LENGTH(100)
         INTEGER EDGES,DIST(100),NEXT,NUMUN,UNDET(100),VERTEX(100)
C
C         INITIALIZE VARIABLES.
C
         EDGES = 0                                              1      1
         NEXT = VO                                              1      1
         NUMUN = M-1                                            1      1
         DO 100 I = 1,M                                         1      1
            UNDET(I) = I                                        M      M
            DIST(I) = A(VO,I)                                   M      M
            VERTEX(I) = VO                                      M      M
  100    CONTINUE                                               M      M
         UNDET(VO) = M                                          1      1
         DIST(VO) = DIST(M)                                     1      1
C
         GO TO 350                                              1      1
C
C         UPDATE SHORTEST DISTANCE TO EACH UNDETERMINED VERTEX.
C                                                               1      M-2
  200 DO 300 I = 1,NUMUN                                        N      (M-2)(M-1)/2
         J = UNDET(I)                                           N      (M-2)(M-1)/2
         JK = L + A(NEXT,J)                                     N,A    (M-2)(M-1)/2,E
         IF ( DIST(I) .LE. JK ) GO TO 300                       B      F
            VERTEX(I) = NEXT                                    B      F
            DIST(I) = JK                                        N      (M-2)(M-1)/2
  300    CONTINUE
C
C         PICK A SHORTEST DISTANCE TO AN UNDETERMINED VERTEX.
C                                                               1      M-1
  350 K = 1                                                     1      M-1
         L = DIST(1)                                            1      M-1
         DO 400 I = 1,NUMUN                                     N,C    (M-1)(M)/2,G
            IF ( DIST(I) .GE. L ) GO TO 400                     D      H
               L = DIST(I)                                      D      H
               K = I                                            N      (M-1)(M)/2
  400    CONTINUE
C
C         ADD EDGE TO SHORTEST PATH TREE.
C
         EDGES = EDGES + 1                                      1      M-1
         FROM(EDGES) = VERTEX(K)                                1      M-1
         TO(EDGES) = UNDET(K)                                   1      M-1
         LENGTH(EDGES) = L                                      1      M-1
         NEXT = UNDET(K)                                        1      M-1
C
C         HAVE WE REACHED W.
C                                                               1,1    M-1,1
         IF ( NEXT .EQ. W ) RETURN
C
C         DELETE NEWLY DETERMINED VERTEX FROM UNDETERMINED LIST.
C
         DIST(K) = DIST(NUMUN)                                  1      M-2
         UNDET(K) = UNDET(NUMUN)                                1      M-2
         VERTEX(K) = VERTEX(NUMUN)                              1      M-2
C
C         ANY UNDETERMINED VERTICES LEFT.
C
         NUMUN = NUMUN - 1                                      1      M-2
         GO TO 200                                              1      M-2
C
         END
```

FIG. 6.2.4 *(Continued)*

VERTICES labeled "undetermined" in Algorithm DIJKSTRA are stored in an array UNDET in SUBROUTINE DIJKST. Vertices relabeled "determined" in the algorithm are removed from the array UNDET in the subroutine. The two columns of statement execution numbers, to the right of the subroutine statements, are explained in the complexity analysis that follows.

The analysis of the worst case performance of SUBROUTINE DIJKST is virtually identical to that for SUBROUTINE PRIM. The column at the extreme right of Fig. 6.2.4 lists the maximum number of times each statement can be executed. By summing these numbers and observing that

$$E + F = \frac{(M-2)(M-1)}{2} \quad \text{and} \quad G + H = \frac{(M-1)M}{2}$$

we can obtain an upper bound of $5M^2 + 8M - 7$ on the number of statements SUBROUTINE DIJKST executes. Thus, the subroutine is worst case $O(M^2)$.

Observe that if we delete the statement

$$\text{IF (NEXT .EQ. W) RETURN}$$

and change the statement GO TO 200 to read

$$\text{IF (NUMUN .GE. 1) GO TO 200}$$
$$\text{RETURN}$$

then the resulting subroutine will compute the shortest distance from V0 to all other vertices in G. Consequently, this shortest-path problem has the same $O(M^2)$ worst case complexity.

Let us now establish a lower bound on the expected performance of SUBROUTINE DIJKST. The algorithm operates iteratively, and each iteration adds one vertex to the determined set. If vertex W is added to the determined set on the nth iteration, the algorithm will terminate. Let $L(n)$ equal the minimum number of statements executed in n iterations. Our objective will be to compute $L(n)$, for $n = 1, 2, \ldots, M-1$, and then to find the average of these values under the assumption that vertex W is equally likely to be added to the determined list at any iteration. This assumption produces a smaller lower bound than what might be observed in practice since, in most applications, W is likely to be a vertex that is fairly far from V0.

It is not difficult to check that if we stop after exactly one iteration, then $L(1) = 7M + 14$. If exactly two iterations are required, the minimum number of instructions executed is

$$L(2) = [L(1) - 1] + 5 + 1 + 5(M - 2) + 3 + 3(M - 2) + 7$$
$$= L(1) + 8M - 1$$

In computing $L(1)$ and $L(2)$, recall that these denote minimum values. Therefore, we always execute the GO TO 300 and GO TO 400 branches in the DO-loops ending at 300 and 400, respectively. Also note that in calculating L(2), we do not execute the RETURN on the first iteration—hence the $L(1) - 1$ term.

The calculations of L(3), L(4), and so forth, are similar. In fact, a little thought shows that the $L(n)$ values satisfy the following recurrence relation:

$$L(1) = 7M + 14$$

$$L(n) = L(n - 1) + 8(M - n) + 15 \qquad \text{for } 2 \leq n \leq M - 1$$

This recurrence relation is immediately apparent from the detailed computation of L(2) in the previous paragraph.

To obtain a closed-form expression for $L(n)$ that does not involve $L(n - 1)$, we proceed as follows:

$$L(n) - L(n - 1) = 8(M - n) + 15$$

$$L(n - 1) - L(n - 2) = 8[M - (n - 1)] + 15$$

$$L(n - 2) - L(n - 3) = 8[M - (n - 2)] + 15$$

$$\vdots$$

$$L(2) - L(1) = 8(M - 2) + 15$$

Now add all $n - 1$ of these equations, and observe the cancellation on the left-hand side. This yields

$$L(n) - L(1) = 15(n - 1) + 18 \sum_{i=2}^{n} (M - i)$$

$$= 15(n - 1) + 8\left[\sum_{i=2}^{n} M - \sum_{i=1}^{n} i + 1 \right]$$

$$= 8n M - 8M - 4n^2 + 11n - 7$$

Thus, $L(n) = 8n M - M - 4n^2 + 11n + 7$.

Assuming that the final vertex W is equally likely to appear at any iteration, a lower bound on the average number of instructions executed by SUBROUTINE DIJKST is given by

$$\text{LBD} = \frac{1}{M - 1} \sum_{n=1}^{M-1} L(n)$$

$$= \frac{1}{M - 1} \left\{ 8M \sum_{n=1}^{M-1} n - M(M - 1) - 4 \sum_{n=1}^{M-1} n^2 + 11 \sum_{n=1}^{M-1} n + 7(M - 1) \right\}$$

$$= \frac{1}{M - 1} \left\{ 4M^2(M - 1) - M(M - 1) - \tfrac{2}{3}M(2M - 1)(M - 1) + \tfrac{11}{2}M(M - 1) + 7(M - 1) \right\}$$

$$= 4M^2 - M - \tfrac{4}{3}M^2 + \tfrac{2}{3}M + \tfrac{11}{2}M + 7$$

$$= \tfrac{8}{3}M^2 + \tfrac{31}{6}M + 7$$

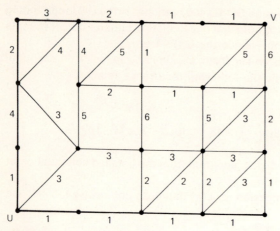

FIG. 6.2.5 Find a shortest path from U to V. (*Hint* : It has length 12.)

Note that the lower bound on the expected performance of the algorithm is still $O(M^2)$. Does this surprise you? What do you think we would find if we computed an upper bound?

Exercises 6.2

6.2.1 Complete Algorithm DIJKSTRA on the network in Fig. 6.2.1 and find a shortest path from LEXINGTON to DANVILLE.

6.2.2 Find a shortest path from LEXINGTON to DANVILLE in time. You will discover a different path than in Exercise 6.2.1.

6.2.3 Find a shortest path from U to V in the network shown in Fig. 6.2.5.

6.2.4 Can a network have two distinct shortest-path trees?

6.3 PROBABILISTIC ALGORITHMS

Selection Sampling

A number of data processing and game problems ask for an unbiased sample of exactly M items to be chosen from a set of N items. For example, one might want to simulate the deal of a poker hand or take a limited sample from a set of records.

One naïve approach to the construction of a sampling procedure is to select each record with probability M/N. This method has the comfortable feature that each item is accepted or rejected as it comes along, and only one pass must be made through the file of items.   Unfortunately, it does not guarantee that exactly M items will be chosen.

To see this, define the random variables for $i = 1, \ldots, N$:

$$X_i = \begin{cases} 1 & \text{if item } i \text{ is chosen} \\ 0 & \text{if item } i \text{ is not chosen} \end{cases}$$

The probability mass function for each X_i is

$$P(X_i = 0) = 1 - \frac{M}{N}$$

$$P(X_i = 1) = \frac{M}{N}$$

The X_i are independent, identically distributed random variables.   Each has mean M/N and variance (M/N)[1 − (M/N)].   The random variable

$$X = X_1 + X_2 + \cdots + X_N$$

denotes the number of items chosen on any trial.   Then

$$E[X] = E[X_1] + \cdots + E[X_N] = N\,\frac{M}{N} = M$$

and $$\text{var}[X] = \text{var}[X_1] + \cdots + \text{var}[X_N] = N\,\frac{M}{N}\left(1 - \frac{M}{N}\right) = M\left(1 - \frac{M}{N}\right)$$

Thus, only the *average* number of items chosen is M, and the large variance implies that the actual number chosen on any trial may be considerably larger or smaller than M.

A second intuitive approach to selecting M integers from a sample of N is to repeatedly generate random integers until M different ones have appeared.   This procedure can be stated algorithmically as follows.

Algorithm TRYAGAIN   To select an unbiased sample of $1 \leq M \leq N$ integers from the set of integers $1, 2, \ldots, N$.   The selected integers will be stored in an array SELECT(1), SELECT(2), ..., SELECT(M).

Step 0. [Initialize] **Set** L ← 0 (the variable L is used to record the number of items selected so far); **and** label all integers from $1, \ldots, N$ as "unselected".

Step 1. [Iterate] **Do through** step 3 **while** L < M **od**; **and** STOP.

Step 2. [Generate a random integer] Generate a uniformly distributed random integer K between 1 and N.

Step 3. [Has K been selected?] **If** K is labeled "unselected" **then set** L ← L + 1; SELECT(L) ← K; **and** label K as "selected" **fi**.

Although Algorithm TRYAGAIN is intuitively appealing and simple, it can be very slow and inefficient. This is due to the fact that a large number of random integers may have to be generated before the next unselected integer occurs. This can be explained by the following analysis.

Let $p_L = (N - L)/N$ be the probability of generating an unselected integer from $1, \ldots, N$, given that L integers have already been selected. Let $q_L = 1 - p_L = L/N$ be the probability of generating one of the L previously selected integers.

If X_L is the random variable which equals the number of integers that are generated before an unselected integer occurs, given that L integers have already been selected, then

$$P(X_L = k) = q_L^{k-1} p_L$$

Thus, X_L has a geometric distribution with

$$E(X_L) = \sum_{k=1}^{\infty} k q_L^{k-1} p_L = \frac{1}{p_L}$$

(See Exercise 2.4.31.)

Thus, for example, if we want to select 97 integers out of 100 using Algorithm TRYAGAIN, and we have already selected 96, it would be necessary to generate, on the average, $100/(100 - 96) = 25$ integers before producing one of the three remaining integers.

If T is a random variable which equals the total number of integers generated in selecting M out of N integers, then

$$E(T) = \sum_{L=0}^{M-1} E(X_L)$$

$$E(T) = 1 + \frac{N}{N-1} + \frac{N}{N-2} + \cdots + \frac{N}{N-(M-1)}$$

$$= N \sum_{k=M-1}^{N} \frac{1}{k}$$

$$= N(H_N - H_{M-1})$$

$$H_N = \sum_{k=1}^{N} \frac{1}{k} \quad \text{(this is the N}th\text{ harmonic number)}$$

Thus, $E(T) = O(N \log_2 N)$.

We would like an algorithm that guarantees that exactly M items will be chosen on every trial, but which also retains the one-pass acceptance/rejection feature of the first procedure described.

Assume that we are about to inspect the $(k + 1)$st item, and that q items have already been selected. What probability should be used for accepting this item? Observe that there are $\binom{N-k}{M-q}$ ways to pick $M - q$ items from the remaining $N - k$. Each way should be considered equally likely, and one must occur if we are to eventually choose M items. Similarly, if the $(k+1)$st item is chosen, there are $\binom{N-k-1}{M-q-1}$ ways to pick $M-q-1$ items from the $N-k-1$ that remain. Of all the ways to choose M items from N items such that q are chosen from among the first k, exactly

$$\frac{\binom{N-k-1}{M-q-1}}{\binom{N-k}{M-q}} = \frac{M-q}{N-k}$$

of these will choose the $(k+1)$st element. We claim that this is the correct probability to use for accepting the $(k+1)$st item.

Before taking up this claim, let us state the entire selection-sampling algorithm.

Algorithm SS (*Selection Sampling*)   To select an unbiased sample of $1 \leq M \leq N$ items from a set of N items.

Step 0. [Initialize] **Set** K←0; **and** Q→0. (K+1 indicates the item being inspected, and Q denotes the number of items currently selected.)

Step 1. [Iterate] **Do through** step 4 **while** Q<M **od; and** STOP.

   Step 2. [Generate a random number] Generate a uniformly distributed random number Y between 0 and 1.

   Step 3. [Test for acceptance or rejection] **If** (N−K)Y<M−Q **then** select item K+1; **and set** Q←Q+1 **fi**.

   Step 4. [Increment K] **Set** K←K+1.

At first glance it is not at all clear that Algorithm SS always selects exactly M items and that the sample is unbiased—that is, the acceptance probability used in step 3 actually gives each item an equal chance of acceptance.

Theorem 6.3.1   Algorithm SS selects exactly M items.

Proof   Clearly, no more than M items are chosen since the algorithm stops as soon as the M*th* item has been selected.

At step 3, observe that if q items have been selected and only $M-q$ items remain to be inspected, then all of the remaining items will be chosen. Thus, at least M items are selected. Therefore, exactly M items are selected.

Theorem 6.3.2   Algorithm SS selects each item in an unbiased fashion.

Consider the $(k+1)$st item. On any trial the probability that we accept this item is $(M-q)/(N-k)$, where q is the number of items already selected. The value of q is a random variable that depends on the selections made during the first k inspections. We would like to show that, for any k, M, and N, the *average* value of $(M-q)/(N-k)$ is exactly M/N. It is in this sense that Algorithm SS is unbiased.

Since the full proof of Theorem 6.3.2 is too complicated for this text, we simply demonstrate its correctness for $k = 2$.

Since $k = 2$, we are considering item 3. The following table of possible outcomes for the first two items is self-explanatory. For the indicated actions on the first two items, the values of q and the probabilities of selecting item 3 are also shown.

Item 1	Item 2	q	P(select item 3)
Accept	Accept	2	$(M-2)/(N-2)$
Accept	Reject	1	$(M-1)/(N-2)$
Reject	Accept	1	$(M-1)/(N-2)$
Reject	Reject	0	$M/(N-2)$

The probability that $q = 2$ is computed as follows:

$$P(q = 2) = P(\text{accept item 1})[P(\text{accept item 2} \mid \text{item 1 accepted})]$$

$$= \frac{M}{N}\frac{M-1}{N-1}$$

In a similar fashion, we can calculate the remainder of the probability mass function for q:

$$P(q = 1) = \frac{M}{N}\left(1 - \frac{M-1}{N-1}\right) + \left(1 - \frac{M}{N}\right)\frac{M}{N-1}$$

$$= \frac{2M(N-M)}{N(N-1)}$$

$$P(q = 0) = \left(1 - \frac{M}{N}\right)\left(1 - \frac{M}{N-1}\right)$$

$$= \frac{(N-M)(N-M-1)}{N(N-1)}$$

Check that $P(q = 2) + P(q = 1) + P(q = 0) = 1$.

The average value of P(accept item 3) is then

$$P_{avg}(k = 3) = \frac{M-2}{N-2}P(q = 2) + \frac{M-1}{N-2}P(q = 1) + \frac{M}{N-2}P(q = 0)$$

$$= \frac{M}{N} \quad \text{(check this!)}$$

Clearly, in the worst case, Algorithm SS will have to inspect every item before it obtains a full M sample. In the best case, only M items will be inspected. As an exercise, try to show that the average value of k when Algorithm SS stops is given by

$$k_{avg} = \frac{M(N+1)}{M+1}$$

Another method of selecting M integers out of N is the following.

Algorithm SELECT To select an unbiased sample of $1 \leq M \leq N$ integers from the set of integers $1, 2, \ldots, N$. The selected integers will be stored in an array SELECT(1), ..., SELECT(M).

Step 0. [Initialize] **For** I ← 1 **to** N **do** set ITEM(I) ← I **od**; set LAST ← N; **and** set L ← 1.

Step 1. [Iterate M times] **Do through** step 4 **while** L ≤ M **od**; **and** STOP.

Step 2. [Generate a random number] Generate a uniformly distributed random integer K between 1 and LAST.

Step 3. [Select next integer] **Set** SELECT(L) ← ITEM(K); **set** L ← L + 1.

Step 4. [Reduce sample size] **Set** ITEM(K) ← ITEM(LAST); **and** LAST ← LAST − 1.

Figure 6.3.1 illustrates the use of Algorithm SELECT in selecting 5 integers out of 10.

It is easy to prove that Algorithm SELECT is unbiased. Let $p_i(k)$ denote the probability that the ith integer is selected on the kth iteration of Algorithm SELECT. The probability p_i of selecting integer i is then

$$p_i = \sum_{k=1}^{M} p_i(k)$$

where

$$p_i(k) = \frac{N-1}{N} \times \frac{N-2}{N-1} \times \frac{N-3}{N-2} \cdots \frac{N-(k-1)}{N-(k-2)} \times \frac{1}{N-(k-1)}$$

$$= \frac{1}{N}$$

Thus,

$$p_i = \sum_{k=1}^{M} \frac{1}{N} = \frac{M}{N}$$

Notice that only a fixed number M of random integers must be generated in order to select M distinct integers out of N using Algorithm SELECT. In fact, the amount of work required is O(N + M); that is, Algorithm SELECT will execute:

N + 2 assignment statements in step 1

4M assignment statements in step 2

M random number calls in step 3

	ITEM	ITEM	ITEM	ITEM	ITEM
1	1	1	1	1	1
2	2	2	2	2	2
3	3	3	3	3	3
4	4	4	4	4	9
5	5	5	5	5	5
6	6	10	10	8	8
7	7	7	9	9	
8	8	8	8		
9	9	9			
10	10				

RANDOM NUMBER

GENERATED

	6	7	6	4	3

BETWEEN

	1-10	1-9	1-8	1-7	1-6

INTEGER

SELECTED

ITEM(6) = 6   ITEM(7) = 7   ITEM(6) = 10   ITEM(4) = 4   ITEM(3) = 3

FIG. 6.3.1   An example using Algorithm SELECT.

Contrast this with Algorithm SS, which executes:

   2 assignment statements in step 0

   O(N) random number calls in step 2

   O(N) tests in step 3

   3M assignment statements in step 3

   O(N) increments in step 4

Notice also that as a byproduct Algorithm SELECT produces a random permutation of the integers $1, \ldots, N$ when $M = N$, thereby increasing its overall usefulness.

Random Number Generators

In Sec. 2.4 we defined *discrete random variables*, that is, random variables whose ranges[1] are finite or countably infinite sets. Random variables whose

[1]Remember, a random variable is a function.

ranges are uncountably infinite sets are called *continuous*. Although most elementary computer science applications of probability and statistics use only discrete random variables, there are two important continuous distributions that arise so frequently that they should be considered explicitly.

A random variable X is continuous if there exists a nonnegative function $f(x)$, defined on the entire real line, having the property that if S is any set of real numbers, then

$$P(X \in S) = \int_S f(x)\, dx$$

The function $f(x)$ is called the *density function* of X.

In particular, if S is the entire real line, then since X must take on *some* value,

$$1 = P(X \in (-\infty, \infty)) = \int_{-\infty}^{\infty} f(x)\, dx$$

Also, if S is some interval $[a, b]$ on the real line, then

$$P(a \le X \le b) = \int_a^b f(x)\, dx$$

The continuous counterpart of a discrete random variable with an equally likely distribution is the *uniform random variable*. If X is a random variable that is equally likely to take on any value in the range $[0, 1]$, its density function would be

$$f(x) = \begin{cases} 1 & 0 \le x \le 1 \\ 0 & \text{otherwise} \end{cases}$$

Then, for example,

$$P(\tfrac{1}{4} \le X \le \tfrac{3}{4}) = \int_{1/4}^{3/4} 1\, dx = \tfrac{3}{4} - \tfrac{1}{4} = \tfrac{1}{2}$$

and

$$P(X = \tfrac{1}{2}) = \int_{1/2}^{1/2} 1\, dx = \tfrac{1}{2} - \tfrac{1}{2} = 0$$

The last result is especially important. The probability that a continuous random variable will equal any particular value X in its continuous range is *always* 0, *not* $f(X)$. We cannot assign finite probabilities to each of a continuous infinity of values since the "sum" of all these probabilities would be infinite (not unity). Think about this carefully. The uniform distribution on the interval $[0, 1]$†—or $(0, 1)$; does it matter?—is essentially the distribution simulated by computer random number generators. That is, a random number generated by a computer is basically a sample of a uniform random variable.

---

†The symbol $U(0, 1)$ will occasionally be used to denote this distribution.

The expected value and variance of a continuous random variable are defined similarly to those of a discrete random variable, with the exception that summations are replaced by integrals. Thus,

$$E[X] = \int_{-\infty}^{\infty} xf(x)\, dx$$

$$\text{var}[X] = \int_{-\infty}^{\infty} (x - E[X])^2 f(x)\, dx$$

For a uniform random variable U on [0, 1], we have

$$E[U] = \int_{-\infty}^{\infty} xf(x)\, dx = \int_{0}^{1} x\, dx = \frac{x^2}{2}\Big|_{0}^{1} = \frac{1}{2}$$

$$\text{var}[U] = \int_{-\infty}^{\infty} (x - E[X])^2 f(x)\, dx = \int_{0}^{1} \left(x - \frac{1}{2}\right)^2 dx = \frac{1}{12}$$

The other continuous distribution of great importance is the *normal distribution*. The density function for a random variable X with a normal distribution with parameters μ and σ^2 is given by

$$f(X) = \frac{1}{\sqrt{2\pi}\sigma}\, e^{[-(x-\mu)^2]/2\sigma^2} \qquad -\infty < x < \infty$$

This is the famous "bell-shaped curve of probability theory." A graph of the function is shown in Fig. 6.3.2. The curve is symmetric about the value μ, sharply peaked for small values of σ^2, and more spread out for larger values of σ^2. A normal distribution with parameters μ and σ^2 is denoted by $N(\mu, \sigma^2)$. The distribution $N(0, 1)$ is called *standard normal*.

Straightforward, but somewhat laborious, calculations show that if X is a normal random variable with parameters μ and σ^2, then $E[X] = \mu$ and $\text{var}[X] = \sigma^2$.

A surprisingly large number of random variables have normal, or near normal, distributions. Many of these random variables tend to exhibit the cumulative, or additive, effects of other random variables. Theoretically, this follows from a number of important theorems, collectively known as *central limit theorems*. Roughly speaking, these theorems state that a random variable that is the sum of many other random variables tends to have a normal distribution.

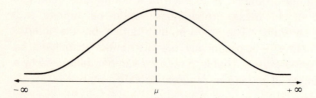

FIG. 6.3.2 Density function for the normal distribution.

The estimators $\bar{X}$ and s^2 can be shown to be unbiased and consistent minimum-variance estimators for μ and σ^2 for any normally distributed random variable. In cases where a random variable is thought to reflect the additive effects of other random variables, a normal distribution with $\bar{X}$ and s^2 (based on statistical observations) can be a good estimator for the entire unknown distribution of the random variable.

In Secs. 2.4 and 4.2, we have seen that it is important to have computer-generated "random numbers" to help test and analyze algorithms. It is therefore important to have efficient algorithms for generating random numbers.

Computer random number generators most often try to behave as though they are producing sample values of a random variable that is uniform on the interval from 0 to 1. Other random variable distributions can then be readily simulated using this basic distribution. Thus, a random-number-generating algorithm attempts to choose a number between 0 and 1 such that the probability that the number lies in any particular subinterval of the unit interval is equal to the length of the particular subinterval.

One obvious mechanical means of doing this is to use a perfectly balanced wheel with unit circumference. The wheel is spun under a fine needle, and the reading under the needle is taken as the next randomly generated number. Why not build such a device into the hardware of the computer? The reason that wheels of this sort are not used is that random numbers can be generated more quickly, cheaply, accurately, and almost as reliably using certain simple algorithms.

Actually these algorithms do not generate random numbers with the same uncertainty as the spinning wheel. In fact, they use simple arithmetic operations to *deterministically* produce a sequence of numbers that only *look* random. These numbers can be predicted *before* they are generated. This fact seems to offend a number of people, but it really should not. The sequences of *pseudorandom numbers* generated by these algorithms appear random and satisfy a number of sophisticated statistical tests that, in effect, "license" them as reasonable.

One of the earliest arithmetic random number generators, due to John von Neumann in 1946, is known as the *middle-square method.*

Algorithm MS (*Middle Square*) To generate K-digit pseudorandom numbers. An initial K-digit number X_0 has to be supplied. For convenience, we assume that K is even and a sequence $X(1), X(2), \ldots, X(M)$ of M random numbers is required (see Exercise 6.3.20).

Step 0. [Initialize] **Set** $X \leftarrow X_0$.

Step 1. [Basic loop] **For** $J \leftarrow 1$ **to** M **do** step 2 **od**; **and** STOP.

Step 2. [Generate new random number X(J)] **Set** $Y \leftarrow X^2$; $X(J) \leftarrow$ (middle K digits of Y); **and** $X \leftarrow X(J)$. (The number Y will have 2K digits, and the next random number X(J) is obtained by removing K/2 digits from each end of Y. It is understood that a decimal point is placed before the first digit of X(J) before it is output as a random number.)

For $K = 4$ and $X_0 = 2134$, the first 10 pseudorandom numbers produced by Algorithm MS are

$$X_0^2 = 04\ 5539\ 56 \qquad X_1 = .5539$$
$$X_1^2 = 30\ 6805\ 21 \qquad X_2 = .6805$$
$$X_2^2 = 46\ 3080\ 25 \qquad X_3 = .3080$$
$$X_3^2 = 09\ 4864\ 00 \qquad X_4 = .4864$$
$$X_4^2 = 23\ 6584\ 96 \qquad X_5 = .6584$$
$$X_5^2 = 43\ 3490\ 56 \qquad X_6 = .3490$$
$$X_6^2 = 12\ 1801\ 00 \qquad X_7 = .1801$$
$$X_7^2 = 03\ 2436\ 01 \qquad X_8 = .2436$$
$$X_8^2 = 05\ 9340\ 96 \qquad X_9 = .9340$$
$$X_9^2 = 87\ 2356\ 00 \qquad X_{10} = .2356$$

In spite of the apparent randomness of the numbers produced by Algorithm MS, it suffers from deficiencies that have led to its abandonment in serious applications. Observe that if a .0000 ever showed up in the sequence, all following numbers would also be .0000. The random number production of Algorithm MS can degenerate in other ways. For $K = 4$ and $X_0 = 1357$, the sequence produced is

$$X_1 = .8414$$
$$X_2 = .7953$$
$$X_3 = .2502$$
$$X_4 = .2600$$
$$X_5 = .7600$$
$$X_6 = .7600$$
$$X_7 = .7600$$
$$\vdots$$
$$X_n = .7600 \qquad \text{for } n \geq 5.$$

This hardly looks random. Even if K and X_0 are chosen more carefully, the sequences generated by this method tend to start repeating themselves quickly and do not perform well when tested against sophisticated statistical criteria.

Of the various deterministic arithmetic procedures for generating random numbers, a class of algorithms known as *linear congruential methods* is the most widely used. A general format for such algorithms is given below.

Algorithm LCM (*Linear Congruential Method*) To generate a sequence X(1), X(2), . . . , X(M) of M pseudorandom numbers. Input values must be given to the following:

X(0) = initial "raw" random number	X(0) ≥ 1; integer
B = multiplier	B ≥ 1; integer
K = increment	K ≥ 0; integer
MOD = modulus	MOD > X(0), B, K; integer

Step 1. [Basic loop] **For** $J \leftarrow 1$ **to** M **do through** step 3 **od**; **and** STOP.

Step 2. [Generate new raw random number] **Set** $X(J) \leftarrow (B * X(J-1) + K)$ (mod MOD).† ($X(J)$ will lie in the range $0 \leq X(J) < $ MOD.)

Step 3. [Generate next random number] **Set** $Y(J) \leftarrow X(J)/$MOD. ($Y(J)$ will lie in the range $0 \leq Y(J) < 1$ and have the desired distribution.)

Let us take $K = 0$, MOD $= 2^{10}$, $B = 101$, and $X(0) = 432$. The first few numbers produced by Algorithm LCM are

$$X_1 = 624 \qquad Y_1 = \tfrac{624}{1024} = .610$$
$$X_2 = 560 \qquad Y_2 = \tfrac{560}{1024} = .546$$
$$X_3 = 240 \qquad Y_3 = \tfrac{240}{1024} = .234$$
$$X_4 = 688 \qquad Y_4 = \tfrac{688}{1024} = .673$$
$$X_5 = 880 \qquad Y_5 = \tfrac{880}{1024} = .859$$
$$X_6 = 816 \qquad Y_6 = \tfrac{816}{1024} = .796$$
$$X_7 = 496 \qquad Y_7 = \tfrac{496}{1024} = .484$$
$$X_8 = 944 \qquad Y_8 = \tfrac{944}{1024} = .923$$

There is a deep and interesting theory on the subject of "good" choices for K, B, MOD, and X(0) which is beyond the scope of this book. It is adequate for our purposes to simply state that there exist choices of these parameters for which Algorithm LCM will generate numbers in the range [0, 1) that appear unpredictable and that satisfy certain statistical criteria. For all practical purposes, these numbers appear to be a sequence of observations of a uniformly distributed random variable.

The density function of a uniform random variable makes it particularly easy to use in order to simulate random variables with other distributions. Let us start with two relatively simple examples.

Let X be a discrete random variable with the following probability mass function:

$$P(X = 1) = .1$$
$$P(X = 2) = .2$$
$$P(X = 3) = .4$$
$$P(X = 4) = .2$$
$$P(X = 5) = .1$$

How can we take computer "samples" of X so that the value $X = 1$ occurs roughly 10 percent of the time, the value $X = 2$ roughly 20 percent of the time, and so forth?

Since all probabilities in the mass function add to unity, it is a straightforward matter to partition the interval [0, 1) into five subintervals and to assign each possible value of X to a subinterval whose length equals the corresponding

---

†By definition, if $a(\text{mod } m) \equiv x$ for integers a and m, then x is the (integer) remainder after dividing a by m. For example, 5(mod 3) $\equiv$ 2.

probability of X actually attaining this value. In our example, we might make the following assignment:

$$
\begin{aligned}
X=1 &\leftrightarrow [0, .1) \\
X=2 &\leftrightarrow [.1, .3) \\
X=3 &\leftrightarrow [.3, .7) \\
X=4 &\leftrightarrow [.7, .9) \\
X=5 &\leftrightarrow [.9, 1.0)
\end{aligned}
$$

To simulate random variable X on a computer, generate a standard (uniformly distributed) random number Z. If $Z \in [0, .1)$, take $X = 1$; if $Z \in [.1, .3)$, take $X = 2$. After obtaining a large number of samples, the observed frequency distribution of X should be quite close to the mass function.

The procedure just described can be applied to any discrete random variable with a finite range; it can also be applied (approximately) to many random variables whose range is a countably infinite set. This technique is used extensively in the design of simulation algorithms.

Now consider the use of a uniformly distributed random number generator to generate normally distributed random numbers. A good, simple algorithm appeals directly to a central limit theorem and a transformation which can be used to convert a $N(\mu, \sigma^2)$ distribution to a $N(0, 1)$ distribution, and vice versa.

The next theorem is the simplest of the central limit theorems, and it is often called *the* central limit theorem.

Theorem 6.3.3 (*central limit theorem*) Let $X_1, X_2, \ldots, X_n$ be a sequence of independent, identically distributed random variables with mean μ and variance σ^2. The distribution of the random variable

$$
Z = \frac{X_1 + X_2 + \cdots + X_n - n\mu}{\sigma \sqrt{n}}
$$

then approaches $N(0, 1)$ as $n \to \infty$.

Theorem 6.3.4 If random variable Y has a $N(\mu, \sigma^2)$ distribution, then

$$
Z = \frac{Y - \mu}{\sigma}
$$

has a $N(0, 1)$ distribution. The converse is also true.

The proof of Theorem 6.3.3 is a bit advanced and is therefore omitted; the proof of Theorem 6.3.4 is straightforward and is left as an exercise.

Algorithm NRN (*Normal Random Numbers*) To generate normally distributed random numbers using a uniform random number generator RANN. The uniformly distributed random numbers are used to produce N(0, 1) random numbers using Theorem 6.3.3. The N(0, 1) random numbers are converted into N(μ, σ^2) random numbers using Theorem 6.3.4. Input values of n, μ, and σ^2 need to be supplied. Assume that a sequence Y(1), (Y)2, ..., Y(M) of M random numbers is required.

Step 1. [Basic loop] **For** J $\leftarrow$ 1 **to** M **do through** step 3 **od; and** STOP.

    Step 2. [Generate new N(0, 1) random number] CALL RANN n times, returning the sequence $X_1, \ldots, X_n$; **set**

$$Z(J) \leftarrow \frac{X_1 + X_2 + \cdots + X_n - (n/2)}{\sqrt{n/12}}$$

    (Since each X_k has a uniform distribution with mean $\frac{1}{2}$ and variance $\frac{1}{12}$, Z(J) will be N(0, 1) by Theorem 6.3.3. In practice, $n = 10$ is adequate for most needs.)

    Step 3. [Generate new N(μ, σ^2) random number] **Set** Y(J) $\leftarrow$ σZ(J) + μ.

Let us now consider two more advanced procedures. We start with the general problem of simulating an arbitrary continuous distribution using a uniform distribution.

For any random variable X, the *cumulative distribution function* $F(a)$ is defined by

$$F(a) = P(X \leq a) \qquad -\infty < a < \infty$$

It is readily verified that any cumulative distribution function has the following properties:

1 $F(a)$ is a nondecreasing function of a

2 $\lim_{a \to \infty} F(a) = 1$

3 $\lim_{a \to -\infty} F(a) = 0$

4 $P(a < X \leq b) = F(b) - F(a)$ for all $a < b$.

If X is a continuous random variable with density function $f(x)$, then

$$F(a) = P(X \leq a) = \int_{-\infty}^{a} f(x)\, dx$$

and, by the fundamental theorem of the integral calculus,

$$\frac{d}{da} F(a) = f(a)$$

If Y has a uniform distribution on $[0, 1)$, then it has cumulative distribution

$$G(a) = P(Y \leq a) = \begin{cases} 0 & \text{if } a \leq 0 \\ \int_0^a 1 \, dy = a & \text{if } 0 < a \leq 1 \\ 1 & \text{if } 1 < a \end{cases}$$

Let random variable X have a cumulative distribution function F, and let random variable Y be uniform on $[0, 1)$. Assume that the inverse function F^{-1} is well-defined. We would like to show that the random variable defined by $X' = F^{-1}(Y)$ has cumulative distribution function F. Then if $\{y_1, y_2, \ldots, y_n\}$ is a sequence of uniform random numbers, the sequence $\{x_1 = F^{-1}(y_1), x_2 = F^{-1}(y_2), \ldots, x_n = F^{-1}(y_n)\}$ will have distribution F.

Thus, we would like to show that

$$P(X' \leq x) = F(x) \qquad \text{if } X' = F^{-1}(Y)$$

and Y has a uniform distribution. This is proven as follows:

$$P(X' \leq x) = P(F^{-1}(Y) \leq x)$$
$$= P(Y \leq F(x))$$
$$= \int_0^{F(x)} 1 \, dy = F(x)$$

where we noted that $F(x)$ is always between 0 and 1, and we used the cumulative distribution function for Y.

Although this procedure is very general and is simple in principle, it is not used as often as might be expected. This is primarily because it is difficult to obtain explicit analytical expressions for the inverse functions of many distributions. However, we shall consider one important case in which this method works very well.

The *exponential distribution* (with parameter λ) has density function

$$f(x) = \lambda e^{-\lambda x} \qquad 0 < x < -\infty$$
$$= 0 \qquad \text{otherwise}$$

The cumulative distribution function for an exponentially distributed random variable is given by

$$F(x) = 0 \qquad\qquad\qquad \text{if } x \leq 0$$
$$= \int_0^x \lambda e^{-\lambda x} dx = (1 - e^{-\lambda x}) \qquad \text{if } x > 0$$

This distribution is fundamental in the study of queues or waiting lines. Exponentially distributed random variables seem well-suited for modeling inter-arrival times.

If Y is uniform, then

$$Y = F(X) = 1 - e^{-\lambda X}$$

Inverting F (that is, solving for X),

$$X = -\frac{1}{\lambda} \ln (1 - Y)$$

Thus, if $\{y_1, y_2, \ldots, y_n\}$ are uniformly distributed random numbers, then

$$\left\{ x_1 = -\frac{1}{\lambda} \ln (1 - y_1),\ x_2 = -\frac{1}{\lambda} \ln (1 - y_2),\ \ldots,\ x_n = -\frac{1}{\lambda} \ln (1 - y_n) \right\}$$

are exponentially distributed random numbers.

It is not possible to use this inverse function procedure to generate normally distributed random numbers. Also, Algorithm NRN has the unfortunate feature of requiring n uniformly distributed random numbers to generate a single normally distributed random number. The great importance of the normal distribution has led to the development of a few efficient algorithms for generating normal random numbers. The next algorithm is one such method.

Algorithm PNRN (*Polar method for generating Normally distributed Random Numbers*). To generate two independent and N(0, 1)-distributed random numbers from two independent, uniformly distributed random numbers. The N(0, 1) distribution can be converted into an N(μ, σ^2) distribution using Theorem 6.3.4.

Step 1. [Generate two uniform random numbers] Generate two independent U(0, 1) random numbers U_1 and U_2; **set** $V_1 \leftarrow 2U_1 - 1$; **and** $V_2 \leftarrow 2U_2 - 1$. (V_1 and V_2 are U(−1, +1) distributed.)

Step 2. [Compute and check S] **Set** $S \leftarrow V_1^2 + V_2^2$; **if** $S \geq 1$ **then go to** step 1 **fi**.

Step 3. [Compute N₁ and N₂] **Set** $N_1 \leftarrow V_1 \sqrt{(-2 \ln S)/S}$; **and** $N_2 \leftarrow V_2 \sqrt{(-2 \ln S)/S}$; **and** STOP. ($N_1$ and N_2 are normally distributed.)

Algorithm PNRN has an important computational advantage over Algorithm NRN in that it will usually generate one normal random number for each uniform random number. Does this compensate for the additional time spent evaluating natural logarithms and square roots?

The proof of Algorithm PNRN is heavily dependent on calculus and analytic geometry, and it is left as an exercise.

Exercises 6.3

6.3.1 Design an algorithm for randomly generating two BINGO cards, as in the following example:

1–15	16–30	31–45	46–60	61–75
B	I	N	G	O
4	17	32	49	73
11	25	42	51	67
12	19	FREE	46	62
8	29	37	54	64
5	30	44	50	74

Make sure that no number is generated twice in the same column.

6.3.2 Algorithm SS is often used to make an unbiased selection of M out of N data files, where N is a large number. Why is the one-pass feature important in this application?

6.3.3 Verify Theorem 6.3.2 for the case $k = 1$.

*L6.3.4 *Algorithm* SS (*testing*). Extensively test Algorithm SS. Try to obtain experimental support for Theorem 6.3.2.

***6.3.5 *Algorithm* SS (*analysis*). Show that the average value of k when Algorithm SS stops is

$$k_{avg} = \frac{M(N+1)}{M+1}$$

6.3.6 Discuss the relative merits of Algorithms SS and SELECT.

6.3.7 *Uniform random variables.* If Y is a uniform random variable over the interval $[\alpha, \beta]$, what is its density function? Compute $E[Y]$ and var$[Y]$.

6.3.8 In this section we described a wheel that could be used to mechanically generate "real" random numbers with a uniform distribution. What are some of the difficulties associated with such a device?

6.3.9 Most random number generators are designed so that the same numbers will be generated each time a program is run unless special care is taken to do otherwise. Why do you think this is done?

6.3.10 If X is an $N(\mu, \sigma^2)$ random variable, show explicitly that $E[X] = \mu$ and var$[X] = \sigma^2$.

6.3.11 Compute the sample variance s^2 for the straight insertion sort experiment of Exercise 2.4.25.

*L6.3.12 *Algorithm* MS (*implementation*). Code Algorithm MS using any convenient values of K and X_0. Generate 10 random numbers and compute the values of the estimators $\bar{X}$ and s^2. How do these compare with the true mean and variance of a uniform random variable? Repeat for 25, 50, and 100 random numbers.

6.3.13 Uniform random variables defined on each of the following open or closed intervals are essentially equivalent: [0, 1], (0, 1], [0, 1), (0, 1). Why?

6.3.14 Is the range of a computer random number generator (such as Algorithm LCM) *really* the continuous interval [0, 1)?

*L6.3.15 *Algorithm* NRN (*implementation*). Code Algorithm NRN using your local random number generator for RANN and $n = 10$ and 20. Conduct some experiments with your program to verify that it produces normally distributed random numbers. Use tables of the normal distribution as a check.

6.3.16 Prove Theorem 6.3.4.

**L6.3.17 *Chi-square test.* It is often necessary to take a sample of a random variable and ask: What distribution underlies this sample? In general, this question must be given a probabilistic answer. There are many tests designed to help answer such questions. The best known is the chi-square test (χ^2 test). Look up this test and learn to use it. Discussions of a number of such statistical tests can be found in Sec. 3.3 of Knuth (1969b).

*6.3.18 In Exercises 2.4, a number of general results were obtained on the means and variances of random variables. At that time, we had only defined discrete random variables. Verify that these results are also true for continuous random variables.

*6.3.19 Let X and Y be two independent random variables. Let $\{X_1, \ldots, X_n\}$ be a sample of n observed values of X and $\{Y_1, \ldots, Y_n\}$ be a sample of n observed values of Y. Find an unbiased estimator for $E[Z]$, where $Z = XY$.

6.3.20 *Random number generators.* No commercial random number generators contain the step 1 DO-loops used in Algorithms MS, LCM, and NRN. What procedure does your local random number generator use to produce a sequence of random numbers?

L6.3.21 *Exponentially distributed random numbers.* Use the procedure developed in this section to generate some exponentially distributed random numbers. Use $\lambda = 1$. Compare the theoretical distribution function with the frequency distribution obtained experimentally.

6.3.22 Calculate the mean and variance, in terms of λ, for an exponentially distributed random variable.

***6.3.23 *Algorithm* PNRN (*proof*). Prove the correctness of Algorithm PNRN. *Hints*: (a) Note that (V_1, V_2) is a random point uniformly distributed inside the unit circle if $S < 1$ in step 2; (b) use polar coordinates with $S = R^2$ (the square of the distance from the origin); (c) compute the probability that $-2 \ln S \le r^2$, for $0 < r < 1$.

*L6.3.24 *Algorithm* PNRN (*testing*). Implement Algorithm PNRN and use it to generate N(0, 1)-distributed random numbers. Compare the theoretical distribution function with the frequency distribution obtained experimentally.

**L6.3.25 *Algorithm* PNRN (*testing, analysis*). Comparatively test the time it takes to obtain normally distributed random numbers using Algorithm PNRN and Algorithm NRN. Analyze the difference by looking into the complexity of calls to your local systems routines for generating uniform random numbers, and for finding square roots and natural logarithms.

*L6.3.26 *Shuffling cards* (*complete development*). Completely develop an algorithm for simulating the shuffling of a deck of cards.

7

SUPPLEMENTARY REMARKS AND REFERENCES

The objective of this chapter is to draw attention to material which supplements the subject matter in this text. It is not intended to be a comprehensive bibliography. An effort has been made to find good, readable references on topics which will be of interest to our readers.

There are two parts to this chapter. The first is an annotated bibliography arranged by chapter and section. The second is an alphabetical listing, by author, of the references given in the first part. Whenever possible, we cite a textbook at the lowest known level rather than a more difficult journal article. The following abbreviations are used to denote level:

E: elementary

I: intermediate

A: advanced

VA: very advanced

An additional symbol M is used to label references which use or develop a significant amount of mathematics. The scale is calibrated by classifying this text as IM.

CHAPTER 1 THE COMPLETE DEVELOPMENT OF AN ALGORITHM

There is no "official" definition of the phrase "the complete development of an algorithm." It appears that most computer scientists find the list given at the end of Sec. 1.1 acceptable.

A palatable introduction to mathematical machines and the formal theory of computation is:

Trakhtenbrot, B. A., *Algorithms and Automatic Computing Machines*, Heath, Boston, Mass., 1963(IM).

A more comprehensive and slightly more difficult introduction is:

Minsky, M., *Computation: Finite and Infinite Machines*, Prentice-Hall, Englewood Cliffs, N.J., 1967(IM).

Although some purists accept nothing less than explicit code as the statement of an algorithm, we find the semiverbal step-by-step statements used here (see Appendix A) and some prose discussion very useful (and often necessary) to get across a basic understanding of how an algorithm works. Many people find it difficult to go straight into code, even if it is well-documented.

It can be argued that the idea of a mathematical model is the most fundamental concept in applied mathematics. In spite of this, we cannot find a good elementary discussion of the subject that is oriented toward computer science.

The original formulation of the traveling salesman problem is attributed to Merrill M. Flood of Columbia University in 1937. It arose in connection with school-bus routing. Journal papers on the problem started emerging in the operations research literature in the early to middle 1950s, and it has been widely studied ever since. Although no polynomial worst case algorithm is known for the problem, there are a number of impressive heuristics and exact (but worst case exponential) solution procedures. References to some of these are given for Sec. 4.4. The following reference describes some "real-life" applications of the traveling salesman problem:

Lenstra, J. K., and A. H. G. Kan Rinnooy, "Some Simple Applications of the Traveling Salesman Problem," Publication BW 38/74, Mathematisch Centrum, Amsterdam, 1974(AM).

A good general discussion of implementation, debugging, and documentation is given in:

Yohe, J. M., "An Overview of Programming Practices," *Comput. Surv.*, **6**: 221–245 (1974) (E).

For a programming "style manual," see:

Kernighan, B. W., and P. J. Plauger, *The Elements of Programming Style*, McGraw-Hill, New York, 1970(E).

Although the polynomial-exponential complexity criterion in Sec. 1.3 seems very obvious to many people, it does not appear to have been widely used until the mid-1960s. The first explicit statement that we have found is in:

Edmonds, J., "Paths, Trees, and Flowers," *Can. J. Math.*, **17**: 449–467 (1965) (AM).

The "big-oh little-oh" notation has become popular in a number of mathematical contexts. Further discussion can be found in Chap. 1 of:

Knuth, D. E., *Fundamental Algorithms, The Art of Computer Programming*, vol. 1, Addison-Wesley, Reading, Mass., 1969a(AM).

CHAPTER 2   SOME BASIC TOOLS AND ALGORITHMS

2.1   Top-down Structured Programming and Program Correctness

The subject of top-down structured programming is both new and controversial. It seems to be rapidly gaining acceptance in the computer science community even though its use is still far from universal. The literature on structured programming is growing exponentially. For further study, we would recommend:

McGowan, C. L., and J. R. Kelly, *Top-Down Structured Programming Techniques*, Petrocelli/Charter, New York, 1975(E).

This book is fairly thorough and contains a brief account of the history of the subject. The following special issues of two popular journals might also be consulted:

Comput. Surv., **6**: (1974)(E).

Datamation, **19**: (1973)(E).

On a more advanced level, there is:

Dahl, O., E. Dijkstra, and C. A. R. Hoare, *Structured Programming*, Academic, New York, 1972(I).

2.2   Networks

The vocabulary associated with networks is still in a state of flux. The world cannot even agree on a common name for these structures. Approximately half of the literature refers to them as *networks*, and the other half calls them *graphs*. Vertices are often called *points* or *nodes*; edges are often called *lines* or *arcs*. We have tried to adopt terminology whose use is reasonably common.

A somewhat encyclopedic study of trees can be found in Knuth (1969a).

A comprehensive, applications-oriented book is:

Deo, N., *Graph Theory with Applications to Engineering and Computer Science*, Prentice-Hall, Englewood Cliffs, N.J., 1974(IM).

Good introductions to applications in switching and coding theory, electrical network analysis, and operations research can be found here. There is also a brief discussion of the use of networks in chemistry.

For a comprehensive, theory-oriented reference, see:

Berge, C., *Graphs and Hypergraphs*, North-Holland, Amsterdam, 1973(AM).

This tome is the most complete mathematical treatment of graphs or networks in the world today, and it is likely to remain so for some time.

Network algorithms are used quite extensively in operations research. The literature in this area is vast. Let us just mention:

Fulkerson, D. R., "Flow Networks and Combinatorial Operations Research," *Am. Math. Mon.*, **73**: 115–138 (1966)(IM).

Frank, H., and I. T. Frisch, *Communications, Transmission, and Transportation Networks*, Addison-Wesley, Reading, Mass., 1971(AM).

Lawler, E., *Combinatorial Optimization: Networks and Matroids*, Holt, Rinehart and Winston, New York, 1975(AM).

Algorithm CONNECT can be found in Deo (1974), as can some additional matrix representations and a number of other network algorithms.

A good heuristic for the isomorphism problem can be found in:

Corneil, D. G., and C. C. Gotlieb, "An Efficient Algorithm for Graph Isomorphism," *J. ACM*, **17**: 51–64 (1970)(AM).

Unfortunately, some of the theoretical claims made in this paper have been shown to be incorrect. However, the main algorithm presented in this article remains one of the best-known general heuristics.

The isomorphism problem has been solved for several special classes of networks, the most important being the class of trees. See:

Corneil, D. G., "Graph Isomorphism," doctoral thesis, Department of Computer Science, University of Toronto, Canada, 1968 (AM); see also *Tech. Rept.* 18, Department of Computer Science, University of Toronto, 1970.

A large number of special programming languages and software packages have been developed to handle networks. The following is merely a sampling of the literature:

Basili, V. R., C. K. Mesztenyi, and W. C. Reinboldt, "FGRAAL: Fortran Extended Graph Algorithmic Language," *Tech. Rept.* 179, Computer Science Center, University of Maryland, 1972(I); see also *Tech. Rept.* 225, 1973(I).

Chase, S. M., "GASP—Graph Algorithm Software Package," *Quart. Tech. Prog. Rept.* (Oct.–Dec. 1969), Department of Computer Science, University of Illinois (I).

Hart, R., "HINT: A Graph Processing Language," *Res. Rept.*, Computer Institute for Social Science Research, Michigan State University, 1969(I).

King, C. A., "A Graph-Theoretic Programming Language," in R. C. Read (ed.), *Graph Theory and Computing*, Academic, New York, 1972, 63–74(I).

Martin, C., and D. S. Richards, "CLAMAR: A Combinatorial Language," *Tech. Rept.* 75-5, Department of Applied Mathematics and Computer Science, University of Virginia, 1975(I).

The last language is notable since it was completely developed by two undergraduates. Although many special languages have been constructed, their use seems limited and localized.

2.3 Some Data Structures

An extensive and readable account of a variety of data structures can be found in Knuth (1969a). Other commonly used texts include:

Berztiss, A. T., *Data Structures: Theory and Practice*, Academic, New York, 1971(IM).

Page, E. S., and L. B. Wilson, *Information Representation and Manipulation in a Computer*, Cambridge, London, 1973(IM).

Stone, H., *Introduction to Computer Organization and Data Structures*, McGraw-Hill, New York, 1972(I).

2.4 Elementary Notions from Probability and Statistics

A readable, applications-oriented introduction to probability theory is:

Ross, S. M., *Introduction to Probability Models*, Academic, New York, 1972(IM).

Chapter 8 of Ross contains a nice introduction to the topic of system reliability—a topic with serious applications in computer science.

A reasonably elementary, yet comprehensive, treatment of discrete events and random variables can be found in Feller's classic:

Feller, W., *An Introduction to Probability Theory and Its Applications*, 2d ed., vol. 1, Wiley, New York, 1957(IM).

For a very elementary, computer-oriented (Basic language) introduction to discrete probability, see:

Snell, J. L., *Introduction to Probability Theory with Computing*, Prentice-Hall, Englewood Cliffs, N.J., 1975(EM).

Expected performance analysis of algorithms is generally quite difficult; the analysis of Algorithm SIS in this section is something of an exception. An expected performance analysis of Algorithm MAX (see Sec. 1.2) can be found in Knuth (1969a). Algorithm ETS (see Sec. 1.3) always performs the same number of operations for any set of N cities. There is so little "play" in Algorithm PRIM that it is hardly worth an expected performance analysis. This assessment is supported by observations on the individual run times obtained in the experimental average performance analysis of Sec. 5.2.

A sampling of references for the applications described at the beginning of Sec. 2.4 are given below.

On the subject of simulation, see:

Fishman, G. S., *Concepts and Methods in Discrete Event Digital Simulation*, Wiley, New York, 1973(IM).

Additional references are given for Secs. 3.6 and 6.3.

For computational statistics, see:

Freiberger, W., and U. Grenander, *A Short Course in Computational Probability and Statistics*, Springer-Verlag, New York, 1971(VAM).

On the topic of random number generation, see:

Knuth, D. E., *Seminumerical Algorithms, The Art of Computer Programming*, vol. 2, Addison-Wesley, Reading, Mass., 1969b(AM).

For bayesian decision theory, see:

Winkler, R. L., *Introduction to Bayesian Inference and Decision*, Holt, Rinehart and Winston, New York, 1972(IM).

DeGroot, M. H., *Optimal Statistical Decisions*, McGraw-Hill, New York, 1970 (VAM).

A fairly complete, introductory account of statistical techniques can be found in:

Mood, A. M., and F. A. Graybill, *Introduction to the Theory of Statistics*, McGraw-Hill, New York, 1963(IM).

On a more elementary level, there is:

Huntsberger, D. V., and P. Billingsley, *Elements of Statistical Inference*, 3d ed., Allyn and Bacon, Boston, Mass., 1973(EM).

For a more advanced introductory treatment, see:

Cox, D. R., and D. V. Hinkley, *Theoretical Statistics*, Chapman and Hall, London, 1974(AM).

CHAPTER 3   ALGORITHM DESIGN METHODS

3.1   Subgoals, Hill Climbing, and Working Backward

Psychologists, mathematicians, and computer scientists have all shared in developing the literature of general problem-solving techniques. Some of the best-known references are the following. By a psychologist:

Wickelgren, W. A., *How to Solve Problems; Elements of a Theory of Problems and Problem Solving*, Freeman, San Francisco, 1974(EM).

By a mathematician:

Polya, G., *How to Solve It*, Doubleday, Garden City, N.Y., 1957(EM).

———, *Mathematical Discovery*, vols. 1 and 2, Wiley, New York, 1962(EM).

By a computer scientist:

Nilsson, N. J., *Artificial Intelligence*, McGraw-Hill, New York, 1971(IM).

Most of the computer science effort in the area of problem-solving techniques can be found under the heading "artificial intelligence." Comprehensive surveys include:

Feigenbaum, E. A., and J. Feldman, *Computers and Thought*, McGraw-Hill, New York, 1963(I).

Meltzer, B., and D. Michie, *Machine Intelligence 7*, Wiley, New York, 1972(AM).

A significant fraction of this literature is concerned with computer game playing. A thorough treatment of the jeep problem can be found in:

Gale, D., "The Jeep Once More or Jeeper by the Dozen," *Am. Math. Mon.*, **77**: 493–501 (1970)(IM).

The technique of working backward has been developed into something between an art and a science, known as *dynamic programming*, by Richard Bellman and others. Readable, introductory accounts can be found in:

Hastings, N. A. J., *Dynamic Programming*, Crane, Russak, New York, 1973(IM).

Kaufmann, A., *Graphs, Dynamic Programming and Finite Games*, Academic, New York, 1967(IM).

3.2 Heuristics

Algorithm GTS2 is "rediscovered" by many undergraduates each year. A much more powerful (and more complicated) heuristic for the traveling salesman problem is given by Lin and Kernighan (1973). Fast, simple (but not especially powerful) heuristics for very large problems are considered in:

Webb, M. H. J., "Some Methods of Producing Approximate Solutions to Traveling Salesman Problems with Hundreds or Thousands of Cities," *Oper. Res. Q.*, **22**: 49–66 (1971)(E).

A clear discussion, with many interesting examples, of scheduling and packing heuristics can be found in:

Graham, R. L., "Bounds on Multiprocessing Anomalies and Related Packing Algorithms," in *Proc. Spring Joint Comput. Conf.*, 205–217 (1972)(IM).

For the analysis of a variety of simple, but effective, heuristics, see:

Johnson, D., "Approximation Algorithms for Combinatorial Problems," *J. Comput. Syst. Sci.*, **9**: 256–278 (1974)(AM).

3.3 Backtrack Programming

This technique has been "rediscovered" many times. For example, see:

Golomb, S. W., and L. D. Baumert, "Backtrack Programming," *J. ACM*, **12**: 516–524 (1965)(I).

A good, general statement of the backtracking procedure can be found in:

Knuth, D. E., "Estimating the Efficiency of Backtrack Programs," *Math. Comput.*, **29**: 121–136 (1975)(IM).

This reference also contains a useful semiexperimental expected performance analysis applicable to any backtrack algorithm.

3.4 Branch and Bound

The algorithm of this section is based on:

Little, J. D. C., K. G. Murty, D. W. Sweeney, and C. Karel, "An Algorithm for the Traveling Salesman Problem," *Oper. Res.*, **11**: 979–989 (1963)(IM).

This paper did much to popularize the branch-and-bound procedure.
For a more advanced and comprehensive discussion, see:

Garfinkel, R. S., and G. L. Nemhauser, *Integer Programming*, Wiley, New York, 1972(AM).

As the last reference indicates, branch-and-bound procedures are very useful for solving optimization problems known as *integer linear programs*. These problems ask for a set of integers which maximize or minimize a linear equation subject to a set of linear constraint equations. Many important problems, including the traveling salesman problem, can be formulated as integer linear programs.
A survey of the work on the traveling salesman problem before 1968 can be found in:

Bellmore, M., and G. L. Nemhauser, "The Traveling Salesman Problem: A Survey," *Oper. Res.*, **16**: 538–558 (1968)(IM).

Two noteworthy contributions to the literature of the traveling salesman problem are:

Bellmore, M., and J. C. Malone, "Pathology of Traveling Salesman Subtour Elimination Algorithm," *Oper. Res.*, **19**: 278–307 (1971)(AM).
Held, M., and R. M. Karp, "The Traveling Salesman Problem and Minimum Spanning Trees, Part II," *Math. Prog.*, **1**: 6–25 (1971)(AM).

Computational experience with these two algorithms is impressive. Note that the Held and Karp (1971) reference uses minimum-weight spanning trees.

One of the most effective heuristics, in terms of speed and quality of solution, for the traveling salesman problem can be found in:

Lin, S., and B. W. Kernighan, "An Effective Heuristic Algorithm for the Traveling Salesman Problem," *Oper. Res.*, **21**: 498–516 (1973)(I).

3.5 Recursion

An excellent reference for recursion is:

Barron, D. W., *Recursive Techniques in Programming*, American Elsevier, New York, 1968(IM).

Recurrence relations arise often in applications, and many techniques exist for finding closed-form solutions to such equations. A good, introductory treatment of this material can be found in:

Liu, C. L., *Introduction to Combinatorial Mathematics*, McGraw-Hill, New York, 1968(IM).

Nilsson (1971) discusses depth-first and breadth-first search methods. Recursive depth-first search has recently been used as the basis for a variety of efficient network algorithms. One of the earliest and most influential papers is:

Tarjan, R., "Depth-First Search and Linear Graph Algorithms," *SIAM J. Comput.*, **1**: 146–160 (1972)(IM).

3.6 Simulation

A tremendous amount of effort has gone into the development of good simulation techniques and languages. This effort has been amply justified by the importance of simulation models for real-life problems. In addition to Fishman (1973), we would recommend:

Gordon, G., *System Simulation*, Prentice-Hall, Englewood Cliffs, N.J., 1969(I).

Both references contain chapters on special simulation languages. Fishman (1973) has a large bibliography which should be consulted by anyone who is seriously interested in the subject.

CHAPTER 4 A COMPLETE EXAMPLE

4.1 The Development of a Minimum-Weight Spanning Tree Algorithm

The algorithm presented in this section was first stated in:

Prim, R. C., "Shortest Connection Networks and Some Generalizations," *Bell Syst. Tech. J.*, **36**: 1389–1401 (1957)(IM).

There are a variety of tricks that can be used to speed up this basic algorithm, but these modifications still leave an O(M²) algorithm. We chose to ignore these tricks and avoid unnecessary complications.

Good introductory discussions of interpolation, extrapolation, and least-squares data fitting can be found in:

Hamming, R. W., *Introduction to Applied Numerical Analysis*, McGraw-Hill, New York, 1971(IM).

Fröberg, C. E., *Introduction to Numerical Analysis*, 2d ed., Addison-Wesley, Reading, Mass., 1969(AM).

4.2 Program Testing

The subject of program testing does not have a well-developed literature. It is not hard to understand why. Published accounts of testing procedures generally reflect guidelines and rules of thumb used by assorted groups in the "real world." To a considerable extent, the material in this section reflects our own ideas and practices. It will probably be some time before any particular set of testing procedures is widely adopted.

A readable, fairly comprehensive account of testing for correctness may be found in:

Van Tassel, D., *Program Style, Design, Efficiency, Debugging, and Testing*, Prentice-Hall, Englewood Cliffs, N.J., 1974(E).

Yohe (1974) also contains some useful guidelines. Some people have worried about rigorous proofs of program correctness, but this line of research has been fairly unfruitful so far. See Yohe (1974) for some references.

Two readable accounts of testing for efficiency are:

Knuth, D. E., "An Empirical Study of FORTRAN Programs," *Software—Pract. Exper.*, **1**: 105–133 (1971)(E).

Ingalls, D. H. H., "FETE: A Fortran Execution Time Estimator," *Tech. Rept.* STAN-CS-71-204, Stanford University, Stanford, Calif., 1971(E).

Programs for producing profiles on other programs are generally large and complicated. However, a good undergraduate is capable of designing and implementing a respectable profiling program:

Ferguson, L., "PROFILE, A CDC Fortran Profiling Program," *Tech. Rept.* 75–6, Department of Applied Mathematics and Computer Science, University of Virginia, 1975(I).

4.3 Documentation and Maintenance

See Kernighan and Plauger (1970), Yohe (1974), Van Tassel (1974), and:

Gunderman, R. E., "A Glimpse into Program Maintenance," *Datamation*, **19**: 99–101 (1973)(E).

Mooney, J. W., "Organized Program Maintenance," *Datamation*, **21**: 63–64 (1975)(E).

CHAPTER 5 COMPUTER SCIENCE ALGORITHMS

5.1 Sorting

Sorting algorithms are perhaps the most widely studied algorithms in all of computer science. Most of what is known on the subject is covered in comprehensive detail in:

Knuth, D. E., *Sorting and Searching, The Art of Computer Programming*, vol. 3, Addison-Wesley, Reading, Mass., 1973(AM).

An excellent survey article is:

Martin, W. A., "Sorting," *Computing Surveys*, **3**: 148–174 (1971)(I).

Other textbook accounts, in increasing order of difficulty, are Page and Wilson (1973), and:

Nievergelt, J., J. C. Farrar, and E. M. Reingold, *Computer Approaches to Mathematical Problems*, Prentice-Hall, Englewood Cliffs, N.J., 1974(IM).

Aho, A. V., J. E. Hopcroft, and J. D. Ullman, *The Design and Analysis of Computer Algorithms*, Addison-Wesley, Reading, Mass., 1974(VAM).

5.2 Searching

A comprehensive treatment of computer searching can be found in Knuth (1973). A more elementary treatment is contained in Page and Wilson (1973).

Both of these references discuss an important technique, known as *hashing*, which we have not covered. Hashing searches for keys by evaluating a function of the key itself. The value of this function specifies the exact or approximate location of the record being sought.

Probabilistic search problems require sophisticated mathematics for their solution—the example given in this section being a notable exception. For a description of some more advanced problems, see DeGroot (1970). References to the original Huffman and Zimmerman papers may be found in Knuth (1969a).

5.3 Arithmetic and Logical Expressions

Further discussion of arithmetic expressions can be found in Knuth (1969a), Nievergelt, Farrar, and Reingold (1974), and:

Wegner, P., *Programming Languages, Information Structures, and Machine Organization*, McGraw-Hill, New York, 1968(I).

5.4 Paging

There are several good sources of information on paging algorithms, including:

Belady, L. A., "A Study of Replacement Algorithms for a Virtual Storage Computer," *IBM Syst. J.*, **5**: 78–101 (1966)(I).

Denning, P. J., "Virtual Memory," *Comput. Surv.*, **2**: 153–189 (1970)(I).

Coffman, E. G., and P. J. Denning, *Operating Systems Theory*, Prentice-Hall, Englewood Cliffs, N.J., 1973(AM).

We have only been able to scratch the surface of the subject of computer system algorithms in Secs. 5.3 and 5.4. Compilers and operating systems are constructed using a wide variety of such algorithms. Some of the previously cited references can be consulted for additional examples. These include all three volumes by Knuth, Hellerman and Conroy (1975), Berztiss (1971), Page and Wilson (1973), Nievergelt, Farrar, and Reingold (1974), Coffman and Denning (1973), and Wegner (1968).

5.5 Parallelism

A description of Illiac IV is given in:

Slotnick, D. L., "The Fastest Computer," *Sci. Am.*, **224**: 76–88 (1971)(E).

A number of interesting articles on parallel computation can be found in:

Traub, J. F. (ed.), *Complexity of Sequential and Parallel Numerical Algorithms*, Academic, New York, 1973(IM to AM).

It appears that M. Sollin never published his parallel minimum-weight spanning tree algorithm. We found a brief discussion in:

Even, S., *Algorithmic Combinatorics*, Macmillan, New York, 1973(IM).

Algorithm PARSORT comes from:

Kautz, W. H., K. N. Levitt, and A. Waksman, "Cellular Interconnections Arrays," *IEEE Trans. Comput.*, **C-17**: 443–451 (1968)(IM).

This algorithm is also presented in Even (1973).

CHAPTER 6   MATHEMATICAL ALGORITHMS

6.1   Games and Combinatorial Puzzles

The literature on games is vast and diversified, and we cannot begin to do it justice.   However, we shall provide enough of a list to keep the interested reader busy for years.

An elementary, semihistorical introduction to magic squares can be found in:

Gardner, M., *The 2nd Scientific American Book of Mathematical Puzzles and Diversions*, Simon and Schuster, New York, 1961(EM).

This reference also cites a number of more advanced sources.

Mr. Gardner's regular column "Mathematical Games" in the *Scientific American* is a must for game enthusiasts.   He has also published or edited over a dozen books on mathematical games and puzzles; for example, see:

Gardner, M., *The Unexpected Hanging and Other Mathematical Diversions*, Simon and Schuster, New York, 1969(EM).

The nimbi game in this section was invented by James Bynum, and it is described by Gardner in his February 1974 column.   The three-way duel problem is a classic.   Gardner (1961) describes its origins.   A slightly more general and advanced treatment than the one given here can be found in:

Freudenthal, H., *Probability and Statistics*, Elsevier, Amsterdam, 1965(IM).

There is a formal, mathematical theory of games which we have not considered since the subject rates its own course at most universities.   The following books provide introductions at several different levels:

Williams, J. D., *The Compleat Strategyst*, McGraw-Hill, New York, 1966(EM).

Singleton, R. R., and W. F. Tyndall, *Games and Programs: Mathematics for Modeling*, Freeman, San Francisco, 1974(IM).

Von Neumann, J., and O. Morgenstern, *Theory of Games and Economic Behavior*, Princeton University Press, Princeton, N.J., 1944(AM).

Luce, R. D., and H. Raiffa, *Games and Decisions*, Wiley, New York, 1957(AM).

As might be expected, much effort has gone into the analysis of serious gambling games. The two references that follow are very thorough, each in its own way.

Scarne, J., *Scarne's Complete Guide to Gambling*, Simon and Schuster, New York, 1961(E).

Epstein, R. A., *The Theory of Gambling and Statistical Logic*, Academic, New York, 1967(AM).

Computer game enthusiasts should consult the literature on artificial intelligence—for example, Feigenbaum and Feldman (1963), Nilsson (1971), and:

Spencer, D. D., *Game Playing with Computers*, Spartan, New York, 1968(E).

Nievergelt, Farrar, and Reingold (1974) also have a good chapter on computer-oriented games.

6.2 Shortest Paths

The problem of finding shortest paths in networks has been studied ad nauseum. In fact, the only problem considered in this text which has been more thoroughly studied is sorting (some subjects, such as searching, are too diversified to be considered as one basic problem). Lawler (1975) contains a good discussion that is much more comprehensive than what we have presented here. Algorithm DIJKSTRA was first stated in:

Dijkstra, E. W., "A Note on Two Problems in Connexion with Graphs," *Numer. Math.*, **1**: 269–271 (1959)(IM).

6.3 Probabilistic Algorithms

The central limit theorem (Theorem 6.3.3) enables us to approximate a number of discrete and continuous distributions with the standard normal distribution $N(0, 1)$. Some examples can be found in Ross (1972). This approximation can often greatly simplify computations.

Knuth (1969b) contains a very comprehensive treatment of random number generators. This reference contains a discussion of how to choose the parameters in Algorithm LCM, and it provides descriptions of a wide assortment of statistical tests for checking the "randomness" of a random number sequence. Some readers may also be interested in his discussion of the question: What is a random sequence? (The material is somewhat advanced, but at least you can get some idea of the effort that has been made to answer this question.)

Knuth (1969b) and Hellerman and Conroy (1975) might be consulted for further theory and examples relating to probabilistic algorithms. Two other viewpoints can be found in the articles by U. Grenander and M. Neuts in:

LaSalle, J. P., *The Influence of Computing on Mathematical Research and Education: Proc. Symp. Appl. Math., vol. 20,* American Mathematical Society, Providence, R.I., 1974(AM).

The subject of statistical evaluation of computer systems performance has attracted considerable recent attention. The interested reader might consult:

Freiberger, W. (ed.), *Statistical Computer Performance Evaluation,* Academic, New York, 1972(A).

Hellerman, H., and T. F. Conroy, *Computer System Performance,* McGraw-Hill, New York, 1975(AM).

Some knowledge of computer organization and/or operating systems is necessary to read this material.

NUMERICAL COMPUTATIONAL COMPLEXITY AND THE NP-COMPLETE PROBLEMS

There are two important topics which we have not been able to cover since their inclusion would require a longer book and some additional course prerequisites. We shall be content merely to mention them and provide some references.

The subject of numerical, or analytic, computational complexity deals with the design and analysis of numerical algorithms. These include algorithms for matrix manipulation, integer and polynomial arithmetic, the solving of algebraic and differential equations, the fast Fourier transform, etc. The interested reader should consult Knuth (1969b), Traub (1973), Aho, Hopcroft, and Ullman (1974), and the article by Traub in LaSalle (1974). A brief and highly readable overview can be found in:

Traub, J. F., "Numerical Mathematics and Computer Science," *Comm. ACM,* **15**: 537–541 (1972)(IM).

It has been shown that a large class of combinatorial problems, including the traveling salesman problem and general scheduling and packing problems (see Sec. 3.2), are equivalent in the sense that either all or none of them can be solved by polynomial algorithms. Thus, if it could be shown that a polynomial worst case performance algorithm could not possibly exist for one of these problems, then no such algorithm could exist for any of the other problems in the class. Conversely, if a polynomial worst case performance algorithm could be found for any one of these problems, then it could be used to produce polynomial algorithms for the others. This group of problems is known as the *NP-complete class.* The most elementary paper on the subject appears to be:

Karp, R. M., "On the Computational Complexity of Combinatorial Problems," *Networks,* **5**: 45–68 (1975)(AM).

For a more advanced treatment, see Aho, Hopcroft, and Ullman (1974).

ALPHABETICAL BIBLIOGRAPHY

Aho, A. V., J. E. Hopcroft, and J. D. Ullman, *The Design and Analysis of Computer Algorithms*, Addison-Wesley, Reading, Mass., 1974(VAM).

Barron, D. W., *Recursion Techniques in Programming*, American Elsevier, New York, 1968(IM).

Basili, V. R., C. K. Mesztenyi, and W. C. Reinboldt, "FGRAAL: Fortran Extended Graph Algorithmic Language," *Tech. Rept.* 179, Computer Science Center, University of Maryland, 1972(I); see also *Tech. Rept.* 225, 1973(I).

Belady, L. A., "A Study of Replacement Algorithms for a Virtual Storage Computer," *IBM Syst. J.*, **5**: 78–101 (1966)(I).

Bellmore, M., and J. C. Malone, "Pathology of Traveling Salesman Subtour Elimination Algorithms," *Oper. Res.*, **19**: 278–307 (1971)(AM).

———, and G. L. Nemhauser, "The Traveling Salesman Problem: A Survey," *Oper. Res.*, **16**: 538–558 (1968)(IM).

Berge, C., *Graphs and Hypergraphs*, North-Holland, Amsterdam, 1973(AM).

Berztiss, A. T., *Data Structures; Theory and Practice*, Academic, New York, 1971(IM).

Busacker, R. G., and T. L. Saaty, *Finite Graphs and Networks*, McGraw-Hill, New York, 1965(IM).

Chase, S. M., "GASP—Graph Algorithm Software Package," *Q. Tech. Prog. Rept.* (Oct.–Dec. 1969), Department of Computer Science, University of Illinois (I).

Coffman, E. G., and P. J. Denning, *Operating Systems Theory*, Prentice-Hall, Englewood Cliffs, N.J., 1973(AM).

Comput. Surv., **6**: (1974)(E).

Corneil, D. G., "Graph Isomorphism," doctoral thesis, Department of Computer Science, University of Toronto, Canada, 1968(AM); see also *Tech. Rept.* 18, Department of Computer Science, University of Toronto, 1970.

———, and C. C. Gotlieb, "An Efficient Algorithm for Graph Isomorphism," *J. ACM*, **17**: 51–64 (1970)(AM).

Cox, D. R., and D. V. Hinkley, *Theoretical Statistics*, Chapman and Hall, London, 1974(AM).

Dahl, O., E. Dijkstra, and C. A. R. Hoare, *Structured Programming*, Academic, New York, 1972(I).

Datamation, **19**: (1973)(E).

DeGroot, M. H., *Optimal Statistical Decisions*, McGraw-Hill, New York, 1970(VAM).

Denning, P. J., "Virtual Memory," *Comput. Surv.*, **2**: 153–189 (1970)(I).

Deo, N., *Graph Theory with Applications to Engineering and Computer Science*, Prentice-Hall, Englewood Cliffs, N.J., 1974(IM).

Dijkstra, E. W., "A Note on Two Problems in Connexion with Graphs," *Numer. Math.*, **1**: 269–271 (1959)(IM).

Edmonds, J., "Paths, Trees, and Flowers," *Can. J. Math.*, **17**: 449–467 (1965)(AM).

Epstein, R. A., *The Theory of Gambling and Statistical Logic*, Academic, New York, 1967(AM).

Even, S., *Algorithmic Combinatorics*, Macmillan, New York, 1973(IM).

Feigenbaum, E. A., and J. Feldman, *Computers and Thought*, McGraw-Hill, New York, 1963(I).

Feller, W., *An Introduction to Probability Theory and Its Applications*, 2d ed., vol. 1, Wiley, New York, 1957(IM).

Ferguson, L., "PROFILE, A CDC Fortran Profiling Program," *Tech. Rept.* 75-6, Department of Applied Mathematics and Computer Science, University of Virginia, 1975(I).

Fishman, G. S., *Concepts and Methods in Discrete Event Digital Simulation*, Wiley, New York, 1973(IM).

Frank, H., and I. T. Frisch, *Communications, Transmission, and Transportation Networks*, Addison-Wesley, Reading, Mass., 1971(AM).

Freiberger, W., and U. Grenander, *A Short Course in Computational Probability and Statistics*, Springer-Verlag, New York, 1971(VAM).

Freiberger, W. (ed.), *Statistical Computer Performance Evaluation*, Academic, New York, 1972(A).

Freudenthal, H., *Probability and Statistics*, Elsevier, Amsterdam, 1965(IM).

Fröberg, C.E., *Introduction to Numerical Analysis*, 2d ed., Addison-Wesley, Reading, Mass., 1969(AM).

Fulkerson, D. R., "Flow Networks and Combinatorial Operations Research," *Am. Math. Mon.*, **73**: 115–138 (1966)(IM).

Gale, D., "The Jeep Once More or Jeeper by the Dozen," *Am. Math. Mon.*, **77**: 493–501 (1970)(IM).

Gardner, M., *The 2nd Scientific American Book of Mathematical Puzzles and Diversions*, Simon and Schuster, New York, 1961(EM).

———, *The Unexpected Hanging and Other Mathematical Diversions*, Simon and Schuster, New York, 1969(EM).

Garfinkel, R. S., and G. L. Nemhauser, *Integer Programming*, Wiley, New York, 1972(AM).

Golomb, S. W., and L. D. Baumert, "Backtrack Programming," *J. ACM*, **12**: 516–524 (1965)(I).

Gordon, G., *System Simulation*, Prentice-Hall, Englewood Cliffs, N.J., 1969(I).

Graham, R. L., "Bounds on Multiprocessing Anomalies and Related Packing Algorithms," in *Proc. Spring Joint Comput. Conf.*, 205–217 (1972)(IM).

Gunderman, R. E., "A Glimpse into Program Maintenance," *Datamation*, **19**: 99–101 (1973)(E).

Hamming, R. W., *Introduction to Applied Numerical Analysis*, McGraw-Hill, New York, 1971(IM).

Hart, R., "HINT: A Graph Processing Language," *Res. Rept.*, Computer Institute for Social Science Research, Michigan State University, 1969(I).

Hastings, N. A. J., *Dynamic Programming*, Crane, Russak, New York, 1973(IM).

Held, M., and R. M. Karp, "The Traveling Salesman Problem and Minimum Spanning Trees, Part II," *Math. Prog.*, **1**: 6–25 (1971)(AM).

Hellerman, H., and T. F. Conroy, *Computer System Performance*, McGraw-Hill, New York, 1975(AM).

Huntsberger, D. V., and P. Billingsley, *Elements of Statistical Inference*, 3d ed., Allyn and Bacon, Boston, Mass., 1973(EM).

Ingalls, D. H. H., "FETE: A Fortran Execution Time Estimator," *Tech. Rept.* STAN-CS-71-204, Stanford University, Stanford, Calif., 1971(E).

Johnson, D., "Approximation Algorithms for Combinatorial Problems," *J. Comput. Syst. Sci.*, **9**: 256–278 (1974)(AM).

Karp, R. M., "On the Computational Complexity of Combinatorial Problems," *Networks*, **5**: 45–68 (1975)(AM).

Kaufmann, A., *Graphs, Dynamic Programming and Finite Games*, Academic, New York, 1967(IM).

Kautz, W. H., K. N. Levitt, and A. Waksman, "Cellular Interconnection Arrays," *IEEE Trans. Comput.*, **C-17**: 443–451 (1968)(IM).

Kernighan, B. W., and P. J. Plauger, *The Elements of Programming Style*, McGraw-Hill, New York, 1970(E).

King, C. A., "A Graph-Theoretic Programming Language," in R. C. Read (ed.), *Graph Theory and Computing*, Academic, New York, 1972, 63–74(I).

Knuth, D. E., *Fundamental Algorithms, The Art of Computer Programming*, vol. 1, Addison-Wesley, Reading, Mass., 1969a(AM).

———, *Seminumerical Algorithms, The Art of Computer Programming*, vol. 2, Addison-Wesley, Reading, Mass., 1969b(AM).

———, "An Empirical Study of Fortran Programs," *Software Pract. Exper.*, **1**: 105–133 (1971)(E).

———, *Sorting and Searching, The Art of Computer Programming*, vol. 3, Addison-Wesley, Reading, Mass., 1973(AM).

———, "Estimating the Efficiency of Backtrack Programs," *Math. Comput.*, **29**: 121–136 (1975)(IM).

LaSalle, J. P., *The Influence of Computing on Mathematical Research and Education: Proc. Symp. Appl. Math., vol. 20*, American Mathematical Society, Providence, R.I., 1974(AM).

Lawler, E., *Combinatorial Optimization: Networks and Matroids*, Holt, Rinehart and Winston, New York, 1975(AM).

Lenstra, J. K., and A. H. G. Kan Rinnooy, "Some Simple Applications of the Traveling Salesman Problem," Publication BW 38/74, Mathematisch Centrum, Amsterdam, 1974(AM).

Lin, S., and B. W. Kernighan, "An Effective Heuristic Algorithm for the Traveling Salesman Problem," *Oper. Res.*, **21**: 498–516 (1973)(I).

Little, J. D. C., K. G. Murty, D. W. Sweeney, and C. Karel, "An Algorithm for the Traveling Salesman Problem," *Oper. Res.*, **11**: 979–989 (1963)(IM).

Liu, C. L., *Introduction to Combinatorial Mathematics*, McGraw-Hill, New York, 1968(IM).

Luce, R. D., and H. Raiffa, *Games and Decisions*, Wiley, New York, 1957(AM).

Martin, C., and D. S. Richards, "CLAMAR: A Combinatorial Language," *Tech. Rept.* 75-5, Department of Applied Mathematics and Computer Science, University of Virginia, 1975(I).

Martin, W. A., "Sorting," *Comput. Surv.*, **3**: 148–174 (1971)(I).

McGowan, C. L., and J. R. Kelly, *Top-Down Structured Programming Techniques*, Petrocelli/Charter, New York, 1975(E).

Meltzer, B., and D. Michie, *Machine Intelligence 7*, Wiley, New York, 1972(AM).

Minsky, M., *Computation: Finite and Infinite Machines*, Prentice-Hall, Englewood Cliffs, N.J., 1967(IM).

Mood, A. M., and F. A. Graybill, *Introduction to the Theory of Statistics*, McGraw-Hill, New York, 1963(IM).

Mooney, J. W., "Organized Program Maintenance," *Datamation*, **21**: 63–64 (1975) (E).

Nievergelt, J., J. C. Farrar, and E. M. Reingold, *Computer Approaches to Mathematical Problems*, Prentice-Hall, Englewood Cliffs, N.J., 1974(IM).

Nilsson, N. J., *Artificial Intelligence*, McGraw-Hill, New York, 1971(IM).

Page, E. S., and L. B. Wilson, *Information Representation and Manipulation in a Computer*, Cambridge, London, 1973(IM).

Polya, G., *How to Solve It*, Doubleday, Garden City, N.Y., 1957(EM).

——, *Mathematical Discovery*, vols. 1 and 2, Wiley, New York, 1962(EM).

Prim, R. C., "Shortest Connection Networks and Some Generalizations," *Bell Syst. Tech. J.*, **36**: 1389–1401 (1957)(IM).

Ross, S. M., *Introduction to Probability Models*, Academic, New York, 1972(IM).

Scarne, J., *Scarne's Complete Guide to Gambling*, Simon and Schuster, New York, 1961(E).

Singleton, R. R., and W. F. Tyndall, *Games and Programs: Mathematics for Modeling*, Freeman, San Francisco, 1974(IM).

Slotnick, D. L., "The Fastest Computer," *Sci. Am.*, **224**: 76–88 (1971)(E).

Snell, J. L., *Introduction to Probability Theory with Computing*, Prentice-Hall, Englewood Cliffs, N.J., 1975(EM).

Spencer, D. D., *Game Playing with Computers*, Spartan, New York, 1968(E).

Stone, H., *Introduction to Computer Organization and Data Structures*, McGraw-Hill, New York, 1972(I).

Tarjan, R., "Depth-First Search and Linear Graph Algorithms," *SIAM J. Comput.*, **1**: 146–160 (1972)(IM).

Trakhtenbrot, B. A., *Algorithms and Automatic Computing Machines*, Heath, Boston, Mass., 1963(IM).

Traub, J. F., "Numerical Mathematics and Computer Science," *Comm. ACM*, **15**: 537–541 (1972)(IM).

—— (ed.), *Complexity of Sequential and Parallel Numerical Algorithms*, Academic, New York, 1973(IM to AM).

Van Tassel, D., *Program Style, Design, Efficiency, Debugging, and Testing*, Prentice-Hall, Englewood Cliffs, N.J., 1974(E).

Von Neumann, J., and O. Morgenstern, *Theory of Games and Economic Behavior*, Princeton University Press, Princeton, N.J., 1944(AM).

Webb, M. H. J., "Some Methods of Producing Approximate Solutions to Traveling Salesman Problems with Hundreds or Thousands of Cities," *Oper. Res. Q.*, **22**: 49–66 (1971)(E).

Wegner, P., *Programming Languages, Information Structures, and Machine*

Organization, McGraw-Hill, New York, 1968(I).

Wickelgren, W. A., *How to Solve Problems; Elements of a Theory of Problems and Problem Solving*, Freeman, San Francisco, 1974(EM).

Williams, J. D., *The Compleat Strategyst*, McGraw-Hill, New York, 1966(EM).

Winkler, R. L., *Introduction to Bayesian Inference and Decision*, Holt, Rinehart and Winston, New York, 1972(IM).

Yohe, J. M., "An Overview of Programming Practices," *Comput. Surv.*, **6**: 221–245 (1974)(E).

APPENDIX A CONVENTIONS FOR STATING ALGORITHMS

This appendix contains an explanation of the conventions which are used to state algorithms in this text. The term "convention" rather than "rule" is used to indicate that they are not meant to be fixed and fast; on the contrary, they are meant to be flexible enough so that any algorithm can be stated in a way that is easy to read and understand.

The following (from Sec. 1.2) is an example of the form used to state algorithms.

Algorithm MAX Given N real numbers in a one-dimensional array R(1), R(2), ..., R(N), to find M and J such that $M = R(J) = \max_{1 \le K \le N} R(K)$. In the case where two or more elements of R have the largest value, the value of J retained will be the smallest possible.

Step 0. [Initialize] **Set** $M \leftarrow R(1)$; **and** $J \leftarrow 1$.

Step 1. [N = 1?] **If** N = 1 **then** STOP **fi**.

Step 2. [Inspect each number] **For** $K \leftarrow 2$ **to** N **do** step 3 **od**; **and** STOP.

  Step 3. [Compare] **If** $M < R(K)$ **then set** $M \leftarrow R(K)$; **and** $J \leftarrow K$ **fi** (M is now the largest number we have inspected, and it is in the K*th* position of the array.)

The remainder of this appendix explains this format.

General format The general format for stating an algorithm is illustrated below.

Algorithm NAME (⠀⠀⠀⠀⠀⠀⠀⠀⠀ **)** A description of the purpose of the algorithm, together with a description of relevant input and output parameters and variables.

Step 0. ⠀⠀⠀ [⠀⠀⠀⠀⠀⠀] Statements.

Step 1. ⠀⠀⠀ [⠀⠀⠀⠀⠀⠀] Statements. _____

_____

_____. (Comments.)

⠀⠀⠀⠀⠀⠀ *Step 2.* [⠀⠀⠀⠀⠀⠀] Statements.

⠀⠀⠀⠀⠀⠀⠀⠀⠀ .
⠀⠀⠀⠀⠀⠀⠀⠀⠀ .
⠀⠀⠀⠀⠀⠀⠀⠀⠀ .

⠀⠀⠀⠀⠀⠀ *Step K.* [⠀⠀⠀⠀⠀⠀] Statements. (Comments.)

Step K + 1. [⠀⠀⠀⠀⠀⠀] Statements.

⠀⠀⠀⠀⠀⠀⠀⠀⠀ .
⠀⠀⠀⠀⠀⠀⠀⠀⠀ .
⠀⠀⠀⠀⠀⠀⠀⠀⠀ .

Step N. ⠀⠀⠀ [⠀⠀⠀⠀⠀⠀] Statements.

Name and description The beginning "**Algorithm NAME (** ⠀⠀⠀⠀⠀⠀ **)**" is rendered in boldface type and starts at the left margin. The description of the algorithm reads like a paragraph, with subsequent lines continuing below and at the left margin.

The name of the algorithm is written entirely in capital letters and should indicate the nature or author of the algorithm. On occasion, the name may be an abbreviation, in which case an italicized full name may follow in parentheses; for example:

Algorithm SIS (*Straight Insertion Sort*)

Algorithm PARSORT (*PARallel Sort*)

The name of the algorithm is immediately followed by a brief description of its purpose, including a description of the input required and the output produced. Where appropriate, a description is also provided of variables which appear in the algorithm whose purpose is not readily apparent.

Steps The numbered steps of the algorithm—*Step i*—are rendered in italic type and start at the left margin. Some steps may be doubly (or triply, etc.) indented to distinguish levels of logic, to improve readability, etc. If the statements within Step *i* require more than one line, subsequent lines start below and to the right of the step number.

The steps of the algorithm are indicated by *Step i*, where *i* is a nonnegative integer. Step numbers are always consecutive and start with either 0 or 1; *Step 0* is generally used for initializing variables and arrays. A step is used to define a meaningful logical unit in the breakdown of an algorithm for which further breakdown is deemed unnecessary to understand the algorithm.

Brackets   Immediately following *Step i* is a brief phrase enclosed in brackets [   ] which describes the purpose of the step.   These brackets may be omitted on occasion if the purpose of the step is obvious and requires no explanation.   Another useful purpose is served by these brackets if they are used as comments or remarks in an implementation of the algorithm; this would help to show directly where the particular step is implemented in the code.

Punctuation and statement comments   Following the phrase in brackets is a sequence of one or more statements separated by semicolons (;) and ending with a period.   Immediately following the last semicolon and preceding the last statement in the sequence, the word **and** may appear for improved readability. Additional comments, enclosed within parentheses, may appear after all statements within a step; they are used to explain features of the algorithm or various stages of a computation.

Statement language conventions   It is intended that all statements can be read like sentences or as a sequence of commands.   Thus, instead of writing COST $\leftarrow 0$, we may write **Set** COST $\leftarrow 0$.   In this case we say that **Set** is a part of the *statement language*, whereas COST is a variable chosen by the designer of the algorithm.   All words of the statement language are rendered in boldface type; these include:

and   do   else   fi   for   goto   if   od

set   then   through   to   while

If these words start a sentence, the initial letters are capitalized—for example, **Set**, **Do**, **If**.

To distinguish variable names and logical operators from words in the statement language, variable names and logical operators appear in full capital letters.   Note the difference between AND and **and** in the following example:

If I < 10 AND J < 10 **then set** I $\leftarrow$ I $+ 1$; **and set** J $\leftarrow$ J $+ 1$ **fi**.

Assignment statements   Assignment statements are written using the arrow ($\leftarrow$).   The word **set** is optional; for example,

Set I $\leftarrow 1$

or   **Set** I $\leftarrow 1$; J $\leftarrow 2$; **and** K $\leftarrow 3$.

If statements   **If** statements have one of two forms, as follows:

If I $<$ J **then set** I $\leftarrow$ I $+ 1$ **fi**

or   **If** I $<$ J **then set** I $\leftarrow$ I $+ 1$

         else set J $\leftarrow$ J $- 1$ **fi**.

Bracketed statements may appear after **then** and **else** if they improve either understandability or readability, or both; for example,

> **If** I < J **then** [delete vertex] **set** I ← I + 1
> **else** [move pointer] **set** PTR ← LEFT(PTR) **fi**.

Normally we recommend the use of **fi** at the end of an **if** statement, particularly when failure to use it can cause a statement to be ambiguous or incorrect. Consider the statement

> **If** I < J **then set** I ← I + 1
> **else set** J ← J + 1; K ← 1.

This can be interpreted in one of two ways:

> **If** I < J **then set** I ← I + 1
> **else set** J ← J + 1; **set** K ← 1 **fi**.

or

> **If** I < J **then set** I ← I + 1
> **else set** J ← J + 1 **fi**; **set** K ← 1.

In the first statement, K is set equal to 1 only if I is not less than J; in the second statement, K is set equal to 1 regardless of the value of I and J.

Iteration statements Iteration statements appear in a variety of forms; for example:

1 *Step i.* [   ] **Do** step $i + 1$ **while** I ≤ M **od**.
   Step i + 1. [   ] **If** COST(I, J) ≤ MIN
                                    then   set   MIN ← COST(I, J);   **and**
                                    I ← I + 1 **fi**.
2 *Step i.* [   ] **Do through** step $i + 3$ **while** J > 0 **od**.
   Step i + 1. [   ] Statements.
   Step i + 2. [   ] Statements.
   Step i + 3. [   ] Statements.
   Step i + 4. [   ] Statements.

The execution of statement 2 is as follows: steps $i + 1$, $i + 2$, and $i + 3$ are executed; a test is *then* made to see if J > 0; if J ≤ 0, then step $i + 4$ is executed next; if J > 0, then steps $i + 1$, $i + 2$, and $i + 3$ are executed again, and J is once again compared with 0, etc.   It is understood that somewhere in steps $i + 1$, $i + 2$, or $i + 3$ the value of J is changed; otherwise the possibility exists of an infinite loop through these steps.

3 *Step i.* [   ] **While** PTR > 0 **do** PTR ← LEFT(PTR) **od.**
4 *Step i.* [   ] **While** J > 0 **do through** step *i* + 2 **od.**
　　　Step i + 1. [   ] Statements.
　　　Step i + 2. [   ] Statements.
　　Step i + 3. [   ] Statements.

The execution of the **while-do** differs from that of the **do-while** only in that in the former the test is performed before the first execution of the step(s) indicated by the **do**, rather than after.   The use of **od**, as in statement 3, serves to define the end of the **do**; its use is identical to that of **fi**.

5 *Step i.* [   ] **For** I ← 1 **to** N **do** step *i* + 1 **od.**

The intent of statement 5 is to permit the execution of a typical DO- or FOR-loop, in increments of 1, rather than having to initialize to the index variable I and increment it within a **do-while** or a **while-do**.

Goto statements   Although the principles of structured programming eliminate the need for **goto**s, we occasionally find situations where the use of a **goto** seems both appropriate and natural.   In such instances the algorithms are usually very short and the use of **goto**s is not detrimental to understanding the logic of the algorithm.   Hence, we use **goto** statements sparingly.

APPENDIX B

SETS AND SOME BASIC SET ALGORITHMS

Sets are the most general of all mathematical structures and, as such, they appear in almost every mathematical model. Often a problem is modeled in terms of sets, and solution algorithms are formulated in terms of basic operations on these sets. In many ways, the implementation of any algorithm involves set representation and manipulation.

This appendix is *not* an "introduction to set theory." Rather, it assumes a basic knowledge of sets and operations on them. It is intended in part to establish the notation used throughout the book, but its primary purpose is to introduce some questions that arise when we use sets to implement algorithms.

B.1 NOTATION

1 Sets are denoted by roman capital letters, and the elements of sets are rendered in italic lowercase letters; for example, $U = \{r, s, t, u, v, w\}$.

2 $v \in U$ v *is an element of the set* U.

        $v \notin U$ v *is not an element of set* U.

        $V \subseteq U$ V *is a subset of* U; that is, every element of V is also an element of U.

        $V \subset U$ V *is a proper subset of* U; that is, there exists an element of U which is not an element of V.

3 $V = \emptyset$ V *is the empty set*; that is, there are no elements in V.

4 $|V|$ *Cardinality of* V; that is, for finite sets the number of elements in V.

5 $U \cup V$ *Union of sets* U *and* V; that is, the set consisting of all elements in U and all elements in V.

        $U \cap V$ *Intersection of sets* U *and* V; that is, the set consisting of all elements that are both in U and in V.

        $V - U$ *Difference of* V *and* U; that is, the set consisting of those elements in V which are not in U.

        $V \subseteq U, \bar{V}$ If V is a subset of U, then $\bar{V}$ denotes *the complement of* V *in* U; that is, $\bar{V} = U - V$.

6 If $V = \{v_1, v_2, \ldots, v_n\}$ is a finite set of real numbers, then

$$\sum_{i=1}^{n} v_i = v_1 + v_2 + \cdots + v_n \quad \text{and} \quad \prod_{i=1}^{n} v_i = v_1 v_2 \cdots v_n$$

denote the sum and product of all elements in V, respectively.

7 $\lceil v_i \rceil$ *Smallest integer greater than or equal to* v_i.

$\lfloor v_i \rfloor$ *Largest integer less than or equal to* v_i.

8 $|V| = \infty$ V *is an infinite set*—that is, it contains a countably infinite number of elements.

$|V| < \infty$ V *is a finite set*.

9 If i, k are positive integers, then $i! = i \times (i - 1) \times \cdots \times 2 \times 1$ is read "i factorial" (see Sec. 4.5). $\binom{i}{j}$ is read "i choose j" and denotes the number of ways of choosing j different objects from i different objects.

10 The *harmonic* sequence is the infinite sequence of rational numbers

$$1 + \frac{1}{2} + \frac{1}{3} + \frac{1}{4} + \cdots + \frac{1}{N} + \cdots$$

$$H_N = 1 + \frac{1}{2} + \cdots + \frac{1}{N} = \sum_{i=1}^{N} \frac{1}{i}$$

is called the N*th* partial sum of the harmonic sequence.

B.2   IMPLEMENTATION OF SETS AND OPERATIONS ON SETS

How do we tell if a given element u is an element of a set V? By looking at V and seeing if u is there, right? The problem, however, is: How can a computer "look" at V and check for the presence of u? This is the problem of representing a set in the computer. One very simple answer will be given here. Other answers are possible.

A particularly simple representation is possible if we assume that all sets to be considered are subsets of some finite universal set U. Let U contain n distinct elements, labeled $1, 2, \ldots, n$ (one distinct integer to each element). We can represent any subset V of U by a string or sequence of 0s and 1s. If the ith position, or bit, in this string is a 1, then the element assigned the integer i, denoted v_i, is in V; and if we find a 0 there, then $v_i \notin V$. For example, if U has six elements then

$$V = (0, 0, 1, 0, 1, 1)$$

represents the set V consisting of elements v_3, v_5, and v_6; and

$$\emptyset = (0, 0, 0, 0, 0, 0)$$

represents the *empty set* (always denoted by $\emptyset$) consisting of no elements, while $U = (1, 1, 1, 1, 1, 1)$. Any such sequence representing a set V is known as the *characteristic vector* (with respect to U) of V.

If U has n elements, how many distinct subsets of U are there?

Note that if $|U|$ is smaller than the number of bits in a word on your computer, then it may be possible to represent any $V \subseteq U$ in a single word of memory.

How then do we test to see if $v \in V$? In the characteristic vector representation we check to see what integer label has been assigned to v. Assume that it is i. We then inspect the ith bit in the sequence representing V. If we find a 0, then $v \notin V$; otherwise $v \in V$.

The operation of set union is easily implemented using characteristic vectors. All we do is "add" the characteristic vector representing A to that of B to obtain $A \cup B$. We do this "addition" one component at a time, subject to the condition that the "sum" of two 1s is another 1. We call this modified addition the *binary-OR* operation and denote it by the symbol $\vee$. The basic rules of this operation are summarized in the four formulas:

$$1 \vee 1 = 1$$
$$1 \vee 0 = 1$$
$$0 \vee 1 = 1$$
$$0 \vee 0 = 0$$

As an example, let $|U| = 7$ and consider the two characteristic vectors

$$A = (1, 0, 1, 0, 1, 1, 0)$$
$$B = (1, 1, 0, 0, 1, 0, 0)$$

Then

$$A \cup B = (1, 1, 1, 0, 1, 1, 0)$$

In many computers this implementation of the union operation can be done in a single operation if $|U| \leq$ the basic machine word size. Otherwise, we may have to use $|U|$ operations.

We can also define a *binary-AND* operation $\wedge$, and we use this to formulate an algorithm for constructing the characteristic vector representation for $A \cap B$ from those of A and B.

Similarly, a .NOT. operation can be defined to represent set complementation.

What are some other operations on sets whose implementations are never considered in mathematics courses but which have to be considered in detail for computer implementation? Think about this question for a moment before reading on.

How about the operation of deleting an element v from a set V, denoted $V - \{v\}$? This takes one step using our characteristic vector representations.

Then there is the problem of finding an element v. Which of our current collection of sets, if any, contains v? This is an example of a *search problem*. More general search problems ask for all elements that have certain properties.

Often the set elements we consider are all real numbers or integers, and they can be ordered in the *natural order*—that is, using the real number relations of "equal to" and "greater than." Other sets of elements may also be ordered in some natural or well-defined fashion. Can you think of some examples?

APPENDIX C   ALGOL AND PL/1 PROGRAMS

This appendix contains implementations of several of the algorithms in this text in the Algol and PL/1 programming languages. These are included as a supplement for the reader who may not be familiar with, or may not use, the Fortran language. The following table lists the contents of this appendix.

Section of text	Algorithm	Language
2.1	KNIGHT'S TOUR	Algol W
2.3	DELETE	PL/1
2.3	INSERT	PL/1
2.4	SIS (Straight Insertion Sort)	PL/1
3.5	DFS (Depth-First Search)	PL/1
3.5	BFS (Breadth-First Search)	Algol W
4.1	PRIM	Algol W
5.1	QUICKSORT	Algol W
5.1	HEAP	Algol W
5.1	HEAPSORT	Algol W
6.2	DIJKSTRA	Algol W

ALGOL W (16JAN72)

```
    BEGIN

    COMMENT************************************************************
            *                                                        *
            * THIS PROGRAM CONSTRUCTS A TOUR OF A KNIGHT ON A CHESSBOARD *
            * USING A CLOCKWISE STRATEGY FOR MOVING TO A NEW POSITION, *
            * WHERE THE INITIAL POSITION IS READ IN.                  *
            *                                                        *
            ************************************************************;

    INTEGER ARRAY BOARD (1::12,1::12);

    INTEGER ARRAY IMOVE,JMOVE (1::8);

    INTEGER IINIT,JINIT,K,I,J,N,INEXT,JNEXT;

    COMMENT************************************************************
            *                                                        *
            * VARIABLE            DESCRIPTION                         *
            *                                                        *
            * BOARD(I,J)          =N MEANS THAT THE SQUARE IN ROW I,  *
            *                     COLUMN J WAS THE N-TH SQUARE VISITED ON *
            *                     THE KNIGHT'S TOUR.                  *
            *                     =0 MEANS THAT THE SQUARE WAS NEVER  *
            *                     VISITED.                            *
            *                     =99 MEANS THAT THE SQUARE IS OFF THE *
            *                     BORDER OF THE BOARD AND IS USED TO  *
            *                     PREVENT THE KNIGHT FROM MOVING OFF THE *
            *                     BOARD.                              *
            *                                                        *
            * IMOVE(K)            THE K-TH POSITION, 1 <= K <= 8 TO WHICH *
            * JMOVE(K)            THE KNIGHT CAN MOVE FROM A GIVEN SQUARE. *
            *                                                        *
            * I,J                 THE CURRENT POSITION OF THE KNIGHT. *
            *                                                        *
            * INEXT,JNEXT         A POSSIBLE NEXT SQUARE TO BE VISITED. *
            *                                                        *
            * N                   THE NUMBER OF MOVES.               *
            *                                                        *
            * IINIT,JINIT         THE INITIAL POSITON.               *
            *                                                        *
            ************************************************************;
    COMMENT************************************************************
            *                                                        *
            * THE MOVES IN THE VECTORS IMOVE AND JMOVE ARE READ IN AS *
            * FOLLOWS:                                                *
            *                                                        *
            *    K           IMOVE           JMOVE                   *
            *    1            -2               1                      *
            *    2            -1               2                      *
            *    3             1               2                      *
            *    4             2               1                      *
            *    5             2              -1                      *
            *    6             1              -2                      *
            *    7            -1              -2                      *
            *    8            -2              -1                      *
            *                                                        *
            ************************************************************;
    FOR I := 1 UNTIL 8 DO
        READON (IMOVE(I),JMOVE(I));

    COMMENT************************************************************
            *                                                        *
            * READ IN THE INITIAL POSITIONS.                         *
            *                                                        *
            ************************************************************;

    READ (IINIT,JINIT);

    COMMENT************************************************************
            *                                                        *
            * ADJUST THE INITIAL POSITIONS SO THAT THEY CORRESPOND TO THE *
            * CORRECT POSITIONS ON THE 12 BY 12 BOARD.               *
            *                                                        *
            ************************************************************;

    IINIT:=IINIT+2;
    JINIT:=JINIT+2;

    COMMENT************************************************************
            *                                                        *
            * INITIALIZE THE BOARD.                                  *
            *                                                        *
            ************************************************************;

    FOR I := 1 UNTIL 12 DO
    FOR J := 1 UNTIL 12 DO
        IF (I<3) OR (I>10) OR (J<3) OR (J>10) THEN BOARD(I,J):=99
                                              ELSE BOARD(I,J):=0;
```

```
COMMENT*****************************************************************
      *                                                               *
      *    INITIALIZE THE VARIABLES.                                   *
      *                                                               *
      ***********************************************************;

K:=1;
BOARD(IINIT,JINIT):=1;
I:=IINIT;
J:=JINIT;
N:=2;


COMMENT*****************************************************************
      *                                                               *
      *    IF ALL THE MOVES FROM THE CURRENT POSITION HAVE BEEN CHECKED *
      *    AND NONE COULD BE MADE THEN K WILL BE > 8 AND THE PROGRAM   *
      *    WILL PRINT OUT THE BOARD AND STOP.  OTHERWISE THIS WILL     *
      *    LOOP AND TRY ALL POSSIBLE MOVES.                            *
      *                                                               *
      ***********************************************************;

WHILE (K<=8) DO


COMMENT*****************************************************************
      *                                                               *
      *    CHECK IF A MOVE CAN BE MADE TO POSITION K.                  *
      *                                                               *
      ***********************************************************;

   BEGIN
   INEXT:=I+IMOVE(K);
   JNEXT:=J+JMOVE(K);
   IF BOARD(INEXT,JNEXT) = 0 THEN


COMMENT*****************************************************************
      *                                                               *
      *    VISIT THE NEW POSITION AND GET THE NEW I,J VALUE.           *
      *                                                               *
      *    RESET K TO 1.                                              *
      *                                                               *
      ***********************************************************;

      BEGIN
      BOARD(INEXT,JNEXT):=N;
      N:=N+1;
      J:=JNEXT;
      I:=INEXT;
      K:=1;
      END
COMMENT*****************************************************************
      *                                                               *
      *    TRY THE NEXT POSITION.                                      *
      *                                                               *
      ***********************************************************;

                              ELSE
      K:=K+1
END;


COMMENT*****************************************************************
      *                                                               *
      *    THE TOUR HAS ENDED, PRINT BOARD AND NUMBER OF MOVES IN TOUR. *
      *                                                               *
      ***********************************************************;

N:=N-1;

WRITE("BOARD IS");

FOR I := 3 UNTIL 10 DO
   BEGIN
   WRITE(" ");

   FOR J := 3 UNTIL 10 DO
       WRITEON (BOARD(I,J))
END;

WRITE("THE NUMBER OF MOVES WAS",N)

END.
```

```
LINK: PROCEDURE OPTIONS(MAIN);
```
```
      LINK: PROCEDURE OPTIONS(MAIN);
```

```
      /*****************************************************************
       *                                                               *
       *                                                               *
       *           THIS PROCEDURE TESTS TWO PROCEDURES DELETE AND INSERT*
       *           WHICH PERFORM OPERATIONS ON A LINEAR LINKED LIST,    *
       *           CONSISTING OF AN INFORMATION PART (INFO) AND A POINTER*
       *           PART (LINK).                                         *
       *                                                               *
       *                                                               *
       *              DELETE    - THIS PROCEDURE WILL DELETE A GIVEN    *
       *              ------       ELEMENT FROM A LINKED LIST           *
       *                                                               *
       *              INSERT    - THIS PROCEDURE WILL INSERT A NEW CELL *
       *              ------       INTO A LINKED LIST.                  *
       *                                                               *
       *           NOTE : ASSUME THAT THE INFO CONTENTS OF THE CELLS IN *
       *           ----    THE LIST ARE ARRANGED IN INCREASING ORDER.   *
       *                                                               *
       *                                                               *
       *****************************************************************/

      DCL (INFO(100),VALUE,NAME) CHAR(100) VARYING,
          (FIRST,NEXT,COND,LINK(100)) FIXED BINARY;

      ON ENDFILE(SYSIN) GOTO END_PRGM;

      /*****************************************************************
       *                                                               *
       *                                                               *
       *           READ IN THE INITIAL CHARACTER VECTOR AND SET UP THE  *
       *           INITIAL LINK VECTOR                                 *
       *                                                               *
       *                                                               *
       *****************************************************************/

      GET LIST(N); /* NUMBER OF NAMES IN THE INITIAL CHARACTER
                      VECTOR                                          */

      FIRST = 0;

      DO I=1 TO N;

          GET EDIT(NAME)
               (COL(1),A(80));

          VALUE=SUBSTR(NAME,1,INDEX(NAME,' '));
          INFO(I)= VALUE;

          CALL INSERT(FIRST,INFO,LINK,I,VALUE);

      END;

      PUT PAGE EDIT('THE INITIAL LIST ARRANGED IN ALPHABETICAL
              ','ORDER IS : ')
              (COL(20),A,A);
      PUT SKIP(3);

      NEXT = FIRST;
      DO WHILE(NEXT ¬= 0);

          PUT SKIP(1) EDIT(INFO(NEXT))
                  (COL(30),A);

          NEXT = LINK(NEXT);

      END;

      PUT SKIP(3);

      /*****************************************************************
       *                                                               *
       *                                                               *
       *           THE INITIAL CHARACTER VECTOR HAS BEEN SET UP AND NAMES*
       *           THAT ARE TO BE ADDED OR DELETED TO/FROM THE LIST ARE *
       *           SUPPLIED WITH THE FOLLOWING INFORMATION :           *
       *                                                               *
       *           VARIABLE   STARTS IN COLUMN   FORM   DESCRIPTION    *
       *           --------   ----------------   ----   -----------    *
       *                                                               *
       *           COND            1              X     = 1 IF THE NAME IS*
       *                                                 TO BE ADDED TO*
       *                                                 THE EXISTING  *
       *                                                 LIST          *
       *                                                               *
       *                                                 = 0 IF THE NAME IS*
       *                                                 TO BE DELETED *
       *                                                 FROM THE      *
       *                                                 EXISTING LIST *
       *                                                               *
       *           NAME           10            70(A)   THE NAME THAT IS TO*
       *                                                 BE ADDED/DELETED*
       *                                                 TO/FROM THE   *
       *                                                               *
```

```
*                                                       EXISTING LIST      *
*                                                                          *
*          NOTE :    X - DENOTES AN INTEGER VALUE                          *
*          ----                                                            *
*                                                                          *
*                   NN(A) - DENOTES NN A'S WHERE A SIGNIFIES A             *
*                           POSITION FOR A CHARACTER VALUE TO APPEAR*      *
*                                                                          *
****************************************************************************/
        DO WHILE('1'B);

            GET EDIT(COND,NAME)
                (COL(1),F(1),COL(10),A(70));

            VALUE = SUBSTR(NAME,1,INDEX(NAME,' '));

            IF COND = 1 THEN DO; /* CALL PROCEDURE INSERT         */

                INFO(I) = VALUE;

                PUT SKIP(2) EDIT('THE FOLLOWING NAME '' ',
                    VALUE,' '' IS TO BE INSERTED IN THE LIST')
                    (COL(20), 3 A);

                CALL INSERT(FIRST,INFO,LINK,I,VALUE);

                I = I+1;

            END;

            ELSE DO;        /* CALL PROCEDURE DELETE             */

                PUT SKIP(2) EDIT('THE FOLLOWING NAME '' ',
                    VALUE,' '' IS TO BE DELETED FROM THE LIST')
                    (COL(20), 3 A);

                CALL DELETE(FIRST,INFO,LINK,VALUE);

            END;

            PUT SKIP(1);

            NEXT = FIRST;

            DO WHILE(NEXT ¬= 0);

                PUT SKIP(1) EDIT(INFO(NEXT))
                    (COL(30),A);

                NEXT = LINK(NEXT);

            END;

        END;
DELETE: PROCEDURE(FIRST,INFO,LINK,VALUE);

/**************************************************************************
*                                                                        *
*                                                                        *
*       THIS PROCEDURE DELETED A CELL C(I) WITH INFO(I) = VALUE          *
*       FROM A LINKED LIST, THE FIRST CELL OF WHICH IS GIVEN             *
*       BY FIRST.                                                        *
*                                                                        *
*                                                                        *
**************************************************************************/

    DCL (INFO(*),VALUE) CHAR(100) VARYING,
        (FIRST,PTR,PREV,LINK(*)) FIXED BINARY;

        PTR = FIRST;             /*   GET FIRST CELL                 */
        PREV = 0;

        DO WHILE(PTR ¬= 0);  /* ENTERS ONLY IF THE CELL IS NOT
                                        EMPTY                         */

            IF INFO(PTR) = VALUE THEN DO; /* THE CELL TO BE DELETED
                                             HAS BEEN FOUND   */

                IF PREV = 0 THEN DO; /* DELETE FROM THE FRONT */

                    FIRST = LINK(PTR);
                    RETURN;

                END;

                ELSE DO; /* DELETE FROM THE INTERIOR             */

                    LINK(PREV) = LINK(PTR);
                    RETURN;

                END;

            END;

            PREV = PTR;              /* GET NEXT CELL              */
```

```
                    PTR = LINK(PTR);

          END;

END DELETE;
INSERT: PROCEDURE(FIRST,INFO,LINK,ROW,VALUE);
    /*********************************************************************
     *                                                                   *
     *                                                                   *
     *          THIS PROCEDURE INSERTS A NEW CELL ROW, WITH INFO(ROW) =  *
     *          VALUE, INTO AN ORDERED LINKED LIST, THE FIRST CELL OF    *
     *          WHICH IS GIVEN BY FIRST.  ASSUME THAT THE INFO CONTENTS  *
     *          OF THE CELLS IN THE LIST ARE ARRANGED IN INCREASING ORDER*
     *                                                                   *
     *                                                                   *
     *********************************************************************/

        DCL (INFO(*),VALUE) CHAR(100) VARYING,
            (FIRST,PTR,ROW,PREV,LINK(*)) FIXED BINARY;

            PTR = FIRST;              /* GET FIRST CELL                */
            PREV = 0;

            DO WHILE('1'B);

                IF PTR = 0 THEN DO;         /* IS THE LIST EMPTY ?     */

                    IF PREV = 0 THEN DO; /* INSERT NEW CELL AS ONLY
                                                    CELL ON LIST       */

                        FIRST = ROW;
                        LINK(ROW) = 0;
                        RETURN;

                    END;

                    ELSE DO;          /* INSERT NEW CELL AT THE END OF
                                                    THE LIST           */

                        LINK(PREV) = ROW;
                        LINK(ROW) = 0;
                        RETURN;

                    END;

                END;
    /*********************************************************************
     *                                                                   *
     *                                                                   *
     *          DOES THE NEW CELL PRECEDE AN EXISTING CELL               *
     *                                                                   *
     *          NOTE :    UNSPEC DETERMINES THE INTERNAL BINARY          *
     *          ----      REPRESENTATION OF THE GIVEN CHARACTER STRING   *
     *                                                                   *
     *                                                                   *
     *********************************************************************/

                IF UNSPEC(VALUE) <= UNSPEC(INFO(PTR)) THEN DO;

                    IF PREV = 0 THEN DO;   /* INSERT NEW CELL AT
                                                    THE FRONT OF THE LIST*/

                        FIRST = ROW;
                        LINK(ROW) = PTR;
                        RETURN;

                    END;

                    ELSE DO;       /* INSERT THE NEW CELL IN THE
                                                    INTERIOR OF THE LIST */

                        LINK(PREV) = ROW;
                        LINK(ROW) = PTR;
                        RETURN;

                    END;

                END;

                PREV = PTR;              /*    GET NEXT CELL           */
                PTR = LINK(PTR);

            END;

END INSERT;
END_PRGM: END LINK;
```

```
MAIN: PROCEDURE OPTIONS(MAIN);

      MAIN: PROCEDURE OPTIONS(MAIN);

      /********************************************************************
       *                                                                  *
       *                                                                  *
       *        THIS MAIN PROCEDURE TESTS THE ALGORITHM SIS               *
       *            *** STRAIGHT INSERTION SORT ***                       *
       *                                                                  *
       *                                                                  *
       ********************************************************************/

         DCL N /* NUMBER OF ELEMENTS IN THE ARRAY I                   */
             FIXED BINARY,

             K FIXED BIN INITIAL(0);

             ON ENDFILE(SYSIN) BEGIN;

                 PUT SKIP(5) EDIT('END OF DATA SETS.')
                     (COL(15),A);
                 GOTO END_PRGM;

             END;

             DO WHILE('1'B);

                 GET LIST(N);
                 K=K+1;

                 BEGIN;

                    DCL I(N) FIXED BINARY; /* DIMENSION AN ARRAY OF
                                              LENGTH N                */

                    GET LIST((I(J) DO J=1 TO N));

                    PUT SKIP(4) EDIT('DATA SET NUMBER ',K)
                        (COL(15),A,F(5));

                    PUT SKIP(3) EDIT('THE UNSORTED ARRAY IS : ')
                        (COL(20),A);

                    M=N/10;
                    PUT SKIP(2) EDIT((I(J) DO J=1 TO N))
                        (R(F1));

                    CALL SIS(I,N);    /* ALGORITHM STRAIGHT
                                         INSERTION
                                         SORT                         */

                    PUT SKIP(3) EDIT('THE SORTED ARRAY IS : ')
                        (COL(20),A);

                    PUT SKIP(2) EDIT((I(J) DO J=1 TO N))
                        (R(F1));

         F1: FORMAT((M) (COL(20),(10) (F(5),X(2))),COL(20),
                        (N-M*10) (F(5),X(2)));
      SIS: PROCEDURE(I,N);

      /********************************************************************
       *                                                                  *
       *                                                                  *
       *        THIS PROCEDURE PERFORMS THE STRAIGHT INSERTION SORT       *
       *        (SIS).  THE ALGORITHM PLACES A SEQUENCE OF INTEGERS       *
       *        I(1), I(2) , ... , I(N) INTO ASCENDING ORDER.            *
       *                                                                  *
       *                                                                  *
       ********************************************************************/

         DCL (I(*), /* ARRAY OF UNSORTED INTEGERS                    */

             N,   /* NUMBER OF ELEMENTS OF THE ARRAY I TO BE SORTED */
             K,L) FIXED BINARY;

             DO J=2 TO N BY 1; /* BASIC ITERATION                   */

                 K= I(J);            /* NEXT INTEGER                 */
                 L= J-1;

                 DO WHILE( K <= I(L) & L >= 1); /* COMPARE WITH SORTED
                                                   INTEGERS          */

                     I(L+1)= I(L);
                     L= L-1;

                 END;

                 I(L+1)= K;         /* INSERT                        */

             END;

             RETURN;

      END SIS;
                 END;
             END;
      END_PRGM: END MAIN;
```

```
DFS: PROCEDURE(ADJ,NEXT,V,TREE,T);
```

NEST

```
    DFS: PROCEDURE(ADJ,NEXT,V,TREE,T);
/****************************************************************
*                                                              *
*        THIS PROCEDURE IS AN ADAPTATION OF TARJAN'S RECURSIVE  *
*        DEPTH-FIRST SEARCH ALGORITHM.  DFS WILL FIND A SPANNING*
*        TREE OF A CONNECTED UNWEIGHTED NETWORK G, HAVING P < 100*
*        VERTICES AND Q EDGES.   THE NETWORK G IS REPRESENTED BY*
*        LINKED LISTS, USING VECTORS ADJ AND NEXT.  DFS PLACES  *
*        THE EDGES CHOSEN FOR THE SPANNING TREE IN ARRAY TREE,  *
*        AND BEGINS ITS SEARCH FOR A SPANNING TREE AT VERTEX V. *
*        IF G IS NOT CONNECTED DFS WILL FIND A SPANNING TREE OF *
*        THE CONNECTED COMPONENT OF G CONTAINING V.             *
*                                                              *
*        VARIABLES        DESCRIPTION                           *
*                                                              *
*        ADJ(K)           VECTOR USED TO STORE THE P LINKED LISTS*
*        NEXT(K)          OF VERTICES ADJACENT TO A GIVEN VERTEX.*
*                         FOR 1 < K < P, ADJ(K)=0, AND IF J=NEXT(K),*
*                         THEN ADJ(J) IS THE FIRST VERTEX ADJACENT*
*                         TO VERTEX K.  THE NEXT VERTEX ADJACENT TO*
*                         K IS CONTAINED IN ADJ(NEXT(J)), ETC.. *
*                                                              *
*        U,V              AT ANY POINT IN TIME, WE ARE VISITING *
*                         VERTEX V HAVING ARRIVED AT V FROM VERTEX*
*                         U USING EDGE UV.                      *
*                                                              *
*        TREE(J,1)        THE J-TH EDGE CHOSEN FOR THE SPANNING *
*        TREE(J,2)        TREE.                                 *
*                                                              *
*        T                THE COUNT OF THE NUMBER OF EDGES CURRENTLY*
*                         IN THE SPANNING TREE.                 *
*                                                              *
*        W                THE NEXT VERTEX ADJACENT TO V.        *
*                                                              *
*        VISIT(V) = I     MEANS THAT VERTEX V WAS THE I-TH VERTEX*
*                         VISITED FOR THE FIRST TIME.  VISIT(V) = 0*
*                         MEANS THAT VERTEX V HAS NOT YET BEEN  *
*                         VISITED.                             *
*                                                              *
*        K                A POINTER USED IN TRAVERSING THE LINKED*
*                         LISTS OF ADJACENCIES.                 *
*                                                              *
****************************************************************/
    DCL (ADJ(*),NEXT(*),TREE(*,*),VISIT(100)) FIXED BIN,
    (V,T,I,W) FIXED BIN;
```

NEST

```
/****************************************************************
*                                                              *
*                    INITIALIZATION                            *
*                                                              *
****************************************************************/
    I = 0;
    VISIT(*) = 0;
    T = 1;

    CALL DFSR(V);

    DFSR: PROCEDURE(V) RECURSIVE;
/****************************************************************
*                                                              *
*        DFSR IS THE RECURSIVE SECTION OF DFS THAT WILL VISIT   *
*        ALL OF THE VERTICES.                                  *
*                                                              *
****************************************************************/
    DCL (V,K) FIXED BIN;

    I = I+1;
/****************************************************************
*                                                              *
*        V IS THE I-TH NEW VERTEX VISITED.                     *
*                                                              *
****************************************************************/
    VISIT(V) = I;
    K = NEXT(V);
```

NEST

```
/****************************************************************
*                                                              *
*        ANY MORE VERTICES ADJACENT TO V ?                     *
*                                                              *
****************************************************************/
```

```
                DO WHILE( K > 0 );
1                       W = ADJ(K);   /* GET THE NEXT VERTEX ADJACENT TO V   */
1                       IF VISIT(W) = 0 THEN DO;   /* HAS VERTEX W ALREADY
                                                      BEEN VISITED ?          */
2                                       TREE(T,1) = V;/* ADD EDGE             */
2                                       TREE(T,2) = W;/* VW TO THE            */
2                                       T = T+1;      /* SPANNING             */
                                                      /* TREE.                */
2                                       CALL DFSR((W));
2                                   END;
1                       K = NEXT(K);  /* GET THE NEXT VERTEX ADJACENT TO V.*/
1               END;
        END DFSR;
      END DFS;
```

```
ALGOL W (16JAN72)

    BEGIN

    COMMENT THIS PROCEDURE IMPLEMENTS A BREADTH FIRST SEARCH ALGORITHM
            FOR FINDING A SPANNING TREE OF AN UNWEIGHTED NETWORK G.;

    PROCEDURE BFS ( INTEGER ARRAY ADJ,
                          NEXT (*);
                    INTEGER VALUE V,P);
    BEGIN

    COMMENT***PARAMETERS***
        ADJ,NEXT   ARRAYS USED TO STORE A LINKED LIST REPRESENTATION OF
                   THE NETWORK G.

        P          THE NUMBER OF VERTICES IN G.

        V          INITIAL VERTEX FROM WHICH BREADTH FIRST SEARCH BEGINS.;

    INTEGER ARRAY VISIT,LIST (1::100);
    INTEGER ARRAY TREE (1::100,1::2);
    INTEGER I,J,K,T,W,U;

    COMMENT***VARIABLES***
        VISIT     IF VISIT(I) IS ZERO THEN THE VERTEX HAS NOT BEEN VISITED.

        TREE      CONTAINS THE VERTEX NUMBERS OF THE EDGES IN THE TREE.

        LIST      LIST IS AN ARRAY OF VERTICES TO BE VISITED FOR THE
                  FIRST TIME.

        U         U IS THE VERTEX CURRENTLY BEING VISITED.

        W         W IS AN ADJACENT VERTEX TO THE ONE CURRENTLY BEING VISITED

        J         J IS THE INDEX WHICH IS USED TO ADD VERTICES TO THE ARRAY
                  LIST.

        K         K IS USED TO POINT TO THE NEXT VERTEX IN ADJ.;

    COMMENT INITAILIZE ARRAYS.;

    FOR I := 1 UNTIL P+1 DO
        BEGIN
        VISIT(I):=0;
        LIST(I):=0
    END;
    J:=1;
    I:=1;
    T:=0;
    COMMENT START AT VERTEX V AND INITIALIZE VISIT(V).;

    LIST(J):=V;
    VISIT(V):=1;

    COMMENT THIS LOOPS WHILE THERE ARE STILL VERTICES.;

    WHILE (LIST(J) ¬= 0 ) DO
        BEGIN

    COMMENT GET THE NEXT VERTEX.;

        U:=LIST(J);
        J:=J+1;

    COMMENT SEE IF THERE ARE ANY ADJACENT VERTICES TO U.;

        K:=NEXT(U);

    COMMENT LOOP WHILE THERE ARE ADJACENT VERTICES.;

        WHILE ( K ¬= 0 ) DO
            BEGIN
            W:=ADJ(K);

    COMMENT IF W IS UNVISITED THEN ADD IT TO LIST AND THE EDGE TO TREE.;
```

```
          IF VISIT(W) = 0 THEN
               BEGIN
               I:=I+1;
               LIST(I):=W;
               VISIT(W):=1;
               T:=T+1;
               TREE(T,1):=W;
               TREE(T,2):=U
          END;


COMMENT GET THE NEXT ADJACENT VERTEX.;


          K:=NEXT(K)
     END
END;
COMMENT OUTPUT THE TREE.;


FOR I := 1 UNTIL T DO
     WRITE(TREE(I,1),TREE(I,2));
END;
END.
```

```
ALGOL W (16JAN72)

   BEGIN
     COMMENT THIS PROCEDURE FINDS A MINIMUN WEIGHT SPANNING TREE (MWST)
             IN A WEIGHTED, CONNECTED NETWORK G USING AN ALGORITHM DUE TO
             PRIM (BEL SYSTEM TECH. J. 36 (NOV. 1957), 1389-1401). THIS
             IMPLEMENTATION IS A MODIFICATION OF A PROGRAM DUE TO V. KEVIN
             AND M. WHITNEY (COMM. ACM APRIL, 1972), ALGORITHM 422).   ;

     PROCEDURE PRIM ( INTEGER ARRAY C (*,*);
                      INTEGER VALUE M;
                      INTEGER ARRAY FROM, TO, COST (*);
                      INTEGER RESULT WEIGHT );

     COMMENT ***FORMAL PARAMETERS***
             C IS THE COST MATRIX PASSED TO THE PROCEDURE
             M IS THE NUMBER OF VERTICES PASSED TO THE PROCEDURE
             (FROM,TO, COST) THE I-TH EDGE IN THE MWST IS FROM VERTEX
             -FROM(I)- TO VERTEX -TO(I)- OF COST -COST(I)-.
             THESE ARE RETURNED FROM THE PROCEDURE.
             WEIGHT IS THE TOTAL WEIGHT OF THE MWST PASSED FROM THE
             PROCEDURE            ;

       BEGIN
       INTEGER EDGES,
               NEXT,
               NUMUN,
               I,J,JK,L,K;

       INTEGER ARRAY LIGHT,
                     UNCHSN,
                     VERTEX   (1::100);

     COMMENT ***PROCEDURE VARIABLES***
             EDGES NUMBER OF EDGES IN MWST SO FAR.
             LIGHT WEIGHT OF LIGHTEST EDGE, FROM VERTEX(I) TO UNCHSN(I).
             NEXT NEXT VERTEX TO BE ADDED TO MWST.
             NUMUN NUMBER OF UNCHOSEN VERTICES.
             UNCHSN ARRAY OF UNCHOSEN VERTICES.
             VERTEX VERTEX OF PARTIAL MWST CLOSEST TO VERTEX UNCHSN.   ;

     COMMENT   INITIALIZE VARIABLES.  ;

       EDGES := 0 ;
       WEIGHT := 0 ;
       NEXT := M ;
       NUMUN := M-1 ;
       FOR I := 1 UNTIL NUMUN DO
              BEGIN
                 UNCHSN(I) := I ;
                 LIGHT(I) := C(I,NEXT) ;
                 VERTEX(I) := NEXT
              END;

     COMMENT THIS LOOPS WHILE THERE IS AN UNCHOSEN VERTEX.    ;

       WHILE (NUMUN ¬= 0 ) DO
             BEGIN

     COMMENT UPDATE LIGHTEST EDGE FROM EACH UNCHOSEN VERTEX
             TO A CHOSEN VERTEX.  ;

                FOR I := 1 UNTIL NUMUN DO
                      BEGIN
                         J:= UNCHSN(I);
                         JK := C(J,NEXT);
                         IF LIGHT (I) > JK THEN
                             BEGIN
                                 VERTEX(I) := NEXT;
                                 LIGHT(I) := JK
                             END
                      END;

     COMMENT PICK A LIGHTEST EDGE FROM AN UNCHOSEN VERTEX
             TO A CHOSEN VERTEX.   ;

                K:=1;
                L:=LIGHT(1);
                FOR I := 1 UNTIL NUMUN DO
                IF LIGHT(I) < L THEN
                      BEGIN
                         L:=LIGHT(I);
                         K:=I
                      END;

     COMMENT ADD EDGE TO MWST.  ;

                EDGES := EDGES + 1 ;
                FROM (EDGES) := UNCHSN(K) ;
                TO (EDGES) := VERTEX (K) ;
                COST(EDGES) := L ;
                WEIGHT := WEIGHT + L ;
                NEXT := UNCHSN(K);

     COMMENT DELETE NEWLY CHOSEN VERTEX FROM UNCHOSEN LIST.    ;

                LIGHT(K) := LIGHT(NUMUN);
                UNCHSN(K) := UNCHSN(NUMUN);
                VERTEX(K) := VERTEX(NUMUN);

     COMMENT DECREMENTS NUMUN FOR THE WHILE LOOP   ;

                NUMUN:=NUMUN-1
             END
       END;
   END.
```

```
ALGOL W (16JAN72)

    BEGIN

    COMMENT THE PROCEDURE QUICKSORT SORTS A SEQUENCE OF N KEYS A(1),A(2)...
                ...A(N), IN PLACE, INTO ASCENDING ORDER.  SUBSEQUENCES OF
                SIZE LESS THAN M ARE SORTED BY STRAIGHT INSERTION SORT (SIS).
                THIS PROCEDURE MAKES USE OF A PUSHDOWN STORE
                (LEFT(K),RIGHT(K)) WHICH CONTAINS THE LEFT AND RIGHT SUBSCRIPTS
                OF SUBSEQUENCES YET TO BE SORTED.         ;
    PROCEDURE QUICKSORT (INTEGER ARRAY A (*);
                          INTEGER VALUE N,M);

    COMMENT***PARAMETERS***
        A     THE VECTOR OF ELEMENTS TO BE SORTED.

        N     THE NUMBER OF ELEMENTS IN A.

        M     SUBSEQUENCES OF LESS THAN SIZE M ARE SORTED BY SIS.;

    BEGIN

    COMMENT***VARIABLES***
        LEFT(K)   THE STACK USED TO STORE THE POINTER TO THE LEFT SIDE OF
                  A SUBSEQUENCE IN A YET TO BE SORTED.

        RIGHT(K)  THE STACK USED TO STORE THE POINTER TO THE LEFT SIDE OF
                  A SUBSEQUENCE IN A YET TO BE SORTED.

        K     THE POINTER TO THE STACKS LEFT AND RIGHT.

        L,R   THE POINTERS TO THE RIGHT AND LEFT SIDES OF SUBSEQUENCES
              IN A TO BE SORTED NOW.

        I,J   THE POINTERS USED TO SORT THE VECTOR A.

        MID   A TEMPORARY LOCATION TO INTERCHANGE ELEMENTS IN A.;
    INTEGER ARRAY LEFT,RIGHT (1::N);
    INTEGER K,L,R,I,J,MID;

    COMMENT INITIALIZE THE STACKS AND THE POINTER;

    K:=1;
    LEFT(K):=1;
    RIGHT(K):=N;

    COMMENT LOOP WHILE THERE ARE STILL SUBSEQUENCES TO BE SORTED;

    WHILE K > 0 DO
        BEGIN

    COMMENT GET THE NEXT SUBSEQUENCE TO BE SORTED;

        L:=LEFT(K);
        R:=RIGHT(K);
        K:=K-1;

    COMMENT SORT THE SUBSEQUENCES WHILE THEY ARE GREATER THAN LENGTH M;

        WHILE (R-L) >= M DO
            BEGIN

    COMMENT INITIALIZE THE POINTERS AND MID;

            I:=L;
            J:=R;
            MID:=A(I);

    COMMENT LOOP WHILE MID < A(J) DECREMENTING J;

    STEP5:        WHILE MID < A(J) DO
                      J:=J-1;

    COMMENT IF J <= I THE PASS IS COMPLETE.
            RESET A(I) AND GOTO STEP 11 SO A SUBSEQUENCE IS STACKED;

                IF J <= I THEN
                    BEGIN
                    A(I):=MID;
                    GOTO STEP11
                END;

    COMMENT INTERCHANGE A(I) AND A(J) AND RESET I;

                A(I):=A(J);
                I:=I+1;

    COMMENT LOOP WHILE A(I) < MID AND DECREMENT I;

                WHILE ( I <= J ) AND (A(I) < MID ) DO
                    I:=I+1;
```

```
COMMENT IF J <= I THEN THE PASS IS COMPLETE.
        RESET A(J) AND GOTO STEP 11 SO A SUBSEQUENCE IS STACKED;

                    IF J <= I THEN
                          BEGIN
                          A(J):=MID;
                          I:=J;
                          GOTO STEP11
                    END;

COMMENT INTERCHANGE A(J) AND A(I) RESET J AND LOOP FOR ANOTHER PASS;

                          A(J):=A(I);
                          J:=J-1;
                          GOTO STEP5;


COMMENT STORE THE CURRENT UNSORTED SUBSEQUENCE POINTERS;

STEP11: K:=K+1;
        IF (R-I) >= (I-L) THEN
              BEGIN
              LEFT(K):=I+1;
              RIGHT(K):=R;
              R:=I-1;
              END
                            ELSE
              BEGIN
              LEFT(K):=L;
              RIGHT(K):=I-1;
              L:=I+1
              END
        END
    END;


COMMENT CALL SIS IF THE SUBSEQUENCE IS LESS THAN LENGTH M;

    SIS (A,L,R)
END
END QUICKSORT;

COMMENT THIS PROCEDURE USES THE STRAIGHT INSERTION SORT ALGORITHM TO
        SORT SUBSEQUENCES FROM QUICKSORT THAT ARE LESS THAN LENGTH M;

PROCEDURE SIS (INTEGER ARRAY A(*);
               INTEGER VALUE L,R);


COMMENT***PARAMETERS***
     A    THE VECTOR TO BE SORTED.

     L,R  THE LEFT AND RIGHT POINTERS TO THE SUBSEQUENCE IN A THAT IS
          TO BE SORTED;

BEGIN

COMMENT***VARIABLES***
     I,J  THE POINTERS TO THE VECTOR A.

     B    A TEMPORARY LOCATION FOR ELEMENTS IN A;

INTEGER I,J,B;

COMMENT WHILE THE SUBSEQUENCE IS UNSORTED LOOP;

FOR J := L+1 UNTIL R DO
    BEGIN

COMMENT INITIALIZE;

    I:=J-1;
    B:=A(J);

COMMENT WHILE B <= A(I) AND THERE ARE STILL ELEMENTS TO BE CHECKED
        EXCHANGE A(I+1) AND A(I) AND DECREMENT I;

    WHILE ( B <= A(I)) AND (I >= L) DO
          BEGIN
          A(I+1):=A(I);
          I:=I-1
    END;

COMMENT INSERT B;

    A(I+1):=B
END

COMMENT RETURN TO QUICKSORT;

END SIS;
END.
```

```
ALGOL W (16JAN72)

    BEGIN
    COMMENT*******************************************************************
                * THIS PROCEDURE PLACES AN ELEMENT A(J) OF THE VECTOR A INTO *
                * IT'S CORRECT PLACE IN A HEAP.                              *
                *************************************************************;

    PROCEDURE HEAP (INTEGER ARRAY A(*);
                    INTEGER VALUE J,M);

    COMMENT***PARAMETERS*****************************************************
                * A        A VECTOR INTO WHICH AN ELEMENT CAN BE HEAPED.     *
                *                                                           *
                * J        THE INDEX OF THE ELEMENT TO BE HEAPED.           *
                *                                                           *
                * M        THE NUMBER OF ELEMENTS IN A.                     *
                *************************************************************;

    COMMENT***VARIABLES******************************************************
                * TEMP     A TEMPORARY LOCATION.                           *
                *************************************************************;

    BEGIN
    INTEGER TEMP;

    COMMENT*****************************************************************
                * THIS LOOPS UNTIL A(J) IS IN IT'S CORRECT LOCATION IN THE *
                * HEAP.                                                    *
                *************************************************************;

    WHILE (2*J+1 <= M) AND ((A(J) < A(2*J)) OR (A(J) <= A(2*J+1))) DO
    COMMENT*****************************************************************
                * THIS DETERMINES WHICH BRANCH OF THE CURRENT NODE A(J) SHOULD*
                * BE PLACED AT.                                            *
                *************************************************************;

    IF A(2*J) > A(2*J+1) THEN
        BEGIN

    COMMENT*****************************************************************
                * LEFT BRANCH.                                             *
                *************************************************************;

            TEMP:=A(J);
            A(J):=A(2*J);
            A(2*J):=TEMP;
            J:=2*J;
            END

    COMMENT*****************************************************************
                * RIGHT BRANCH.                                            *
                *************************************************************

                            ELSE
            BEGIN
            TEMP:=A(J);
            A(J):=A(2*J+1);
            A(2*J+1):=TEMP;
            J:=2*J+1
    END;

    COMMENT*****************************************************************
                * IF A(J) WAS THE SMALLEST NUMBER IN THE HEAP IT IS PLACED *
                * AT A(M).                                                 *
                *************************************************************;

    IF (( 2*J) = M) AND (A(J) < A(2*J)) THEN
        BEGIN
        TEMP:=A(J);
        A(J):=A(2*J);
        A(2*J):=TEMP
    END

    COMMENT*****************************************************************
                * RETURNS.                                                 *
                *************************************************************;

    END HEAP;

    COMMENT*****************************************************************
                * THIS PROCEDURE PLACES INTO ASCENDING ORDER ELEMENTS OF   *
                * THE VECTOR A USING A HEAP.                               *
                *                                                         *
                * THE HEAP IS CREATED BY PROCEDURE HEAP.                   *
                *************************************************************;
```

```
PROCEDURE HPSORT (INTEGER ARRAY A(*);
                  INTEGER VALUE N);
COMMENT***PARAMETERS*********************************************************
         * A          A VECTOR OF N ELEMENTS TO BE SORTED.                  *
         *                                                                  *
         * N          NUMBER OF ELEMENTS IN A.                              *
         ***********************************************************************;

COMMENT*** VARIABLES*********************************************************
         * M          THE CURRENT NUMBER OF UNSORTED ELEMENTS IN A.         *
         *                                                                  *
         * I          THE POSITION OF THE ELEMENT TO BE PLACED IN THE       *
         *            HEAP.                                                  *
         *                                                                  *
         * TEMP       A TEMPORARY LOCATION.                                 *
         ***********************************************************************;

BEGIN
INTEGER M,I,TEMP;

COMMENT*********************************************************************
         * INITIALIZE M,I                                                   *
         ***********************************************************************;

I:=N;
M:=N;

COMMENT*********************************************************************
         * CALLS HEAP REPEATEDLY UNTIL EVERY ELEMENT HAS BEEN PLACED        *
         * IN THE HEAP.                                                     *
         ***********************************************************************;

WHILE I >= 1 DO
    BEGIN
    HEAP(A,I,M);
    I:=I-1
END;
COMMENT*********************************************************************
         * THIS CALLS HEAP REPEATEDLY WITH A(1) AND M-1 ELEMENTS UNTIL      *
         * THE VECTOR A IS SORTED.                                          *
         ***********************************************************************;

WHILE M > 1 DO
    BEGIN

COMMENT*********************************************************************
         * THIS INTERCHANGES THE LARGEST ELEMENT A(1) AND A(M) AND          *
         * THEN CALLS HEAP WITH M:=M-1 TO PLACE THE NEW A(1) IN IT'S        *
         * CORRECT POSITION.                                                *
         ***********************************************************************;

    TEMP:=A(1);
    A(1):=A(M);
    A(M):=TEMP;
    M:=M-1;
    HEAP(A,1,M)
END
END HPSORT;
END.
```

```
ALGOL W (16JAN72)

    BEGIN

    COMMENT THIS PROCEDURE DETERMINES THE SHORTEST DISTANCE FROM AN
            INITAL VERTEX VO TO A FINAL VERTEX W IN A NON-NEGATIVELY
            WEIGHTED, CONNECTED NETWORK G, USING AN ALGORITHM DUE TO
            DIJKSTRA (NUMERISCHE MATHEMATIK, VOL. 1, PP. 269-271.)
            THIS IMPLEMENTATION IS A MODIFICATION OF A PROGRAM DUE TO
            V. KEVIN AND M. WHITNEY (COMM. ACM (APRIL, 1972), ALGORITHM
            422).  THE OUTPUT OF THIS SUBROUTINE IS A SHORTEST PATH TREE
            ROOTED AT VO.           :

    PROCEDURE DIJKST( INTEGER ARRAY A(*,*);
                      INTEGER ARRAY FROM, TO, LENGTH (*);
                      INTEGER VALUE M,VO,W;
                      INTEGER RESULT EDGES);

    COMMENT***PARAMETERS***
    A        THE MATRIX WHICH CONTAINS THE LENGTHS OF THE EDGES BETWEEN
             ANY TWO VERTICES.
    VO       THE INITIAL VERTEX.
    W        THE FINAL VERTEX.
    M        THE NUMBER OF VETICES.
    FROM(I)  CONTAINS THE I-TH EDGE IN THE SHORTEST PATH TREE,
    TO(I)    FROM VERTEX -FROM(I)- TO VERTEX -TO(I)-
    LENGTH(I) OF LENGTH -LENGTH(I)-.
    EDGES    NUMBER OF EDGES IN THE SHORTEST PATH TREE

    BEGIN

    INTEGER ARRAY DIST,UNDET,VERTEX (1::100);
    INTEGER NEXT, NUMUN,I,J,JK,L,K;


    COMMENT***VARIABLES***
    UNDET        LIST OF UNDETERMINED VERTICES.
    VERTEX       VERTEX OF PARTIAL SHORTEST PATH TREE ON SHORTEST PATH
                 FROM UNDET TO VO.
    DIST         THE SHORTEST DISTANCE FROM UNDET(I) TO THE PARTIAL
                 SHORTEST PATH TREE.
    NEXT         NEXT VERTEX TO BE ADDED.
    NUMUN        NUMBER OF UNDETERMINED VERTICES


    COMMENT INITIALIZE VARIABLES;

    EDGES:=0;
    NEXT:=VO;
    NUMUN:=M-1;
    FOR I := 1 UNTIL M DO
       BEGIN
          UNDET(I):=I;
          DIST(I):=A(VO,I);
          VERTEX(I):=VO
    END;
    UNDET(VO):=M;
    DIST(VO):=DIST(M);


    COMMENT   LOOPS UNTIL THE FINAL VERTEX IS DONE;

    WHILE (NEXT ¬= W) DO
       BEGIN


    COMMENT   UPDATE SHORTEST DISTANCE TO EACH UNDETERMINED VERTEX;

       IF EDGES ¬= 0 THEN
          FOR I := 1 UNTIL NUMUN DO
             BEGIN
                J:=UNDET(I);
                JK:=L+A(NEXT,J);
                IF DIST(I) > JK THEN
                   BEGIN
                      VERTEX(I):=NEXT;
                      DIST(I):=JK
                END
    END;


    COMMENT   PICK A SHORTEST DISTANCE TO AN UNDETERMINED VERTEX;

       K:=1;
       L:=DIST(1);
       FOR I :=1 UNTIL NUMUN DO
          IF DIST(I) < L THEN
             BEGIN
                L:=DIST(I);
                K:=I
       END;


    COMMENT   ADD EDGE TO SHORTEST PATH TREE;
```

```
        EDGES:=EDGES+1;
        FROM(EDGES):=VERTEX(K);
        TO(EDGES):=UNDET(K);
        LENGTH(EDGES):=L;
        NEXT:=UNDET(K);
```

COMMENT DELETE NEWLY DETERMINED VERTEX FROM UNDETERMINED LIST;

```
        DIST(K):=DIST(NUMUN);
        UNDET(K):=UNDET(NUMUN);
        VERTEX(K):=VERTEX(NUMUN);
```

COMMENT   DECREMENT NUMUN;

```
        NUMUN:=NUMUN-1
    END
END;
END.
```

INDEX